Scottish Coal Miners in the Twentieth Century

JIM PHILLIPS

EDINBURGH
University Press

Edinburgh University Press is one of the leading university presses in the UK. We publish academic books and journals in our selected subject areas across the humanities and social sciences, combining cutting-edge scholarship with high editorial and production values to produce academic works of lasting importance. For more information visit our website: edinburghuniversitypress.com

First published in hardback by Edinburgh University Press 2019

Edinburgh University Press Ltd
The Tun – Holyrood Road
12 (2f) Jackson's Entry
Edinburgh EH8 8PJ

Typeset in 10/13 Giovanni Std by
IDSUK (DataConnection) Ltd, and
printed and bound by CPI Group (UK) Ltd,
Croydon, CR0 4YY

A CIP record for this book is available from the British Library

ISBN 978 1 4744 5231 1 (hardback)
ISBN 978 1 4744 5232 8 (paperback)
ISBN 978 1 4744 5233 5 (webready PDF)
ISBN 978 1 4744 5234 2 (epub)

Contents

Figures and Tables

Figures

Tables

Acknowledgements

Scholarship is the enemy of romance, according to Billy Bragg, the Bard of Barking, but it is also a rich scene of collegiality and friendship. This book has been written with help, advice and support from many people.

Thank you to past and present colleagues in Economic & Social History at the University of Glasgow, where work-in-progress seminar discussions have been invaluable. Rose Elliot, Jeff Fear, Angus Ferguson, Mike French, Annmarie Hughes, Jeff Meek, Chris Miller, Sumita Mukherjee, Malcolm Nicolson, Neil Rollings, Duncan Ross, Catherine Schenk, Ray Stokes, Jim Tomlinson, Val Wright and Helen Yaffe have all contributed to the development and completion of this book. Thank you to Roma French for supplying the Gillesbie 'electric' houses detail. Thank you also to Ewan Gibbs, an outstanding student in Economic & Social History at Glasgow when I started researching this book and a formidable early career lecturer at the University of the West of Scotland by the time it was finished.

I extend a grateful thank you to Rab Wilson for his poem, *The Auld Union Banner*, and to Phillipa MacInnes and her colleagues at East Ayrshire Leisure for the cover image, which inspired the structure of this book. Thanks to Stewart Maclennan, Gregor Gall and other comrades, friends and teachers in the Scottish Labour History Society. Thank you to Terry Brotherstone for his continued advice and friendship.

The research was conducted at Glasgow Caledonian University Archives, Kirkcaldy Art Gallery and Museums, Methil Heritage Centre, the Mining Institute in Newcastle, the National Archives at Kew, the National Library of Scotland, the National Mining Museum of Scotland in Newtongrange, where David Bell kindly arranged permissions for the eight black and white images used in the book, the National Records of Scotland, and the University of Glasgow Archives and Library. I am grateful to everyone employed or volunteering in these archives and libraries. In preserving social memory they lead the struggle against politicised ignorance and prejudice.

The book's ideas, findings and conclusions were developed through discussion at various conferences, public talks, seminars and workshops. So thank you to those who organised and participated in the Mineurs du Monde Colloque International at Lens in April 2013, 'Swan Songs? Reconsidering the Death of Industrial Britain (ca. 1970–1990)' at the German Historical Institute London in October 2013, the Riots in Regions of Heavy Industry conference at the University of Tübingen in 2014, the Contemporary History Seminar at the University of Tübingen in June 2015, the Economic History Society annual conference at Robinson College, Cambridge in March–April 2016, the End of Coal conference at the University of Nottingham in June 2016, the Fife Mining Heritage Preservation Society meeting at Kirkcaldy in March 2017, the Friends of the National Mining Museum of Scotland 'First Fridays' talk at Newtongrange in November 2017, and the first meeting of the Coal and Steel history group at the National Mining Museum, England, in December 2017. I am especially grateful to Jörg Arnold of the University of Nottingham, a learned protagonist in four of these events, to Arne Hordt for inviting me to Tübingen (twice), to Freddy Dickson, Duncan Gilfillan and Elizabeth McGuire of the Fife Mining Heritage Preservation Society, and Jim Waugh of the Friends of the National Mining Museum of Scotland.

In a previous book I thanked several former miners who I interviewed between 2009 and 2011. I have remained in contact with a number of these men, and take the opportunity here to restate my gratitude to Rab Amos, Iain Chalmers and Nicky Wilson.

Billy Bragg was only half-right. At a crucial moment in my life scholarship was not the enemy of romance. My greatest thanks are to Anna Robertson, who I met at the University of Aberdeen in 1989. I dedicate this book to her, with love and respect, and to our two fine sons, Robert Phillips and Matthew Phillips.

Abbreviations

AUEW	Amalgamated Union of Engineering Workers
BSC	British Steel Corporation
CISWO	Coal Industry Social Welfare Organisation
CPGB	Communist Party of Great Britain
DEA	Department of Economic Affairs
EWO	Essential Work Order
FCC	Fife Coal Company
FCKMA	Fife, Clackmannan and Kinross Miners' Association
FKCMA	Fife, Kinross and Clackmannan Miners' Association
FMHPS	Fife Mining Heritage Preservation Society
ILP	Independent Labour Party
MAGB	Mining Association of Great Britain
MFGB	Miners' Federation of Great Britain
MMC	Militant Miners' Committee (1940s)
MMC	Monopolies and Mergers Commission (1980s)
NAT	National Arbitration Tribunal
NCB	National Coal Board
NUM	National Union of Mineworkers
NUMSA	National Union of Mineworkers Scottish Area
NUSMW	National Union of Scottish Mineworkers
NUWM	National Unemployed Workers' Movement
OMS	Output per Manshift
SCEBTA	Scottish Colliery Enginemen, Boilermen and Tradesmen's Association
SNP	Scottish National Party

SSEB	South of Scotland Electricity Board
SSHA	Scottish Special Housing Association
TUC	Trades Union Congress
UCS	Upper Clyde Shipbuilders
UDM	Union of Democratic Mineworkers
UMS	United Mineworkers of Scotland

The Auld Union Banner

Banners sic as this aince flew abune
Battlefields like Bannockburn; Culloden,
Juist as proodly, an wi nae less purpose.
The uniforms o thaim wha haud it heich,
Oan this braw Simmer's day in Auchinleck,
Are sweatshirt, t-shirt, casual jeans an trainers –
Scotland's fowk, stuill mairchin wi that purpose
That saw their graundsires bleed fir ither causes;
The Somme, Dunkirk, aye, an e'en Orgreave Cokeworks,
(tho medals werenae gien oot fir the latter!)
But, the battle, an the war, is aye the same,
See it here, an read it here, the day.
These are the people wha focht fir the people,
The graund auld cause, that's spelt oot here in rid,
Nae revolution, juist fair shares fir aa.
Ye've mind o thon puir boy wha askt fir mair?
Ah've mind when miners goat the same short shrift,
Frae baton-wieldin bully boys oan horses,
Wha chairged doun throu the years frae Peterloo.
This banner flew aince at the heid o thoosans,
Led bi Scargill, Clarke, an Mick McGahey,
Sae dinnae think, because the day we're few,
The cause is deid, the struggle bin abandoned,
See it here, an read it here, the day;
Tae Legislate, Educate, aye, an Organise.
Alang Well Road an Barbieston it gangs,

Back Rogerton Crescent, then doun past the shoaps,
Whaur auld men stoap, respectfully, tae stare
At an eemage they'd aamaist forgotten;
Twa miners tyauvin in the mirk o nicht,
Wha'll win throu yet tae tak their share o licht.

Rab Wilson

Introduction: Scottish Coal Miners and Economic Security

This book frames the history of Scottish coal miners from the 1920s to the 1980s in terms of collective economic security. It shows how Scottish miners campaigned for material improvement that was only partly won with nationalisation of the coal industry in 1947, and then defended working class welfare during a prolonged process of deindustrialisation from the 1950s onwards. This involved leading labour movement demands for political-constitutional reforms that eventually resulted in the establishment of the Scottish Parliament in 1999.

The three-part structure of this book – Legislate, Educate, Organise – is inspired by *The Auld Union Banner* of Rab Wilson's poem. The banner belonged to the Barony and Killoch Colliery branches of the National Union of Mineworkers (NUM) in Ayrshire, and 'spelt out' in bold red letters the 'graund auld cause' of socialism. A coal miner's helmet lamp beamed a bright shaft of life-affirming light, with the familiar industry symbols of pit bing and colliery winding gear in the background, and two other workers striving underground to win the black diamonds. The banner is pictured on the front cover of this book. Peter Ackers and Alastair J. Reid might see *The Auld Union Banner* as misdirection. They argue that labour historians have been preoccupied with false assumptions about the socialist aspirations of British workers in the twentieth century. Workers were not united politically: their diverse economic, social and cultural worlds shaped a rich plurality of political ambitions. Many workers, Ackers and Reid assert, saw life in a liberal state and employment in privately owned

firms as reliable paths to rising living standards, eschewing centralised economic planning and nationalisation of industry.[1] Scottish
coal miners, however, were less heterogeneous in economic and
social terms than the generality of British workers, and their political
values were probably less diverse. Competing political movements
certainly found adherents in the Scottish coalfields, where rivalries
especially between Labour and Communist forces were often acute.
But very few Scottish miners opposed the nationalisation of coal in
1947, and hardly any supported the privatisation of what remained
of the industry in 1994. Ownership clearly mattered, at least to this
group of British workers.

Socialism is nevertheless an ambiguous term, and not all miners would have regarded themselves as socialists. This book was
researched and written in a prolonged period of political, economic
and social precariousness. Permanent austerity in public finances
from 2010, along with oppressive anti-trade union government legislation and private sector employment practices, framed the growth
of a highly insecure labour regime.[2] This encompassed zero-hours
contracts and the gig economy, with its bogus self-employment, lost
wages coupled with fines for workers reporting sick and digital-era
mechanisms for policing employees.[3] The drawn-out imbroglio of
Brexit from 2016 onwards heightened the atmosphere of political
crisis and social instability across the UK. From this twenty-first-
century perspective the most striking feature of the history of Scottish coal miners in the twentieth century is their collective pursuit of
economic security. Socialism might have been a divisive as well as
unifying force in the coalfields, as Ackers and Reid imply, but miners in Scotland unambiguously campaigned for stable employment,
safe workplaces, and viable communities.

In this respect Mike Savage's reading of the working class of Preston in Lancashire from 1880 to 1940 offers a useful guide to the
study of Scottish miners in the twentieth century. Preston's workers,
many of whom laboured in the cotton industry, sought to minimise
the insecurity which arose from their separation from the means
of their own subsistence, as Savage puts it. Three approaches or
types of struggle were adopted: 'mutualist', where workers avoided
the insecurities of the open market by developing their own goods
and services, through co-ops, friendly societies, churches, clubs and

institutes; 'economist', where workers sought to gain some control over the deployment of their own labour through trade unions and collective bargaining; and 'statist', with legislation and other forms of local and national government regulation geared to the reduction of working-class insecurity.[4] Another valuable point of reference is Guy Standing's advocacy of universal basic income, which he and many others argue is the key to improved security across the globe in the twenty-first century. Standing identifies two linked 'meta-securities': income security, and voice security. Each is a prerequisite for the exercise of 'republican freedom', the capacity of citizens to participate meaningfully in the construction and exercise of democracy.[5]

The analysis in this book, following Savage and Standing, emphasises the central linkage between economic security and political voice. The book examines the interaction between various economic actors: miners and their trade union and elected political representatives; private and then public sector coal industry employers; and policy-makers, primarily at central government level. There is an emphasis on the highly contested nature of security in the coalfields. Employers and policy-makers at different times contributed to its extension. Private coal firms and then the National Coal Board (NCB), which operated the industry after nationalisation in 1947 on behalf of the British state, provided employment and a range of welfare services; government policy, particularly from the 1940s to the 1970s, involved a degree of wealth redistribution and economic management that broadly advanced the material position of miners. The NCB was a more responsible and progressive employer than many of the private companies which it succeeded. Colliery closures and other changes that threatened the security of miners and their communities were negotiated rather than imposed; union voice was heard on safety and many other important issues. Lost employment and pit closures were off-set with the opening of new mines and opportunities for younger men that endured until the early 1980s.[6] But these improvements were won by the miners through their own union and political organisation and activity. At times, especially in the 1920s and then in the 1980s, the ambitions and actions of both employers and the state destabilised the security of miners, their families and communities.

Perceptions of security among miners in the Scottish coalfields were shaped to a large extent by macro-economic conditions and UK government policy. Clement Attlee's 1945–51 Labour governments consolidated and extended the trend initiated by Winston Churchill's war-time coalition to an enlarged state with greater economic-interventionist powers. Changes in the 1940s were not entirely abrupt. Governments in the 1930s had made significant 'corporatist' interventions to stimulate aggregate demand, which anticipated the limited Keynesian 'revolution' that followed the Second World War. But there was an important strategic innovation in the 1940s, governments accepting a responsibility to maintain high levels of employment. This marked a clear dividing line from the inter-war years of persistent and heavy unemployment, and shaped Britain's economic direction from the 1950s to the 1970s.[7] In the coalfields this change in direction strengthened security. Before the Second World War precariousness in mining communities was acute. About one-third of coal industry employment in Scotland was lost between the 1926 national lockout and the global trade slump in 1932. Unemployment was accompanied by lower wages for those who retained their jobs and the more or less permanent threat of redundancy. This was often targeted at workplace union activists who sought to challenge their employers and defend their workmates.[8] The risks of underground injury and death increased in the late 1920s and 1930s, perhaps as a result of the attack on union voice and in the context of intensifying competitive pressures during the great depression. After nationalisation the average annual rate of fatality per manshift was roughly halved, comparing the 1950s with the 1930s. Coalfield security was also strengthened after the Second World War by the 1944 White Paper, *Employment Policy*. This stated that governments should protect workers from unemployment, but in reciprocal terms emphasised that workers would have to be flexible, willing to change jobs and occupations as national priorities developed over time.[9] On this question Margaret Thatcher's personal copy of the paper is worth examining. Paragraphs detailing the onus on workers to accept the inevitability of changes and occupational mobility were underlined in red and blue pencil by the future Conservative Prime Minister.[10]

NCB employment in Scotland peaked in 1957–8, and deindustrialisation was managed carefully thereafter, within the spirit of the
1944 White Paper. Coalfield security was broadly maintained, with
many miners finding work in alternative industrial occupations. UK
government regional policy incentives to manufacturers to locate
in the south of Wales, northern England and central Scotland were
increased significantly, 'sixteen-fold in real terms' from 1962–3
to 1969–70, as the Labour governments led by Harold Wilson
attempted to secure more rapid economic growth in part through
widening employment opportunities in the coalfields.[11] Wilson's
government admittedly oversaw an acceleration of coal industry
job losses, but responded positively to calls from miners' union
representatives for changes in the timing and pace of coal closures.
Job losses in coal were offset by the regional policy-funded provision of alternative industrial employment in the coalfields, in engineering and various forms of assembly goods manufacturing. This
broad approach was abandoned, however, in the 1980s. Thatcher's
Conservative governments, first elected in 1979, initiated a radical
strategic reverse, scaling back the state and abandoning Keynesian
demand management.[12] The rapidity of change in the 1980s, as in
the 1940s, should not be over-emphasised. The 'neoliberal' turn
under Thatcher's leadership was based on long-running dialogue
between elite Conservative Party activists, business leaders and
economic thinkers, which commenced in the 1950s.[13] The extent
to which Thatcher then secured a permanent economic revolution
after 1979 has also been exaggerated: in the 1990s Conservative and
then New Labour governments both followed interventionist and
expansionist policies.[14] Two unambiguous changes after 1979 can
nevertheless be detected, each of which greatly destabilised coalfield security: the widening of inequality, and the acceptance of
higher unemployment. A standard measure of income distribution
is the Gini coefficient, usually expressed as a figure between 0 and
1, rising as inequality increases. After taxes and benefits the Gini
coefficient in the UK was 0.42 in 1938. Redistribution of income on
progressive lines reduced this to 0.24 in 1961 and 0.23 in 1977. The
Thatcher effect was remarkable, widening the Gini coefficient to
0.34 in 1987, where it has more or less plateaued since.[15] Increased
inequality resulted from various changes to fiscal, budgetary and

social security policy, and the state abandoning its commitment to high levels of employment. Job stimulation through regional incentives gave way to an emphasis in policy on re-training, with limited positive impact on the re-employment of redundant industrial workers, particularly older citizens.[16] Ex-industrial workers were maintained through the social security system, which included incentives encouraging them to withdraw from economic activity altogether on disability grounds. This masked the 'real' level of unemployment, which was often double the official social security benefit claimant count.[17]

The coal industry was targeted for disinvestment and then privatisation by the Conservative government. The strike of 1984–5 was in defence of collieries threatened with closure in the new political economy of Thatcherism, and also an attempt to protect the democratic basis of policy-making which the miners had won in pursuit of enhanced security. The government and its allies within the NCB were seeking the right of management to manage, unchecked by union voice. A restoration of the less regulated and privately owned industry of the 1920s and 1930s was envisaged. In the more intensively competitive energy markets of the later 1980s and 1990s, however, coal production in Scotland was marginalised. Deindustrialisation accelerated, and with minimal government regard for its casualties. No meaningful employment alternatives were put in coal's place and insecurity in mining areas was arguably even more pronounced by the end of the 1980s than it had been in the 1920s.[18] The state's pursuit of employment creation was only partly re-joined in the 1990s.[19] Coal communities became significantly less secure, a process exacerbated in the 2010s by further reductions in the relative value of welfare benefits and a narrowing of the eligibility terms for welfare claimants.[20]

These changes in economic direction in the 1940s and then the 1980s were both shaped, as David Marquand has argued, by public policy decisions that were mediated by moral economy arguments. A mid-twentieth century 'solidaristic' view of the moral economy was shared by social democratic and 'middle way' Conservative policy-makers: hence the reciprocity element, stressing the rights and responsibilities of workers, in *Employment Policy*. The Thatcherite turn encompassed 'market fundamentalist' arguments about the duties of individuals that were rooted in an opposing moral vision of the economy.[21] Each of these moral economies was initially elitist in scope, devised by policy-makers, but attracted wider support over time.[22] Thatcher's picture of the self-responsible and diligent individual, with limited obligations to others, as private interests superseded public goods, acquired cultural as well as political capital as the 1980s progressed.[23] Yet the appeal of Thatcherism can be exaggerated. The Conservative Party won big Parliamentary majorities from fairly thin electoral margins, securing less than 44 per cent of the vote in 1983 and just over 42 per cent in 1987. Resistance was especially pronounced in industrial areas of England, including London, a manufacturing city in terms of employment and economic activity in the 1970s, along with Wales and Scotland. Scottish opposition to both Thatcherism and deindustrialisation was couched in terms of class and nation. The UK government's shift in economic direction was presented and widely understood as an attack on the working class, and on the distinct interests of Scotland more broadly, where the limited and dwindling electoral support for the Conservative governments and their radical policies pointed to the existence of a democratic deficit.[24]

Anti-Thatcher resistance in the 1980s was bolstered substantially by a distinct working class moral economy which had developed from the 1940s onwards. This resembled the moral economy of the eighteenth century English crowd, memorably examined by E. P. Thompson, composed of plebeian customs and expectations that were transgressed by employers and traders in a period of rapid economic and social change.[25] The workers' moral economy interacted from the 1950s to the 1970s with the 'solidaristic' policy-makers' variant that Marquand has identified, which heightened working class expectations of improvement, placing further demands in turn on policy-makers. These two moral economies developed interactively, and within the broader trend to greater state regulation of market forces that was taking place across capitalist societies in the mid-twentieth century. Understanding this general shift to greater government control of economic life was central to *The Great Transformation*, written by Karl Polanyi, and first published in 1944. Polanyi argued that industrialisation across the eighteenth and nineteenth centuries was a dehumanising experience. Governments had enabled market mechanisms and competitive forces to override social imperatives and cooperation. This produced a delayed reaction in the twentieth century, with economic actors seeking to protect themselves or their clients against market insecurity through various forms of collective action, from government regulation to political and revolutionary movements, and trade union organisations.[26] The mutualist, economist and statist approaches to security that were pursued by workers in Preston, from 1880 to 1940, illustrate this general trend.[27]

The liberalising transformation of the eighteenth century identified by Polanyi involved a direct change to the conditions of labour in coal mining in Scotland. Scottish miners had been made indentured servants by Acts of Parliament in 1606 and 1641, unable to leave their place of employment without permission from their 'master'. This has been likened to slavery and was remembered in the 1970s by Iain Chalmers, then a young NUM activist in Fife, as a deeply embedded historical factor shaping the militancy of Scottish miners in the twentieth century.[28] But emancipation, while welcomed by miners, came via legislation passed in 1774 and 1793 after lobbying from coal masters who shared the opinion of Adam Smith that slavery included various social costs which made it more expensive than free labour. A different form of servitude ensued in the nineteenth century, according to Robin Page Arnot, Communist author of a history of Scottish miners written early in the 1950s. Owners were no longer obliged to maintain workers and their family members in lean times, but required only to pay market wages in exchange for labour and production. Demand from miners for nationalisation from the late nineteenth century onwards eventually secured the vital change of ownership in 1947.[29]

Polanyi termed this process – social action to minimise the damage of economic change – the 'double movement'. Industrialisation induced higher 'market-ness', which was then lowered by social democracy in the twentieth century. This underlined the tendency of economic liberalisation to be met by 'counter-movement' coalitions which included policy-makers and organised workers.[30] The competing mid-twentieth century moral economies were part of a 'counter-movement' but articulated contrasting ends. Policy-makers were seeking to re-embed economic activity within a social framework, to subvert political action in favour of more egalitarian wealth redistribution.[31] Workers, by contrast, were claiming a share in the taking of decisions about resources, and in the process challenging the authority of both private sector employers and policymakers. The double movement therefore involved a continuation of class conflict. Social developments in the UK on the 'Home Front' during the Second World War anticipated the longer-term survival of industrial tension. Workers won improvements to their employment conditions and secured greater access to material resources through social policy, but these were resisted by employers and at times grudgingly yielded by policy-makers, particularly Conservatives in Winston Churchill's Coalition government.[32]

In Scotland the working class moral economy shaped popular understanding of industrial changes from the 1950s onwards, and influenced collective action which compelled policy-makers to prioritise security. The Upper Clyde Shipbuilders (UCS) work-in of 1971–2 illustrates the interaction between the policy-maker and popular moral economies. In the 1960s there were significant losses of shipyard employment, but policy-makers were unconcerned because redundant workers were finding jobs in new industries. Major alternatives included the car plant at Linwood in Renfrewshire, established in 1963 within daily travelling distance of the Glasgow waterfront.[33] The work-in was prompted by less propitious economic circumstances: there were fewer alternatives to shipbuilding by 1971–2. When the UCS entered liquidation in June 1971 the workers refused to accept redundancy. 'No rank, no honour can compare with the honour of belonging to the Scottish working class', said Jimmy Reid, one of several charismatic UCS shop stewards. 'We refuse to accept the philosophy that economics control men', he continued; 'men must and shall control economics'.[34] A major political campaign developed in support of the yards and the workers, blending themes of working class dignity and Scottish national identity, each offended by 'distant' and 'faceless' Whitehall governance. The Conservative government was pushed to concede a major package of re-investment which retained substantial shipbuilding employment on the Upper Clyde.[35]

Coal miners were central to the projection and impact of the popular moral economy. Generational influence was important.

Abe Moffat, elected President of the National Union of Scottish Mineworkers (NUSMW) in 1942 and then foundation President of the National Union of Mineworkers Scottish Area (NUMSA) in 1945, was born in 1896 and joined the Communist Party of Great Britain (CPGB) in 1922.[36] Moffat belonged to a generation of union officials across the British coalfields who were shaped as young men by the First World War and the industrial struggles of the 1920s, including Communists from South Wales, notably Arthur Horner and Will Paynter,[37] and Labour figures from England, such as Will Lawther in Northumberland and Sam Watson in Durham. These miners welcomed nationalisation in 1947 as an unambiguous victory. It was their 'utopia', according to David Hopper, General Secretary of the Durham Miners' Association in the 2010s.[38] They were circumspect in their criticisms of the NCB,[39] pressing union members to increase output and condemning unofficial strikes and absenteeism in forceful terms.[40] On closures they were especially cautious, although started making the case in the 1950s and early 1960s for economic diversification to stabilise coal communities. In Scotland a second generation of union leaders, born in the 1920s with different formative experiences and political expectations, was more assertive in its criticism of the nationalised industry, particularly on closures. Key figures were Michael McGahey, elected NUMSA President in 1967 and NUM Vice President in 1972,[41] and Lawrence Daly, elected NUMSA General Secretary in 1965 and NUM General Secretary in 1968.[42] In moral economy terms pit closures required the agreement of workers and their representatives, and the security of affected miners and communities had to be preserved, through transfer to nearby pits or local provision of comparably paid alternative employment. This position, articulated hesitantly by the first generation, was expressed more forcefully by the McGahey-Daly generation, and secured a significant slowing of coalfield deindustrialisation from the late 1960s onwards.

*   *   *

In providing an original analysis of Scottish coal miners, organised around the theme of their struggle for economic security, this book adopts a structure influenced by the Barony-Killoch union banner. Thematic approaches are blended with chronological narrative. The banner's three steps to Socialism – Legislate, Educate, Organise – are used to explore the changing ways in which miners understood and sought to advance their individual and collective security across the twentieth century.

Part One is *Legislate: Ownership and Welfare*. It comprises three chapters, each analysing the impact on coalfield security of broad structural changes over time. Chapter 1 examines nationalisation and changing employment structures; Chapter 2 scrutinises mining communities, including their class and gender dimensions, and establishing the importance of changes associated with migration, re-housing and the character of collieries; and Chapter 3 explores the shifting hazards of work underground, showing that public ownership and the related growth of trade union voice had highly beneficial consequences. Part One ranges from the 1920s to the late 1960s, with an emphasis on how UK-level developments affected security in Scotland. Part Two is *Educate: Political Learning and Activity*, emphasising the informal schooling of everyday coalfield life and politics, and the ways in which Scotland's miners came to understand coalfield security as a distinctly Scottish question. Chapter 4 shows how formative workplace and industrial experience conditioned the evolution of social identity and coalfield politics. Generational differences are highlighted, and the discussion moves chronologically from the 1920s to the 1950s. Chapter 5 extends the generation theme to analyse developments in the 1960s and 1970s. The key role of the Scottish miners in advancing working class and trade union support for Home Rule for Scotland is highlighted. Part Three, *Organise: For Jobs, Wages and Communities*, reiterates the importance of UK-level policy and the Scottish miners' sense of nation as well as class, but there is greater emphasis on the defence of security at pit-level. Chapter 6 picks up the chronological thread from Chapter 1, moving the discussion of deindustrialisation forward from the mid-1960s. It demonstrates how miners advanced their collective security in the late 1960s and 1970s by mobilising against closures, and in pursuit of improved wages. Chapter 7 evaluates the prolonged attempt to preserve jobs and pits in the great strike of 1984–5.

The analysis is based on a wide range of sources. It engages with social science and historical literature on the economy, 'high' politics, working class culture, labour and gender, as well as specialist writings on the coal industry, coal miners and coal communities. These include valuable books on Scottish miners by Alan Campbell, published in 2000, and Robert Duncan, in 2005, which explore some aspects of the twentieth century within a longer-running chronological narrative that reaches back into the nineteenth century. Campbell's two-volume study ends in 1939, and Duncan's compresses the twentieth century into sixty or so pages.[43] Government publications – annual reports, fatal accident inquiries, special investigations – furnish much of the rich detail. Further original perspective is drawn from unpublished material in UK government, coal industry and mining union archives. Of particular value are the pit-level records of the NCB, which illuminate the colourful pattern and complex texture of production and labour in the nationalised industry from the 1940s to the 1980s. Two sets of interviews with coalfield actors are also used. The first was conducted by Willie Thompson in 1985–6, with men and women who had led the strike against closures just twelve months earlier. I conducted the second set of interviews from 2009 to 2011 while writing a book on the strike.[44] There are obvious methodological challenges in integrating perspectives from these interviews, conducted by separate historians, 25 years apart, and organised around the highly specific event of the strike. But each of the interviews selected for analysis here encompassed discussion of longer-run events and phenomena, including industrial and gender relations, the restructuring of the 1950s and 1960s, and the national disputes of the 1970s. The interviews undertaken from 2009 to 2011 were organised around a life course format, and provided wide-ranging perspectives on the big question examined in this book: how coal miners struggled to improve collective economic security in the Scottish coalfields across the twentieth century.

Notes

1. Peter Ackers and Alastair J. Reid, 'Other Worlds of Labour: Liberal-Pluralism in Twentieth-Century British Labour History', in Peter Ackers and Alastair J. Reid, eds, *Alternatives to State-Socialism in Britain: other*

Worlds of Labour in the Twentieth Century (Palgrave: London, 2017), pp. 1–27.

2. Guy Standing, *The Precariat: the New Dangerous Class* (Bloomsbury: London, 2011).

3. Union of Construction, Allied Trades and Technicians, False Self Employment, https://www.ucatt.org.uk/false-self-employment, accessed 15 March 2017.

4. Michael Savage, *The Dynamics of Working-Class Politics. The Labour Movement in Preston, 1880–1940* (Cambridge University Press: Cambridge, 1987), with the schema summarised at pp. 20–8.

5. Guy Standing, *Basic Income: and how we can make it happen* (Penguin: London, 2017), pp. 68–9.

6. Royce Logan Turner, 'Post-War Pit Closures: The Politics of De-Industrialisation', *Political Quarterly*, 56.2 (April 1985), pp. 167–74.

7. Alan Booth, 'New Revisionists and the Keynesian Era: an Expanding Consensus?', *Economic History Review*, 56 (2003), pp. 125–30.

8. Alan Campbell, *The Scottish Miners, 1874–1939. Volume One: Work, Industry and Community* (Ashgate: Aldershot, 2000), pp. 21–2, 26, and *Volume Two: Trade Unions and Politics* (Ashgate: Aldershot, 2000), pp. 238–43.

9. *Employment Policy*, Cmd. 6527 (HMSO: London, 1944).

10. http://www.margaretthatcher.org/document/110368, pp. 13, 19–20, accessed 14 March 2017.

11. Peter Scott, 'Regional development and policy', in Roderick Floud and Paul Johnson, eds, *The Cambridge Economic History of Modern Britain. Volume III, Structural Change and Growth, 1939–2000* (Cambridge University Press: Cambridge, 2004), pp. 332–67.

12. Peter Hall, *Governing the Economy: The Politics of State Intervention in Britain and France* (Polity: Cambridge, 1986).

13. Ben Jackson, 'The Think-Tank Archipelago: Thatcherism and Neo-Liberalism', in Ben Jackson and Robert Saunders, eds, *Making Thatcher's Britain* (Cambridge University Press: Cambridge, 2012), pp. 43–61; Neil Rollings, 'Cracks in the Post-War Keynesian Settlement? The Role of Organised Business in the Rise of Neoliberalism before Margaret Thatcher', *Twentieth Century British History*, 24 (2013), pp. 637–59.

14. Jim Tomlinson, 'Tale of a Death Exaggerated: How Keynesian Policies Survived the 1970s', *Contemporary British History*, 21 (2007), pp. 429–48.

15. A. B. Atkinson, 'The Distribution of Income in the UK and OECD Countries in the Twentieth Century', *Oxford Review of Economic Policy*, 15 (Winter 1999), pp. 56–75.

16. Tim Strangleman, 'Networks, Place and Identities in Post-Industrial Mining Communities', *International Journal of Urban and Regional Research*, 25.2 (2001), pp. 253–67.
17. Christine Beatty and Stephen Fothergill, 'Labour Market Adjustment in Areas of Chronic Industrial Decline: The Case of the UK Coalfields', *Regional Studies*, 30.7 (1996), pp. 627–40.
18. Mike Foden, Steve Fothergill and Tony Gore, *The State of the Coalfields: economic and social conditions in the former mining communities of England, Scotland and Wales* (Coalfields Regeneration Trust and Sheffield Hallam University: Sheffield, 2014).
19. Jim Tomlinson, 'De-industrialization not Decline: a New Meta-Narrative for Post-War British History', *Twentieth Century British History*, 27.1 (2016), pp. 76–99.
20. Christine Beatty, Steve Fothergill and Tony Gore, *The real level of unemployment 2012* (Centre for Regional Economic and Social Research, Sheffield Hallam University: Sheffield, 2012).
21. David Marquand, *Mammon's Kingdom. An Essay on Britain, Now* (Allen Lane: London, 2014).
22. Jim Tomlinson, 'Re-inventing the Moral economy in post-war Britain', *Historical Research*, 84 (2011), pp. 356–73.
23. Andy Beckett, *Promised You a Miracle. Why 1980–82 Made Modern Britain* (Allen Lane: London, 2015), especially Part Four, 'Revolution in the Head', pp. 183–288.
24. James Mitchell, *Conservatives and the Union. A Study of Conservative Party Attitudes to the Union* (Edinburgh University Press: Edinburgh, 1990), pp. 117–21; Jim Phillips, *The Industrial Politics of Devolution: Scotland in the 1960s and 1970s* (Manchester University Press: Manchester, 2008), pp. 178–83; Charles Woolfson and John Foster, *Track Record: the story of the Caterpillar Occupation* (Verso: London, 1988).
25. E. P. Thompson, 'The Moral Economy of the English Crowd in the Eighteenth Century', *Past and Present*, 50 (1971), pp. 76–136.
26. Karl Polanyi, *The Great Transformation: the political and economic origins of our time* (Beacon Press: Boston, MA, 1944).
27. Savage, *The Dynamics of Working-Class Politics*.
28. Chalmers, Iain, Untitled Manuscript Talk on The Scottish Colliers, 1606 to 1799, undated; copy in author's possession.
29. R. Page Arnot, *A History of the Scottish Miners* (George Allen & Unwin: London, 1955), pp. 4–13, 267–78.
30. Ewan Gibbs, 'The Moral Economy of the Scottish Coalfields: Managing Deindustrialization under Nationalization c.1947–1983', *Enterprise and Society*, 19.1 (2018), pp. 124–52.

31. Guy Standing, *Work After Globalization. Building Occupational Citizenship* (Edward Elgar: London, 2009), pp. 1–9.
32. Geoffrey G. Field, *Blood, Sweat and Toil. The Remaking of the British Working Class, 1939–1945* (Oxford University Press: Oxford, 2011), pp. 79–128, 299–334.
33. National Records of Scotland (hereafter NRS), SEP 10/312, Ministry of Labour, monthly reports on employment position in Scotland, January 1963 to December 1964.
34. Cinema Action, *UCS 1* (1971). This film is included in *Tales from the Shipyard*, a two-disc DVD set published by the British Film Institute in 2011.
35. John Foster and Charles Woolfson, *The Politics of the UCS Work-in: Class Alliances and the Right to Work* (Lawrence and Wishart: London, 1986).
36. R. Page Arnot, *Scottish Miners*, pp. 271–9.
37. W. Paynter, *My Generation* (Allen & Unwin: London, 1972).
38. Interview with David Hopper, Inky Thomson, Stan Pearce, *The Spirit of '45* (Sixteen Fly Limited/The British Film Institute, 2013), directed by Ken Loach.
39. Ben Curtis, *The South Wales Miners, 1964–1985* (University of Wales Press: Cardiff, 2013), p. 72.
40. Huw Beynon and Terry Austrin, 'The Performance of Power. Sam Watson, a Miners' Leader on Many Stages', *Journal of Historical Sociology*, 28 (2015), pp. 458–90.
41. John McIlroy and Alan Campbell, 'McGahey, Michael (Mick), (1925–1999)', in Keith Gildart and David Howell, eds, *Dictionary of Labour Biography. Volume XIII* (Palgrave Macmillan: Basingstoke, 2010), pp. 242–51.
42. Jean McCrindle, Obituary, Lawrence Daly, *The Guardian*, 30 May 2009.
43. Campbell, *The Scottish Miners, 1874–1939. Volume One* and *Volume Two*; Robert Duncan, *The Mineworkers* (Birlinn: Edinburgh, 2005).
44. Jim Phillips, *Collieries, Communities and the Miners' Strike in Scotland, 1984–85* (Manchester University Press, 2012).

Part One

Legislate: Ownership and Welfare

CHAPTER 1

Changing Ownership and Employment

Coal mining is an extractive and therefore dynamic industry. Across the developed world there has been recurrent tension between stability and temporality in the coal industry.[1] Scottish miners sought to ensure that economic and social changes were made to strengthen rather than weaken coalfield security from the 1920s to the 1980s. The emphasis in this chapter and the one that follows is on the restructuring of the coalfields through public policy: nationalisation in 1947; government-guided changes in economic and social structures, especially from the mid-1950s, with employment diversification; and measures that conditioned greater economies of scale in mining. The examination of policy-shaped restructuring involves a focus on the interaction between UK-level developments and economic security across the Scottish coalfields. Miners and their trade union representatives engaged with policy-makers, pressing moral economy demands for consultation and guarantees of collective security. This approach influenced the operation of the policy-makers' 'solidaristic' moral economy, identified by Marquand,[2] which, in turn, further strengthened the miners' expectations of justice and security. Progress was neither straightforward nor sustained. Insecurity arose especially from pit closures in the years immediately following nationalisation, and resurfaced amid the significant contraction of coal industry employment after the post-Second World War peak in 1957–8.

The chapter opens with an examination of the shift from private to public ownership of the coal industry. Literature on nationalisation tends to be highly critical, from both a private enterprise perspective and a labour tradition. The argument here is that nationalisation was a highly positive force in the coalfields. The NCB was broadly a responsible and responsive employer. Changes were generally introduced carefully, with the agreement of union representatives. The industry became significantly safer, an invaluable improvement that is analysed in Chapter 3. The second part of the chapter analyses coalfield employment. From the mid-1950s UK government fuel policy encouraged alternatives to coal. There was a deliberate rundown in coal industry employment, 'releasing' labour for deployment in higher value-added manufacturing. Private sector firms were incentivised to locate in mining areas, while coal production was increasingly concentrated in a smaller number of larger collieries. Restructuring and diversification provided new opportunities in paid employment for women as well as men, contributing to changes in gender relations. The process of restructuring is related in this chapter to deindustrialisation, carefully managed in the coalfields through dialogue between workers, employers and the state, until the election in 1979 of Margaret Thatcher's Conservative governments, which were hostile to public enterprise and trade unionism.

Nationalisation

The coal industry was nationalised in 1947 by Clement Attlee's Labour government, elected two years earlier. It was a landmark event in the coalfields, and appears prominently in many mining memoirs, autobiographies and oral testimonies.[3] The Labour government was animated by both pragmatic and ideological concerns in taking coal and other industries and services – 20 per cent of the entire economy – into public ownership. This was the second phase of Polanyi's 'double movement' examined in the Introduction, with the government re-embedding economic activity in a stronger pattern of social security. 'Market-ness' was lowered. Nationalisation was a response to market failure in the 1930s and 1940s, with the private sector unable to secure necessary investment and scale economies. It was also designed to strengthen government direction of future economic activity through control of the 'commanding heights' of coal, iron and steel, the railways, elements of road transport and the utilities.[4] The social and economic priorities embodied in coal nationalisation were reflected in the government's periodic expressions of debt and gratitude to the miners. 'Dear Friend', wrote Attlee to all NCB employees in January 1951. The Prime Minister thanked them for their positive response to a recent call from union leaders to increase output and work additional Saturday shifts, with the aim of supporting post-war economic recovery and maintaining the jobs and living standards of workers in other industries. The 'nation looks to you', Attlee concluded, implicitly appealing to the miners' sense of working class solidarity.[5]

Nationalisation has been criticised, chiefly from a private enterprise perspective, as an economic failure, motivated by allegedly sectional interest. Margaret Thatcher, Prime Minister from 1979 to 1990, saw nationalisation as primarily serving Labour's trade union supporters. The Labour government certainly had a substantial trade union base. More than a quarter of its 393 MPs were sponsored by the NUM, and nationalisation was strongly supported by miners. A Gallup opinion poll in March 1944 found that 90 per cent of them were in favour. But the same poll showed that nationalisation of coal was also endorsed by 63 per cent of professional, executive and salaried group respondents, and 60 per cent of all respondents.[6] Thatcher also claimed that nationalisation was inefficient. Taking industries and services 'back' into private ownership, including coal in 1994, helped to establish a more competitive economic environment, it was argued, stimulating productivity and macro-economic growth.[7] These private enterprise criticisms have been challenged. Nationalisation was extended on various grounds after the 1940s by both Labour and Conservative governments. Strategic national goals rather than sectional interests were generally involved. Public ownership was used to maintain selected firms, notably Rolls Royce in 1971 and British Leyland in 1975, or whole sectors, shipbuilding in 1976 being one example, which were in financial difficulty but too important economically or politically to lose.[8]

The case of coal indicates, moreover, that if broader economic and social criteria are applied, then nationalisation can be regarded as successful. The NCB supplied energy in quantities required by domestic and commercial users at stable prices, and was a relatively progressive employer, balancing production with significant

Figure 1 Working in the nationalised industry: men coming off shift at Killoch, Ayrshire, 1963. © NMMS

improvements in employee welfare. In this respect, and responding to pressure from miners and their representatives, the NCB was an important agent in extending economic security in the coalfields. Major collieries opened by the Board in Scotland after 1947 were of central value in this respect, and included Killoch in Ayrshire, depicted in Figure 1. These new units are examined in detail in Chapter 2.

The Board oversaw the establishment of an industry mineworkers' pension scheme in 1951. Where standard contributions from employer and member were determined by the scheme's Actuary to be insufficient to meet liabilities, then the NCB agreed to pay additional defining contributions.[9] During radical contraction in the 1960s it also helped to 'recycle' hundreds of thousands of workers into other sectors, including manufacturing, thereby aiding the growth of the productive economy, and at minimal social cost.[10] Furthermore, the NCB assumed much greater responsibility for the well-being of its employees than many of the private firms which preceded it. Workers injured in the course of their work, or weakened by occupational illness, were not routinely discarded. Ex-miners often recall the efforts made by NCB managers, admittedly in dialogue with union representatives, to place disabled workers in less strenuous roles.[11] Some even talk about the NCB recruiting young adults with learning difficulties, school leavers among them, such was the social mission that it accepted.[12]

Nationalisation has nevertheless been criticised from a labour perspective. Three specific and related charges have been made. First, the terms of compensation to private owners were overly generous, burdening the NCB with large debts that inhibited subsequent development and performance. The official historian estimated that the NCB overpaid by about 18 per cent for the industry's physical assets.[13] Second, nationalisation was overly centralised and managerial. The NCB was a public corporation, answerable to Parliament, but there was no transformational shift towards industrial democracy, with limited workers' involvement in the development of long-term strategy. Workers were not enthused by the adopted model of nationalisation, which arguably contributed to the initially slower than anticipated improvement in output.[14] The NCB was directed by a Chairman, appointed by the government, who oversaw a national secretariat with divisional responsibilities for production, finance, marketing and manpower. The huge and varied coalfield was managed, top-down, through regional and sub-regional areas. The Scottish Division, for instance, had North and South areas, each with their own sub-units for production, finance, marketing and manpower. Third, within this structure at everyday level miners reported limited practical changes, in terms of local and even regional management. Many pits had been operated before nationalisation by large, multi-colliery firms. In Scotland the Fife Coal Company operated seventeen collieries that were acquired by the NCB.[15] Pit-level and company-level Fife Coal Company managerial personnel naturally sought and obtained equivalent positions within the new

NCB structures. Ex-private industry managers were reinforced by recruits from elsewhere, including the armed forces, which tended to reinforce the sense of class division and social hierarchy.[16] Eric Clarke, later General Secretary of the NUMSA, began his working life in Midlothian just after nationalisation, managed by former Lothian Coal Company officials and ex-army officers. Interviewed six decades later, he emphasised the indignities of manual labour under the 'new' regime, which included queuing outside – unsheltered from the elements – to collect weekly wages from the office window on a Friday afternoon. The window in question, at the Lady Victoria Colliery in Newtongrange, was yards away from the office in the National Mining Museum of Scotland where this interview was being conducted.[17] Such frustrations were common to other parts of the British coalfields, recalled by ex-miners from Durham and South Wales in Ken Loach's 2013 film, *The Spirit of '45*.[18]

The complex class effects of nationalisation impressed social scientists in the 1950s. The influential study by Norman Dennis, Fernando Henriques and Clifford Slaughter, *Coal Is Our Life*, drew out the persistence of class feeling and antagonism in the Yorkshire coalfield, shaped by the history of the privately owned industry, and surviving into the early years of nationalisation. Adversarial relations in the workplace were the norm. Many miners were suspicious of almost any managerial initiative, interpreted as a covert intensification of their exploitation. Some complained also that union representatives had become too close to management, and less willing or able to articulate and defend the distinct interests of workers.[19] A similar pattern of conflict was identified in a study of two Lancashire collieries in the 1950s.[20] The existence of tension between workers and union officials illuminates the complexities and ambiguities of the new regime, but it should also be emphasised that industry unions – especially the NUM – did not share the NCB's industrial and political agenda entirely. Joint industrial partnership was plainly qualified by the attachment of union officials as well as workers to adversarial collective bargaining.[21] History was a powerful element in incubating these feelings of class. In *Coal Is Our Life*, the Yorkshire miners drew upon a shared collective memory of conflict, even although this was in the fairly deep past. Many in the 1950s were still talking about the 1893 national lockout, when two miners in the town of Featherstone were killed by the South Staffordshire infantry regiment, which had been mobilised to suppress crowd action after the Riot Act had been read.[22]

In Scotland a similar collective memory of class conflict was present in the 1950s, shaping the attitudes and behaviour of miners and their union representatives.[23] The key point of reference was the vindictive behaviour of industry employers between the wars, particularly around the 1921 and 1926 lockouts.[24] Abe Moffat, born in 1896, was President of the NUSMW from 1942, and then President of NUMSA from its foundation in 1945 until his retirement in 1960. Abe and his brother Alex Moffat, born 1903, NUMSA President from 1960 until 1967, were schooled in these conflicts. They belonged to a generation of miners leading the NUM after the Second World War, in England and Wales as well as Scotland, who had been formed politically by the inter-war political and industrial environment. Fittingly, the memoir of one of this cohort, Will Paynter, was called *My Generation*.[25] Paradoxically, while continuing to recognise the powerful dimensions of class and eschew closer involvement in the management of the industry, members of this generation were reluctant to challenge openly the broad structures and operations of the NCB.[26]

The generation of miners' representatives who led the union in the 1960s and 1970s, by contrast, were shaped by the early frustrations of nationalisation, specifically – as in Eric Clarke's testimony – the presence of ex-private industry personnel, compounded by the initial mishandling of pit closures in the 1950s. This generation worked to strengthen union voice in workplaces and within the broader management of the industry. The details of this process are examined in Chapters 4 and 6, but a valuable initial illustration of strengthened workforce representation can be offered here. Joint industrial regulation under nationalisation pushed unresolved local grievances upwards, so national union officials, with greater knowledge and experience, could protect the security of their members. A Scottish Divisional Disputes Committee met periodically. In August 1968 Michael McGahey, elected President of the NUMSA the previous year, used this committee to safeguard earnings of miners who had been transferred to work at Seafield Colliery in Fife. NCB officials claimed that they were committed under an existing agreement to paying up to 80 per cent of previous earnings. McGahey had a clearer appreciation of this agreement's wording than management, procuring an acknowledgement that men were guaranteed earnings 'not less than' 80 per cent. A pay increase was secured.[27]

If progress towards security in the coalfields was incremental and contested after nationalisation, then this was true of working class life more generally in the 1940s and 1950s. In *The Uses of Literacy*, published in 1957, Richard Hoggart emphasised the distinct persistence of class-based inequalities and the related survival of working class identity, despite the emergence of a class-less mass culture.[28] Other left intellectuals were likewise struck by powerful continuities: nationalisation and welfare improvements narrowed income inequalities but broader structures of class power and privilege were undisturbed; and there was no move in workplaces to greater employee involvement in the organisation of production,[29] although this was plainly more advanced in coal than in many other industrial sectors.[30] Sociologists emphasised that conflicts of interest in the workplace were as much a feature of nationalised industries as private enterprises. An NCB Scottish Divisional research officer recognised this in the early 1970s, nearly thirty years after nationalisation. In attempting to understand the phenomenon of Monday and Friday absenteeism, this officer, J. C. H. Melanby Lee, paraphrased the influential work of Alan Fox.[31] Workers did not share the goals of their employers, Melanby Lee noted. Conflict was therefore 'endemic', even in the NCB, the 'primary function' of which was to produce coal rather than advance the 'welfare of men'. Absenteeism was characterised as a rare form of 'disorganised' conflict in the industry, as opposed to 'organised' conflict, which was channelled more effectively through joint industrial dialogue on wages and broad conditions of service.[32] The 'Affluent Worker' debate, initiated by the study of manual employees in three Luton factories in the 1960s,[33] tended to reinforce this impression of continuity in class relations and identity. Looking back on this debate from the twenty-first century, Savage and others have shown that improvements in working class living standards were broadly contingent on the modest growth of wages from strenuous labour, secured only through bargaining with sometimes reluctant employers who carefully protected their control of workplaces.[34]

The theme of continuity is further illustrated by the longer history of collective state action in the coal industry, which predated nationalisation. The Miners' Federation of Great Britain (MFGB), the NUM's forerunner, to which the various Scottish district trade unions were affiliated, had adopted support for state ownership and control of coal mines, along with land and railways, as early as 1897.[35] The aim of improving security through legislation, foregrounded on the Ayrshire NUM banner in the late twentieth century, was based on substantial historical precedent. In this respect the mid-nineteenth century had provided two key legacies: the ban on women and children working underground, and the Mines Inspectorate, which, from highly constrained beginnings, contributed to an industrial and political environment where dangers were seen as manageable, and casualties avoidable.[36] Successive catastrophes plus the accumulated attrition of injuries and fatalities highlighted the weaknesses of the safety regime, but broadened the scope of the miners' political ambition. A perceived link between private ownership and underground danger was established. Specifically, the pursuit by private employers of profit was seen as inimical to the safe winning of coal. A national strike for a minimum wage in 1912 consolidated the trend both to pan-British labour cooperation and state intervention. The Liberal government of Herbert Asquith and David Lloyd George acknowledged market failure as fact, stating that miners were often unable to secure a 'reasonable minimum wage', but – bending to the interests of employers – opposed a national wage, recommending district rates instead. Minimum wage legislation, with district rates, was passed.[37]

The introduction of various state controls during the First World War represented further important incursions on market forces and managerial sovereignty in the coal industry. Crucially, these included national wage minima. In August 1918, emboldened by the new situation, the MFGB restated the pre-war demand for nationalisation, along with enhanced workplace representation and a standard fixed price for coal.[38] This proposed transformation was resisted strongly by the owners and the state, shaping the conduct and outcomes of three major crises: a threatened strike in 1919, and then two lockouts, in 1921 and 1926. The lockouts are examined in Chapter 4. The owners, working in alliance with Liberal-Conservative and then Conservative governments, attained their goals: avoiding nationalisation in 1919, consolidating private ownership and managerial sovereignty in 1921, and then securing a return to market-driven wages in 1926.[39] But state regulation was developed in another way. The 1920 Mining Industry Act made some attempt to ameliorate the social problems that underpinned the miners' case for nationalisation. A national Miners' Welfare Fund was established, 'to be applied for such purposes connected with the social well-being, recreation and conditions of living of workers in or about coalmines and with mining education and research'. The financial basis of this initiative was a levy on the owners of 1d per ton of coal output. A national Committee dispensed funds to 25 district committees, composed of representatives of owners and miners, which allocated resources in response to local applications. In the context of continued conflict, the Conservative government elected late in 1924 strengthened the fund in two ways. First, an additional levy of 5 per cent on existing royalties paid by mining companies to landowners was established in 1925. In 1927 this added about £250,000 to the £1 million raised through the output levy. Second, the 1926 Mining Industry Act was introduced. While primarily designed to promote efficiency through larger aggregations of capital, this also required employers to finance 'accommodation and facilities for workmen taking baths and drying clothes'.[40] This contributed directly to the growth of colliery baths and other facilities in the 1930s,[41] assessed in Chapter 2. Two elements of this enhanced welfare provision can be emphasised: the state had overseen significant improvements to everyday life prior to nationalisation in 1947; and these improvements were funded by the private owners, but only after they were compelled to do so through state policy, itself stimulated by the collective action of miners. The Miners' Welfare Fund was abolished in 1952. Recreation, education, convalescence and retirement were henceforth the responsibilities of the newly established Coal Industry Social Welfare Organisation (CISWO), funded by an annual grant from the NCB, which itself took direct and sole responsibility – 'as the proper function of good management' – for pit-level baths, medical treatment rooms, canteens and cycle storage areas.[42]

This separation of colliery and social welfare was a departure. A brief but telling episode from the early life of the CISWO in Scotland nevertheless reinforces the strong impression that changes arising from nationalisation were partial and contested. Among its various commitments, the CISWO organised weekend drama training courses. In May 1953 Tam Galbraith, Unionist MP for Glasgow Hillhead, forwarded a complaint from one of his constituents, a male drama teacher, to Geoffrey Lloyd, the Conservative government's Minister of Fuel and Power. The teacher had attended a drama weekend near Gorebridge in Midlothian, and was displeased by a number of its alleged features: the cost of £5 to 'the tax-payer' per student; the limited interest in dramatic arts of the students, who passed a whole evening dancing; the carriage by bus of the students to a 'local' pub on Saturday night, and a Catholic service on Sunday morning; and 'immoral happenings' in the camp grounds after supper.[43] This complaint can be read as an articulation of anti-working class prejudice, many examples of which populate literature on the expansion of state welfare and social democracy in Britain in the 1940s and 1950s.[44] The drama teacher's allegations were given serious consideration at the Ministry of Fuel and Power. Officials sought advice from T. W. S. Morgan of the CISWO Scottish Divisional Welfare Committee, who provided a detailed roll of the 234 students. The majority, 143, were female; all were members of 'bona fide' drama clubs in Ayrshire, Clackmannan, Fife, Lanarkshire, Midlothian and West Lothian. The funding was itemised carefully. Each student paid a booking fee of five shillings, yielding £61. A grant of £28 from the Scottish Education Department (SED) left a balance of £211 on the total cost, which was £300. The CISWO paid this from its NCB block grant. The 'tax-payer' had therefore directly borne only the SED's small share – less than 10 per cent – of the overall cost. Morgan explained further that students had been bussed to Gorebridge on Saturday evening for about an hour, and some had enjoyed a quick drink in a pub, before the evening dance, which included assessed performances of songs and recitals. While the Catholic students were at Sunday mass a short service had been held in the camp by the Reverend A. C. Orr, where a collection of £4 7s 6d was taken for the Church of Scotland Building Extension

Fund. Morgan characterised the 'immoral happenings' allegation as 'malicious and completely untrue', citing the camp manager's commendation of the students as having behaved throughout 'in an exemplary manner'. Sir Hubert Houldsworth, the NCB Chairman no less, wrote to Tam Galbraith, reprising Morgan's account of working class coalfield respectability, adding that he had 'no hesitation in saying that community drama and other similar cultural activities do increase the output of coal in that they foster a spirit of healthy and happy cooperation'. In setting out this prospectus of strengthened community and culture supporting improved production, Houldsworth was challenging the drama teacher's politicised criticism of nationalisation, which had been channelled, remember, by a Unionist MP. Yet the theme of gradual innovation as opposed to radical reconstruction was also present: in cultural provision, Houldsworth asserted, the NCB was simply 'continuing the policy of our predecessors'.[45]

Changing Coalfield Employment

The restructuring of employment in the Scottish coalfields by policy-makers illustrates the pattern of gradual but contested progress towards greater security for miners. The privately owned industrial order of the 1920s, with limited new growth and investment, and where trade union influence was circumscribed by authoritarian management, gave way after the Second World War and nationalisation to targeted development and greater partnership between employers and employees. The manner of these changes qualifies both the private enterprise and the labour tradition critiques of nationalisation. NCB and government investment from the 1950s to the 1970s improved economic security even as the coal industry contracted as producer and employer. Long-run employment changes in Scotland's deep coal mines are shown in Table 1.1. In the mid-1920s more than 10 per cent of Scotland's occupied population were employed in coal mining. Radical contraction followed, in the context of disrupted international trade in the late 1920s and early 1930s. Employment rose gradually after nationalisation, peaking across NCB Scottish Division holdings at 87,373 in February 1958, with 34,520 face workers.[46]

Table 1.1 Collieries and employment in deep coal mines in Scotland (thousands), selected years, 1925 to 1987

Year	Number of Collieries	Employment (thousands)	Average Number of Workers per Colliery
1925	388*	126.0	325
1932		82.3	
1947	207**	77	372
1957	164**	86	500
1967	48**	36	667
1977	21**	21	1,000
1987	8	6	750

Notes: *figure for 1927; **approximate numbers
Sources: Campbell, *Scottish Miners. Volume One*, pp. 22–3, 26; Oglethorpe, *Scottish Collieries*, p. 20; Department of Energy and Climate Change, *Historical Coal Data: Coal Production, 1853 to 2014* (https://www.gov.uk/government/statistical-data-sets/historical-coal-data-coal-production-availability-and-consumption-1853-to-2011, accessed 8 January 2019)

The drop in coal mining employment that followed was precipitous. The annual average loss of nearly 6 per cent in Scotland was steeper than the industry rate across Britain. Scotland's share of NCB employment fell from 12.2 per cent in 1957 to 10.2 per cent in 1972–3, as investment was concentrated increasingly in Yorkshire and the Midlands. These territories increased their share of NCB output from 51.9 per cent in 1957 to 63.8 per cent in 1972–3, and in the same period their portion of manpower grew from 42.6 per cent to 53.5 per cent.[47]

Lost employment was accompanied in Scotland by pit closures, and compromised the security apparently won through nationalisation. The union response is examined in Chapters 4, 5 and 6. Policy-makers were challenged to explain and rationalise the disproportionately large scale of contraction in Scotland. Chaired from 1961 to 1971 by Lord Robens, a Cabinet Minister in Attlee's government, the NCB was pursuing the aims of Conservative and then Labour government policy. This was informed by broad economic priorities, of course, but the distinct role and strategy of the Ministry of Power was highly significant. From 1957 onwards this Ministry was apparently exhibiting an anti-coal bias that would become pronounced later in the 1960s, and even more so at its institutional successor, the Department of Energy, in the 1970s and 1980s. In November 1959 Richard Wood, newly in post as Minister of Power, told MPs that his Conservative government's fuel policy was based on supplying energy 'efficiently and at lowest cost, with due regard to all relevant social and economic factors'. Market demand for coal, he added, was falling, and only the stock-piling of reserves was inhibiting faster growth of closures and redundancies.[48] Wood, the Old Etonian son of Lord Halifax and a disabled military veteran of the Second World War, has been characterised as a centrist or even leftish Tory, whose desire for accommodation with trade unions irritated many party colleagues.[49] But his stint at the Ministry of Power helped to establish a powerful narrative of coal as a high cost market loser, with important long-run consequences. He was the first of several Conservative energy ministers who deflected criticism by characterising pit closures as resulting from decisions taken by the NCB rather than the government.[50] This was disingenuous, ignoring the impact on the coal industry of government efforts to stimulate alternative energy forms. Coal's share of energy supplied in the UK fell from 73.7 per cent in 1960 to 46.6 per cent in 1970.[51] Coal production in Scotland was stable at around 22–23 million tonnes from 1947 to 1957, but then fell to about 18 million tonnes in 1960, slightly less than 15 million tonnes in 1965, and 11–12 million tonnes in 1970.[52]

Within this broader policy framework, in 1961 the Ministry of Power convened a committee of Whitehall officials to examine the coal industry's performance in Scotland, drawn from the Treasury, the Scottish Office, the Board of Trade, the Ministry of Labour and the NCB. Ministry of Power officials guided this committee to accept two important narratives: first, that Scottish coal was expensively produced; and second, that the economic costs of winning coal at each colliery ought to match the revenue from its sale. Collieries where mining was unprofitable could face closure, irrespective of the quantity of their coal reserves. The committee established that pre-nationalisation Scottish coal firms had obtained comparative advantage and enhanced profitability because their employees were paid less than the industry average across Britain. After nationalisation, with industry-wide collective bargaining in place, wage rates for

Scottish miners matched those in the industry generally, reversing the localised bargaining imposed by employers in 1926. The wage burden rose steadily after 1947, but the NCB had not exploited the sellers' market conditions. In the early and even mid-1950s prices to domestic and business customers were below the overall cost of production. This remained the case in 1961, despite the closure of less productive collieries and the loss of roughly one job in four since the end of 1957. The Whitehall committee supported an NCB proposal to raise the price of Scottish coal by 12 per cent to reflect more accurately the costs of production. It was reckoned that this would increase the cost of supplying electricity and gas in Scotland by 4 per cent and add 0.5 per cent to the overall cost of living. Steel production costs would probably rise by up to 2.5 per cent, although costs to broader industry would increase by less than 0.5 per cent. The committee knew that more expensive coal would lower demand, and accelerate the rundown of manpower in Scotland. Without a price rise employment could be pegged at around 60,000 in 1965; the decision to increase it would reduce the workforce to 49,000.[53]

The price increase took its effect, as did the impact of the gradual shift from coal to other sources of fuel, so much so that employment had dipped to 42,000 by the autumn of 1966, below the Whitehall committee's projection. Department of Economic Affairs (DEA) officials advised their Secretary of State, George Brown, that coal job losses had been absorbed at minimal social cost since 1957. The chief explanation for this was an average annual wastage rate of 15 per cent, which enabled the NCB to redeploy miners from pits that were closing to those that were remaining open. But this approach was becoming less sustainable as employment continued to contract, complicating redeployment in the event of further closures.[54] Brown, who was also Deputy Prime Minister to Harold Wilson in the Labour government, was preparing for a meeting with representatives of the Scottish Trades Union Congress (STUC). The labour movement's resistance to the employment effects of coalfield deindustrialisation was stiffening in Scotland and becoming more effective. A distinct and slower phase of contraction developed from 1967 to 1979, when the average annual job loss was 2.8 per cent, less than half the rate observable between 1957 and 1966. The phased nature of deindustrialisation was evident across

Table 1.2 NCB manpower in Scotland, 1968 to 1972

	Scottish North Area	Scottish South Area	Total
End March 1968	14,656	21,251	35,907
End March 1969	13,437	18,060	31,497
End March 1970	13,312	16,824	30,136
End March 1971	13,495	16,643	30,138
End March 1972	12,874	15,498	28,372

Sources: NCB, *Report and Accounts for 1967–68*, HC 401 (HMSO: London, 1968), p. 40; *for 1968–9*, HC 446 (HMSO: London, 1969), p. 35; *for 1969–70*, HC 130 (HMSO: London, 1970), p. 33; *for 1971–2*, HC 445 (HMSO: London, 1972), p. 31

the British coalfields from the 1940s to the 1980s,[55] but in Scotland a slowdown in the rate of contraction after 1967 was especially pronounced. Thirteen pits closed in 1968, but only two more followed in 1969. There was a single closure in 1970 and none in 1971. From 1972 to 1977 just twelve more closed.[56] Lawrence Daly, NUM General Secretary, observed when meeting Wilson in May 1969 that the falling number of closures was deceptive, given that the affected pits were larger than average and job alternatives in the areas concerned were scant.[57] Yet the general trend to a softening of deindustrialisation was clear. Table 1.2 provides closer details. In the Scottish North Area, comprising Stirlingshire, Clackmannan and Fife, the average annual rate of employment contraction was less than 1.4 per cent per annum in the three years from March 1969, compared with 4.7 per cent in the Scottish South Area, comprising Ayrshire, Lanarkshire and the Lothians, and over 8 per cent across all NCB holdings.[58]

The changing rate of employment loss in coal is a key element in this book's analysis of miners and their economic security. It is best understood in terms of the manner in which workers mobilised to influence the management of industrial contraction. Deindustrialisation – in output and employment terms – was commonly experienced across Organisation for Economic Co-operation and Development countries in the final third of the twentieth century, but accelerated more rapidly in the United Kingdom than in any other comparable economy from the 1980s.[59] So marked was this change that deindustrialisation can be seen as one of the UK's defining economic and social characteristics since the 1960s, but it has often been misunderstood.[60] The rapid contraction of industrial employment in the 1980s captured political attention, but obscured the longer history of deindustrialisation, commencing with the peak of employment in the 'staples', in textiles, metals and shipbuilding as well as coal in Scotland in the late 1950s, and in manufacturing in the late 1960s.[61] The longer history is important: these earlier changes were carefully managed and even encouraged by policy-makers who were intent on diverting labour and capital resources into higher value-added assembly manufacturing. The development especially of electrical and then electronic engineering, it was felt, would produce more rapid increases in growth and living standards.[62] Unemployment, low by historic standards in the 1950s and 1960s, would be further eliminated. This was a particularly important goal in Scotland, where the greater proportionate reliance on the staples was a factor in its higher than UK average rate of unemployment: 3 per cent compared to 1.6 per cent on average per annum, from 1953 to 1959.[63] Policy changes secured some convergence of growth and employment rates in the decade from 1964: Scotland's GDP per capita rose from 88 to 94 per cent of the UK's, and the ratio of Scottish to UK unemployment fell from about 2:1 to 1.7:1.[64]

The Labour government elected in 1964, with Wilson talking about industrial and technological modernisation, placed a special premium on planning for more rapid economic growth.[65] A key instrument was regional assistance, set out in the Labour government's 1965 *National Plan*.[66] Various financial incentives were offered to businesses moving to areas of slower economic growth. These, as noted in the Introduction, were increased 'sixteen-fold in real terms' from 1962–3 to 1969–70.[67] What this meant for the coal-fields was spelt out by Scottish Development Department officials in 1965, emphasising that alternative industrial employment would be built up significantly in mining areas, to attain the *National Plan*'s objectives, and allow for further NCB employment shrinkage.[68] This was partial recognition of the demands from miners and their trade union representatives for employment diversification, examined in Chapter 5. The NCB's Scottish Division, looking at the implications of closures in 1965, was advised by Ministry of Labour officials that 6,400 additional jobs could follow in Fife in the next three years, 2,300 of these explicitly 'for males'. This helped the NCB to rationalise the shutdown of all remaining pits in Central Fife, with the further proviso that a major new colliery at Seafield, to the west of Kirkcaldy, would provide jobs 'for all those fit, willing and able to accept them'.[69]

Fife was the core of the Scottish coalfield by the 1960s. This marked a significant change from the 1920s when Lanarkshire was the key area, responsible for roughly half of Scottish production and employment. In the inter-war decades pits in Fife and the Lothians were already larger on average than those in Lanarkshire and Ayrshire, signalling the greater industrial efficiencies which stimulated a shift to the east and north in coal's regional distribution, which started under private ownership and was then accelerated by the NCB.[70] In 1925 about one in five of Scotland's miners were employed in Fife, rising to about one in three by 1951.[71] More than 7,000 miners and their families left Lanarkshire between 1947 and 1954, mainly for Fife but also to the Lothians, organised with financial incentives from the NCB. Younger miners and their wives especially were encouraged to move, enabling older miners to remain in Lanarkshire.[72] The NCB portrayed this positively, highlighting the advantages of stable employment and modern housing in Fife, but in the late 1940s and early 1950s under-estimated the ruptures of extended family separation and community abandonment, and the depth of workforce resentment.[73] These tensions are explored further in Chapters 4 and 6, where it is shown that closures were managed more carefully in later years as a result of union pressure.[74]

The changing employment position in Lanarkshire illuminates the largely positive nature of this restructuring. Coal contracted from 15.5 per cent of male employment in 1951 to 2.8 per cent in 1971, by which point most miners were employed at two large pits in North Lanarkshire: Cardowan near Stepps, and Bedlay, near Glenboig. Closures immediately after nationalisation had been around Shotts, in the late 1940s; a second wave followed from the mid-1950s, also in South Lanarkshire, around Hamilton. Cardowan's workforce in the winter of 1964–5 numbered 1,639. Like the Central Fife miners travelling to Seafield, more than

700 South Lanarkshire miners made a daily return journey of 20 miles or more from Blantyre, Bothwell, Burnbank, Cambuslang, Hamilton, Larkhall and Uddingston.[75] Despite the shrinkage of coal manpower, industrial employment in Lanarkshire remained stable. Mainly as a result of UK government regional incentives, engineering increased its share of male employment from 9.9 in 1951 to 25.6 per cent in 1971. So the male employment share of engineering plus coal actually *increased* across this twenty-year period from 25.4 per cent to 28.4 per cent.[76] An important illustration of this overall pattern of restructuring was Caterpillar Tractors. In 1956 the US multinational firm opened a factory to build bulldozers at Uddingston, near Hamilton. Scotland's largest single industrial unit by the mid-1960s, this was built on the site of a demolished ex-coal village, Tannochside.[77] At its peak, in 1968, Caterpillar employed around 2,500 relatively well-paid engineering workers.[78]

A similar process of managed restructuring was evident in Fife. In 1951 one in four of the county's employed men, 24,000 in total, worked in coal. One in 10 working men were still in coal by 1971, when 44 per cent of all male jobs were in industrial categories. This was down from 56 per cent in 1951, but above the Scottish national average of 40 per cent, and other industries had increased their share from 31 to 34 per cent.[79] The major innovations were in engineering, in and around Glenrothes, which was developed initially to aid the expansion of coal production, trumping an alternative proposed development adjacent to Cowdenbeath and Lochgelly.[80] Glenrothes housed families of miners who moved eastwards from Lanarkshire, working at a major new pit, Rothes, which opened in 1957 but closed in 1962 owing to geological difficulties and extreme flooding.[81] But the local labour market was stabilised, with other employers attracted through regional policy,[82] including US multinationals such as Hughes Electronics and Burroughs Machines. Workers travelled daily to the town's factories from the Central Fife coalfield and settlements to the east. Glenrothes grew in population, and high concentrations of manufacturing activity were established. By 1971 roughly 65 per cent of male jobs and 55 per cent of female jobs were in industrial categories. One-third of the town's economically active women were employed in electrical engineering.[83]

The growth generally of female employment was a major benefi-cial aspect of restructuring, which strengthened the sustainability of coal communities. Mining households were becoming less reli-ant on male earnings. Gender divisions in economic terms there-fore became less pronounced, encouraging the progressive shift in relations between men and women in the coalfields that a number of scholars have recently emphasised. Women in the coalfields in the 1960s and 1970s were not passive victims of gender oppres-sion. They articulated a wider range of social and cultural ambitions than women of previous generations.[84] The breadwinner ideology nevertheless remained central to working class male esteem in the early 1980s according to Daniel Wight, in his study of Cauldmoss, a pseudonym for a small town in central Scotland on the boundary between the West Lothian and Lanarkshire coalfields. In Cauldmoss the performance by men of domestic labour tasks was still seen as exceptional in the 1980s. Male shoppers were mildly derided as the 'carrier bag brigade'. Men in this minority emphasised their ancil-lary or 'helping' role: helping, that is, the woman who was primarily responsible for designing and completing the schedule of domestic labour.[85] The availability of part-time and shift work in the new factories was therefore an important asset,[86] accommodating the existing gender division of domestic labour by providing female workers with time for child care, shopping, cleaning and other vital but unpaid tasks of social reproduction.

Security in the coalfields was duly advanced in a number of ways through post-1947 restructuring. The process nevertheless con-tained three distinct challenges. First, many workers experienced a difficult adjustment to the regime of factory employment. There were workplace tensions between new employers, particularly US multinationals, and their employees, mainly over job design and control over production. Some workers, coming with craft skills from mining or a metals background, found factory employment to be a demotivating exercise in de-skilling. Second, struggles were often necessary to win union recognition. Inward investors, espe-cially from the USA, were reluctant to admit a trade union pres-ence to their factories.[87] Third, and perhaps most problematic of all, there were early signs of the 'retreat' of multinational firms. Employment in overseas-owned factories often peaked early, 10 or

15 years before their eventual closure in the late 1970s and early 1980s. Total volume of employment in these units did not peak until 1975, but their rate of growth from the late 1960s was no longer sufficient to offset the loss of jobs elsewhere in manufacturing in Scotland. Hence there was an overall fall in manufacturing employment which proved to be lasting.[88] This concerned policy-makers greatly, particularly as it coincided with the Labour government's plans for renewed contraction of coal production and employment. In 1967 the Ministry of Power published *Fuel Policy*, a White Paper which projected a further fall in coal's market share from 58 per cent in 1966 to 34 per cent in 1975, with employment across the UK industry to be more than halved, from 425,000 to 195,000.[89]

Fuel Policy was opposed openly by the NUM in ways that earlier industrial contraction was not. This resistance, a key generational shift in the miners' collective approach to closures, is examined in Chapter 6. Here it is worth emphasising that the DEA established a Working Party to estimate the social costs of *Fuel Policy*. The strategy would result in the loss of 1 per cent of all male employment in Scotland, and not just in coal. The geographical concentration of the coal industry meant that there would be highly acute localised effects. Particular problems were forecast for Ayrshire, where industrial diversification had been less effective than elsewhere in the coalfields. This concern had been raised by Ayr County Council with Willie Ross, the Labour government's Secretary of State for Scotland, in October 1965. The local authority was seeking a concentration of regional assistance in coalfield areas, to stimulate jobs for men, especially in and around the East Ayrshire settlements of New Cumnock and Auchinleck, where 'modern housing and community facilities' had been established before the disinvestment in coal.[90] The pessimism of DEA officials in 1967 focused on the South Ayrshire town of Sanquhar, where unemployment at 7 per cent was already more than double the Scottish average, and *Fuel Policy* would eliminate half of the remaining male jobs. Officials were more optimistic about the position in West Fife, where a giant coal-fired electricity power station at Longannet was coming into operation. This had been approved in principle by the NCB and the Ministry of Power in 1964–5,[91] and was adapted under pressure from the NUM to accommodate additional coal burn and therefore extra employment after 1967. Two new drift mines, Solsgirth and Castlehill, would employ almost 1,700 at their peak between 1971 and 1975. DEA officials were also confident about Midlothian, where two major new collieries, Bilston Glen and Monktonhall, were now established, but less sanguine about West Lothian and Lanarkshire as well as Ayrshire. These areas were vulnerable to employment losses in steel as well as coal, and a major effort would be required to stimulate alternatives.[92]

Table 1.2 emphasised the falling rate of employment contraction in the Scottish coalfields, which was especially pronounced by this point in the north area encompassing Fife. The linkage between coal and broader industrial employment, and the managed nature of change, is the underlying explanation for this. Coal jobs were preserved after 1967 partly because the NCB had achieved intended economies in scale and concentration, but also in response to concerted union pressure as the growth of alternatives was slowing. The NCB recognised its special duty to consult 'men and unions' when considering closures and redundancies, and mitigate their social effects. In 1968–9 this meant slowing the rate of contraction.[93] Economic stagnation was particularly visible in Fife, and troubled UK government officials. Special incentives for attracting new industry to Glasgow and its environs, usually the top priority for policy-makers worrying about unemployment-related social unrest, were extended to Glenrothes,[94] where new businesses were providing fewer than anticipated jobs. Burroughs, for example, operating in a £4 million factory provided by the UK government,[95] had proposed recruiting 1,000 workers,[96] but by the end of 1974 employed only 270 men and 160 women.[97] In 1969 Willie Hamilton, Labour MP for Fife West, pressed the case for re-opening Michael Colliery in East Wemyss, closed by the NCB in 1967 after a disastrous and fatal fire. Reginald Freeson, Parliamentary Secretary to the Minister of Power, responded by outlining the government's commitment to Fife. This involved the planned expansion of factory capacity in the Kirkcaldy, Leven and Methil, Glenrothes and Burntisland employment exchange areas, where the level of joblessness – following Michael's closure and the slowed process of wider diversification – now exceeded the Scottish average, 4.8 per cent against 3.5 per cent in July 1969. A projected 4,754 new jobs, 2,723 of them 'for men', were anticipated for the area in the coming thirty-month period.[98] At least one important initiative followed, the Distillers Company Limited establishing a blending and bottling plant in Leven which was employing 900 workers by 1973, including 350-plus men.[99]

Conclusion

Collective state and employee action were important in the restructuring of the coalfields from the 1920s onwards, and especially after the Second World War when moral economy arguments were highly influential. Security was emphasised by miners as their key priority. In pursuing their ambitions of higher growth and rising living standards for the population generally, policy-makers were persuaded to accommodate the needs of the coalfields as miners defined them. Human and capital resources were shifted out of basic industry, including coal, and into higher value-added manufacturing. Coal jobs in this sense were not so much 'lost' as more or less consciously exchanged for other industry jobs. New factories were established in the coalfields, mainly in mechanical engineering and then electrical engineering, with jobs for women as well as men. This latter point was important. In gender terms miners can be seen as defending a system of security that privileged the interests of male wage-earners, but this process was changing. A reconfigured pattern of social relations emerged gradually, with more opportunities for women and less gender inequality.

The process of restructuring was initially clumsy, insensitive to the costs of community destabilisation and even abandonment in the 1950s. But over time the process was achieved through multiactor dialogue and agreement, involving the state, the NCB, and mining unions, and provided greater security, at least in the 1960s and 1970s. Changes experienced in the 1920s and 1930s were accelerated by nationalisation and the related contraction overall of production and employment. Operations were concentrated in a smaller number of larger collieries from the late 1950s onwards. Literature on nationalisation – from free enterprise and labour tradition perspectives – has been critical of the manner in which the Labour government took coal into public ownership. But this overlooks the interaction of the workforce and policy-maker moral economies, which combined to ensure that the NCB generally was a responsible employer, keeping coal communities sustainable and recycling workers at minimal social cost. It is true that nationalisation involved limited innovation in the sense of enhanced industrial democracy, but the NCB was operating in the context of a broader redistribution of esteem which strengthened worker voice. Workers were organising and this ensured that policy-makers were responsive. Miners and their union representatives made nationalisation work as a positive force for collective economic and social security in the coalfields.

Notes

1. Sylvie Aprile, Matthieu de Oliveira and Béatrice Touchelay, 'Introduction', in Sylvie Aprile, Matthieu de Oliveira, Béatrice Touchelay and Karl-Michael Hoin, *Les Houillères entre l'État, le marché et la société* (Septentrion Presses Universitaires: Villeneuve d'Ascq, 2015), pp. 17–19.
2. David Marquand, *Mammon's Kingdom. An Essay on Britain, Now* (Allen Lane: London, 2014).
3. Gibbs, 'Moral Economy of the Scottish Coalfields', pp. 16–18; Keith Gildart, 'Mining Memories: Reading Coalfield Autobiographies', *Labor History*, 50 (2009), pp. 139–61.
4. Jim Tomlinson, *Democratic Socialism and Economic Policy: the Attlee Years, 1945–1951* (Cambridge University Press: Cambridge, 1997), pp. 97–103.
5. The Mining Institute, Newcastle (hereafter TMI), David Douglass Archives (hereafter DDA), General papers relating to mining industry, Box 1, Copy of letter from C. R. Attlee, 11 January 1951.
6. Field, *Blood, Sweat and Toil*, p. 119.
7. Leslie Hannah, 'A failed experiment: the state ownership of industry', in Roderick Floud and Paul Johnson, eds, *The Cambridge Economic History of Modern Britain. Volume III, Structural Change and Growth, 1939–2000* (Cambridge University Press: Cambridge, 2004), pp. 84–111; N. Crafts, 'Economic growth during the long twentieth century', in R. Floud, J. Humphries and P. Johnson, eds, *The Cambridge Economic History of Modern Britain, Vol. II, 1870 to the present* (Cambridge University Press: Cambridge, 2014), pp. 26–59.
8. J. Foreman-Peck and R. Millward, *Public and Private Ownership of British Industry, 1820–1990* (Clarendon: Oxford, 1994), pp. 306–14, 323–8.

9. TMI, DDA, General Papers relating to the mining industry, Box 3, *Coal Industry Mineworkers' Pension Scheme* (NCB, 1958).

10. Jim Tomlinson, 'A "failed experiment"? Public Ownership and the Narratives of Post-war Britain', *Labour History Review*, 73 (2008), pp. 199–214.

11. Arthur McIvor, 'Deindustrialization Embodied: Work, Health and Disability in the United Kingdom since the Mid-Twentieth Century', in Steven High, Lachlan MacKinnon and Andrew Perchard, eds, *The Deindustrialized World: Confronting Ruination in Postindustrial Places* (University of British Columbia Press: Vancouver, 2017), pp. 25–45, and especially pp. 32–5.

12. Ewan Gibbs, *Deindustrialisation and Industrial Communities: The Lanarkshire Coalfields c.1947–1983*, University of Glasgow PhD, 2016, pp. 79–80.

13. W. Ashworth, *The History of the British Coal Industry, Volume Five, 1946–1982: the nationalised industry* (Oxford University Press: Oxford, 1986), pp. 29–31.

14. Mark Tookey, 'Three's A Crowd?: Government, Owners, and Workers during the Nationalization of the British Coalmining Industry, 1945–47', *Twentieth Century British History*, 12.4 (2001), pp. 486–510.

15. Miles K. Oglethorpe, *Scottish Collieries. An Inventory of the Scottish Coal Industry in the Nationalised Era* (Royal Commission on the Ancient and Historical Monuments of Scotland: Edinburgh, 2006), p. 310.

16. Andrew Perchard, *The Mine Management Professions in the Twentieth-Century Scottish Coal Mining Industry* (Edwin Mellan: Lampeter and Lewiston, 2007).

17. Eric Clarke, Interview with Author, Newtongrange, 25 August 2009.

18. *Spirit of '45*, directed by Ken Loach.

19. Norman Dennis, Fernando Henriques and Clifford Slaughter, *Coal Is Our Life: an Analysis of a Yorkshire Mining Community* (Tavistock: London, 1969), pp. 9–10, 15–17, 26–33, 56–63.

20. W. H. Scott, Enid Mumford, I. P. McGivering and J. M. Kirby, *Coal and Conflict. A Study of Industrial Relations at Collieries* (Liverpool University Press: Liverpool, 1963), pp. 20–2.

21. Rebecca Zahn, 'German Codetermination without Nationalization, and British Nationalization without Codetermination: Retelling the Story', *Historical Studies in Industrial Relations*, 26 (2015), pp. 1–28.

22. Dennis, Henriques and Slaughter, *Coal Is Our Life*, 80–3.

23. Ian Gareth Anderson, *Scottish Trade Unions and Nationalisation, 1945–1955: a Case Study of the Coal Industry*, University of Glasgow PhD, 1999, pp. 232–61.

24. Alan Campbell, 'Reflections on the 1926 Mining Lockout', *Historical Studies in Industrial Relations*, 21 (2006), pp. 143–81.
25. Paynter, *My Generation*.
26. Curtis, *South Wales Miners*, p. 72; Huw Beynon and Terry Austrin, 'The Performance of Power. Sam Watson, a Miners' Leader on Many Stages', *Journal of Historical Sociology*, 28.4 (2015), pp. 458–90.
27. The National Archives (hereafter TNA), COAL 75/1863, Minutes of Meeting of the Scottish Disputes Committee, Green Park, Edinburgh, 23 August 1968.
28. Richard Hoggart, *The Uses of Literacy* (Penguin: London, 1957).
29. Alexandre Campsie, 'Mass-Observation, Left Intellectuals and the Politics of Everyday Life', *English Historical Review*, 131 (2016), pp. 92–121.
30. Jim Phillips, 'Participation and Nationalization: the case of British coal from the 1940s to the 1980s', in Stefan Berger, Ludger Pries and Manfred Wannöffel, eds, *The Palgrave International Handbook of Workers' Participation* (Palgrave Macmillan, Basingstoke, 2018).
31. Alan Fox, *Industrial Sociology and Industrial Relations. Royal Commission on Trade Unions and Employers' Associations, Research Papers, 3* (HMSO: London, 1966).
32. TNA, COAL 101/488, J. C. H. Melanby Lee, A paper for consideration by the Scottish Area Monday and Friday Absence Committee, meeting 8 August 1973.
33. John Goldthorpe, David Lockwood, Frank Bechhofer and Jennifer Platt, *The Affluent Worker: Industrial Attitudes and Behaviour* (Cambridge University Press: Cambridge, 1968); *The Affluent Worker: Political Attitudes and Behaviour* (Cambridge University Press: Cambridge, 1968); *The Affluent Worker in the Class Structure* (Cambridge University Press, Cambridge: 1969).
34. Mike Savage, 'Working Class Identities in the 1960s: revisiting the Affluent Worker Studies', *Sociology*, 34 (2005), pp. 929–46; Selina Todd, 'Affluence, Class and Crown Street: Reinvestigating the Post-War Working Class', *Contemporary British History*, 22 (2008), pp. 501–18; Richard Whiting, 'Affluence and Industrial Relations', *Contemporary British History*, 22 (2008), pp. 519–36.
35. Page Arnot, *Scottish Miners*, pp. 93–6.
36. Roy A. Church, *The History of the British Coal Industry. Vol. 3, 1830–1913: Victorian pre-eminence* (Oxford University Press: Oxford, 1986).
37. Page Arnot, *Scottish Miners*, pp. 122–33; Lewis Mates, *The Great Labour Unrest: Rank and file movements and political change in the Durham Coalfield* (Manchester University Press: Manchester, 2016).
38. Page Arnot, *Scottish Miners*, p. 144.

39. M. W. Kirby and S. Hamilton, 'Sir Adam Nimmo', in A. Slaven and S. Checkland, eds, *Dictionary of Scottish Business Biography. Volume 1: The Staple Industries* (Aberdeen University Press: Aberdeen, 1986), pp. 57–9; Keith Laybourn, 'Revisiting the General Strike', *Historical Studies in Industrial Relations*, 21 (2006), pp. 109–20.

40. W. John Morgan, 'The Miners' Welfare Fund in Britain, 1920–1952', *Social Policy & Administration*, 24.3 (1990), pp. 199–211.

41. Charles McKean, *The Scottish Thirties. An Architectural Introduction* (Scottish Academic Press: Edinburgh, 1987), pp. 116–17.

42. Morgan, 'Miners' Welfare Fund', p. 209.

43. TNA, BX 6/13, H. Atkinson, Ministry of Fuel and Power, to T. W. S. Morgan, Divisional Welfare Officer, CISWO, Scottish Division, 26 May 1953.

44. Selina Todd, *The People: the Rise and Fall of the Working Class* (John Murray: London, 2014), pp. 152–98.

45. TNA, BX 6/13, Morgan to Atkinson, 28 May 1953; Chairman, NCB, to T. G. D. Galbraith, MP, 3 June 1953.

46. National Records of Scotland (hereafter NRS), CB 51/2, NCB Scottish Division, Manpower, week beginning 8 February 1958.

47. Ashworth, *British Coal Industry*, pp. 253, 261 and 264, Table 6.2, Regional distribution of output and manpower, 1957 and 1972–3.

48. *Parliamentary Debates, Fifth Series, Commons*, Vol. 614, 42–158, 23 November 1959.

49. Obituary, Lord Holderness (Richard Wood), 1920–2002, *The Telegraph*, 15 August 2002, http://www.telegraph.co.uk/news/obituaries/1404416/Lord-Holderness.html, accessed 27 July 2017.

50. *Parliamentary Debates, Fifth Series, Commons*, Vol. 631, 837–8, 5 December 1960.

51. Ashworth, *British Coal Industry*, pp. 38–9, 678–9.

52. Oglethorpe, *Scottish Collieries*, p. 20.

53. TNA, COAL 31/96, Ministry of Power, Scottish Coal Committee, Report, 11 October 1961.

54. TNA, EW 8/294, Department of Economic Affairs, Brief for Secretary of State ahead of meeting with STUC, September 1966.

55. Turner, 'Post-War Pit Closures'.

56. Jim Phillips, 'Deindustrialization and the Moral Economy of the Scottish Coalfields, 1947 to 1991', *International Labor and Working Class History*, 84 (Fall 2013), pp. 99–115; detail at p. 100.

57. TNA, PREM 13/2769, Note of meeting between Prime Minister and representatives of the Labour Party National Executive Committee and the NUM, 8 May 1969.

58. NCB, *Report and Accounts for 1967–68*, HC 401 (HMSO: London, 1968), p. 40; *for 1968–69*, HC 446 (HMSO: London, 1969), p. 35; *for 1969–70*, HC 130 (HMSO: London, 1970), p. 33; *for 1971–72*, HC 445 (HMSO: London, 1972), p. 31.

59. Michael Kitson and Jonathan Michie, 'The De-industrial Revolution: The Rise and Fall of UK Manufacturing, 1870–2010', in R. Floud, J. Humphries and P. Johnson, eds, *Cambridge Economic History of Modern Britain*, vol. 2, *1870 to the Present* (Cambridge University Press: Cambridge, 2014), pp. 312–14.

60. Tomlinson, 'De-industrialization not decline'.

61. Ewan Gibbs and Jim Tomlinson, 'Planning the new industrial nation: Scotland, 1931–1979', *Contemporary British History*, 30.4 (2016), pp. 585–606.

62. Jim Tomlinson, 'Re-inventing the Moral economy in post-war Britain', *Historical Research*, 84 (2011), pp. 356–73.

63. Committee of Inquiry appointed by the Scottish Council (Development and Industry) under the Chairmanship of J. N. Toothill, *Report on the Scottish Economy* (SCDI: Edinburgh, 1961), pp. 17, 20–3.

64. Fraser of Allander Institute, *The Scottish Economy: Main Trends, 1964–1973*, https://pure.strath.ac.uk/portal/files/38985955/FEC_1_1_1975_Scottish_Economy.pdf, accessed 25 February 2017.

65. Jim Tomlinson, *The Labour Governments, 1964–70. Volume 3: Economic policy* (Manchester University Press, Manchester 2004), pp. 75–83.

66. Department of Economic Affairs, *The National Plan*, Cmnd. 2764 (HMSO: London, 1965), pp. 97, 100.

67. Scott, 'Regional development and policy'.

68. NRS, SEP 14/1894, Scottish Development Department note, 7 October 1965.

69. NRS, CB 305/5/1, NCB Scottish Division, Closure of Glencraig, no date, but presumed March 1966; Oglethorpe, *Scottish Collieries*, pp. 158–9.

70. 'Replanning a Coalfield', *Mining Review*, 2nd Year, No. 10 (1949), directed by Peter Pickering, produced for Data Film Productions, sponsored by the National Coal Board (hereafter NCB), commentary by John Slater. The film features on the DVD, *National Coal Board Collection, Volume One, Portrait of a Miner* (London, 2009).

71. Campbell, *Scottish Miners. Volume One*, pp. 22–3; General Registry Office (hereafter GRO), *Census 1951 Scotland. Volume IV: Occupations and Industries* (HMSO: Edinburgh, 1956), Table 13.

72. National Coal Board Scottish Division, *Scotland's Coal Plan* (NCB: Edinburgh, 1955), pp. 29–30.

73. Duncan, *Mineworkers*, p. 257.
74. Hazel Heughan, *Pit Closures at Shotts and the Migration of Miners* (Edinburgh University Press: Edinburgh, 1953).
75. NRS, CB 51/4, NCB – Scottish Division – Central Area, Places of Work and Residence of Mineworkers and Industrial Workers as at 28 November 1964.
76. Gibbs, 'Moral Economy of the Scottish Coalfields'.
77. NRS, DD 10/380, Scottish Home Department, Note for Under Secretary of State, Note on Company and Tannochside Project, 21 August, 1959.
78. NRS, SEP 2/49, 'Strike by 1100 at Tannochside', *Glasgow Herald*, 12 June 1968.
79. *Census 1951 Scotland*, Table 13, and General Registry Office, Edinburgh, *Census 1971 Scotland. Economic Activity: County Tables, Part II* (HMSO: Edinburgh, 1975), Table 3.
80. Roger Smith, 'The New Town Ideal for Scottish Miners: the Rise and Fall of a Social Ideal (1945–1948)', *Scottish Economic and Social History*, 9 (1989), pp. 71–9.
81. Robert S. Halliday, *The Disappearing Scottish Colliery* (Scottish Academic Press: Edinburgh, 1990), pp. 49–77.
82. David Cowling, *An Essay For Today: Scottish New Towns, 1947–1997* (Rutland Press: Edinburgh, 1997), pp. 29–30.
83. *Census 1971 Scotland*, Table 3.
84. Jean Spence and Carol Stephenson, '"Side by Side With Our Men?" Women's Activism, Community and Gender in the 1984–5 British Miners' Strike', *International Labor and Working Class History*, 75 (2009), pp. 68–84; Florence Sutcliffe-Braithwaite and Natalie Thomlinson, 'Women's Activism During the Miners' Strike: Memories and Legacies', *Contemporary British History*, 32.1 (2018), pp. 78–100.
85. Daniel Wight, *Workers Not Wasters. Masculine Respectability, Consumption and Employment in Central Scotland* (Edinburgh University Press: Edinburgh, 1993) pp. 36–47.
86. W. W. Knox and A. McKinlay, 'American Multinationals and British Trade Unions', *Labor History*, 51.2 (2010), pp. 211–29.
87. Alan McKinlay and Bill Knox, 'Working for the Yankee Dollar. US Inward Investment and Scottish Labour, 1945–1970', *Historical Studies in Industrial Relations*, 7 (1999), pp. 1–26.
88. Neil Hood and Stephen Young, *Multinationals in Retreat: the Scottish Experience* (Edinburgh University Press: Edinburgh, 1982), pp. 5–6, 30–7.
89. Ministry of Power, *Fuel Policy*, Cmnd. 3428 (HMSO, 1967), pp. 36, 71.

90. NRS, SEP 17/16, Clerk, Ayr County Council, to Willie Ross, October 1965.

91. TNA, POWE 52/137, Ministry of Power Coal Division, Longannet Colliery Project, 17 August 1964.

92. TNA, POWE 52/113, Fuel Policy Working Party, Regional Implications of Possible Developments in the Coal Industry, Ministry of Power, 16 March 1967, and 'Colliery Closures' in Scotland, Fuel Policy Working Party, Regional Implications of Possible Developments in the Coal Industry, Ministry of Power, 7 June 1967.

93. TMI, DDA, General papers relating to mining industry, Box 1, NCB, *Coal In Britain Today* (NCB: London, January 1970).

94. NRS, SEP 4/57, I. R. Duncan, Regional Development Division, St Andrew's House, to A. H. J. Herpels, EEC Social Affairs Division, 21 September 1971.

95. NRS, SEP 4/3869, W. Mackenzie, Regional Development Division, Burroughs Machines: background note, 23 December 1970.

96. NRS, SEP 4/57, Regional Development Division, St Andrew's House, Note for Lady Tweedsmuir's Visit to Glenrothes on 2 March 1971.

97. NRS, SEP 4/57, Glenrothes Develoment Corporation, Progress Report, Quarter Ended 31 December 1974.

98. *Parliamentary Debates, Fifth Series, Commons*, Vol. 786, 1723–32, 10 July 1969.

99. NRS, SEP 4/2334, Miss M. J. Alexander, Regional Development Division, 'The Closure of Michael Colliery and Industrial Development in the Leven Area of Fife', 19 October 1970.

CHAPTER 2

Changing Communities and Collieries

Changes in ownership and employment in the coalfields were accompanied by important long-term shifts in the character of communities and collieries. Miners mobilised frequently in defence of community, but the term was highly ambiguous, concealing important divisions of class and gender. Workplace tensions between employers and employees were an ever-present reminder of the limits of cross-class social solidarity in mining communities. Intra-working class divisions were observable too, however, especially in times of stress such as the lockouts of the 1920s and the strike in 1984–5. In gender terms the male breadwinner ideology was deeply embedded in the coalfields and the defence of jobs and collieries at times appeared to privilege male interests.

The conflicts of gender and class are examined in the first part of this chapter. Analysis then moves to migration and changes in the built environment. The broader pattern of economic and social restructuring examined in Chapter 1 included the migration of large numbers of miners within Scotland from west to east, and to the expanding regions of the English coalfields, in Yorkshire, Nottinghamshire and Leicestershire. Security in the Scottish coalfields was strengthened with a move to public sector housing, reducing the miners' social dependence on their employers. Re-housing nevertheless had complex long-term effects. It was a factor in loosening the relationship between coalfield workplace and residence, along with the concentration of production in a smaller number of larger collieries and the introduction of new employment in purpose-built industrial estates. This is examined in the third part of the chapter, focusing on the evolution of coal production from the 1920s onwards. The importance of transitional points is emphasised, with three phases of industrial development identified, embodied in the establishment of distinct types of production unit: the Village Pit of the 1900s, the New Mine of the 1930s, and the Cosmopolitan Colliery of the 1960s. These different units represented ever-increasing scale. New production techniques were also involved, plus changes in workforce composition as employees were drawn from a progressively wider locale. These colliery types are related to three generations of miners' union leaders with distinct formative experiences and expectations. Generational changes arising from restructuring were important to the development of the miners' moral economy, and their defence of coalfield security.

Community in the Coalfields

Community is a positive and inclusive term, which partly explains why it is often used to frame understanding of localities, and also of interest groups, sometimes spread over a broad and even international geographical area. 'Imagined Communities', the term applied by Benedict Anderson to nations, could equally hold for other dispersed collectives formed by political ideology, ethnicity, faith, occupational background or even leisure activity.[1] Given this wide application, however, community is also ambiguous and problematic. The cohesion of mining communities was qualified by class divisions and gender inequalities. Diverse in character and changing over time, these localities were less stable and homogeneous than the term 'mining community' implies. The varied nature of mining communities is well recognised in US as well as British literature. The 'isolated mass' thesis in particular has been interpreted as both useful and a misdirection in making sense of communities which varied substantially in scale, occupational profile and proximity to larger urban centres.[2]

Given these theoretical and empirical ambiguities, coal communities are perhaps best understood in dual terms: as economic localities and ideological communalities.[3] The 'ideal type' of occupational community hypothesised by Michael Bulmer, where coal absorbed an overwhelming proportion of male employment, was increasingly unusual in Britain after the Second World War,[4] possibly excepting the South Wales valleys,[5] and in Scotland parts of Ayrshire. A key factor in generating variety was the process of economic diversification examined in Chapter 1. To recap, coal production from the late 1950s was increasingly concentrated in a smaller number of larger pits. The established connection between workplace and residence was disrupted. Increasing numbers of miners lived in coal villages where pits had closed, and travelled daily to work in the 'Cosmopolitan Collieries' opened by the NCB in the 1960s. The alternative employment track, work in regional policy factories, was available to women as well as men. The contrasting employment profiles of Scotland's five New Towns, designed and developed to relieve housing congestion in Glasgow after the Second World War,[6] indicate that restructuring as a whole had a less beneficial impact in Ayrshire than in Lanarkshire, the Lothians and Fife. In 1971 in Cumbernauld, in the historic coalfield of North Lanarkshire, one-third of male jobs were in mechanical engineering. In Irvine, 20 miles from the South Ayrshire mining towns of Cumnock and Auchinleck, less than one-fifth of male jobs were in this category. In 1981, two years into the Thatcher-era acceleration of industrial job loss, 10.6 per cent of men in Cumbernauld were unemployed and looking for work. Less successful diversification in Ayrshire in the 1960s and 1970s meant that 15.3 per cent of Irvine's men were now in this position. New opportunities for women were also unevenly shared across the coalfields. In Fife the ratio of males to females in employment was 2.6 to 1 in 1961 but just 1.5 to 1 in 1981.[7] More than 9 per cent of all women in Fife were employed in electrical engineering in 1971, most of these in Glenrothes. In Irvine, by contrast, the largest industrial employer of women was the older and contracting sector of textiles. Across Scotland the post-1945 expansion of the public sector was important too: state education, the National Health Service and other welfare services, provided an increased range and volume of jobs open to coalfield women.[8] These various changes bolstered the economic sustainability of most coal communities, with Ayrshire a partial exception, and gradually altered social relations in progressive ways.[9]

Social divisions within coal communities were stark in the 1950s. *Coal Is Our Life*, the classic study of coalfield social relations by Dennis, Henriques and Slaughter, was based on miners in 'Ashton', a pseudonym for Featherstone in West Yorkshire. A powerful sense of class was prevalent, with simmering workplace tensions between employees and their managers.[10] Class feeling was powerful in Scottish communities too. The 1921 and 1926 mining lockouts were major expressions of social conflict with strong localised dynamics. Locked-out miners and their supporters attempted to impose significant costs on employers, destroying their private and industrial property, and fought with police officers. After 1926 the owners exacted punitive wage cuts on their workers and victimised union representatives, including the Moffats of Lumphinnans.[11] This was one of the 'Little Moscows' of Central Fife,[12] where the Red Flag was flown annually above Cowdenbeath Town Hall to celebrate the anniversary of the October Revolution.[13] Class remained a powerful and compelling force after nationalisation. This would be evident in workplace politics in the 1950s and 1960s, examined in Chapter 4, the national pay disputes of the 1970s, explored in Chapter 6, and the strike against pit closures in 1984–5, analysed in Chapter 7. But intra-working class unity was tempered by significant political and religious fissures. Some miners were socially conservative, and sectarianism was a significant force. *The Scottish Miner*, a monthly newspaper, was established by the NUMSA in 1954. Its title conveyed the union's ambition to construct greater political unity among Scotland's miners. Differences of locality and region were more easily overcome than divisions of politics and religion. The union's leadership worked hard to build a common identity around the twin themes of class and nation. It campaigned on the basis that miners in Scotland occupied a distinct political position: members of a British and indeed global working class, but with values and interests particular to plebeian citizens of the Scottish Nation.[14]

Social solidarity was further compromised by gender inequalities in the coalfields. Everyday experience was unambiguously structured by gender,[15] which 'is centrally implicated in the very formation of all types of working-class politics'. This observation was made by Savage in 1987,[16] boldly, but more than thirty years later class and gender are generally accepted as points of intersectionality with race in shaping collective and individual social identity.[17] The male breadwinner ideology featured strongly within working class male identity and esteem in the coalfields,[18] and permeated gender relations. Reading *Coal Is Our Life* in the 2010s, the most striking inequality is between working class men and working class women. Organised leisure was structured around the activities of male wage earners. A variety of social and recreational facilities were established in the coalfields in the 1930s and 1940s by the Miners' Welfare Committee and its successor body, the Miners' Welfare Commission. Women gradually acquired greater access to these amenities, particularly the welfare institutes, which were key institutions of coalfield leisure along with working men's clubs. In 1944 one-third of mining institutes had women members and organised joint activities for women and men, and one-quarter had women's groups.[19] In the 1950s and 1960s female participation in these institutes and clubs expanded, but was still circumscribed in a highly gendered social world. The Coal Industry Social Welfare Organisation oversaw an annual 'Retired Mineworkers' Indoor Games Competition' in Scotland. Men and women competed in gender-segregated whist and dominoes, while men alone contested darts.[20]

Gender roles were similarly demarcated in families and households. The needs of women were subordinate to those of men. Dennis, Henriques and Slaughter acknowledged these inequalities, but nevertheless emphasised the primacy of class loyalty and identity. Married women especially, they implied, were reconciled to gender inequality because 'they share the sense of injustice felt by miners and support their husbands against the enemy'.[21] This argument appears in Scottish literature also. Alan Campbell makes qualified reference to women's enforced monopoly of domestic labour before 1939 as an exercise in working class solidarity, enabling men to earn the family wage and fight the employers for improved living standards.[22] The partnership was far from equal, however, with women fulfilling a supporting and therefore subordinate role within the broader pattern of class relations. This was a major qualifier to the ideological unity of coal communities, and a reminder that the miners' pursuit of security was at least partly a defence of their gendered privilege as male wage-earners.

Social cohesion within coal communities was nevertheless strengthened over time. Writing of the areas that broadly supported the 1984–5 strike, which included Scotland, Raphael Samuel argued that the prolonged experience of crisis had rebuilt 'community'.[23] Economic and industrial changes since 1945 had eroded the centrality of coal employment; the linkages between residence and work had become more diffuse over time; and the acceleration of deindustrialisation after the strikers' defeat further diminished the economic viability of coal settlements. But in many localities the strike – mobilising against the unambiguous class enemies of Thatcher's Conservative government and NCB management – solidified the ideological and political basis of community. The changes in gender relations were neither sudden nor transformational. Sexism remained a repellent feature of coalfield social relations but ebbed as women assumed a greater diversity of economic and social responsibilities. This was an important paradox of deindustrialisation, confirmed in Chapter 7. Coalfield communities became stronger in ideological terms as the industry's share of economic activity dwindled. The communal values of miners retained currency in these post-industrial localities, as 'resources of hope', Raymond Williams' phrase, encouraging women and men to maintain their struggle for economic and social security in the twenty-first century.[24]

Migration and Housing

Three factors stimulated changes to the character of coalfield localities: migration, mainly within Scotland but also within the UK, which arguably weakened security; the widening 'locale' or catchment area of pits, as production was concentrated in a smaller number of collieries, with an ambiguous impact on security; and the construction of new housing, with the expansion of public sector provision significantly strengthening security.

Migration was an established feature of coalfield life. In the nineteenth century it was often seasonal. Economic dislocation and social conflict were nevertheless major triggers. Many miners left in the three or four decades before the First World War to evade unemployment and victimisation. Some travelled within Scotland and Britain; others emigrated within the British Empire and to the USA. Among them was Philip Murray, Vice President of the United Mineworkers of America from 1920 to 1942, President of the United Steelworkers of America from 1942 to 1952, and President of the Congress of Industrial Organisations from 1940 to 1952. Murray was born into a mining family in Bothwell, Lanarkshire in 1884, and moved to the Pennsylvania coalfields in 1902 with his father, William, whose working life as a union activist was interrupted by unemployment and disputes with employers.[25] Migration in the 1920s and 1930s was likewise shaped by economic and social disruption. Campbell points out that several leading figures in the NUMSA from the 1960s to the 1980s experienced enforced migration to England in childhood after their activist fathers had been victimised by employers in the 1920s and 1930s.[26]

The scale of coalfield migration before the Second World War is hard to quantify, but NCB data provides a more precise measure of movement after 1947. This was shaped in the first instance by the changing regional distribution of the coal industry, noted in Chapter 1, as the relative importance of Yorkshire and the Midlands grew. The NCB encouraged migration through two distinct schemes which commonly met the costs of relocation and assisted miners in housing themselves and their families, usually in local authority estates. The Inter-Divisional Transfer Scheme (IDTS) was launched in 1962, shifting miners in NCB employment from one coalfield area to another. This was supplemented from 1964 by the Long Distance Re-entrants Scheme (LDRS), encouraging ex-miners to re-join the NCB and move to the higher production areas. By March 1971 a total of 15,000 miners had moved under the two schemes.[27] Scots represented a substantial number of these migrants, along with many from Northumberland and Durham. Ministry of Power data, supplied in a House of Commons written answer in December 1966, showed that 2,768 miners left Scotland from April 1962 to March 1966 under the IDTS and 606 under the LDRS, amounting to 39.7 per cent of the NCB total under the combined schemes.[28]

Migration could be unsettling. David Hamilton, future NUM delegate at Monktonhall in Midlothian, moved to Nottinghamshire as a young man in the late 1960s, with Jean, his wife. They appreciated the social life and friendships in the community, but David disliked what he saw as an overly authoritarian workplace, with miners obliged to address their overseers as 'sir'. This was a jarring contrast with the easier and more democratic underground culture in Midlothian. Monktonhall's expansion offered David and Jean a welcome opportunity to return home within a year.[29] Ian Terris, originally from Lanarkshire, was working at Rothes in Central Fife when it closed in 1962. He was transferred under the IDTS to Thurcroft, near Rotherham in South Yorkshire. The move was short-lived. Within days Terris was rebuked by a workmate for speaking 'informally' to an under-manager who had shone a light in his eyes. Likening these relationships to 'serfdom', he returned shortly afterwards to Fife, accepting lower paid employment with Alexander's buses.[30] Other miners had a far more positive experience of migration. Jimmy Hood, born in 1949, began his working life as a mining engineer at Auchlochan in South Lanarkshire. This closed in 1968, and Hood accepted redeployment to Ollerton Colliery in Nottinghamshire. Hood, who served as Labour MP for Clydesdale from 1987 to 2015, looked back on the transfer as a valuable opportunity to secure his economic future. He was glad to have made the move, despite the difficulties he encountered as a union branch official supporting the strike in 1984–5 while the vast majority at Ollerton continued working.[31]

Migrants shaped their new environment as well as being influenced by it. When a new colliery opened in 1964 in Cotgrave, five miles south-east of Nottingham, the village of several hundred inhabitants was transformed into a small mining town of several thousands.[32] NCB documents show that these new residents were accommodated in three and four bedroom houses, roughly half of which were equipped with garages, itself a sign of expanding material horizons in this part of the English coalfield.[33] Large numbers of miners from the Cumnock area of Ayrshire were redeployed in the early 1960s to Whitwick and Bagworth collieries in the Leicestershire conurbation known as Coalville.[34] With their families they inhabited a new local authority housing estate in Thringston. Officially named the Woodside Estate, this was widely referred to in Coalville as the 'Scotch Estate'. The fabric of culture assumed distinctly Scottish elements. Hogmanay was celebrated and New Year's Day became an unofficial local holiday. Ex-Ayrshire miners were prominent in founding the Thringston Rangers Supporters Club in 1968,[35] a social facility as well as a football fans' association still operating in the late 2010s.[36]

Migration was part of the broader dispersal of older mining localities. This occurred in Lanarkshire and Ayrshire especially, and within the Scottish coalfields more generally the process of re-housing contributed to a spatial distancing of workers from surviving pits. In the 1920s the Fife Coal Company employed roughly three in four of the occupied population in the conurbation of Cowdenbeath, Lumphinnans and Lochgelly. It was a dominant force also in the settlements immediately to the north and east: Kelty, Lochore, Glencraig, Ballingry and Cardenden.[37] Changes in colliery scale and production regime from the 1920s to the 1970s are discussed below, but the impact of these on community 'closeness' can be gauged here. Lochhead in Coaltown of Wemyss in East Fife was an old Village Pit, opened in 1890. When it closed in 1970 there were 156 face workers seeking redeployment. Of these there were 26, exactly one in six, who lived less than two miles away, in West Wemyss, Coaltown of Wemyss or East Wemyss. Family connections were evident among these men: J. and T. Christie both lived in West Wemyss; D. and J. Penman and H. and J. Reekie all resided in Coaltown of Wemyss; and G. Rodger of East Wemyss was perhaps a relative of R. Rodger in Coaltown of Wemyss. Another 93 of the Lochhead face workers lived within four miles, in Buckhaven, Methil, Leven, Windygates and Kennoway to the east, or Dysart and Kirkcaldy to the west. At this long-established colliery, to summarise, less than than a quarter of the workforce lived more than four miles away.[38] Community 'closeness' was less evident at younger pits. At Comrie, a New Mine which opened just before the Second World War in West Fife, there were 1,458 miners employed in 1964–5. Only 297 of these lived in the nearest settlement, Oakley, with a larger number, 364, travelling daily from Dunfermline, five miles away, and another 400 from Cowdenbeath and Kelty, 10 miles away.[39] Bilston Glen, a Cosmopolitan Colliery south of Edinburgh, employed 2,124 in December 1965, close to its eventual peak of 2,367 in 1970. Residentially these miners were even more scattered. Roughly half lived five or more miles away, including 163 spread across Edinburgh and Leith, with about one in four at least nine miles distant by road, including 194 from Prestonpans and 111 from Tranent.[40] This resembled the pattern at Cardowan, the largest survivor in Lanarkshire, where half the workforce also lived more than five miles from the colliery by the mid-1960s.[41]

Iain Chalmers, a Central Fife miner who was active in the NUM at Seafield in East Fife in the 1970s and 1980s, said in 2009 that in Glenrothes the local authority made deliberate use of housing allocation to place miners in streets alongside factory, shop and local authority ancillary workers. This countered the effect on solidarity of concentrating large volumes of miners in the new Cosmopolitan Collieries, including Seafield. The widening locale of these collieries could frustrate union efforts to build common feeling among miners who lived in different villages and towns, distant from each other and their workplace.[42] The internal NCB discussion about absenteeism in the early 1970s was noted in Chapter 1. This involved some emphasis on housing changes, which were mapped to contrasting 'expressive' and 'instrumental' work attitudes. A miner living in the same village as his pit had an expressive attitude: 'he was involved in his work and had a sense of duty and obligation'. His status in a small community was more important to him than the 'economic rewards' which were supposedly prioritised instead by miners with 'instrumental' attitudes, and prepared to travel beyond their immediate community for employment. This was a problematic argument, overlooking the blurring of 'intrinsic' and 'extrinsic' rewards as the 'Affluent Worker' study put it, but the increasing frequency and vehemence of pay disputes in the late 1960s and early 1970s provided some rationale for this internal NCB perspective. 'Many pits have a cosmopolitan work force and a man's status at home depends much more on being a conspicuous consumer'.[43] The 'Affluent Worker' study saw no tension between wage bargaining disputes and an emphasis by manual employees on family life and domestic material comfort.[44] But solidarity on other questions, notably closures affecting miners at some but not all pits, was potentially being weakened, along with the longer term security of the coalfields. Willie Clarke, another Central Fifer who led the NUM at Seafield, believed that rehousing and the move to bigger collieries 'divorced' the social life of miners from the job. Building solidarity in this environment was sometimes difficult.[45]

Where migration and the loosening connection between work and home had uncertain effects on coalfield security, broader changes in housing were an unambiguous source of improvement. A key factor was the growth of public provision in housing. In the north ward of Cambuslang in Lanarkshire, boyhood home of Michael McGahey, tuberculosis rates were reputedly higher than anywhere else in Western Europe in 1939.[46] Campbell's assessment of housing in the pre-nationalised coalfields is bleak. The rows of Lumphinnans in central Fife, shown in Figure 2, were typical. Much of the stock was owned by private employers or their agents, compounding the miners' insecurities.

Figure 2 The poverty of social conditions before nationalisation: housing in Lumphinnans, Central Fife. © NMMS

The implications were clear: confronting an employer also meant challenging a landlord. Dismissal from work was often followed by eviction from home, a terrible class punishment on mining families.[47] Memories of such dispossession influenced the singular character of housing provision in the Scottish area of the UK coalfields after 1947. The NCB agreed to establish a Housing Association to build and manage new homes for miners in England in the 1950s. The NCB Scottish Division avoided this commitment, unwilling to depart, as a Ministry of Fuel and Power official put it, 'from the sound principle that employers should not be responsible for housing the people'.[48] Tied housing, tolerated by workers in England, 'would be entirely unacceptable to the Scottish NUM and was not worth considering', according to the NCB's Scottish Divisional Deputy Chairman in 1952.[49] The same thinking shaped the abolition of the Miners' Welfare Commission in the same year, with the CIWSO assuming responsibility from the NCB for social welfare.

Opposition to tied housing was expressed during a debate in the early 1950s about whether home-building in Scotland's coalfields should be conducted by the NCB's Housing Association – as in England – or remain the province of the Scottish Special Housing Association (SSHA), along with local authorities. The SSHA was established in 1937 in parallel with the limited economic stimulus of the 1934 Special Areas Act. In 1944 the SSHA and the Department of Health for Scotland agreed a Miners' Housing Programme, with a projected target of 13,806 homes. This played a major role in the west to east transfer of miners in the early years of nationalisation: 9,509 houses were completed by July 1952, of which almost 2,500 were in East and West Fife combined, with more than 2,000 in the Lothians, and almost 1,200 in Alloa. The NCB Scottish Division, supported by the Ministry of Fuel and Power, resisted pressure from other government departments led by the Treasury to accept direct responsibility for housing provision, and the SSHA built another 2,500 homes in the two years to July 1954.[50] This was good progress, given the scarcity of building materials and labour.[51]

Some pre-1939 housing was admittedly in good condition and of relatively favourable amenity, particularly in parts of East Fife and Midlothian. The villages of Coaltown of Wemyss and Newtongrange exemplify the best of this stock, built before the First World War, carefully laid out in well-ordered avenues. In Newtongrange the semi-detached, single-storey cottages were built in residential streets running west to east, away from the Lady Victoria Colliery, numerically sequenced from First to Tenth, south to north. But much housing elsewhere in the coalfields was of poor quality: cramped and of limited facility. Even in the 1930s and 1940s electrification was by no means widespread. Water for baths, washing dishes and clothes had to be heated by coal fire. This accentuated gender divisions and inequalities, extending the complexity and time-intensity of domestic labour undertaken by women. The 1920s and 1930s witnessed only limited expansion and improvement. Robert Duncan has emphasised the value of some local authority initiatives, but the legacy of the privately owned industry was severe shortage after the Second World War.[52]

Housing scarcity briefly melded with industrial tension in the Stirlingshire village of Plean in the summer of 1946. The Plean Colliery Company attempted to recruit new workers from outside the village by offering homes which it owned. Local men sensed injustice and occupied some of these homes. This direct action was part of a broader social movement that summer across Scotland, Wales and England. The Plean squatters were evicted, like many in other communities, and prosecuted and fined. An unofficial strike at the colliery in their support nevertheless produced an undertaking from the company that the housing requirements of miners already employed would be prioritised more strongly in the future.[53] The NCB inherited a limited quantity of houses in Scotland in 1947, but – conscious of the conflict of interest inherent in housing its employees – sought to pass this on to local authorities. Where the NCB remained a landlord difficulties were readily apparent. In Lochore in Central Fife there were a small number of NCB houses in 1959–60. Workers at the local Mary Colliery, especially those on a lengthy waiting list, resented the allocation of houses to 'strangers' employed at other pits. One of these Mary miners, Andrew Summers, was living in 1960 with his wife and baby son in one room with no coal fire or alternative source of heating.[54]

These problems were gradually resolved by the trend over time to local authority construction and tenure. Exceeding 50 per cent of households in the mining communities of Ayrshire, Fife, Lanarkshire and Midlothian by 1961, local authority tenure across Scotland's coalfields reached 74 per cent in 1981.[55] The substantial reconstruction of mining communities through local authority provision brought great relief, easing the burden especially on women. Local authority houses were better equipped and more spacious than most of the pre-1939 stock. This had a big impact on collective comfort, and is an important element in social memory. In Gillesbie, on the southern fringes of the ex-Lanarkshire coalfield, children in the 1990s were still explaining the geography of their village to a new teacher in terms of the distinction between the 'electric' houses, built by the local authority in the 1950s, and older homes that were only wired long after their original construction.[56] The parallel extension of pit-level welfare amenities from the 1930s onwards further eased the weight of domestic labour. This equipped women with more time, enabling widespread take-up of the new job opportunities arising in the 1950s and 1960s. This proved an important factor in sustaining the solidarity of the strike in 1984–5. The cost of striking was reduced through a combination of female earnings, and the response to the crisis of Labour-controlled councils in Fife, the Lothians, Lanarkshire and Ayrshire, which deferred or lowered housing rents.[57] The contrasting structural position in Nottinghamshire, where the majority of miners neither observed nor supported the strike, is instructive. There were important ideological and geological distinctions which divergences in housing tenure underlined, accentuating the variety of social conditions and material aspirations in different parts of the British coalfields.[58] In Nottinghamshire there was a clear shift to increased owner-occupation, which provided material incentive to work rather than strike in 1984–5. In Mansfield in North Nottinghamshire 42 per cent of households were owner-occupied in 1961, rising to 53 per cent in 1971; in the Ashfield area in South Nottinghamshire owner-occupation increased from 47.4 per cent in 1971 to 58.5 per cent in 1981.[59]

Village Pits, New Mines and Cosmopolitan Collieries

The changing employment and housing position in the coalfields reflected a strong trend to industrial concentration in Scottish coal mining. The general movement, with miners progressively labouring in larger average-sized economic units, was summarised in the

Table 2.1 Predominant types of production unit in the Scottish coal industry

	Village Pit	New Mine	Cosmopolitan Colliery
Established	1900s	1930s	1960s
Production	Semi-mechanised, with cutting of coal; stoop and room, then long wall	Greater mechanisation of cutting and conveyance; long wall	Full mechanisation, with power-loading from long wall faces
Scale, location and employer	Employment 500–1000; communal solidarity of village; industrial concentration, with multi-pit owner	Employment 1000+; adjacent to or apart from village; workers travelling short distance (3–6 miles); multi-pit owner	Employment 2,000+; adjacent to village or town; workers travelling longer distance (7–15 miles); NCB
Collieries	Valleyfield 1 & 2, Fife (1908–1978); Bedlay, Lanarkshire (1905–1981)	Comrie, Fife (1936–1986); Cardowan, Lanarkshire (1924–1983)	Killoch, Ayrshire (1960–1987); Seafield, Fife (1966–1988)

final column of Table 1.1. In 1957 the mean scale of employment per colliery was 500. It doubled to 1,000 by 1977. This reinforces the argument developed in Chapter 1 that nationalisation secured investment which private ownership could not achieve. Table 2.1 sets out a schema for conceptualising this growth of scale.

Three successive and distinctive predominant forms of economic unit are identified. Each represented an ever larger economy of scale, and substantial qualitative changes in coalfield employment. 'Village Pits', a designation adopted here, opened at the end of the nineteenth century, concentrated upwards of 500 miners, and were larger than older units. The labour process was changing too. The established stoop and room method of coal-getting prevailed in many Village Pits. Known outwith Scotland as pillar and stall, this advanced the coal face by digging out discrete galleries or rooms (or stalls), divided by walls or stoops (or pillars) of coal that were left to support the roof. As the face advanced these walls were then partly removed, creating a grid-like structure underground. This method was still being used in some Scottish pits in the 1950s, such as Kames in Ayrshire,[60] but longwall extraction was probably the norm by the 1920s in most Village Pits. In this method the face was advanced by cutting from a continuous stretch or length of coal, usually bounded at each end by a roadway leading back to the main mineshaft. One roadway brought in air; the other took it away. A stretch of roof wide enough to navigate the length of the face was supported by props that advanced with the cutting, leaving the roof behind to fall beneath the weight of the ground above. More productive than stoop and room, with a greater rate of extraction, longwall mining facilitated increased application of mechanisation over time, but new dangers also arose, primarily from roof falls. These are examined in Chapter 3. Subsidence above ground was an additional social cost of longwall production.[61]

The mixed extraction methods were one element of the industry's uneven development in the 1920s and 1930s. The privately owned industry was highly variegated in Scotland. The 388 separate collieries in 1925 were operated by 153 private companies, with many marginal enterprises running one or two pits. Large-scale capitalism was, however, increasingly predominant. The Fife Coal Company (FCC), marking its golden jubilee in 1922, operated 24 collieries, from Valleyfield in the south west of the county to Leven 1 & 2 in the east. Eighteen of the FCC's units were in Central Fife.[62] Seventeen FCC pits were still in operation and nationalised in 1947, all but five of which were established before the First World War, including Lumphinnans 11 & 12, known locally as Peeweep because miners could hear the lapwing birdsong as they walked to work.[63] The firm's limited investment in the 1920s and 1930s can further be adduced from the age-profile of the steam engines it used to shunt coal from collieries to preparation plants and docks. Nineteen locomotives passed from the FCC to the NCB at the end of 1946. Only six had been acquired since the First World War, four of which were 'Austerity' locomotives, supplied by central government during the Second World War.[64] In Lanarkshire, Bairds & Scottish Steel Limited ran 10 collieries taken into public ownership in 1947, all pre-dating 1905, the largest being Bedlay. Bairds & Scottish Steel was an amalgamation in 1938 of William Baird & Co. and the Scottish Iron & Steel Co. The FCC and William Baird & Co. were major industrial firms. Like others in the sector, notably the Alloa Coal

Company, the Lothian Coal Company and the Wemyss Coal Company, they were connected to the larger worlds of Scottish, British and Imperial capital through inter-locking directorships and commercial activity.[65]

Many Village Pits survived for much of the twentieth century. Table 2.2 details the twenty-one NCB production units operating in Scotland in 1977. Nine of these were Village Pits, pre-dating the First World War in vintage, although crucially, and underlining the positive impact of nationalisation, each was substantially redeveloped by the NCB after 1947, as were two even older survivors, Frances in Fife and Pennyvennie in Ayrshire. Valleyfield 1 & 2, opened by the FCC in 1908, still employed 885 miners in the winter of 1964–5, and did not close until 1978. The pit was in High Valleyfield, home to half of its employees.[66] The continued importance of the Village Pits in the 1960s and 1970s is worth emphasising, certainly when measured against the New Mines established in the 1930s. Two New Mines still operated in 1977: Cardowan, owned by Nimmo and Dunlop, and Comrie in West Fife, established by the FCC. The two firms were linked by Sir Adam Nimmo, Chairman of the FCC from 1923 who, as past President and continuing Vice President of the Mining Association of Great Britain (MAGB), was a major political figure in the industry.[67] Comrie was the subject of a publicity film, *The New Mine*, in 1945, which provides the designation for this production unit type.[68] New Mines employed upwards of a thousand, and longwall extraction was the norm. Coal was machine-cut, then hand-loaded onto mechanical conveyors. These collieries were equipped with better welfare amenities than the Village Pits, and drew on a wider residential locale. New Mines were followed from the late 1950s by Cosmopolitan Collieries, engaging two thousand-plus in longwall extraction with combined cutting and loading machinery, feeding an integrated system of mechanised conveyance. Killoch in Ayrshire and Seafield in Fife are two examples of this type of unit. The term 'Cosmopolitan' was used in South Wales to describe pits which employed a spatial mix of workers transferring in as other units closed.[69] In Scotland Cosmopolitan also implied an amalgamation of miners from a widened catchment area. They came together with sometimes highly differentiated experience of geological conditions and workplace culture.

These three distinct units can be mapped to the three generations of mining leaders identified at various points in this book. This generational story is examined in Chapter 4. In brief, the first generation commenced work as young men in Village Pits, the second in New Mines, and the third in Cosmopolitan Collieries. Differences in ownership, production regime, scale and location were important in forming the contrasting political outlooks of these three generations. Members of the New Mine generation were more willing than their elders to challenge the structures and operations of the nationalised industry. Their ascendancy facilitated a stronger moral economy resistance to pit closures from the late 1960s onwards. By this point the Cosmopolitan Collieries were being established. These contributed to a further shift in the predominant political outlook of the NUMSA. Cosmopolitan Colliery miners were required to accept unpalatable local closures. Daily travelling added a significant additional burden of time: a Killoch miner from New Cumnock and a Seafield miner from Cowdenbeath in the 1970s would be away from home each day for a minimum of 10 hours, while being paid only for the seven hour shift. But this change came with a promise of a more sustainable industry, operating in bigger units, with larger reserves and achieving greater rates of output per man shift. Moral economy expectations of future security were therefore encouraged, a vital factor both in obtaining workforce and community compliance for the changes being effected, and as a basis for the final resistance to deindustrialisation in 1984–5. By 1982 the seven Cosmopolitan Collieries were responsible for 75 per cent of production in Scotland.[70]

Table 2.2 shows the relatively minor profile by the 1970s of the New Mines. Only two units opened in the 1920s and 1930s, to reiterate, were still operating. Village Pits retained their importance because the NCB had identified them for redevelopment in *Scotland's Coal Plan* of 1955, along with the establishment of the Cosmopolitan Collieries.[71] Reconstructions in the 1950s and 1960s included Barony, Kinneil, Manor Powis, Polmaise, Polkemmet and Valleyfield. The necessity of this public investment highlights the limited legacy of the privately owned industry. Michael McGahey started his working life at the age of fourteen in Gateside Colliery in Lanarkshire in 1939. Fifty years later he remembered the relentless physical demands of the job: 'Hard, brutal work. Pick and shovel'.[72]

Table 2.2 NCB collieries in Scotland, 1977

Colliery	Type	Opened/ Closed	Peak NCB Employment and Year
Barony 1, 2, 3 & 4, Ayrshire	Village Pit	1910–1989	1,695 in 1958
Bedlay, Lanarkshire	Village Pit	1905–1981	870 in 1959
Bilston Glen, Midlothian	Cosmopolitan Colliery	1963–1989	2,367 in 1970
Bogside, West Fife	Cosmopolitan Colliery	1959–1986	1,000 in 1971
Cardowan, Lanarkshire	New Mine	1924–1983	1,970 in 1959
Castlehill, West Fife	Cosmopolitan Colliery	1969–1990	770 in 1972
Comrie, West Fife	New Mine	1936–1986	1,498 in 1963
Dalkeith 5 & 9	Village Pit	1903–1978	898 in 1964
Frances, East Fife	Pre-Village Pit	1850–1988	1,482 in 1957
Highhouse, Ayrshire	Village Pit	1894–1983	467 in 1947
Killoch, Ayrshire	Cosmopolitan Colliery	1960–1987	2,305 in 1965
Kinneil, West Lothian	Village Pit	1890–1982	1,268 in 1960
Lady Victoria, Midlothian	Village Pit	1895–1981	1,765 in 1953
Monktonhall, Midlothian	Cosmopolitan Colliery	1967–1997	1,786 in 1971
Pennyvennie 2, 3 & 7, Ayrshire	Pre-Village Pit	1872–1978	725 in 1961
Polkemmet, West Lothian	Village Pit	1913–1985	1,959 in 1960
Polmaise 3, 4 & 5, Stirlingshire	Village Pit	1904–1987	778 in 1957
Seafield, East Fife	Cosmopolitan Colliery	1966–1988	2,466 in 1970
Solsgirth, Clackmannan	Cosmopolitan Colliery	1969–1990	1,007 in 1975
Sorn 1 & 2, Ayrshire	NCB drift mine	1953–1983	294 in 1970
Valleyfield 1 & 2, Fife	Village Pit	1908–1978	1,052 in 1959

Source: Oglethorpe, *Scottish Collieries*
General note: Barony consisted of four shafts: the first two sunk in 1910, the third in 1945 and the fourth in 1965; Bogside, Castlehill and Solsgirth were each connected via underground conveyance to the South of Scotland Electricity Board power station at Longannet; Monktonhall was mothballed by the NCB in 1987, and operated intermittently as private enterprise and then miners' co-operative from 1992 before final closure in 1997

There were, admittedly, some important developments in productive capacity between the wars. Scotland's two largest pits in 1957, the peak year of employment after nationalisation, were neighbours in East Fife: Wellesley in Buckhaven, employing 2,603, and Michael, three miles along the Forth shore in East Wemyss, employing 3,353. Wellesley opened in 1885 and Michael in 1905, and both of these Village Pits were redeveloped in the 1930s by the Wemyss Coal Company. The firm protected part of its investment after 1947 by insisting that the Wemyss Private Railway existed as a separate company, although it had operated more or less entirely to move coal from Michael and Wellesley as well as Lochhead Colliery to a washer facility at Denbeath and thence to Methil docks. In this way private capital retained some force in the East Fife coalfields after nationalisation.[73] Wellesley's prowess was recognised early in the nationalised era, winner of the *News of the World* 3,150 Guineas Coal Competition for the best NCB pit in its size category in 1952.[74] At Michael the Wemyss Coal Company had enlarged the original shaft to improve ventilation and added a second shaft, along with baths, a canteen and a first aid room.[75] Robert S. Halliday, who joined the NCB after leaving the Indian Civil Service in 1948, claimed that 'nationalisation proved disastrous for Michael', with its average annual output from 1935–9 of 949,000 tons drifting downwards in the 1940s and 1950s, partly because of overinvestment in other Fife pits, notably Rothes.[76] This assertion is contentious. The colliery's lowered output actually stemmed from a lengthy programme of NCB development from 1949 to 1962. One shaft was substantially deepened and locomotive haulage was introduced.[77] The baths were also extended, from a surface area of 13,500 to 20,300 square feet.[78] Further investment followed from 1963 to 1966, to expand daily output from 3,350 to 4,000 tons, concentrating on the deeper workings at 450 fathoms.[79] Michael was one of the NCB's favoured fifty pits for development in 1967, with 'priority in recruitment, capital investment and managerial expertise',[80] and producing an annual average tonnage of 845,000, at an annual average profit of £445,000.[81] NCB officials were planning the colliery's further growth in the mid-1960s, to yield an annual average exceeding 900,000 tonnes,[82] and with a smaller workforce and greater output per manshift than achieved under private ownership. Ministry of

Power officials shared this highly positive view when preparing *Fuel Policy* in 1967. By 1980, they predicted, coal production in Scotland would largely be concentrated on four collieries feeding Longannet. All other Scottish pits would be closed, except Michael.[83]

The strongest case for the health and positive contribution of the private industry before the Second World War was Comrie, the FCC's largest inter-war initiative, with development underway from 1936 on the site between Saline and Oakley, west of Dunfermline. *The New Mine*, produced by Gaumont British Instructional Films in collaboration with the company, presented Comrie as an exemplar of a 'new story' for coal. The rural and isolated location was emphasised. Because of its distance from housing, the colliery contributed to improved living conditions, with workers arriving by bus. The principles of 'safety, efficiency and economy' were demonstrated by the testing for firedamp, the cutting machinery, the semi-mechanised loading of cars brought to the bottom of the shaft, and the upward winding of coal to be discharged from skips for cleaning, with the waste conveyed aerially to a distant bing. A further novelty was the provision of welfare amenities: showers, canteen and first aid room. The film concluded with the improbable claim that miners in such an environment 'don't suffer fatigue'. The broader message, however, was straightforward. To paraphrase Ross McKibbin, the 'New Mine' offered clear social improvement and a redistribution of esteem in favour of the workers.[84] Given the gendered division of coalfield domestic labour, this had a positive impact on the lives of women also, freed from the burden of heating water and drying clothes after their men came home.[85]

William Reid, whose career in mine management straddled the transition from private to public ownership, ascribed much of the credit for Comrie's innovative employee welfare characteristics to the far-sighted generosity of his father, Charles Reid, the FCC's General Manager in the 1930s.[86] The firm and its Managing Director in the 1920s and 1930s, Charles Augustus Carlow, have also been presented as progressive when measured against others in the privately owned industry, establishing high standards of employee safety and welfare.[87] Private industry action, however, was stimulated by state intervention. The 1926 Mining Industry Act, as noted in Chapter 1, structured the establishment of pithead baths at more than fifty collieries in Scotland before the Second World War, including Comrie.[88] These amenities were financed by levies on coal output and royalties paid to landowners. The output levy was reduced by the government, under pressure from mining firms near the bottom of the depression in 1932, from 1d per ton to ½d per ton, and then restored to 1d per ton in better trading conditions in 1938.[89] The fund was centrally administered and disbursed to private companies by the Miners' Welfare Committee, which was reconstituted as the Miners' Welfare Commission in 1939, responsible for recreational facilities as well as workplace amenities.[90]

The FCC worked closely with the Miners' Welfare Committee and its national and district officials when planning Comrie.[91] The blurred boundaries between the private and public ownership eras are further illustrated by subsequent developments. The Miners' Welfare Committee met more than half the costs associated with the laying of a one-and-a-half mile long drainage pipe at Comrie, along with an enclosed, brick-built cycle storage facility, with capacity for 250 cycles, and the first aid and ambulance room.[92] The construction of the baths, completed in 1942, was funded entirely by the Miners' Welfare Commission. Payment of their running costs was more complex. A Pithead Baths Management Committee was established in October 1940, with an equal number of employer and employee representatives, although convened by K. H. McNeill of the FCC. Running costs would include wages for a superintendent and two attendants, and were to be met not by the firm or the Miners' Welfare Commission, but by a weekly levy on each miner employed at the pit. This was the general approach to the funding of welfare running costs,[93] which meant that miners were usually contributing more each year in total than the owners were paying through the royalties levy.[94] The *New Mine* was silent on this element of welfare expansion: workers were self-funding an important element of the improvement. When it emerged that the workers' levy initially would not meet the total running costs of the Comrie baths, Charles Reid advanced a loan. This was to be repaid in full by the Baths Management Committee once the colliery was operating at fuller capacity, with sufficient miners employed and paying the levy for the amenity to move into financial surplus.[95]

So the miners had an important role in securing improvement: indirectly, through the industrial struggles that led to the Mining

Industry Act; and directly, through levies that funded the operational costs of the baths and other facilities. This was an important further element in the miners' attachment to the idea of nationalisation: their employers were reluctant reformers. The scale of progress by 1941 in Fife and Clackmannan alone, with provision of baths for more than 13,000 mineworkers, with further large facilities at Valleyfield and Comrie close to completion also, is set out in Table 2.3. A number of these facilities employed women surface workers, sorting and cleaning coal. Each of the installations was financed by the Miners' Welfare Committee and Commission.

Herbert Morrison, Deputy Prime Minister, who helped to design and implement the Labour government's broader programme of

Table 2.3 Selected pithead baths in Fife and Clackmannan, 1941

Colliery	Date	Number of Workers	Private Owner
Completed			
Blairhall	6 March 1930	1,056	Coltness Iron Company
Lochhead	16 August 1930	802	Wemyss Coal Company
Devon	11 February 1931	616	Alloa Coal Company
Frances	3 October 1931	864	Fife Coal Company
Lumphinnans	29 April 1933	608	FCC
Aitken	25 August 1934	912	FCC
Minto	14 March 1935	940 men, 64 women	Lochgelly Iron & Coal Company
Michael	27 February 1937	2,552 men, 96 women	WCC
Bowhill	30 July 1938	1,512 men, 26 women	FCC
Wellesley	6 April 1940	1,800 men, 36 women	WCC
Glencraig	4 October 1941	1,300	Wilsons & Clyde Coal Company
Under Construction			
Comrie		1,008	FCC
Valleyfield		1,008	FCC

Source: NRS, CB 3/178, Miners Welfare Fund: Fife, Clackmannan, Kinross and Sutherland, Annual Report, 1941

nationalisation, visited Comrie in September 1946. He was hosted by William Reid, then a senior manager at the FCC, and accompanied by Joe Westwood, Secretary of State for Scotland, who was a former Fife miner. Nationalisation of coal was just three months away, and Morrison related his optimism about the future to the progressive productive and welfare amenities that were on display at Comrie. 'If I had not seen it', he was reported as saying, 'I would almost think it was a vision, a painting of fifty years hence under nationalisation'. Some journalists, critical of Morrison and the Labour government from a free enterprise perspective, filed reports emphasising Comrie's virtues as a triumph of private ownership. Why, they asked, was Morrison so blind to this that he was contemplating the nationalisation of iron and steel along with coal?[96] Such criticism overlooked the role of collective action in improving this aspect of coalfield security. It was the combination of workforce pressure and state legislation that produced the Miners' Welfare Committee and Commission, and the related compulsion on private owners to invest in new facilities. Nationalisation continued this trend from 1947, with public enterprise making good the limited legacy of private ownership.

Conclusion

Changes in communities and collieries reinforced the broader tendency to greater security in the coalfields. Communities were subject to substantial divisions of class and gender. After nationalisation – and perhaps because of the erosion of coal industry employment – they became socially more cohesive. A key long-term factor was the diversification of the coalfield economy, with new industries bringing a widening range of opportunities for women. Gender divisions gradually became less stark. This theme is examined in greater detail in Chapter 7. Communities were also affected by migration, which was a difficult process. The importance of place within the coalfields was under-estimated by policy-makers, a theme explored further in Chapter 4. Relatively few miners accepted various NCB offers to transfer long-distance from Scotland to the expanding areas of Yorkshire and the East Midlands in England. There was greater take-up of transfers within Scotland, chiefly from Lanarkshire to the Lothians,

Clackmannan and Fife. Security was amplified in all communities by the growth of public ownership of homes. The linkage between employment and housing tenure was largely removed. This was a victory for miners, rooted in personal and communal memory of the 1920s and 1930s, where whole families of workplace union activists were forced from their homes, vindictively punished by recalcitrant employers. The structure of housing ownership in the coalfields after nationalisation was distinct in Scotland, with local authorities assuming the largest share, and the NCB's role negligible. Re-housing, buttressed by secure local authority tenure, was a major factor in the social improvement won by miners and their families in the twentieth century.

At workplace level the trend to greater security was also contested, and hard won. There were continuities from private to public ownership. The Village Pits established by bigger private firms prior to the First World War were redeveloped by the NCB and remained an important part of the industry's productive capacity in the 1970s. New Mines in the 1920s and 1930s pioneered more efficient mining methods, and were accompanied by significantly enhanced welfare amenities. But these, continuing the theme of gradual change that was developed in Chapter 1, were secured from policy-makers pressed into action by trade union pressure, and workers contributed directly to their operation through levies on their wages. The expanded role of public enterprise and legislation after the Second World War was anticipated in the coordinating role of the Miners' Welfare Committee and then Commission, guiding collective action in improving amenity before nationalisation. The Cosmopolitan Collieries opened by the NCB from the late 1950s represented a further advance in the scale and methods of production, but came at a cost to communities that lost their local pits, with miners compelled to travel greater distances to work. Expectations of future security and stability were encouraged, however, enabling workers to accept this cost. So the process of restructuring was broadly reflective of workforce and community concerns. This, to reiterate, was the outcome of the interactive relationship between the priorities of policy-makers and workers in the coalfields. The miners' moral economy expectations were raised by the state's pursuit of full employment and social security from the 1940s onwards.

Miners asserted their expectations as rights: to be consulted when changes were being considered; and to be protected when pits were closed, offered new jobs at other pits, within daily travelling distance, or employment in industrial alternatives established in their localities via regional policy. Restructuring was accepted so far as it improved the economic and social security of the coalfields.

Notes

1. Benedict Anderson, *Imagined Communities: reflections on the origins and spread of nationalism* (Verso: London, 1983), pp. 6–7.
2. Hester Barron, *The 1926 Miners' Lockout: meanings of community in the Durham coalfield* (Oxford University Press:, Oxford, 2010), pp. 4–13, 268–72; Martin Bulmer, 'Sociological Models of the Mining Community', *Sociological Review*, 23 (1975), pp. 61–92; Campbell, *Scottish Miners, Volume One*, pp. 6–13, 159–207; David Gilbert, *Class, Community and Collective Action. Social Change in Two British Coalfields, 1850–1926* (Oxford University Press: Oxford, 1992); Alessandro Portelli, *They Say in Harlan County* (Oxford University Press: Oxford, 2011), pp. 118–34; C. Kerr and A. Siegel, 'The Interindustry Propensity to Strike: An International Comparison', in A. Kornhauser, R. Dubin and A. Ross, eds, *Industrial Conflict* (McGraw-Hill: New York, 1954), pp. 189–212; Andrew J. Richards, *Miners on Strike. Class Solidarity and Division in Britain* (Berg: Oxford, 1996), pp. 16–38; Wight, *Workers Not Wasters*.
3. Jim Phillips, 'The Meanings of Coal Community in Britain since 1947', *Contemporary British History*, 32.1 (2018), pp. 39–59.
4. Bulmer, 'Sociological Models of the Mining Community', pp. 76–84.
5. Curtis, *South Wales Miners*, pp. 227–8.
6. Cowling, *Scottish New Towns*.
7. General Registry Office, Edinburgh, *Census 1961 Scotland. Volume Six. Occupation, Industry and Workplace. Part III Workplace Tables* (HMSO: Edinburgh, 1966), Table 1, Population in Employment by Areas of Residence and Workplace; Registry General Scotland, *Census 1981. Report for Fife Region, Volume 1* (HMSO: Edinburgh, 1982), Table 13, Usually Resident Population, etc.
8. Registry General Scotland, Census 1981. New Towns. Volume 1 (HMSO: Edinburgh, 1983), Table 12; General Registry Office, Edinburgh, *Census 1971 Scotland. Economic Activity: County Tables, Part II* (HMSO: Edinburgh, 1975), Table 3.
9. Phillips, *Miners' Strike in Scotland*, pp. 119–22.

10. Dennis, Henriques and Slaughter, *Coal Is Our Life*, pp. 9–10, 15–17, 26–33, 56–63.

11. Campbell, *Scottish Miners. Volume One*, pp. 289–92, 303, and *Volume Two*, pp. 229–32; Page Arnot, *Scottish Miners*, pp. 178–80.

12. Stuart Macintyre, *Little Moscows: Communism and Working-Class Militancy in Inter-war Britain* (Croom Helm: London, 1980), pp. 48–78.

13. Abe Moffat, *My Life With the Miners* (Lawrence & Wishart: London, 1965), pp. 9–16, 26, 28–33.

14. Page Arnot, *Scottish Miners*, p. 415.

15. Annmarie Hughes, '"A clear understanding of our duty": Labour women in rural Scotland, 1919–1939', *Scottish Labour History*, 48 (2013), pp. 136–57.

16. Savage, *Dynamics of Working-Class Politics*, p. 18.

17. Diarmaid Kelliher, *Solidarity, Class and Labour Agency: Mapping Networks of Support between London and the Coalfields during the 1984–5 Miners' Strike*, University of Glasgow, PhD, 2016.

18. Wight, *Workers Not Wasters*, pp. 87–112.

19. Colin Griffin, 'Not just a case of baths, canteens and rehabilitation centres: The Second World War and the recreational provision of the Miners' Welfare Commission', in N. Hayes and J. Hill, eds, *'Millions Like Us'? British Culture in the Second World War* (Liverpool University Press: Liverpool, 1999), pp. 267–8.

20. TNA, BX 6/13, CISWO, Scottish Welfare Committee, Retired Mineworkers' Games Competitions, Low Waters Miners' Welfare Society and Social Club, Hamilton, 28 February 1968.

21. Dennis, Henriques and Slaughter, *Coal Is Our Life*, pp. 141–62; 170–245, 227.

22. Campbell, *Scottish Miners. Volume One*, pp. 234–42.

23. Raphael Samuel, 'Introduction', in Raphael Samuel, Barbara Bloomfield and Guy Bonas, eds, *The Enemies Within: Pit Villages and the Miners' Strike of 1984–5* (Routledge & Kegan Paul: London, 1986), pp. 6–12.

24. Raymond Williams, 'Mining the Meaning: Key Words in the Miners' Strike', in Robin Gable, ed., *Resources of Hope: Culture, Democracy, Socialism* (Verso: London, 1989), pp. 120–7.

25. Liam Ó Discin, 'Philip Murray: Scotland and the formation of an American union leader', *Scottish Labour History*, 51 (2016), pp. 95–112; Pat Kelly, *Scotland's Radical Exports. The Scots Abroad – How They Shaped Politics and Trade Unions* (Grimsay Press: Edinburgh, 2011), pp. 41–74.

26. Alan Campbell, 'Reflections on the 1926 Mining Lockout', *Historical Studies in Industrial Relations*, 21 (2006), pp. 143–81.

27. Ashworth, *British Coal Industry*, pp. 261–2.
28. *House of Commons, Debates*, Fifth Series, Vol. 738, Written Answers, c. 124, 14 December 1966.
29. David Hamilton, Interview with Author, Dalkeith, 30 September 2009.
30. Ian Terris, *Twenty Years Down the Mines* (Stenlake: Ochiltree, 2001), pp. 87–92.
31. Ewan Gibbs, '"The Chance Tae Move Anywhere in Britain": Scottish Coalfield Restructuring and Labour Migration, c. 1947–74', *'By the People, for the People': The Nationalisation of Coal and Steel Revisited*; first workshop of the Coal and Steelworkers' Study Group, National Coal Mining Museum for England, 7–8 December 2017; 'Jimmy Hood: Obituary', by Brian Wilson, *The Guardian*, 5 December 2017.
32. David Amos and Natalie Braber, *Coal Mining in the East Midlands* (Bradwell Books: Sheffield, 2017), p. 105.
33. TNA, COAL 75/1033, Coal Industry Housing Association, Architect's Certification of Completion of Dwelling Houses, Cotgrave, 24 July 1963.
34. Amos and Braber, *Coal Mining in the East Midlands*, pp. 17–18, 25–6.
35. Jeane Carswell and Tracey Roberts, *Getting the Coal: impressions of a twentieth century mining community* (Alden Press: Oxford, 1992), pp. 107–8, 119.
36. http://www.thringstonebranchrangerssupportersclub.co.uk/page.php?id=14, accessed 18 May 2018.
37. Daniel Gray, *Stramash. Tackling Scotland's Towns and Teams* (Luath: Edinburgh, 2010), p. 53.
38. NRS, CB 346/5/5, NCB, SNA, Colliery Closure, Manpower Department Category: Face Worker, List of men given notice with addresses and dates of birth, no date, presumed January 1970.
39. NRS, CB 51/4, National Coal Board, Scottish Division, Alloa Area, Places of Work and Residence of Mineworkers and NCB Industrial Workers at 28 November 1964.
40. NRS, CB 51/4, NCB, Scottish Division, Lothians Area, Places of Work and Residence of Mineworkers and NCB Industrial Workers as at 4 December 1965.
41. NRS, CB 51/4, NCB, Scottish Division, Central Area, Places of Work and Residence of Mineworkers and Industrial Workers as at 28 November 1964.
42. Iain Chalmers, Interview with Author, Cowdenbeath, 30 July 2009.
43. TNA, COAL 101/488, Melanby Lee, A paper for consideration by the Scottish Area Monday and Friday Absence Committee, 8 August 1973.

44. Goldthorpe, Lockwood, Bechhofer and Platt, *Affluent Worker: industrial attitudes and behaviour.*

45. Willie Clarke, Interview with Author, Ballingry, 13 November 2009.

46. Kenneth Roy, 'Fear of the Famous', *Scottish Review 2012*, http://www. scottishreview.net/KennethRoyJuly003a.html, accessed 20 July 2017.

47. Campbell, *Scottish Miners, Volume One*, pp. 213–23.

48. TNA, COAL 26/598, Bernard Gottlieb, Ministry of Fuel and Power, to J. F. Macdonald, NCB Manpower and Welfare Department, 31 March 1952.

49. TNA, COAL 26/598, Macdonald, 'Scottish Special Housing Association', 7 October 1952.

50. TNA, COAL 26/598, Macdonald to R. Gottlieb, 14 March 1952, and NCB Draft Note, July 1954.

51. Tomlinson, *Democratic Socialism and Economic Policy*, pp. 245–7.

52. Duncan, *Mineworkers*, pp. 207–10.

53. Don Watson, *Squatting in Britain: Housing, Politics and Direct Action, 1945–1955* (Merlin Press: London, 2016), pp. 121–2.

54. NRS, CB 353/3/1, William Page, Secretary, Mary Consultative Committee, to Mr Gough, NCB Scottish Division, Assistant Surface Estates Manager, 20 September 1960.

55. General Registry Office, *Census 1961 Scotland. County Reports* (HMSO: Edinburgh, 1963–64), Table 15, Dwellings by Tenure and Rooms; Registry General Scotland, *Census 1981 Scotland. Reports for Central Region, Fife Region, Lothian Region*, and *Strathclyde Region, Volumes 1 and 4* (HMSO: Edinburgh, 1982).

56. Personal information supplied by Roma French, a friend of the author, who worked as a teacher in Gillesbie in the 1990s.

57. Phillips, *Miners' Strike in Scotland*, pp. 120–1.

58. Jörg Arnold, 'Vom Verlierer zum Gewinner – und zurück. Der Coal Miners als Schlüsselfigure der Britishen Zeitgeschichte', *Geschichte und Gesellschaft*, 42 (2016), pp. 266–97; Colin Griffin, '"Notts. have some very peculiar history": Understanding the Reaction of the Nottinghamshire Miners to the 1984–85 Strike', *Historical Studies in Industrial Relations*, 19 (2005), pp. 63–99.

59. *Census 1961 England & Wales. County Report, Nottinghamshire* (HMSO: London, 1964), Table 15, Dwellings by Tenure and Rooms; *Census 1971 England & Wales. Country Report, Nottinghamshire, Part II* (HMSO: London, 1973), Table 19, Enumerated households, etc., and Table 20, Enumerated households, etc.; *Census 1981 England & Wales. County Reports, Nottinghamshire, part 1* (HMSO: London, 1982), Table 20, Private Households with usual residents.

60. Ministry of Power, *Explosion at Kames Colliery, Ayrshire, 19 November 1957, Report by Sir Harold Roberts*, Cmnd. 467 (HMSO: London, July 1958), p. 4.

61. Campbell, *Scottish Miners, Volume One*, p. 89.

62. And. S. Cunningham, *The Fife Coal Company Limited. The Jubilee Year, 1872–1922* (Fife United Press Limited: Leven, 1922), end papers, map showing Fife Coal Company pits.

63. The Fife Psychogeographical Collective, 'Searching For Storione – A walk with the ghosts of Little Moscow', posted 25 May 2013, http://fifepsychogeography.com/2013/05/29/searching-for-storione-a-walk-with-the-ghosts-of-little-moscow, accessed 27 May 2015.

64. Tom Heavyside, *Fife's Last Days of Colliery Steam* (Stenlake: Ochiltree, 2014), pp. 6, 9.

65. Campbell, *Scottish Miners, Volume One*, pp. 26, 34, 38, 44; Oglethorpe, *Scottish Collieries*, p. 309.

66. NRS, CB 51/4, National Coal Board, Scottish Division, Alloa Area, Places of Work and Residence of Mineworkers and NCB Industrial Workers at 28 November 1964.

67. Kirby and Hamilton, 'Sir Adam Nimmo'.

68. Gaumont British Instructional Films, *The New Mine* (1945), directed by Irene Wilson and produced by Donald Carter, http://film.british-council.org/the-new-mine.

69. Curtis, *South Wales Miners*, pp. 49–50.

70. Monopolies and Mergers Commission, *National Coal Board. A Report on the efficiency and costs in the development, production and supply of coal by the National Coal Board, Volume Two*, Cmnd. 8920 (HMSO: London, 1983), Appendix 3.5 (a).

71. NCB, *Scotland's Coal Plan*, p. 12.

72. Roy, 'Fear of the Famous'.

73. Heavyside, *Last Days of Colliery Steam*, pp. 30–1.

74. Methil Heritage Centre (hereafter MHC), Box 9, L-15-8, Wellesley, *News of the World, Well Done Wellesley!*, 1952.

75. Oglethorpe, *Scottish Collieries*, pp. 139–40, 146, 152–3.

76. Halliday, *Disappearing Scottish Colliery*, pp. 43–4, 113–14, 179–81.

77. Guthrie Hutton, *Fife: the Mining Kingdom* (Stenlake: Ochiltree, 1999), pp. 90–2.

78. NRS, CB 260/14/1, NCB Scottish North Area, Proposed Schedule of Buildings to be Demolished at Michael Colliery, May 1968.

79. TNA, COAL 29/913, NCB, Scottish Division, Fife Area, Michael Colliery, Stage II Submission, July 1963, and Stage II Submission, February 1966.

80. 'Six die, two saved in pit fire trap', *The Observer*, 10 September 1967, p. 1.

81. NRS, CB 360/21/1, NCB, SNA, Michael Colliery: Brief Report on Future Prospects, 18 September 1967.

82. NRS, CB 360/29/2, NCB, Scottish Division, Finance Department, 'Michael Reorganisation Project – Comparative Figures for 1970–71', no date but presumed 1965.

83. TNA, POWE 52/113, Department for Economic Affairs, Working Group on Regional Implications of Fuel Policy and Natural Gas (RIFP). Possible Reductions in Employment Opportunities through Colliery Closures, Note by the Secretary, A. J. Surrey, 30 May 1967.

84. *The New Mine*, directed by Wilson and produced by Carter; Ross McKibbin, *Classes and Cultures: England, 1918–1951* (Oxford University Press: Oxford, 1999), p. 161.

85. Macintyre, *Little Moscows*, p. 144.

86. William Reid, 'Sir Charles Carlow Reid', in Anthony Slaven and Sydney Checkland, eds, *Dictionary of Scottish Business Biography. Volume 1: the staple industries* (University of Aberdeen Press: Aberdeen, 1986), pp. 60–2.

87. Quentin Outram, 'Carlow, Charles Augustus (1878–1954)', *Oxford Dictionary of National Biography* (Oxford University Press: Oxford, April 2016).

88. McKean, *Scottish Thirties*, p. 117.

89. Morgan, 'Miners' Welfare Fund', p. 201.

90. Griffin, 'Not just a case of baths, canteens and rehabilitation centres', p. 266.

91. NRS, CB 3/177, C. Augustus Carlow to J. A. Dempster, Chief Architect, Miners' Welfare Committee, 10 June 1935.

92. NRS, CB 3/176, A. R. Cook, Secretary, Miners Welfare Committee, to FCC, 12 July 1938.

93. Duncan, *Mineworkers*, p. 211.

94. McKean, *Scottish Thirties*, p. 116.

95. NRS, CB 3/178, Comrie Colliery Pithead Baths Management Committee. Minutes of Inaugural Meeting, 10 October 1940; K. H. McNeill to McArthur, FCC Secretary, 23 October 1940; McArthur to McNeill, 9 November 1940; Charles Reid to McArthur, 15 November 1940.

96. NRS, CB 65/21, *Comrie Colliery 1940–1980. 40 Years of Coal*, preface by T. Clark, Colliery General Manager; and CB 3/179, various un-labelled press clippings, September 1946.

CHAPTER 3

Improving Safety

Injuries at work and occupational illness were major threats to economic security in the coalfields. Reduced earnings through enforced absence from employment had a major negative impact on households. Even worse was the permanent loss of a wage-earner in fatal cases. The dangers of work underground have frequently been emphasised, often as a factor in the solidarity of miners. Hazards created mutual inter-dependence underground. Fatal accidents brought workers and their families closer together, pitting them starkly against private owners.[1] Members of each of the three distinct generations of Scottish miners' leaders identified in this book had direct formative experience or premonition of disaster. Abe and Alex Moffat, prominent within the Village Pit generation, were in their teens when their father was badly hurt in Central Fife by a roof fall.[2] Alex Eadie of the New Mine generation, Labour MP for Midlothian from 1966 to 1992, was a young man when his father was killed underground in East Fife.[3] David Hamilton, one of Eadie's successors as Labour MP for Midlothian, was a Cosmopolitan Colliery generation figure. David left school in 1965, following his father and two elder brothers into mining, but started at a pit where no other family members were employed. This was a conscious effort to limit the potential impact on the family of a single accident underground.[4]

The risks of mining increased in the 1920s and 1930s. Alan Campbell's *Scottish Miners* related the rising incidence of accidents to two waves of mechanisation either side of the First World War.[5] Barry Supple, writing in the 1980s, noted that there was 'little or no amelioration' of the industry's poor safety record in the inter-war years, which he ascribed to the owners' tendency to reward risk-taking.[6] The parallel dangers of occupational illness have featured in more recent research. A key contribution is the study of respiratory diseases among British miners by Arthur McIvor and Ronald Johnston.[7] A growing international literature has likewise examined the long-term consequences of dust inhalation,[8] with casualties in developing economies, notably China.[9]

In this contested sphere of economic security miners in Britain made clear gains as a result of nationalisation. Workplaces became safer, with a permanent fall in the rate of fatal casualties.[10] Analysis presented in this chapter shows that the rate of fatal injury was cut roughly by half when comparing the 1950s and 1960s with the 1920s and 1930s. Serious injuries arising from accidents also occurred much less frequently, although danger remained ever-present, and greater mechanisation introduced additional hazards. More machines, especially the combined shearer-loaders, increased geological disturbance and contributed to greater incidence of roof falls. They also made workplaces dustier, elevating the risks of respiratory disease. These various difficulties were tempered, however, by enhanced trade union voice after nationalisation. This chapter examines the improved overall safety record of the industry in Scotland from the 1920s to the late 1960s. The position in Scotland relative to other parts of the British coalfield was mixed. Pneumoconiosis was a relatively small problem in Scotland, certainly in comparison with South Wales. But fatality and serious injury rates in Scotland exceeded the British average after nationalisation as well as before, and the non-fatal injury rate crept back upwards in the 1960s.

In Scotland there were also a number of large-scale fatal accidents after nationalisation. These disasters had different causes, although only one arose from explosion or fire after 1959, at Michael Colliery in 1967, and there were none at all after 1973. David Selway has recently shown that major disasters in South Wales attracted significant civic and political responses, but smaller accidents – routinely ignored outwith coal localities – actually exerted a greater toll of injury and death.[11] This was broadly the position in Scotland too, until the nationalised era when the number of smaller fatal accidents fell and the relative weight of major disasters duly increased. Between

1951 and 1956 annual fatalities fluctuated between 47 and 58. Two disasters in 1957, at Kames in Ayrshire and Lindsay in Fife, resulted in 26 deaths, inflating that year's total to 72. In 1958, as the overall scale of employment started to fall, 30 miners were killed, before the largest disaster of the nationalised period, at Auchengeich in Lanarkshire in 1959, when 47 deaths raised the annual toll to 95. In 1960, by contrast, when four men died in a single accident at Cardowan, Auchengeich's neighbour, total deaths across Scotland numbered 45, at that point the lowest annual tally since nationalisation other than 1958.[12] The devotion of public and political attention to disasters was therefore understandable after 1947. The continued human costs strengthened the miners' moral economy claims for enhanced coalfield security. The broad position of improvement arising from nationalisation is examined in the first half of the chapter. The second half provides a detailed analysis of the disasters. These show some continuities from the private to the public ownership eras, but broadly reinforce the conclusion that nationalisation strengthened union voice and communal security.

Safety, Ownership and Union Voice

Occupational health in coal mining was compromised by the greater application over time of mechanisation. Drilling and cutting generated more dust, key to the contraction of respiratory diseases, notably pneumoconiosis and silicosis. Mechanisation also accentuated the potential for repetitive strain injuries, such as vibration white finger or hand-arm vibration syndrome. Coal Workers' Pneumoconiosis was recognised as a compensatable condition in 1942 and a huge spike in the number of cases followed. By the mid-1950s the NCB had responded by establishing a 'comprehensive health and safety infrastructure', with a Mines Medical Service which oversaw X-rays of all new miners and regular health checks on continuing employees. This is evidence of the NCB's greater willingness to assume responsibility for the welfare of its employees than pre-1947 private firms. Incubation periods for pneumoconiosis and silicosis were of such length that miners diagnosed with these conditions in the 1950s possibly contracted them in the 1930s. The NCB was confronting a problem neglected and even wilfully obscured by employers in the 1920s and 1930s,[13] and akin, perhaps, to the pent-up demand for spectacles and false teeth unleashed by the foundation of the National Health Service in Britain in 1948.[14] McIvor and Johnston nevertheless conclude that the NCB's overall effort, particularly in reducing dust levels, was inadequate to the scale of the problem.[15]

Dust shortened and ruined the lives of many Scottish miners, but the incidence of respiratory diseases in Scotland was appreciably smaller than elsewhere. McIvor and Johnston report the annual average rates of pneumoconiosis diagnosis among tested miners by area in Britain from 1959 to 1963. The overall average was 12.1 per cent, but 25.3 per cent in South Wales, where the highly dusty anthracite coal was prevalent.[16] NCB annual reports show that from 1964 to 1968 its periodic X-ray scheme tested about 93 per cent of miners employed in Scotland for pneumoconiosis. The average annual rate of positive diagnosis in this period was 3.3 per cent in the Scottish North Area and 3.2 per cent in the Scottish South Area. Across all British areas the annual average was 10.7 per cent. The position then deteriorated in Scotland, possibly in the context of improved diagnostic technique. From 1969 to 1971, with 93 per cent of men again X-rayed, the average annual rates of positive diagnosis were 5.6 per cent in the North Area and 3.8 per cent in the South Area. In Britain the average was stable from the previous period, at 10.8 per cent, and in South Wales it was still around 25 per cent.[17]

Scotland's distinct position was partly a question of geology. Pits tended to be damp and relatively dust-free. McIvor and Johnston compiled testimony from retired union officials who accepted that geology was important, but emphasised more strongly the positive role of workforce advocacy. George Bolton, NUMSA Vice President from 1978 to 1987, and then President until his retirement in 1996, compared dust suppression practices in Scottish pits favourably with those applied in the Stoke area, where he worked for a time in the 1960s. NUMSA lobbying of the Department of Health for Scotland resulted in the late 1950s in the establishment of pneumoconiosis research facilities at teaching hospitals in Dundee, Edinburgh and Glasgow, and specialist clinics in West Lothian, Glasgow and Bridge of Earn. Alec Mills, a leading NUM official in Ayrshire, reinforced Bolton's narrative of union voice leading to safer working conditions, referring to the adoption of water-infused blast-borers and the practice of cutting coal under the application of water.[18]

McIvor and Johnston add another factor to their analysis of the dust problem: the risks taken by coal miners in pursuit of production and earnings, influenced by an idealised form of working class masculine identity. Various time-expensive safety precautions were eschewed by miners after nationalisation, elevating the incidence of illness. It is ventured that the likelihood of accidents was also heightened by a macho approach to risk-taking.[19] This is a compelling argument, but an alternative reading of class, gender and risk might equally be posed. Proletarian manliness in the mines and other heavy industries was expressed in the adversarial conduct of workplace relations. Confronting employers and overseers in class terms on working conditions, including safety, was an important element in the constitution of this form of male identity. Jimmy Reid's famous 'no bevvying' speech, early in the 1971–2 UCS work-in, is apposite. Reid was a major figure in the Communist Party of Great Britain as well as a leading workplace union representative at the UCS, and emphasised the responsibility that workers held to themselves, their workmates and communities.[20] Obviously not all miners adhered to this approach, but many were encouraged to do so through the politics and culture of the NUMSA, which are examined in Chapters 4 and 5. Winning improved safety, to strengthen the security of mining communities, was a powerful and validating expression of this form of coalfield manliness, which privileged stoicism and restraint.[21]

Trade union voice and collective action certainly underpinned the broader advance of nationalisation, which transformed the industry's accident record. The narrative of fatally and seriously injured workers in the privately owned industry as victims of capitalist violence featured in George Orwell's examination of the Yorkshire and Lancashire coalfields, *The Road to Wigan Pier*, originally published in 1937. Orwell offered a close reading of five weekly wage slips, passed to him by a Yorkshire miner. Three were 'rubber-stamped with the words "death stoppage"', an agreed deduction taken by the employer for a subscription to the widow of a fatally injured miner. 'The significant detail here', Orwell added, 'is the *rubber stamp*'. Death was a matter of routine bureaucracy: 'casualties are taken for granted almost as they would be in a minor war'. Orwell reckoned that a miner who worked for 40 years stood a 1 in 20 chance of being killed.[22]

Collective action by miners won improvements to this dismal picture, starting in the late 1930s and accelerating after nationalisation. The data in Table 3.1 is partly drawn from a Royal Commission on Safety established by the Conservative-dominated coalition government in response to pressure from trade union representatives, who were pushing for action on a range of issues, including ownership structures as well as the rate of accidents. This

Table 3.1 Coal miners killed by accident in Scotland and Britain, 1922 to 1972–3; average annual rates, per 100,000 man shifts

	Killed in Scotland	Killed in Britain
1922–1926		0.40
1927–1931	0.53*	0.43
1932–1936	0.47	0.44
1937–1941	0.45	0.42
1942–1946**	0.36	0.36
1947–1951***	0.26	0.27
1952–1956	0.24	0.22
1957–1961	0.31+	0.21
1962–1966****	0.23	0.19
1967–1973++	0.21+++	0.13

Notes: *1930–1 for Scotland; **1942–5; ***1949–51; ****1962, and then 1963–4 to 1966–7; +includes 1957, when 17 were killed at Kames and nine at Lindsay, and 1959, when 47 were killed at Auchengeich; ++1967–8 to 1972–3; +++unpublished NCB data for Scottish North Area, includes 1967, when nine died at Michael, and 1971–2, when there were no deaths
Sources: *Royal Commission on Safety in Coal Mines. Report*, Cmd. 5890 (HMSO: London, 1938), Table 13; National Coal Board, *Report and Accounts* (House of Commons, various years, 1950–66); NRS, CB 398/13/12, NCB – Scottish Area, Seafield Inquiry, Dossier, 1973, Note on Accidents; J. N. Williamson, 'Ten Years of Safety Work in a Scottish Colliery Group. Safety Record of the Fife Coal Company, Ltd., 1936–1945', *Transactions of the Institution of Mining Engineers*, Vol. 106 (1946–7), pp. 231–69, Table XIII

reported in 1938.[23] A valuable way of appreciating the extent of progress from the 1940s is to think about the number of miners employed, and the man shifts worked each day. Between 1927 and 1931 there were, on average, roughly 100,000 miners employed in Scotland. One miner was killed every two working days in the Scottish mines in this period. In the five years from 1962 to 1966 there were roughly 50,000 miners employed in Scotland, and one was killed every eight working days. From this it can be concluded that the rate of death under private ownership from 1927 to 1931 was double that from 1962 to 1966 under public ownership.

Private owners in Scotland in the 1920s and 1930s sought to minimise their obligations to workers disabled by mining accident or illness. The contested move to greater employee welfare was emphasised in Chapters 1 and 2. This included the establishment of convalescent homes in the 1920s. Employers were involved in this process. The Fife Coal Company gifted the Charles Carlow Convalescent Home at Culross, opened in 1927 to commemorate the firm's deceased Chairman and Managing Director. The running costs, however, were funded by the workers themselves, through their weekly 1d contributions channelled through the Miners' Welfare Fund. Homes in Ayrshire and Lanarkshire were established and funded in the same manner.[24] Workers injured in their employment were frequently subjected to searching physical examination, as employers attempted to classify them fit for lighter work, and thereby less eligible for financial compensation. In the difficult inter-war economic and political environment union representatives had to show considerable mettle when challenging these cost-controlling employer practices, often through cases heard in Sheriff Courts.[25]

Such expression of union voice was central to improved safety. Progress preceded nationalisation, in the late 1930s and during the Second World War. The FCC makes an illuminating case study. In the later 1920s and early 1930s the firm tightened supervision of production. The Moffats and other workplace advocates were sacked.[26] The annual rate of fatal accidents in the firm's pits exceeded the Scottish annual average from 1930 to 1936, but then the position changed. Despite the deaths of 35 men in a single accident at Valleyfield in

1939, the annual average rate of fatalities in FCC pits from 1937 was regularly under 0.40 per 100,000 man shifts and lower than the Scottish average, which was also falling. The firm made a significant effort to enhance safety,[27] but union voice was also reinvigorated by the significant drop in unemployment arising from rearmament. The Moffat brothers returned to the pits in 1938.[28]

The voice-safety hypothesis is amply demonstrated by the sustained drop in fatal accident rates after nationalisation. The NCB was committed to protecting 'the health and safety of those they employ'.[29] The broader policy framework constructed by the Labour government elected in 1945 increased the likelihood that this commitment would be realised. Valuable innovations included full employment and comprehensive social protection, illustrated by the 1946 Industrial Injuries Act which strengthened provision for those disabled by workplace accidents. Social policy and stronger trade union bargaining presence combined to raise the expectations of manual workers generally.[30] The limited immediate impact of nationalisation in everyday terms in the coal industry was considered in Chapter 1. But over time the new institutional arrangements and procedures had positive results, countering the ideology of managerial prerogative which had prevailed in the pre-nationalised coal sector, and which characterised practices in other branches of British industry in the 1950s and 1960s.[31] NCB pit-level consultative committees met regularly, enabling miners to discuss production, safety and other workplace matters with managers. The NCB was proud of these consultative arrangements and its safety record. Both elements featured in public information films screened in cinemas. *Nines Was Standing*, distributed in 1950, showed 'the way a pit consultative committee works', with representatives of management and workers resolving difficulties that were holding up production on one coalface.[32] *Safety First*, from 1949, emphasised the positive impact of shorter working hours and investment underground, with more secure roof supports. Greater mechanisation was depicted as an asset, with conveyer belts gradually eliminating the danger of runway tubs on roadways, which were being made safer through increased attention to levelling.[33] Improvement was relative rather than absolute. In September 1950 at Valleyfield a miner called David Miller was killed after being hit by runaway tubs, the very hazard identified in *Safety First* as receding.[34]

Policy-makers were preoccupied by the continued presence of serious dangers in mining. The contraction of mining employment from the late 1950s was analysed in Chapter 1. Policy-makers were seeking increased growth and living standards, but rationalised the employment changes partly with reference to the physical risks encountered by miners. Richard Marsh, Minister of Power in Wilson's Labour government from 1966 to 1968, was responsible for the 1967 White Paper, *Fuel Policy*, proposing a further acceleration of coal closures. According to Tam Dalyell, a Labour MP with miners among his West Lothian constituents, Marsh acutely disliked coal mining, appalled by its human costs.[35] Margaret Thatcher's attitude to miners in the 1980s is often related to her experience as a member of Edward Heath's Conservative government that unsuccessfully confronted the NUM in two national disputes, in 1972 and 1973–4.[36] In her own memoirs she emphasised the formative importance of these strikes herself.[37] But one of Thatcher's biographers, John Campbell, points out that she was the Conservative Party's Shadow Minister of Power from 1967 to 1970. In this role Thatcher was even more critical of mining than Marsh, fusing a critique of the industry's alleged economic inefficiencies with an argument that its dangers were futile as well as socially unacceptable.[38]

The linkage between the necessity of economic restructuring and the hazards of coal was emphasised by government and opposition speakers in the House of Commons Second Reading of the 1967 Coal Industry Bill, which made increased financial provision for the enhanced social costs of closures arising from *Fuel Policy*. Exchequer grants to the NCB were to be raised from £30 million over five years to £45 million over four years. 'It is the price', Marsh said, 'and a very large price indeed – which the community will have to pay to minimise the massive problems which stem from the decision to accept change in practice as well as in theory'. The move to a smaller coal industry was highly positive, he claimed, concentrating production in mines where conditions were safer. Closures would be targeted on 'the sort of pits which no Member in the House would send his children down if he had a choice'. Thatcher's reply was critical of the Bill's additional financial protection for miners and mining communities, including the proposed 'intensification' – Marsh's word – of regional assistance. But she endorsed the rationale for further contraction. 'It seems futile to have more men than are necessary going down the pits in conditions in which there will certainly be some deaths, and much danger, to dig up coal that no one wants to buy.' She also deployed the 'responsible parent' motif used by Marsh, asking whether union leaders who opposed closures would favour sending their own sons to work underground.[39]

Thatcher and Marsh were criticised by Alex Eadie for 'distorting' the debate through conflation of pit closures and miners' safety, which were separate issues. A miner for thirty years in East Fife, Eadie said that for many parents – all less fortunate in their circumstances than Thatcher – coal mining was the only meaningful form of employment available to their sons.[40] Other Labour MPs reinforced Eadie's message about the value of mining employment in the coalfields, but there were those who claimed that further shrinkage was desirable. 'I am not one of those who will ever enthusiastically campaign for the opening or reopening and keeping open of coal mines', said Willie Hamilton, Labour MP for West Fife, in a later House of Commons debate, in 1969. 'My father worked in the pits for most of his working life, and he is now choking with pneumoconiosis', he continued, arguing that the core aim of government policy in the coalfields should be further employment diversification. 'I hope to see the day', he concluded, 'when no man has to go underground'.[41] The social provisions of the 1967 Bill encapsulated the careful management of change that Hamilton and other Labour MPs identified as central to future security in coal communities. This was the miners' moral economy in action. Miners enjoyed special protection against economic insecurity in the 1960s and 1970s, Jörg Arnold concludes, precisely because politicians like Marsh recognised the extent of past sacrifices and ongoing hazards in the coalfields.[42]

The continued loss of life underground was accompanied by an upward movement in reportable injuries in Scotland in the late 1950s and 1960s. The latter were 'caused by accidents or dangerous occurrences immediately reportable to H. M. Inspector of Mines, because of either the severity of the resulting injury or the nature

Table 3.2 Reportable injuries in Scotland and Britain; average annual rates, per 100,000 man shifts, 1930–3 to 1972–3

	Scotland	Britain
1930 to 1933	1.68	1.59
1934 to 1937	1.75	1.58
1938 to 1941	1.34	1.51
1942 to 1945	1.19	1.42
1951 to 1954	1.21	1.11
1955 to 1958	1.23	1.11
1959 to 1962	1.34	1.14
1963–4 to 1966–7	1.35	1.13
1967–8 to 1972–3	1.43*	1.03

Note: *unpublished NCB data for Scottish North Area
Sources: Williamson, 'Ten Years of Safety Work', Table XIII; NCB, *Report and Accounts*, House of Commons (various years); NRS, CB 398/13/12, NCB – Scottish Area, Seafield Inquiry, Dossier, 1973, Note on Accidents

of the occurrence', such as an explosion, especially of gas or coal dust.[43] The changing incidence of such injuries from the 1930s to the 1970s is summarised in Table 3.2.

The trend in reportable injuries until the 1950s was similar to that in fatalities. In Scotland and Britain the average annual injury rate was about one-third lower in the 1950s than it had been in the 1930s. But from 1959 there was a sustained increase in Scotland that was not matched elsewhere. There were peaks of 1.44 per 100,000 man shifts in 1960 and 1.43 in 1965–6. In the Scottish North Area the median rate between 1967–8 and 1972–3 was 1.51.[44]

The Royal Commission on Safety in Coal Mines had reported in 1938, establishing that the principal causes of accidents were explosions, mainly of gas ignited by shotfiring prior to machine cutting, and roof collapses. The latter were associated with unstable geological conditions, but made more likely by over-rapid and undersupported advance.[45] A Mines Inspector for Scotland reported to the Commission that the 50 per cent increase in serious accidents from 1924 to 1938 was related to the intensification of production, with 'more rush and bustle'. This was the general view of union activists and officials, who also saw mechanisation and work de-skilling as contributory causes.[46] Across three major collieries operated by the Lothian Coal Company – Easthouses, Lady Victoria and Lingerwood – there was a jump in reported accidents from 208 in 1924 to 309 in 1927. The pattern was consistent with the reported correlation between mechanisation and danger. Eighty-five of the accidents in 1927 included materials falling from roof or face, where mechanised under-cutting was the likely cause, and 103 involved conveyers, engines, bogeys and hutches. Roughly two accidents in three, in other words, were probably or directly relatable to the application of machinery underground.[47] The Royal Commission confirmed the distinct nature of danger in Scotland, where fatality and reportable injury rates were above the British average, and mechanisation was more advanced. The portion of coal cut by machinery in Scotland in 1928 was at least double the rate in Northumberland, Durham, the Midlands and Yorkshire. Some convergence followed but in 1936 Scotland retained a substantial lead in the proportional rate of machine-cutting, a third greater than the British average. Scotland also led significantly in the rate of coal conveyed mechanically: 25 per cent to Britain's 11 per cent in 1928, 42 to 25 per cent in 1932, and 55 to 48 per cent in 1936.[48]

Scotland's lead in mechanisation had disappeared by the 1940s. But a linkage between production methods and safety can still be traced. The key innovation was the cutting and loading of coal by a combined machine. This method, power-loading, increased its share of coal produced in Scotland from 39.6 per cent in 1961 to 78.4 per cent in 1966, 85.9 per cent in 1971 and 90.1 per cent in 1974.[49] Its fuller utilisation contributed to the escalation of reportable accidents from 1958 onwards. Machinery was involved in a number of fatal accidents in these years. At Valleyfield in August 1957 Thomas O'Neill, a miner from Dunfermline, was killed after being struck by a runaway coal cutting machine.[50] Six years later George Johnston, another Dunfermline miner, was killed in the same colliery after being hit by coal that fell having been cut by power-loading machinery.[51]

The major causes of fatal accidents below ground from the mid-1950s to mid-1960s are set out in Table 3.3. Explosions of firedamp and coal dust, plus fire, along with roof falls, were the main causes of serious accidents identified by the Royal Commission in 1938.

Table 3.3 Miners killed underground in Scotland's NCB pits, by major cause, annual averages, 1955 to 1966-7

Cause	1955 to 1958	1959 to 1962	1963–4 to 1966–7
Fall of ground – face	16.25	17.5	9.75
Fall of ground – roads	1.5	2.75	0.5
Haulage and transport	10.25	10.75	8.5
Machinery	2.75	3.5	1.25
Gas, coal dust and fires	6.75	13	0
Shafts	1.75	1.75	0.5
Explosives	0	0.75	0
Use of tools and appliances	0	0.25	0.5
Stumbling, falling, slipping	0.25	0	0
Other	3.25	3.25	1.25
Total Underground	**43**	**53.25**	**25.25**

Sources: NCB, *Annual Reports, 1955 to 1966–7*

Although gas, coal dust and fire remained significant hazards through-out the 1950s, and four men were killed by an ignition of firedamp at the 'notoriously gassy' Cardowan in July 1960,[52] accidents caused by these elements were progressively eliminated. This can be seen in the data for 1963–4 to 1966–7. There was only one fatal fire in Scot-land after the 1959 Auchengeich disaster, at Michael in September 1967. So established was this trend across Britain that from 1967–8 the NCB ceased publishing explosions of gas, coal dust and fires as discreet causes of fatal accidents in its annual reports.

The main causes of danger were now haulage and transport, and fall of ground at the face, as a string of fatal accidents at Seafield in East Fife illustrated from 1968. These culminated in a disaster in May 1973, when five miners cutting up a steep gradient in the colliery's Dysart Main area were killed after an extensive roof fall. Under pressure from the NUM, the Department for Trade and Industry appointed a public inquiry,[53] which took place in Kirk-caldy in August 1973, chaired by J. W. Calder, Chief Inspector of Mines and Quarries.[54] Ahead of the inquiry, the NCB's Scottish Area

Safety Engineer compiled data on accidents at the colliery since 1968. This showed seven other fatal face accidents prior to May 1973. In each of them steep gradient was a factor. George Duncan, a power-loader, was killed in May 1968 when a large stone fell from waste, knocking out roof supports. Joseph McDonald, also a power-loader, stumbled and fell in April 1969, dying five months later from severe head injuries. Stephen Nardone, a sump cleaner, was found dead in March 1972, under the leading wheels of a man-riding locomotive. Peter Law, a deputy, was knocked down and killed in July 1972 by a runaway bogie. Andrew Carson was killed in September 1972, when the locomotive he was travelling on crashed head-on with another locomotive. In the same period, from 1968 to 1972, there were 19 serious reportable injuries at the colliery involving falling objects and 18 arising from haulage incidents. Five more were the consequence of incidents with machinery or tools.[55] Calder's inquiry established that the combination of power-loading and steep gradient had contributed to the May 1973 accident also, in two ways. First, in attempting to follow the seam, the miners lost the horizon, cutting above the coal into stone and weakening the roof. Second, the roof was being held by a sequence of hydraulic roof supports, but these were not stable enough to cope with the steep gradient. Sitting on an irregular floor with coal spillage beneath, the supports were not bracing the roof at optimal pressure. When the roof began to fall, weakened by the lost horizon cutting, it was not held in place by the supports, 61 of which were displaced over a length of 200 feet.[56] James Holmes, Thomas Kilpatrick, Angus Guthrie, Robert Henderson and James Comrie were all killed. David Dickson, Edward Downs, James McCartney and James Todd were rescued from the affected area.[57]

This evidence from Seafield supports the hypothesis that mechanisation in general, and power-loading in particular, contributed negatively to underground safety. The 1973 disaster, involving a combination of power-loading and hydraulic roof supports, could not have happened 15 or even 10 years earlier. Reportable injuries similarly arose from accidents caused by the presence of powerful machines, and the adjustments to working practices that these entailed. Another related correlation might be suggested, however, between dangers and the labour process. The contraction of the coal industry – in production and employment terms – was a reflection of coal's progressively insecure position in the energy market from the late 1950s, examined in Chapter 1. The pressure on management and workers at pit-level to produce has been emphasised as a factor in generating dangerously high levels of dust underground, which contributed to the incubation of serious respiratory illnesses among miners.[58] The production imperative may have added also to the rate of reportable injuries. Idle machinery increased the financial costs – and nominal losses – of coal production. Pit-level officials reporting to Scottish Divisional management were clearly obliged to minimise such costs and losses. Viewed from this perspective, however, it is nevertheless impressive that the rate of reportable injuries in the 1960s remained significantly lower than it had been for most of the 1930s. Enhanced safety was secured and sustained, despite mechanisation and the greater urgency of production pressures. It can even be ventured that the upward movement in the rate of reportable injuries was the product of a stronger safety culture. The balance between disincentives and incentives to reporting accidents changed with nationalisation and the establishment of greater economic security. Workers missing shifts through minor injuries would not fear dismissal or lost income: they would be compensated financially and given time to recover before returning to work. This reduced their risk of further injury and benefited those not required to work beside a debilitated colleague.[59] Trade union voice continued to act in the later 1970s as a means of winning further improvements. Across NCB holdings the rate of fatal injuries arising from accidents fell from 0.12 per 100,000 man shifts in 1975 to 0.08 per 100,000 man shifts in 1977. NUM officials saw this progress in terms of safer powered support installations, post-Seafield. Students at a union safety school at Ruskin College, Oxford in 1980 were nevertheless advised that 'to achieve safety is a constant fight'. George Montgomery of the NUMSA emphasised that union advocacy was central to victory in this relentless struggle.[60]

Mining Disasters in Scotland

The contested path to a safer industry in Scotland is illustrated by the six disasters selected for detailed examination here: Valleyfield in 1939, Knockshinnoch in 1950, Kames and Lindsay in 1957, Auchengeich in 1959, and Michael in 1967. The basic elements of these disasters, along with Seafield in 1973, are summarised in Table 3.4. Each had a major impact on the security of surrounding communities. The post-1947 disasters show that work underground remained highly perilous even after nationalisation and the overall

Table 3.4 Selected disasters in the Scottish coal industry

Colliery	Date	Approximate Cause	Number Killed	Average Age of Killed	NCB/Industry Average Age
Valleyfield, Fife	28 October 1939	Gas explosion ignited by shot-firing	35	39.8	
Knockshinnoch, Ayrshire	7 September 1950	Inrush of peat and moss from surface	13	46.3	40.2
Kames, Ayrshire	19 November 1957	Coal dust explosion ignited by gas explosion ignited by smoker's match – in 'safe' pit	17	38.6	40.5
Lindsay, Fife	14 December 1957	Gas explosion ignited by contraband smoker's match – in 'safety lamp' pit	9	46.6	40.5
Auchengeich, Lanarkshire	18 September 1959	Fire from overheated fan belt; deaths by CO poisoning	47	41.9	41.3
Michael, Fife	9 September 1967	Fire arising from spontaneous combustion of coal, lighting polyurethane insulation and conveyer belt; deaths by asphyxiation	9	51	43.5
Seafield, Fife	10 May 1973	Lengthy roof fall at coal face	5	43.6	43.7

Sources: Valleyfield, 28 October 1939, http://www.scottishmining.co.uk/33.html, accessed 20 January 2017; Cmd. 8180; Cmnd. 467; Cmnd. 485; Cmnd. 1022; Cmnd. 3657; Cmnd. 5485; Ashworth, *British Coal Industry*, Table A1

improvement in safety. At Knockshinnoch, Lindsay and Michael the average age of those killed was significantly above industry average. These disasters took place during the evening or night. A greater share of preparation and development work in the 1950s and 1960s was undertaken on the back or night shift, often involving older men.

The outbreak of the Second World War in 1939 had a limited impact on industrial relations in Britain. There was no immediate transition to industrial peace in workplaces where conflict had been the pre-war norm.[61] In the Scottish coalfields production continued to be interrupted by management-worker disputes.[62] A number of these struggles involved the Fife Coal Company, owner of Valleyfield. The immediate cause of the disaster on 28 October was an explosion of firedamp. This was triggered by shotfiring, 1,920 feet below the surface, and 1,700 yards from the pit bottom. Of the 110 men working underground at the time, 35 were killed.[63] Shot firing was a common practice in stoop and room as well as longwall mining, the method used at Valleyfield. Explosives were placed in the coal face and remotely ignited. This loosened coal prior to mechanical cutting, but required prior testing for gas. The volume and flammability of surrounding coal dust also had to be carefully monitored. FCC managers and officials at Valleyfield made two significant errors on this occasion. First, there was no testing for gas between shots fired at the coal face. Second, too much inflammable coal dust had been allowed to build up in surrounding roads. Gas was released from the face by the first shot and ignited by the second shot. This resembled closely the cause of a disastrous explosion which killed 11 miners at Cardowan in November 1932, where gas was also released by a first shot and ignited by a second.[64] At Valleyfield in 1939 the ignition of gas caused a second and larger detonation, of coal dust. Some men were killed instantly by the first or second explosion: others died shortly afterwards, overcome by the gas. George Crichton, leader of the mines rescue party and a trade union official, told reporters that some of the dead were found 'lying on their side with their hands beneath their face, just as if they had gone to sleep'.[65]

The chief causes of the disaster were established at a public inquiry appointed by the Board of Trade, and held in Edinburgh in January 1940. This led to a prosecution under the 1911 Coal

Mines Act of the FCC as colliery owners, alongside its agent and area manager, Kirkwood Hewitt McNeill, and the pit's general manager, Robert Aitchison. The company prepared its defence at length and cost. J. Ivon Graham of the Royal School of Mines in South Kensington, London, spent a weekend ahead of the trial in Fife with C. Augustus Carlow, Managing Director, and Charles Reid, General Manager, probing the prosecution's case that coal dust levels at Valleyfield were dangerously high.[66] The FCC as a corporate body evaded conviction, demonstrating that under Section 102 of the Coal Mines Act it was not in the habit of managing the mine. This placed responsibility for the accident on McNeill and Aitchison, agent and general manager, who were found guilty in March 1941 on the single charge of failing to administer adequate testing for coal dust, and fined £3 each. On the charge of not testing for gas between shots they were found not guilty. The Sheriff, Neil A. Maclean, found that McNeill and Aitchison were vigilant 'policemen' with strong reputations as disciplinarians, who would not have countenanced such malpractice. Responsibility for the lapse was attributed solely to the dead shotfirer.[67]

The disaster's human effects were highly localised. Of the 35 men killed, 24 lived in Low and High Valleyfield, including a father and son from the same address. Others were from settlements nearby: Blairhall, Culross and Oakley.[68] The response by the company, other mining industry leaders and policy-makers was careless of feeling in these communities. In December 1939 a preliminary hearing to establish the terms of the Board of Trade-appointed inquiry was held in Edinburgh. Representatives of the Fife, Clackmannan and Kinross Miners' Association, and the solicitor for the families of those killed, called for this inquiry to be held in Dunfermline, closer to Valleyfield and the grieving communities. The Board of Trade's Commissioner, R. P. Morison, K. C., steered the discussion instead to the convenience of witnesses who would be travelling from London and other parts of Scotland, and ruled that the inquiry would be held in Edinburgh.[69] Limited concern with the human casualties can also be read in FCC correspondence that followed the trial, which demonstrates the class solidarity of coal owners. J. M. Davidson, General Manager and Secretary of the Scottish Mine Owners' Defence Association, congratulated Carlow, alluding to the contested workplace and industrial politics of wartime. 'So far as directed against the owners it [the prosecution] had the appearance of something approaching vindictiveness', he wrote, 'but it was no doubt inspired by an attempt to placate labour and to ensure there would be no complaints about the owners having been let off'. Carlow replied with thanks, regretting only 'that the Sheriff could not have seen his way to let the Manager and Agent off' the coal dust charge. Davidson wrote again to Carlow, reiterating his relief that the firm had been found not guilty of all charges, which would minimise greatly its financial obligations in terms of compensation to the injured, and to the dependents of those killed.[70]

Shortly after nationalisation the FCC published a company history which emphasised the firm's commitment to worker safety and welfare. This contained no reference at all to the Valleyfield disaster, where the proven neglect of its officials had caused the deaths of 35 miners.[71] The NCB displayed a similar indifference in response to the first major disaster in Scotland after nationalisation, at Knockshinnoch in Ayrshire in September 1950. As with the FCC and Valleyfield, the NCB denied corporate responsibility and was ungenerous in dealings with casualties and their dependents. Knockshinnoch was a mile from New Cumnock, its workings beneath a basin of moss and peat roughly 150 by 300 yards in dimension. The main seam was being mined upwards. At a particularly steep section, rising one in two, this tunnel penetrated the bottom of the basin. The effect was like removing a plug from a sink full of water. A torrent of moss and peat, intensified by unusually heavy rainfall, rushed downwards, flooding miles of underground roadways, tunnels and faces.[72] Thirteen men were killed, all from New Cumnock, and 116 others cut off from safe exit. They were rescued two days later through the nearby abandoned workings of Bank Colliery, the operation complicated by the presence of dangerously high volumes of gas.[73]

This major effort captured significant public and political attention, evoked in James Robertson's 2010 novel, *And The Land Lay Still*, with the action moved to the fictional setting of Borlanslogie in Stirlingshire.[74] Philip Noel-Baker, Minister of Fuel in the Labour government, visited Knockshinnoch and the survivors who were recovering in nearby hospitals. He told reporters that no-one could have anticipated the combination of events that led to the disaster. This was a premature evaluation. Sir Andrew Bryan, Chief Inspector of Mines, also came to Knockshinnoch,[75] and was appointed by the government to chair a public inquiry, held in Ayr County Buildings from 13 to 16 November 1950. The NUMSA had pressed hard for this inquiry, where Abe Moffat cross-examined NCB officials, including the pit manager, William Halliday, and area agent, John Bone. Moffat uncovered their ignorance of conditions above ground, and failure to observe regulations from 1920 requiring mining operations to remain more than 60 feet beneath moss and peat deposits. Bryan's report heavily criticised the officials on each of these counts.[76]

Under pressure from NUMSA officials the NCB removed first Bone and then Halliday from their positions at Knockshinnoch, allowing the pit to resume working in March 1951.[77] Bone and Halliday were prosecuted along with Alexander McNab Stewart, area production manager, and Alexander Gardener, area planning organiser, for contravening the Coal Mines Act and the 1920 moss and peat regulations. At the trial in Ayr Sheriff Court in October 1951 Stewart and Gardener were defended by R. P. Morison, K. C., who had chaired the Valleyfield disaster inquiry. David L. McCardel, area general manager, questioned by Morison, emphasised that neither the area production manager nor the area planning organiser had any control over the 'cause to which contravention or non-compliance' with the law had taken place. Duty in this area was the preserve of the pit manager and the agent.[78] The Sheriff, W. Clarke Reid, found that the production manager and planning officer had probably been in possession of 'essential information' which they did not bring to the attention of the colliery agent and manager, but reasonable doubt existed as to whether the specific charges of contravention or non-compliance with the law could be attached to any of the accused. In reaching this finding Clarke Reid in effect identified an important deficiency in the law.[79] Nationalisation had apparently diminished the clarity of the Coal Mines Act in apportioning individual responsibility for the different areas of safety transgressed at Knockshinnoch. The 1954 Mines and Quarries Act duly required the NCB to ensure that the 'duties of everyone acting between owner and colliery manager' were to be 'defined in writing and communicated to the Mines Inspector'.[80]

The NCB's corporate unwillingness to accept responsibility for Knockshinnoch recalled the FCC's evasive response to Valleyfield. So did the NCB's reluctance to accept obligations to those killed, injured and widowed. The Scottish Divisional Deputy Chairman, William Reid, had worked for the FCC, and was the son of its General Manager in 1939, Charles Reid. William Reid led the NCB's negotiations with NUMSA officials, who sought compensation for eight widows and their children of between £4,000 and £10,000, depending on family size and the age of the lost father, which determined lost potential income over time. One of the widows had given birth to her fourth son on the morning of the disaster.[81] Reid offered a maximum widows' payment of £1,750, and claimed that Scottish courts would award younger widows less, on the basis that they could secure employment, or safeguard their economic future by re-marrying. Even by the gender norms of the 1950s this was callous and coercive. As NCB headquarters were in London, NUMSA officials threatened to take the cases through the English legal system instead, where damages tended to be significantly higher. Improved settlements followed, each widow receiving a minimum of £3,000 plus adjustments for family size, and the non-fatally injured victims won much-enhanced terms also.[82]

Continuity of a different order was apparent in the two fatal explosions that killed 17 miners at Kames in Ayrshire and nine in Lindsay in Fife in November and then December 1957. Two hangovers from the private order were present: smoking underground, and workplace tensions between managers and employers. Each disaster highlighted the continued difficulty of apportioning responsibility for death and injury underground, and the limited agency of both NCB and unions in optimising safety. Kames employed 510 miners below ground and 130 on the surface in 1957. It was one of many collieries still designated 'naked light'. Smoking was permitted, in other words. Prior to the disaster on 17 November there had been no recorded instances of firedamp detection at the pit, which was in Muirkirk, 15 miles north-east of Knockshinnoch. All 17 of the miners killed were from Muirkirk. Their funerals on 22 and 23 November were attended by senior NCB officials, including Ronald Parker, Scottish Divisional Chairman, and NUMSA officials, led by the Moffats.[83] A public inquiry in Ayr County Buildings in February 1958, chaired by Sir Harold Roberts, Chief Inspector of Mines, established that there was a mixture of firedamp and air near the face of an unventilated mine heading. This exploded when a miner lit a cigarette, raising an inflammable cloud of coal dust which also ignited. The miner, Roberts emphasised, was entitled to smoke because of the colliery's 'naked light' status. Abe Moffat drew attention to the method of 'grunching' used in the pit's stoop and room workings. Coal was blasted directly out from the face without under-cutting, increasing the volume of dust and the size of the secondary explosion. Roberts was unconvinced that grunching generated more dust than the alternative combination of blasting, cutting and shearing, but concluded that colliery officials had become complacent in their inspections for gas. He recommended prohibition of naked flames below ground, proposing 31 December 1960 as a deadline for extending 'safety lamp' status to all pits. Roberts underlined his confidence that the NUM and other industry unions would support this measure and help to secure workforce compliance.[84]

Lindsay Colliery was in Kelty, Central Fife, where 790 men were employed underground and 170 on the surface in 1957. Nine miners were killed after an explosion of firedamp, ignited by a smoker's match, early on 14 December 1957. Unlike Kames, Lindsay was a 'safety lamp' mine. The match and cigarette were 'contraband', smuggled underground. The ineffectiveness of contraband inspections by managers and the complicity of workers in dangerous practices were scrutinised in a very difficult public inquiry, again chaired by Roberts, in Dunfermline's St Margaret Hall in March 1958. His report included diagrams depicting the scene of the disaster, No. 3 unit face in the pit's Mynheer area, 1,260 feet below ground. The locations of the men as they were found by the rescue team were marked in the diagrams, along with further details noted by a lengthier investigation conducted on the following day, by the District Inspector of Mines. A spent match and unsmoked cigarette, established as the immediate triggers of the explosion, were shown adjacent to the body of the machine-man who was about to cut the face. Other smoking paraphernalia were strewn along the 120-yard face and round the corner on the tailgate road. More were found by police officers in the clothing of some of the dead. The coal-cutting machine and other electrical equipment were tested and found to be in good working order. Firedamp was present in significant volume only in the area adjacent to the machine-man's body. The inescapable conclusion was that the firedamp exploded when the machine-man struck a match to light a cigarette.

This explanation was accepted by union representatives as well as management officials, but Moffat focused attention also on the colliery's contraband inspection procedures. Managers said these complied with guidelines established by the divisional Mining Inspectorate. Ten per cent of men were searched before going underground. Moffat's questioning established that men evaded these searches by secreting materials in their under-clothing. Roberts exculpated management of responsibility, however. His conclusions can be read as a frustrated commentary on the survival of class solidarities within the nationalised industry. The practice of smoking was evidently widespread at Lindsay, despite the efforts made to eradicate it by the colliery manager, another William Reid. Miners who refused to support their manager on this question imperilled their own lives in acting from a misguided sense of loyalty to their workmates who ignored the dangers and smoked. 'The people who indulge in it [smoking] are not being brave and clever', Roberts concluded, 'but are, in fact, showing an utterly irresponsible, callous and selfish disregard for the lives of their fellows and the happiness of their friends and relations. The possible consequences are so appalling that I appeal to the whole mining community – management, unions, officials, workmen and, if I may, their womenfolk – to try to stamp out this evil practice.'[85] This minority smoking culture was not immediately eradicated, however, at least in Fife. In the late 1950s Ian Terris moved from Cardowan to Rothes, where he was surprised to find men being searched for smoking materials before going underground. Such practice had been unnecessary at Cardowan, well-known as a gassy pit. Terris confronted a group of workers who he believed had been smoking underground at Rothes. Challenged to a fight, Terris punched one of the men in the face and told the others that they would have been 'dead meat' if caught smoking in Lanarkshire.[86]

The combined fatalities at Kames and Lindsay, 28, were more than doubled in the worst disaster of the nationalised era, at Auchengeich in Chryston, North Lanarkshire. A total of 840 men were employed at the colliery, with 340 in the No. 2 pit, where the disaster occurred at the start of the day shift on Friday, 18 September 1959. A total of 140 men were entering just as the fire was developing. The cause was an over-heated belt on a giant fan, 1,710 yards in from the pit bottom, on the return airway. Auchengeich was gassy, like Cardowan, and the fan was dispersing fumes down the airway. The belt slipped from the fan then heated, smouldered and caught fire. Flames transferred from belt to fan, igniting oil, then jumped to wood props and laggings in the return airway. Timing was central to the loss of life. A first locomotive had come up the return airway as the fire was escalating, carrying more than 40 miners towards the face. They disembarked at the terminus adjacent to the fan, and escaped from the smoky atmosphere through safety doors to the inward airway and thence by foot to the pit shaft. Meanwhile a second train, carrying the 47 men who were killed, was following up the return airway. At the terminus the men signalled the danger to the engine box at the bottom of the pit shift and the train was brought back, but its occupants were overcome by carbon monoxide poisoning. Only one man survived.[87]

In the public inquiry and subsequent prosecution of the colliery's manager and under-manager there were two core questions: was there an avoidable fault with the fan, specifically its belt, and why had the fire escalated, despite the presence of officials and other NCB employees underground? There had been intermittent difficulties with the fan for almost three months. It had been accelerated by colliery management in mid-June, from 490 to 540 revolutions per minute, to provide cleaner air. On 11 July the belt was replaced because it was recurrently slipping from the fan. The new belt was found to be slipping on Monday, 7 September, and another fitted on Wednesday, 16 September.[88] This third belt, of the Balata variety, was the focus of subsequent scrutiny. It came to Auchengeich through a larger NCB order from a new supplier, Henry A. Cole & Co. Ltd. After the disaster NCB officials, including H. L. Willett, Deputy Director-General, whose remit included safety, emphasised that local management was responsible for ensuring the belt's proper installation and maintenance. Willett attended two meetings with colliery managers in Lanarkshire in November 1959, ahead of the public inquiry, to make this point.[89] The narrative evident in the

Valleyfield and Knockshinnoch inquiries, pushing responsibility onto local management, was being reprised. But then NCB investigation established that the Auchengeich belt contained 31 oz. duck, lighter in weight than the required 33½ oz. standard of measurement for the cloth.[90] During the public inquiry, held in Glasgow's Justiciary Court and again chaired by Sir Harold Roberts, it was established that the belt had further contravened required specifications by not showing the maker's name or the relevant British Standard number.[91]

This diminished the corporate pressure on the NCB, and apparently the personal culpability of colliery manager, J. Smellie, and under-manager, A. Pettigrew. The NCB's legal counsel argued in the public inquiry that the fire had arisen from an error committed by a person over whom the Board had no responsibility, a representative of the supplier in other words. Union officials did not accept this. Abe Moffat accused the manager and under-manager of 'a complete lack of responsibility' in neglecting safety regulations and precautions.[92] Smellie and Pettigrew were shaken, the NCB's legal adviser noted, by the way in which Moffat's summation at the inquiry was 'framed against them'.[93] Moffat's depiction of negligent management had significant traction. Smellie and Pettigrew were prosecuted. The charge of failing to ensure that the Balata belt was in good condition was found not proven in January 1961. This reflected the NCB's success in raising doubts about the responsibility of its officials for equipment supplied by an external agent. But on two other charges Smellie and Pettigrew were found guilty: failing to appoint persons to oversee the fan during the night shift, and failing to secure adequate supply of water to the place where the fire occurred. These were deemed serious omissions of planning and provision: the fan was unsupervised during the night shift, and men disembarking at the terminus from the first train had found two adjacent fire extinguishers inoperable, and no ready supply of water. On the first charge Smellie and Pettigrew were admonished, and on the second each fined £100.[94]

Auchengeich was another reminder that security in the coalfields was contested and precarious. There were, however, signs of significant change at the NCB. James Cowan, Production Director for the Scotland West Central Area, invited Abe Moffat to inspect the colliery and provided him with detailed underground plans before the public inquiry.[95] Ronald Parker, NCB Scottish Chairman, was horrified by the huge loss of life, so soon after the traumatising disasters at Kames and Lindsay. He told his officials that he was extremely concerned about morale, among 'the men' as well as management. Parker wrote to the relatives of each of the 47 killed, on Sunday, 20 September, just two days after the disaster. Along with union officials, Parker and senior NCB managers attended the funerals that followed, at St Barbara's Chapel in Muirhead, Chryston Parish Church, and St Mary's Church in Kirkintilloch.[96] Twenty-three of those killed were from these and adjacent settlements, within two miles of the colliery, but there were wider ripples of loss too. Eighteen others had been travelling to work from addresses six miles distant or more, including a sizeable portion from South Lanarkshire, where collieries had been closing since the early 1950s. Bellshill, Blantyre, High Blantyre, Bothwellhaugh, Hamilton and Uddingston, along with Coatbridge and Bargeddie, all lost men in the disaster.[97]

Clear advancement in safety across the NCB's Scottish Division followed Auchengeich, which re-opened and continued producing coal until closure in 1965.[98] Selway's analysis of mining disasters in South Wales, to recap, shows that miners were ambivalent about the attention paid to major fatal accidents, which in aggregate terms resulted in fewer deaths than those accumulating in smaller but frequent incidents. In Scotland, as the death rate dropped after nationalisation, large disasters assumed an increasing share of fatal casualties. Auchengeich was followed by a renewed effort that led to the further improvement in underground safety shown in Table 3.1. The death rate among miners in Scotland dropped significantly in the 1960s after the 1957–9 spike caused by the disasters at Kames, Lindsay and Auchengeich. Two qualifications can nevertheless be made. First, the greater application of power-loading contributed to the upward rise in reportable injury rates examined in the opening half of this chapter, and caused a number of fatal accidents, including the roof fall at Seafield in May 1973. Second, there was one further major accident involving underground fire, at Michael, on the night shift of 9 September 1967. Figure 3 shows the pithead on the desperate morning that followed.

Figure 3 The aftermath of disaster: Michael Colliery, East Fife,
September 1967. © NMMS

Nine miners were killed at Michael, asphyxiated by gases released in the conflagration. The escape of 302 other men was a major feat of collective self-discipline, with significant acts of individual heroism subsequently recognised. Andrew Taylor, a 43-year old deputy, was awarded the Edward Medal. He was killed when searching for miners who he feared had been lost in the smoke. David Hunter, 59, also a deputy, won the George Medal after making his way deep into the workings, to warn men and lead their escape. Willie Shaw, 39, led the rescue team, rushing to the scene in the early hours with pit clothes pulled on over his pyjamas, and won the Queen's Medal.[99]

Shaw's team retrieved six of the bodies, five of them from the colliery's Sea mine area, but the other three were permanently entombed behind a series of seals that were the only means of containing the fire. A public inquiry, again established after pressure from NUMSA officials,[100] was held in Kirkcaldy, and chaired by Henry Stephenson, H. M. Chief Inspector of Mines and Quarries. Stephenson concluded that the fire had been caused by spontaneous combustion of coal, which ignited polyurethane foam insulation lining on a roadway in the mine, and then a conveyor belt within that roadway. The polyurethane had been applied as a barrier between air and coal that had been heating in the roadways in the days before the disaster. But it failed in two respects. First, air reached the heating coal, causing it to combust. Second, the foam was not treated as it ought to have been with a flame retardant. So it caught fire too, which spread through coal and timber. The NUMSA's acting President, Michael McGahey, cross-examined NCB officials at the inquiry, and secured an admission that polyurethane had been chosen over other fire-depressants on grounds of economy.[101] Stephenson recommended that polyurethane should not be used as insulation underground. He praised the bravery and self-discipline of the survivors, but noted that they owed their escape to personal knowledge of the many roadways that were used to evade the worst of the smoke, fumes and flames.[102] John McArthur, aged 62, guided his workmate John McEneamy, 46, to safety, through a highly circuitous route over the course of several hours.[103] Stephenson observed that the establishment of clearer underground signage was therefore a priority for the NCB in all collieries. He also noted the NCB's post-Michael commitment that all miners should be fitted with self-rescuing breathing equipment, to prevent carbon monoxide poisoning. This final point bears emphasis. McGahey, formally elected NUMSA President at the end of 1967, had made the universal provision of self-rescuers a central union demand following the disaster,[104] and he regarded the NCB's universal provision of this equipment from 1973 as his highest achievement as leader of the Scottish mineworkers.[105] Self-rescuers might not have saved the Michael men, not all of whom had died of carbon monoxide poisoning, but their development and introduction had been recommended by Sir Andrew Bryan after the Knockshinnoch disaster, where the agony of the rescue would have been shortened if the apparatus had been available.[106] Self-rescuers would certainly have increased the prospects of saving life at Auchengeich in 1959, where all 47 men were overcome by carbon monoxide. Now the union – across England and Wales as well as Scotland – succeeded in pressing the NCB to make universal provision of this vital equipment.[107]

Conclusion

Economic security in the coalfields was intimately connected with underground safety. Hazards were mediated by the effectiveness of trade union representation. Where employers attacked workplace trade unionism, the risks to workers of death, serious injury and illness were increased. This was the pattern in the 1920s and 1930s, when private owners excluded forceful union advocates from the industry. Fatality and serious injury rates increased. The reverse was observable in the 1950s and 1960s, when nationalisation facilitated stronger union voice. The rate of fatality was cut by one half as a result. On this most fundamental of all questions, life and death, nationalisation was an unambiguous success, strengthening coalfield security. Explosions of gas and coal dust, and fires, were all but eliminated as major causes of underground death by the end of the 1950s. The catastrophe in Michael in 1967 was the first of its kind since 1959 in Scotland, and such horrifying underground fire was never repeated. It is also notable that public inquiries into the post-1947 disasters at Knockshinnoch, Kames, Lindsay, Michael and Seafield were held within or closely adjacent to the coalfields: in Ayr, Dunfermline and Kirkcaldy rather than Edinburgh, as with Valleyfield in 1940. This was an important symbol of the progressive redistribution of political and social authority under nationalisation. Another is the contrast between the FCC's silence on Valleyfield in its company history and the NCB's close engagement with the communities affected by disasters in Ayrshire, Fife and Lanarkshire in 1957 and 1959. Ronald Parker, Scottish Chairman of the NCB, wrote to the bereaved and, with his officials, attended each of his employee's funerals. This was a significant shift from the initial NCB approach, embodied in the repugnant treatment of the Knockshinnoch widows by William Reid in 1950.

So the dangers of mining were diminished after nationalisation, but not eradicated. The continued toll in death and disability helped policy-makers to rationalise the further shrinkage of the coal industry in the 1960s. But hazards also strengthened the miners' moral economy interpretation of industrial restructuring after the peak of coal employment in 1957–8. Society's debt to the miners was all the greater because of the costs paid in illness, injury and death. The security of the coalfields was duly strengthened further, as the expectations of miners were broadly met by policy-makers, with the establishment of the Cosmopolitan Collieries and significant employment alternatives stimulated through regional policy. In the Cosmopolitan Collieries there were new dangers. The rapid growth of power-loading in the early 1960s contributed to a rise in the rate of reportable injuries and the Seafield disaster in 1973. But even in these difficult years – from the late 1950s to the early 1970s – the injury rate was lower than in the 1930s. There is, moreover, a strong impression that this very increase in reportable injuries was itself a demonstration of improved safety. Miners were empowered by union voice and public ownership to report accidents, knowing that they would be compensated when missing shifts because of injury or illness. This was unmistakable progress towards greater security in the coalfields.

Notes

1. Page Arnot, *Scottish Miners*, pp. 60–2, 242–4, 369–71.
2. Moffat, *My Life With the Miners*, pp. 9–16.
3. Obituary, Alex Eadie, *The Telegraph*, 26 January 2012.
4. Hamilton, Interview.

5. Campbell, *Scottish Miners. Volume One*, pp. 117, 139–40.

6. Barry Supple, *The History of the British Coal Industry, Volume Four, 1913–1946: the political economy of decline* (Oxford University Press: Oxford, 1987), pp. 426–8.

7. Arthur McIvor and Ronald Johnston, *Miners' Lung: A History of Dust Disease in British Coal Mining* (Aldershot: Ashgate, 2007).

8. Olivier Kourchid, 'Les Mineurs du Nord et du Pas-De-Calais face à la silicose, à la pneumoconiose at aux insufficances respiratoires: techniques de soins et politiques de la santé dans les années 1990', in Sylvie Aprile, Matthieu de Oliveira, Béatrice Touchelay and Karl-Michael Hoin, *Les Houillères entre l'État, le marché et la société* (Septentrion Presses Universitaires: Villeneuve d'Ascq, 2015), pp. 99–114; Portelli, *They Say in Harlan County*, pp. 151–6.

9. A. Chan, 'A "race to the bottom": globalisation and China's labour standards', *China Perspectives*, 46 (2003), pp. 41–9.

10. Ashworth, *British Coal Industry*, pp. 547–9.

11. David Selway, 'Death Underground: Mining Accidents and Memory in South Wales, 1913–74', *Labour History Review*, 81.3 (2016), pp. 187–209.

12. Ministry of Power, *Explosion at Cardowan Colliery, Lanarkshire, on 25 July 1960, by H. R. Houston, C.B.E., H. M. Deputy Chief Inspector of Mines and Quarries*, Cmnd. 1260 (HMSO: London, 1961).

13. Andrew Perchard and Keith Gildart, '"Buying brains and experts": British coal owners, regulatory capture and miners' health, 1918–1946', *Labor History*, 66 (2015), pp. 459–80.

14. Charles Webster, *The Health Services Since the War. Volume I: Problems of Health Care: the National Health Service Before 1957* (HMSO: London, 1988), pp. 133–77.

15. McIvor and Johnston, *Miners' Lung*, pp. 182–3.

16. McIvor and Johnston, *Miners' Lung*, p. 57.

17. NCB, *Annual Report 1968–69*, p. 43, and *Annual Report 1971–72*, pp. 41–2.

18. McIvor and Johnston, *Miners' Lung*, pp. 206–8, 220–2.

19. Arthur McIvor and Ronald Johnson, 'Voices From the Pits: Health and Safety in Scottish Coal Mining Since 1945', *Scottish Economic and Social History*, 22 (2002), pp. 111–33; Hilary Young, 'Being a Man: Everyday Masculinities', in Lynn Abrams and Callum G. Brown, eds, *A History of Everyday Life in Twentieth-Century Scotland* (Edinburgh University Press: Edinburgh, 2010), pp. 131–52.

20. Alan McKinlay, 'Jimmy Reid: Fragments from a Political Life', *Scottish Labour History*, 46 (2011), pp. 37–52.

21. Wight, *Workers Not Wasters*, pp. 103–8.
22. George Orwell, *The Road To Wigan Pier*, in *Orwell's England*, edited by Peter Davison (Penguin: Harmondsworth, 2001), pp. 83–4.
23. Supple, *British Coal Industry*, pp. 426–8.
24. Jenny Cronin, *The Origins and Development of Scottish Convalescent Homes, 1860–1939*, University of Glasgow PhD, 2003, pp. 115–18.
25. Angela Turner and Arthur McIvor, '"Bottom dog men": Disability, Social Welfare and Advocacy in the Scottish Coalfields in the Interwar Years, 1918–1939', *Scottish Historical Review*, 96.2 (2017), pp. 187–213.
26. Campbell, *Scottish Miners. Volume One*, p. 60; Moffat, *My Life*, pp. 49–51.
27. J. N. Williamson, 'Ten Years of Safety Work in a Scottish Colliery Group. Safety Record of the Fife Coal Company, Ltd., 1936–1945', *Transactions of the Institution of Mining Engineers*, Vol. 106 (1946–47), p. 263.
28. Campbell, *Scottish Miners. Volume Two*, p. 238.
29. National Coal Board, *Report and Accounts for 1950*, HC 188 (HMSO: London, 1951), para. 43.
30. McKibbin, *Classes and Cultures*, p. 161.
31. Fox, *Industrial Sociology and Industrial Relations*.
32. *Nines Was Standing*, directed by Humphrey Swingler, Greenpark Productions, NCB, 1950; this film is on *Portrait of a Miner*, a two-DVD NCB film collection issued by the British Film Institute in 2009.
33. *Safety First*, directed by Peter Pickering, Data Film Productions, NCB, *Mining Review*, 2nd Year, No. 11, July 1949.
34. NRS, SC 21/11/1950/15, Fatal Accident Inquiry, 3 November 1950.
35. Tam Dalyell, 'Dick Marsh', in Greg Rosen, ed., *Dictionary of Labour Biography* (Politicos: London, 2001), pp. 381–3.
36. Kenneth O. Morgan, *The People's Peace: British History, 1945–1990* (Oxford University Press: Oxford, 1992), pp. 325–56; Andrew Taylor, *The NUM and British Politics. Volume 2: 1969–1995* (Ashgate: Aldershot, 2005), pp. vii–viii, 50–72.
37. Margaret Thatcher, *The Path to Power* (HarperCollins: London, 1995), pp. 201–22.
38. John Campbell, *Margaret Thatcher. Volume One: The Grocer's Daughter* (Vintage: London, 2001), pp. 177–81.
39. *Parliamentary Debates, Fifth Series, Commons*, Vol. 755, col. 245–61 (Marsh) and col. 261–76 (Thatcher), 28 November 1967.
40. *Parliamentary Debates, Fifth Series, Commons*, Vol. 755, col. 372–6, 28 November 1967.
41. *Parliamentary Debates, Fifth Series, Commons*, Vol. 786, 1723–32, 10 July 1969.

42. Arnold, 'Death of Sympathy'.
43. National Coal Board, *Report and Accounts for 1957*, HC 181 (HMSO: London, 1958), p. 107.
44. NRS, CB 398/13/12, NCB – Scottish Area, Seafield Inquiry, Dossier, 1973, Note on Accidents.
45. *Royal Commission on Safety in Coal Mines: Report*, Cmd. 5890 (HMSO: London, 1938).
46. Campbell, *Scottish Miners. Volume One*, pp. 117, 139–40.
47. National Mining Museum of Scotland (NMMS), Lothian Coal Company, Accident Report Book, 1914–33.
48. Cmd. 5890, Tables 8 and 9.
49. The Scottish Office, *Scottish Abstract of Statistics*, No. 9/1980 (HMSO: Edinburgh, 1980), Table 12.9, 'NCB Mines: Employment and Productivity'.
50. NRS, SC 21/11/1957/11, Fatal Accident Inquiry, 1 November 1957.
51. NRS, SC 21/11/1963/3, Fatal Accident Inquiry, 13 November 1963.
52. Cmnd. 1260, p. 4.
53. 'Pit inquiry pledge', *The Guardian*, 12 May 1973.
54. Department of Trade and Industry, *Extensive Fall of Roof at Seafield Colliery Fife, 10 May 1973, Report by J. W. Calder, Chief Inspector of Mines and Quarries*, Cmnd. 5485 (HMSO: London, 1973).
55. NRS, CB 398/13/12, Memo, Seafield Colliery, Accidents, prepared by NCB Scottish Area Safety Engineer for G. Gillespie, NCB Scottish Area Chief Mining Engineer, 4 July 1973.
56. NRS, CB 398/13/8, DTI Press Notice, Seafield Colliery Accident Inquiry Report, 14 December 1973; Cmnd. 5485, pp. 20–1.
57. NRS, CB 398/13/12, NCB – Scottish Area, Seafield Inquiry. Dossier; Cmnd. 5485, 'Plan of Incident Area'.
58. McIvor and Johnston, *Miners' Lung*, pp. 149–52.
59. Ashworth, *British Coal Industry*, pp. 547–9; round-table discussion at meeting of Fife Mining Heritage Preservation Society, Kirkcaldy, 20 March 2017, attended by author.
60. TMI, DDA, Papers relating to Health & Safety, NUM Safety School, Ruskin College, Oxford, 27 September to 3 October 1980.
61. Field, *Blood, Sweat and Toil*, pp. 86–93, 111–19.
62. Keith Gildart, 'Coal Strikes on the Home Front: Miners' Militancy in the Second World War', *Twentieth Century British History*, 20.2 (2009) pp. 121–51; John McIlroy and Alan Campbell, 'Beyond Betteshanger: Order 1305 in the Scottish Coalfields during the Second World War, Part 1: Politics, Prosecutions and Protest', *Historical Studies in Industrial Relations*, 15 (2003), pp. 27–72, and 'Part 2: The Cardowan Story', *Historical Studies in Industrial Relations*, 16 (2003), pp. 39–80.

63. '35 Dead in Pit Disaster. Firedamp Explosion in Scottish Colliery', *Manchester Guardian*, 30 October 1939, p. 4.

64. Mines Department, *Explosion at Cardowan Colliery, Lanarkshire, on 16 November 1932, by Sir Henry Walker, C.B.E., H. M. Chief Inspector of Mines*, Cmd. 4309 (HMSO: London, 1933).

65. Excerpt from report in *The Scotsman*, 30 October 1939; http://www. scottishmining.co.uk/33.html, accessed 20 January 2017.

66. NRS, CB 420/13/1, Ross & Connel, FCC Solicitor, to Ivon Graham, 13 January 1941; Ivon Graham to Ross & Connel, 15 January 1941; C. Augustus Carlow to J. Ivon Graham, 17 January 1941.

67. NRS, CB 420/13/1, Finding and Judgement by Sheriff Neil MacLean, Sheriff Court Dunfermline, 6 March 1941; FCC, Legal Fees, March 1941.

68. Valleyfield, 28 October 1939, http://www.scottishmining.co.uk/33. html, accessed 20 January 2017.

69. NRS, CB 420/13/3, Proceedings at a Preliminary Hearing of a Public Inquiry by the Board of Trade regarding explosion at Valleyfield Colliery, Fife, on 28 October 1939, Edinburgh 11 December 1939.

70. NRS, CB 420/13/1, J. M. Davidson to Augustus Carlow, 6 March 1941; Carlow to Davidson, 7 March 1941; Davidson to Carlow, 8 March 1941.

71. Augustus Muir, *The Fife Coal Company Limited: A Short History* (Fife Coal Company: Leven, approximately 1948).

72. 'Field Subsides into Scots Pits: 125 Trapped, 13 Feared Dead', *Manchester Guardian*, 8 September 1950.

73. 'Descent Through Crater in Pit Search', *Glasgow Herald*, 11 September 1950; Ministry of Fuel and Power, *Accident at Knockshinnoch Castle Colliery, Ayrshire, 7 September 1950, by Sir Andrew Bryan, H. M. Chief Inspector of Mines*, Cmd. 8180 (HMSO: London, 1951), pp. 12–20.

74. James Robertson, *And The Land Lay Still* (Hamish Hamilton: London, 2010), pp. 176–201.

75. 'No Hope For Trapped Men', *Glasgow Herald*, 12 September 1950.

76. Cmd. 8180, pp. 31–5, 45–6.

77. 'Colliery Agent Retiring', *Manchester Guardian*, 24 March 1951, p. 7.

78. 'Coal Board Officials Accused', *Manchester Guardian*, 2 October 1951, p. 5.

79. 'Mining Officials Acquitted: Knockshinnoch Charges', *Manchester Guardian*, 9 October 1951, p. 9.

80. 'New Bill as "Safety Charter" for the Miners', *Manchester Guardian*, 22 January 1954, p. 2.

81. 'Descent Through Crater in Pit Search', *Glasgow Herald*, 11 September 1950.

82. Page Arnot, *Scottish Miners*, pp. 376–96.
83. James Taylor, Kames Colliery Disaster, compiled from the files of *The Muirkirk Advertiser*; http://www.ayrshirehistory.com/pdf/kamesdisaster.pdf, accessed 20 February 2017.
84. Cmnd. 467, pp. 4–5, 11, 16–17.
85. Ministry of Power, *Explosion at Lindsay Colliery, Fifeshire, 14 December 1957, by Sir Harold Roberts*, Cmnd. 485 (HMSO: London, 1958), Plan no. 2, Glassee Seam Mynheer Mine Area, Plan View of No. 3 Face, and pp. 4–6, 9, 11–16, 19–20.
86. Terris, *Twenty Years Down the Mines*, p. 74.
87. Ministry of Power, *Underground Fire at Auchengeich Colliery, Lanarkshire, 18 September 1959, by T. A. Rogers, H. M. Chief Inspector of Mines and Quarries*, Cmnd. 1022 (HMSO: London, 1960), Plan No. 1, Auchengeich Colliery No. 2 Pit, and pp. 2–3, 21–6.
88. Matt O'Neill, *Lanarkshire's Mining Disasters* (Stenlake: Catrine, 2011), pp. 77–9.
89. NRS, CB 207/39/3/1, NCB Auchengeich Colliery, Meeting of 2 November 1959, Action remit to Messrs Willett, Anderson and Skidmore, note 1 December 1959.
90. NRS, CB 207/39/3/1, NCB Scottish Division, Production Department, Fire at Auchengeich – Central West Area, Appraisal of various papers, 22 December 1959.
91. NRS, CB 207/13/7, Legal Adviser to Chairman, NCB Scottish Division, 20 January 1960.
92. 'Q. C. says an unexplained error caused pit disaster. N. C. B. "not responsible" for faulty belt', *Manchester Guardian*, 16 January 1960.
93. NRS, CB 207/13/7, Legal Adviser to Chairman, NCB Scottish Division, 20 January 1960.
94. NRS, CB 207/13/7, NCB Scottish Division, Production Department, Auchengeich Colliery – Prosecution of Manager and Under-Manager, 10 January 1961.
95. NRS, CB 207/39/3/2, James Cowan to Abe Moffat, 17 December 1959.
96. NRS, CB 207/13/7, Notes of Informal Meetings, NCB Scottish Division Board, 19 September 1959 and 21 September 1959; P. O. Osbourne, Secretary, NCB Scotland Central West Area, to K. G. Smith, Secretary, NCB Scottish Division, 24 September 1959; and Note on Funeral Arrangements, Auchengeich, 25 September 1959.
97. NRS, CB 207/39/3/2, Assistant Area Safety Engineer to J. R. Cowan, Production Manager, NCB Scotland Central West Area, List of Auchengeich Fatal Casualties, 30 September 1959; author calculations.

98. NRS, CB 207/24/1, Minute of Meeting, Proposed Closure of Auchengeich Colliery, 25 February 1965.

99. MHC, Box 9, L-15-9, Michael Colliery, clipping, 'Medals for Michael heroes', *Courier & Advertiser*, 17 July 1968.

100. TNA, POWE 52/202, Lawrence Daly, NUMSA General Secretary, to Ray Gunter, Minister of Labour, 19 September 1967.

101. MHC, Box 9, clipping, 'Safety Is Our Resolution in 1968', *Scottish Miner*, January 1968.

102. Ministry of Power, *Fire at Michael Colliery, Fife, 9 September 1967. Report by H. S. Stephenson, H. M. Chief Inspector of Mines and Quarries*, Cmnd. 3657 (HMSO: London, 1968), pp. 2, 10, 16–17.

103. MHC, Box 9, clipping, 'Two Saved From Fife Disaster Pit', *Sunday Post*, 19 September 1967.

104. *Scottish Miner*, October 1967.

105. Duncan, *Mineworkers*, pp. 251–2.

106. Cmd. 8180, p. 46.

107. Cmnd. 3657, pp. 28–9.

Part Two

Educate: Political Learning and Activity

CHAPTER 4

Generational Learning: from the 1920s to the 1950s

The Scottish miners' central political goal was economic and social security. Their interpretations of what this meant and how it could be achieved varied over time. An important generational element was involved in this process of political learning. There were three distinct generations of Scottish miners in the twentieth century. Their members came of age in the successive types of predominant workplace introduced in Chapter 2. The Village Pit generation, born in the 1890s, viewed security in terms of nationalisation, obtained in 1947. The New Mine generation, born in the 1920s, saw problems in the nationalised order that its predecessor could not. Its members were more vigilant on pit closures and the wider employment position in the coalfields in the late 1950s and 1960s, and exerted greater workforce control over the industry. The Cosmopolitan Colliery generation, born in the 1950s, found its standard of living challenged in the late 1960s and early 1970s by falling real wages. In the 1980s it faced NCB management incursions on union rights, and pit closures without workforce agreement or alternative employment provision. The strike of 1984–5, to protect union rights as well as jobs and collieries, is presented in Chapter 7 as a movement of generation as well as class and community.

This chapter examines the generational process of political learning among Scottish miners from the 1920s to the late 1950s. It expands on an earlier discussion of generational change in the Scottish coalfields.[1] Analysis is organised in three parts. First, the conflicts of the 1920s and 1930s are detailed, showing how these formed the politics of the Village Pit generation, and strengthened their demand for nationalisation. Second, the industrial tensions of the Second World War are examined as formative influence on the New Mine generation. Third, pit closures in the 1950s are presented to show how the New Mine generation adopted a more assertive defence of coalfield security than the Village Pit generation. Chapter 5 then takes the chronological discussion of political learning forward to the 1980s.The Communist politics of the miners' union leaders feature throughout this chapter. These politics were informed by everyday life in the coalfields as well as international developments, and were periodically problematic. Village Pit generation leaders admired the Soviet Union, where workers had rid themselves of private owners and, it was believed, obtained enhanced security.[2] But this created difficulties in the coalfields, especially evident in the Second World War, when defending the strategic interests of the Soviet Union led Communist trade union officials to adopt positions and pursue actions at odds with their members' demands.

Political Learning in the 1920s and 1930s

What makes a generation? Formative experience is vital. The Rhondda, wrote Will Paynter, the South Wales Communist born in 1903, was 'the oven which moulded me into the kind of man I was to become'.[3] Karl Mannheim, writing when Paynter was entering adulthood in the 1920s, saw generational location and social class as twin elements in the construction of identity. He argued that generations acquire their distinct identity from shared 'concrete experience' as young adults, especially in circumstances of crisis such as political revolution, military conflict and economic depression.[4] Mannheim's model is almost a century old, but historical scholarship in the 1990s and 2000s revived the value of generation as analytical category.[5] Martin Roseman's study of coal mining in the Ruhr from 1945 to 1958 is an exemplar in this respect. Reconstruction after Nazism was influenced by inter-generational differences between younger miners and older union officials, industry managers and policy-makers. Younger men, shaped by military conscription and service, coupled with the trauma of national defeat and occupation by external powers, resisted authoritarian managerial entreaties to work harder for limited wages and rations after 1945. Yet they were also flexible and less receptive to Communist and radical left politics than their employers and social democratic union officials feared. Younger men 'had had enough shouting', Roseman concluded, and helped to establish social partnership and workplace co-determination in the Ruhr, contributing to the German economic 'miracle' of the later 1950s and 1960s.[6]

Political learning among Scottish miners from the 1920s onwards was shaped in generational terms by the same combination of political, industrial and everyday experience that structured developments in the Ruhr after 1945. Abe Moffat, President of the NUMSA from 1945 to 1961, was born in 1896; his brother and successor as NUMSA President, Alex, was born in 1903. As young men they worked at Lumphinnans 11 & 12 in Central Fife, in an industry that was becoming different in business organisation and production scale from that of their coalmining father's youth. Industrial concentration and growth from the 1890s and 1900s meant that big firms such as the Fife Coal Company, the Moffats' employer, were major political as well economic operators.[7] Sir Adam Nimmo, Chairman from 1923 until his death in 1939, was a former President of the Mining Association of Great Britain (MAGB).[8] Charles Augustus Carlow, Managing Director of the FCC from 1923 and then Nimmo's successor as Chairman, was another prominent figure in the UK industry, elected President of the Institution of Mining Engineers in 1937.[9] The presence of large-scale capital enterprise had a major formational influence on the Moffats and other members of their Village Pit generation. Expanding firms, larger units and increased mechanisation flattened divisions between workers, who were stimulated to greater collective action on wages, conditions and the broader organisation of industry and society. Lumphinnans was one of three 'Little Moscows' identified in Stuart Macintyre's analysis of inter-war working class militancy in Britain,[10] and appears in a more recent survey of 'Small-Place Communism' across Western Europe, comparable with Sallaumines in Pas-de-Calais and Penzberg in Bavaria.[11] The Italian-French political activist, Lawrence Storione, was attracted to the area, where he became a miner and founded the Anarchist Communist League in 1908.[12] In his memoirs, published in 1965, and an interview recorded shortly before his death in 1975, Abe Moffat related his personal radicalisation to village politics, the industrial culture and dangerous working conditions of the pits, and the purposeless slaughter of workers on the Western Front in the First World War, which he witnessed as an infantryman. Storione persuaded him to join the CPGB in 1922.[13]

The Moffats shared formative experiences and politics with others across the Scottish coalfields. In East Fife John McArthur was born in Buckhaven in 1899 and David Proudfoot in Methil in 1892. After leaving school both men worked in mines owned by the Wemyss Coal Company. A significant share of the Parish Council area's housing stock belonged to the firm also. McArthur and Proudfoot were founder members of the CPGB in 1920. While Proudfoot left the Party in 1931 and withdrew from front-line union leadership thereafter, serving in the 1940s and early 1950s as a Town and County Councillor, McArthur was a member of the NUMSA executive and Fife District Secretary from 1946 to 1964.[14] Willie Allan, born in 1900, started in 1914 at Craighead Colliery in Blantyre, Lanarkshire. This was owned by Baird & Co., another multi-operational outfit. Allan joined the CPGB in 1923,[15] influenced in 1921 by the lockout and attending John Maclean's Scottish Labour College classes in Glasgow, where he studied with McArthur and five other young miners, all sponsored by their unions.[16] Allan, McArthur, the Moffats and others of the Village Pit generation were the 'militant miners' who, according to Alan Campbell, wrested leadership of coal industry trade unionism and politics in the 1920s from the preceding generation of 'bureau-cratic reformists'.[17] William Adamson, born in 1863, secretary of the Fife county union since 1908, and Labour MP from 1910 to 1931, was one of many older figures who lost ground after the First World War when encouraging miners to accept wage cuts in falling market conditions, just as members of the Village Pit generation were pressing for a more combative approach to negotiations with the private owners.[18]

This generational struggle in the coalfields is a key motif of William McIlvanney's 1975 novel, *Docherty*, where the eponymous Tony dies in 1922, age 53, in a pit accident, after experiencing defeat in the 1921 lockout. Tony's son Mick, who lost his right arm when serving in the army during the war, joins the CPGB and tells younger brother Conn why they need to break with the past: 'We came an' stood in line wi' oor bunnets oot. An a' we goat wis a bunnetfu' o' air. Ah mean, we've been waitin' in a queue for hunners o' year'. Mick laments the fixation of their labour movement elders with legal methods. 'But whit's legal? Legal is whit they need tae keep whit they've goat. We hiv tae brek in. An' we hiv tae batter onybody that gets in oor road oot o' existence'.[19] John McArthur, recording his inter-war memories in conversation with Ian Mac-Dougall between 1969 and 1971, recalled this struggle for control of the labour movement explicitly in generational terms. 'The war and the Bolshevik Revolution had created a schism', he said, 'and we young ones were told we had "no patience"'.[20]

Industrial conflict after the First World War was multi-faceted, but ownership and wages predominated, central as they were to collective security in the coalfields. The conduct and outcome of this struggle shaped the political outlook of the Village Pit generation with effects that lasted into the 1950s and even 1960s. The private coalfield order had been qualified by state controls in the First World War, with national wage minima. In August 1918 the MFGB's annual conference reprised a pre-war demand for nationalisation, plus stronger workplace representation and a standard fixed price for coal to remove the destabilising effect of market pressure on wages. The owners were pursuing a restoration of the pre-war situation: district wage-setting, without national minimum, and freedom from government control. They achieved their primary goal, avoiding nationalisation, in 1919. The coalition government of Liberals and Conservatives averted a national strike by establishing the Coal Commission, under Mr Justice Sankey. This had union members, including Robert Smillie of the Scottish Miners' Federation, who favoured nationalisation, as did a slight majority of government-appointed economists, Sidney Webb and R. H. Tawney among them. Led by Nimmo of the Fife Coal Company, however, employer representatives on the Commission forced the government to oppose nationalisation, although a significant pay increase was conceded.[21]

Employers opposed national pay bargaining as well as nationalisation.[22] The national minimum wage strengthened security across the coalfields with an element of state subsidy and the pooling of profits between companies and across districts. The MAGB lamented this structure for generating the supposed 'evils of high prices, low output and inefficient working'.[23] The next major crisis, the 13-week lockout that began on 1 April 1921, was framed by the owners' aim of ending national agreements. It took place within the radical slowdown in economic activity across Britain towards the end of 1920, and followed the abrupt cessation of government control of coal on 31 March 1921.[24] The miners were in a weaker bargaining position than 1919, trying to protect an industry-wide wage with the goal of nationalisation now growing distant. Where the government was in some ways sympathetic to the miners in 1919, a closer coalition of interest between state and owners was now evident. The Liberal Prime Minister, David Lloyd George, told representatives of unions and employers early in the lockout that the government opposed subsidy from general taxation. As negotiations continued, the government also stated that the national pooling of profits to sustain equalisation of wages across the industry was undesirable.[25]

The coalition of interest between ministers and owners had a further complex element. The government wanted to restore the Gold Standard, the mechanism for determining sterling's value in currency markets. This required raising the bank rate to encourage investors to hold sterling reserves, at a cost to industrial borrowers of capital and, as the value of the pound appreciated, exporters. The financial position of many coal producers was adversely affected as a result, but the balance of power in the industry was shifted decisively in their favour by lower economic activity and rising unemployment.[26] While employers in Scotland experienced heavy commercial losses arising from the lockout their victory resulted in major labour cost-savings. Basic pay across the Scottish coalfields was cut by half from January to December 1921, although the national minimum was preserved.[27] Nimmo and other owners offered no public criticism of the Gold Standard strategy, which was accelerated by the election of Stanley Baldwin's Conservative government in October 1924. Sterling returned to the Gold Standard in March 1925. This over-valued the pound against the dollar and the mark by at least 10 per cent according to John Maynard Keynes. Demands from owners for further substantial wage cuts followed, including an end to the national minimum. Railway workers, dock labourers and other groups of unionised workers were organising in support of the miners, and the government averted a crisis with a nine-month subsidy to the coal industry starting at the end of July 1925, using this hiatus to prepare for a predicted coal lockout and General Strike, both of which began at the start of May 1926.

The General Strike is a central political event in Britain's twentieth century history. Around two million mostly male workers in various industrial and transport sectors were officially on strike in support of the locked out miners. They were joined unofficially by several hundreds of thousands of other workers, including many women. The strike was brought to an end after nine days by the leadership of the Trades Union Congress (TUC) which was coordinating the action, on the insubstantial promise of negotiations on miners' wages and working conditions. These did not materialise.[28] John McArthur assessed this outcome four decades later. With competing systems of social organisation and economic distribution the strike was 'becoming a struggle between an embryo workers' political state that was being set up and the power of the capitalist state'. The TUC leadership, attached to the 'legal' strategy criticised by Mick Docherty in McIlvanney's novel, called the strike off.[29] The mining lockout continued until late November because the owners refused to yield, seeking to strengthen their control with wages fixed by market prices and without national minimum.[30]

Division between owners and miners was sharpened greatly by the lockouts. The prolonged absences of male wages resulted in intense material deprivation. Few women in mining communities were engaged in paid employment in the 1920s, a possible factor in securing coalfield compliance for economic diversification in the 1950s and 1960s. Widening opportunities for women strengthened economic security. The lockouts made alternative forms of social organisation necessary. Systems of collective sustenance were improvised and then consolidated. The Burnbank soup kitchen, Hamilton, in Figure 4 was one of hundreds around the Scottish coalfields.

Figure 4 Alternative forms of social organisation: women at Burnbank Soup Kitchen, Lanarkshire, 1926. © NMMS

In East Fife in 1926 miners compelled the Wemyss Parish Council to fund communal kitchens operated by the Trades Council. Miners applied for public assistance *en masse*; those who registered worked in the kitchens, which ordered food through co-operative stores, paid for by the Parish.[31] Basic provision was supplemented by the rustling of sheep, goats and cows. Miners apprehended while stealing these animals were punished with prison sentences, in some cases exceeding 12 months. Women in Scotland led the organisational and political effort, operating the kitchens and bolstering collective morale, as in Durham where wives, mothers and sisters strengthened resistance on class lines.[32] Women gathered outside collieries during both lockouts in Scotland to prevent working miners from entering. They also mustered at the homes of 'scabs', drawing attention in gendered terms to their alleged unmanliness.[33] Willie Adamson, the 'bureaucratic reformist', embarrassed himself at a public meeting in East Fife in 1926 by decrying 'scabs' as 'women' rather than 'men'. David Proudfoot later remembered that the crowd's response to this objectionable stereotype was like 'Hell with the lid off'.[34]

Mining men and women attempted to impose costs on employers, attacking their property. In the first week of the 1921 lockout there were major crowd actions in Central Fife. An estimated 2,000 forcibly stopped pumping at Bowhill Colliery on 4 April, unsuccessfully trying to flood the pit and nearby Glencraig. On 5 April another large crowd entered the Fife Coal Company's Kirkford Colliery and extinguished the boiler, again seeking to flood the mine. The crowd then occupied Dalbeath Colliery and apprehended the company's agent, William Spalding. Viewed as an overly zealous disciplinarian, Spalding was marched through Cowdenbeath and Lumphinnans. Publicly ridiculed and threatened, he was rescued by police officers. There were similar incidents elsewhere in 1921, in Lanarkshire, Ayrshire and Midlothian.[35] Collective violence was less pronounced initially in 1926, but became more intense as some miners returned to work and the owners' goal of enforcing wage cuts became clearer. There were crowd attacks on working miners and owners' property in Lanarkshire and across Fife. More than 300 miners 'stormed the pithead' at Glencraig on 22 November, destroying the boiler and fighting with working miners and police officers, the latter regarded as agents of a hostile government and unambiguous allies of the employers.[36]

Allan, the Moffats and McArthur were among many arrested in 1926: Willie was found not guilty of offences under the Conspiracy and Protection of Property Act; Abe was convicted and fined for leading 'a riotous mob'; Alex was imprisoned for two months under the government's Emergency Regulations; and John was exonerated by the Sheriff on the charge of sedition after publicly criticising the policing at Glencraig. Union activists were victimised after each lockout, sacked and 'blacklisted' by other employers. Allan experienced this in 1921, the Moffats in 1926, and McArthur and Proudfoot on both occasions. Allan, the Moffats and Proudfoot became checkweighers, elected by workers under Coal Mines legislation. When the Moffats led a local strike in 1929, such involvement beyond their checkweighers' purview, the FCC successfully applied legal interdicts to have them removed. Abe did not work again in the coal industry until 1938.[37] After 1926 Proudfoot and McArthur served as workmen's safety inspectors, safeguarded under coal industry legislation. This provided them with access to the men for organising and propaganda, but was poorly paid. McArthur, like Abe Moffat, was unable to secure waged employment underground until 1938. The Wemyss Coal Company and other employers extended the victimisation to encompass his father, brother, son and three daughters, all of whom found work difficult to obtain in the 1930s.[38]

The McArthurs and the Moffats were among the tens of thousands of unemployed coal miners in Scotland, as the industry's overall manpower contracted by a third from around 126,000 in 1925 to just over 82,000 in 1932. This predicament and its social costs were not accepted passively. Miners were a key constituency in Scotland of the UK-wide National Unemployed Workers' Movement (NUWM), formed in 1921, mainly by CPGB members. The NUWM campaigned for government action to stimulate jobs and significant increases in out-of-work benefits. Its activists targeted the means testing of unemployment maintenance as a particularly vindictive example of anti-working class social policy. Local, regional and national demonstrations were organised. These included a sequence of marches to petition Parliament, between 1922 and 1936. The route of the 1934 march reinforces the centrality of miners to the NUWM. It left Glasgow on 22 January, passing through the coalfields of Ayrshire, Cumbria, Lancashire and the West Midlands, before arriving in London on 25 February.[39] Scottish miners led lively actions locally, and demonstrated in the streets of Edinburgh, targeted as Scotland's capital.[40]

Unemployment and the employers' anti-unionism did not bring peace to the pits. Union activists in some areas resisted managerial control underground. In FCC units by the late 1930s 'a culture of guerrilla war and lightning strikes had become entrenched'.[41] It will be remembered from Chapter 3 that fatal and reportable accident rates rose after 1926, a further stimulus to union action. A trend to greater militancy in coalfield politics was complicated, however, by shifts in Communist analysis and strategy, which contributed to the intermittent existence of rival union organisations. Across the Scottish coalfields there were eight regional or 'county' unions, affiliated to a relatively loose federation, the National Union of Scottish Mineworkers (NUSMW), formed in 1914, and the MFGB. Adamson headed the Fife, Kinross and Clackmannan Miners' Association (FKCMA). After the 1921 lockout Communists established a rival Mineworkers' Reform Union of Fife, Kinross and Clackmannan, which operated until 1927. Then, after the damaging defeat of 1926, Communists sought to unify the miners' reduced forces in the FKCMA, in a more combative defence of wages and working conditions. This partly generational struggle was shaped initially by the Communist International's 'United Front' approach, encouraging adherents to operate within existing working class political and industrial structures.[42]

The position was then transformed by two developments. First, seeking to marginalise his younger and militant rivals, Adamson established a new organisation in 1928, the Fife, Clackmannan and Kinross Miners' Association (FCKMA), as distinct from the FKCMA. He persuaded his allies in the NUSMW and then the MFGB to disaffiliate the FKCMA, on the pretext that it was financially insolvent, and recognise the FCKMA instead.[43] Second, in 1929 a new Communist rival was established, the United Mineworkers of Scotland

(UMS). This sprang from the first articulation of the Communist International's 'Third Period' analysis. Socialist revolution was regarded as imminent, following after the First World War and its revolutionary sequels (first period), including the establishment of the Soviet Union and the Communist International, followed by capitalism's temporary stabilisation (second period). Communists in capitalist societies were urged to show the 'social fascist' character of labour representatives. The UMS was intended to isolate reformists and promote greater unity across the Scottish coalfield. It was led initially by Allan, but achieved little headway in attracting members or influencing employers in Ayrshire, the Lothians or even Lanarkshire. Non-Communist miners were alienated by the Third Period criticisms of Labour and county union representatives.[44] The UMS increasingly focused on Fife. Allan was replaced as General Secretary in 1930 by Proudfoot, who was succeeded the following year by Abe Moffat.[45] The union made substantial gains in FCC pits in the Lochgelly–Lumphinnans–Cowdenbeath conurbation, and the big Wemyss Coal Company units, Wellesley and Michael. Both firms were forced to recognise the UMS and negotiate with its officials.[46]

The seizure of power in Germany by the Nazis in 1933 showed that the Third Period had been disastrous, creating absolute divisions between Social-democratic and Communist workers. The leaders of the Soviet Union and the Communist International then developed the Popular Front strategy, identifying the need for common struggles with anti-fascist 'progressive' forces. This eased the pressure on Communist coalfield organisers. The CPGB liquidated the UMS in 1936, although Communists were already pursuing accommodation with district unions.[47] In this context Communism claimed a significant victory in the 1935 General Election. Willie Gallacher, Clydeside engineering union activist and founder member of the CPGB, was an enthusiastic advocate of the Popular Front, and won West Fife with 37.4 per cent of the vote, ahead of Willie Adamson's 35.7 per cent and the Unionist Charles Black Milne, winner of the seat in 1931.[48] John McArthur recalled in 1969–71 the role in this election of workplace politics. Adamson and his FCKMA officials had failed, he claimed, to provide Valleyfield miners with effective leadership when the FCC forced through unattractive changes to pay rates shortly beforehand. Valleyfield's workforce comprised a sizeable portion of Gallacher's electorate.[49]

The 1935 General Election was followed shortly afterwards by the publication of *Revolt on the Clyde*, Gallacher's memoir of First World War industrial struggles and meetings with Lenin at the Second Congress of the Communist International in Moscow in 1920. Gallacher linked these experiences directly to the efforts made on behalf of miners by Communist trade unionists in the coalfields.[50] *Revolt on the Clyde* in this respect was part of a strategic effort to establish the CPGB as ideological heir to the various working class struggles of the 1910s. This claimed lineage was restated in the 1970s when a new edition of the book appeared with a foreword by Michael McGahey, NUMSA President.[51] Gallacher's 1935 victory in West Fife helped to embed Communism in the area's coalfield politics. While Labour regained the Parliamentary constituency in 1950, Communist candidates attracted greater support here than anywhere else in Scotland. Alex Maxwell, born in 1930, and Willie Clarke, born in 1935, who encountered Gallacher as a young miner at Glencraig in the 1950s, were both elected as Communist councillors in Central Fife in 1973. Both earned strong reputations as public servants and local champions, and were recurrently re-elected. Maxwell served in Cowdenbeath until retirement in 2012. Clarke was Councillor for Ballingry and then Benarty until retirement in 2016, the occasion marked by a House of Commons Early Day Motion sponsored by Roger Mullin, Scottish National Party MP for Kirkcaldy and Cowdenbeath, emphasising his long and valuable service in various political and trade union roles.[52]

The Communist and militant legacies of the 1920s and 1930s were also evident in the family histories of coalfield activists. Alan Campbell has written about the 'genealogies of victimization and radicalism' established in the 1920s.[53] Within four years of returning to the pits, in 1942 Abe Moffat was elected President of the NUSMW. In 1945 he was elected the first President of the newly constituted NUMSA, in which position he was succeeded by Alex in 1960 and McGahey in 1967. Abe's son, Abe Moffat, born in 1925, and daughter, Ella Egan, born in 1933, along with McGahey, were leading New Mine generation figures in the labour movement.[54] The younger Abe was a tradesman in the coal industry. He was President of NUMSA's trade union ally, the Scottish Colliery Enginemen, Boilermen and Tradesmen's Association (SCEBTA) before and during the 1984–5 strike. Ella convened the Scottish women's support groups formed in 1984, and her son, a miner at Monktonhall, was on strike for the duration.[55] Michael McGahey, born in 1925, was a son of Jimmy McGahey, a Communist imprisoned and then sacked in 1926.[56] Michael was a Communist, and served the NUMSA alongside Lawrence Daly, elected General Secretary in 1965. Daly was born in 1924, son of Jimmy, a Central Fife Communist also dismissed from employment in 1926. Lawrence became a Communist too but left the Party in 1956.[57] In 1984–5 Michael McGahey's son, also Michael, a Bilston Glen miner and Communist, was sacked by the NCB.[58] In 1926 John Bolton was sentenced to three months' hard labour for rustling sheep. His nephew, George Bolton, born in 1934, became NUMSA Vice-President in 1978, and succeeded McGahey as President in 1987. Guy Bolton, John's brother and George's father, was 77 when arrested in 1984–5 for an 'alleged breach of the peace outside a blackleg's house'. The case was dismissed.[59]

This rich familial story has significant generational dimensions. The Village Pit generation emerged from the 1920s and 1930s determined to eradicate the power of the private owners who had imposed punitive costs on their workmates and communities. Its members had experienced the results of disunity during the struggles with older union leaders in the 1910s and early 1920s, and in the damaging Communist-inspired Third Period.[60] They learned to be wary of internal union divisions which employers could exploit. When leading the NUSMW during the Second World War and then the NUMSA after nationalisation, they were suspicious of dissent. Members of the New Mine generation were formed politically by conflicts in the Second World War and in the first decade of nationalisation. Members of this younger generation derived distinct conclusions from the 1940s and early 1950s, less convinced than their elders that public ownership was in principle a guarantor of security. Generational difference would be particularly apparent on the issue of unofficial action and strikes, seen by the Moffats as disruptive, but by McGahey and Daly as a measure of coalfield discontent to be mobilised against closures and for improved pay and working conditions in the 1960s.[61]

The New Mine Generation and the Second World War

The prolonged national emergency from 1939 to 1945 shifted the terms of security in the coalfields. Miners viewed victory for the allied powers as vital for their collective welfare, but in its class and political dimensions the war was nevertheless complex. A fully successful outcome for the miners meant defeating the private owners as well as the Nazis. The Valleyfield disaster in November 1939 was salutary. The Fife Coal Company's evasive response reminded many miners that private ownership was socially unjust and aggravated the dangers of working underground. Nationalisation re-emerged as a realistic prospect with the miners' increased bargaining power in an extended period of labour scarcity. The miners' two priorities – winning the war and fighting the employers – were not always in harmony, however. There was tension between maximising production, to support the military effort, and defending wages and workplace rights. Industrial disputes were generally illegal under war-time emergency regulations, and in any case were avoided by union leaders who prioritised military victory, particularly after the Soviet Union became an ally in 1941. Communist mining leaders saw unofficial strikes as a threat to coalfield security but this outlook was partly generational. For members of the New Mine generation, including Communists, the defence of workplace rights and wages took precedence. This was their contribution to the war effort and the advance to greater collective security. The politics of this generation, whose members included Michael McGahey and Lawrence Daly, who starting working in 1939, were formed in part by unofficial struggles that placed them at odds with the government, their employers, union leaders and older relatives.[62]

The balance of power between labour and capital shifted during the Second World War. Government controls reduced the autonomy of private coal owners. A crucial mechanism was the Essential Work Order (EWO), introduced by Ernest Bevin, Minister of Labour and National Service in Winston Churchill's Coalition government. Bevin was founding General Secretary of the Transport & General Workers' Union in 1922. As Minister of Labour he saw the war as an opportunity to bolster the strength and prestige of unions and manual workers. This involved reciprocity: workers gained employment security but lost some privileges, notably the freedom to move between jobs and withdraw their labour. Applied to the coal industry, the EWO eroded the owners' control over their workplaces. The removal of dismissal as an instrument of discipline was welcomed by miners but resented by employers, who saw the gradual rise in absenteeism, from 6.5 per cent in 1939 to over 12 per cent in 1942–3 across Britain as the undesirable consequence. Employers claimed that absenteeism led to production shortfalls and so compromised the war effort. At the same time, however, the EWO prevented miners from leaving the pits to take better-paid jobs elsewhere, notably in the many munitions factories that were established in the coalfields.[63] These changing labour market regulations and structures greatly destabilised the fragile 'micro-politics' of many mining settlements, not least in gender terms, with female earnings in munitions matching and sometimes even exceeding male wages in coal.[64]

A further and more stringent disciplinary mechanism was the Conditions of Employment and National Arbitration Order, commonly known as Order 1305. Introduced in 1940, this attempted to ban strikes and lockouts. Parties to an industrial dispute were obliged to submit their case to the Ministry of Labour & National Service or, in the coalfields, to the Ministry of Fuel & Power. Where parties could not settle their differences in consultation with the relevant state official, the dispute was referred for binding settlement to a National Arbitration Tribunal (NAT). This consisted of three members selected by the Minister of Labour: one each from panels approved by the TUC and the British Employers' Confederation, plus an 'independent'. Only where the case was not referred to the NAT by either party to the original dispute within 21 days were strikes or lockouts legal. There are competing interpretations of the Order's impact.[65] Evidence from private sector engineering in England indicates that NAT decisions tended to operate more in favour of workers than employers,[66] but miners frequently experienced the Order in negative terms. Ministry of Fuel & Power officials were more inclined to pursue prosecutions against workers than their Ministry of Labour equivalents, and miners were reluctant to submit grievances to the arbitration authorities. Strikes arising from continued workplace tension and wage disputes resulted in mounting political difficulty, with numerous prosecutions, convictions and prison sentences for workers. A major crisis arose early in 1942 after the prosecution of 1,085 striking miners from Betteshanger in Kent who were fined, with three of their pit-level representatives imprisoned.[67] These miners had been in dispute with their employer and Ministry of Fuel & Power officials over output levels and payment rates in difficult seams. The miners refused to pay the fines, and articulated their resistance to Order 1305 in language of patriotism and justice.[68]

The Betteshanger crisis was reflective of the general trend in the British coalfields to greater conflict as the war progressed. The low pay issue was compounded as work became harder. More was demanded from a workforce that contracted by 10 per cent across Britain, from 773,000 in 1939 to 701,000 in 1944.[69] Anticipating future nationalisation, employers were reluctant to invest in production methods and welfare amenities. The government attempted to alleviate these difficulties in June 1942 with *Coal*, a White Paper. Regional controllers, with input from workers' representatives, were empowered to remove pit managers who were obstructing increased output, and enhanced medical services would be established to reduce the time and production lost through injuries and illness.[70] A committee of inquiry into coal industry wages was also appointed, resulting in a substantial increase, moving miners from 59th to 23rd in the government's 'league table' of industrial earnings.[71] Miners secured a national minimum wage, removing the link between earnings and prices, an important gain which industry unions had unsuccessfully sought to defend after the First World War.[72] But with a growing labour shortage and escalating production pressures there were further strike waves across the British coalfields in 1943 and early in 1944.[73]

In Scotland the incidence of strike action followed a distinct and politically significant path, as Table 4.1 illustrates. This reproduces Ministry of Labour & National Service data compiled and presented by McIlroy and Campbell in 2003. Throughout the war around 12 per cent of the mining workforce was employed in Scotland, so from 1939 to 1941 and again in 1945 there were a disproportionately high number of working days lost to recorded disputes in Scottish pits. The intervening years from 1942 to 1944 were different. This requires careful explanation.

Table 4.1 Working days lost in recorded disputes in coalmining, Scotland and the UK, 1939 to 1945

	1939	1940	1941	1942	1943	1944	1945
Scotland	234,409	205,039	201,694	113,419	218,092	344,103	385,125
UK	565,015	505,148	332,575	840,121	886,405	2,480,774	640,768
Scotland as % of UK	41.5%	40.6%	60.6%	13.5%	24.6%	13.9%	60.1%

Source: John McIlroy and Alan Campbell, 'Beyond Betteshanger: Order 1305 in the Scottish Coalfields during the Second World War, Part 1: Politics, Prosecutions and Protest', *Historical Studies in Industrial Relations*, 15 (2003), p. 53

Campbell and McIlroy use the data to argue that Scottish miners resisted the war-time industrial regime, which included an important role for Communist trade unionists. The Moffats and others of the Village Pit generation attained leadership of the NUSMW in the late 1930s and early 1940s. After Nazi Germany's invasion of the Soviet Union and the start of the 'Great Patriotic War' in June 1941 these Communist union leaders worked more closely with the state and employers. Campbell and McIlroy show that this created space for alternative 'militant' voices in the Scottish coalfields, particularly members of the Independent Labour Party (ILP), who combined with a smaller fraction of Trotskyists in the Militant Miners' Committee (MMC), formed in 1942.[74] This theme has been developed by Keith Gildart, who emphasises that ILP critiques of the CPGB gained traction in Cumberland and South Wales as well as Scotland.[75]

McIlroy and Campbell present support for the MMC as challenging rather than over-turning Communist ascendency in Scottish coalfield trade unionism. Table 4.1 suggests indeed that the CPGB was successful in containing militancy. The effects of the August 1939 pact between Nazi Germany and the Soviet Union may be seen in the data for the first three calendar years in the table. The CPGB was compelled by the pact to oppose British military action against Nazi Germany, and Communists in the NUSMW strongly criticised the EWO and Order 1305, likening Bevin's regime – particularly the ban on strikes – to the Nazis' oppression of trade unionism.[76] Hence, perhaps, the relatively unchanging volume of working days lost in Scotland's coalfields from 1939 to 1941. But then comes 1942, the first full calendar year after the Nazi invasion of the Soviet

Union. In Scotland, reflecting the influence of Communist coalfield leadership, the number of working days lost almost halved where elsewhere it more than doubled. The number of lost days increased in Scotland in 1943 and especially in 1944 at a much slower rate than in England and Wales. Communists were therefore influential in Scotland in limiting the workforce anger that contributed to a trebling of days lost to disputes in Britain as a whole from 1943 to 1944. This escalation prompted the introduction of Defence Regulation 1AA, making it an offence, punishable with up to five years' penal servitude, to incite strike action in essential industries. Only in 1945 did the pre-1941 trend re-emerge in mining, with a disproportionately high volume of days lost to disputes in Scotland. Military victory in Europe had been achieved in early May, and the CPGB was relaxing its emphasis on maximising production.[77]

Defence Regulation 1AA triggered action from constabularies in Edinburgh, Midlothian and Lanarkshire. Short unofficial strikes at Newcraighall and Lingerwood collieries, to the east and south of Edinburgh, the latter spreading briefly to Lady Victoria and Easthouses, were reported by the police to the Ministry of Labour & National Service in May 1944. In each instance government officials advised that there was no evidence of subversion and prosecutions were unwarranted. W. O. Kerr, Superintendent in Lanarkshire Constabulary at Baillieston, east of Glasgow, submitted 10 near-identical reports to the Ministry between May 1944 and September 1945, alleging contraventions of the regulation at various pits, but no action followed.[78] In fact, no workers were prosecuted at any time under the Regulation, which was introduced hurriedly by Bevin when presented with claims that a small number of Trotskyists – who probably totalled fewer than 1,000 across Britain in 1944 – were 'encouraging' leaders of unofficial strikes with potential to disrupt industrial production on the eve of the allied Normandy landings.[79]

Bevin's officials had learned from the tumults arising from the application of Order 1305. There were distinct problems in Scotland, where legal authorities made much greater use of the instrument than in England and Wales. Between 1940 and 1945 there were 111 cases prosecuted under the Order in Great Britain, of which 72 were in Scotland. About half of these related to strikes in coal mining, with 1943 the peak year, when 28 cases were prosecuted in Scotland and six in England and Wales. This adds texture to the strike data shown in Table 4.1. More than four out of five prosecutions against miners under Order 1305 in 1943 were in Scotland, even although Scottish miners represented just 12 per cent of the British industry's workforce and were involved that year in only about a quarter of the days lost to strikes in mining across Britain. Ariane Mak has shown that the key to understanding this distinct usage in Scotland of Order 1305 is the high preponderance of short-lived strikes in Scottish mines. Employers placed substantial pressure on the legal authorities to enforce the emergency regulation. The typical brevity of these strikes meant that they had a limited impact in terms of overall working days lost, and was perhaps reflective of official union efforts to maintain production.[80]

Generational learning was involved in these conflicts, with younger miners coming to appreciate the hazards of demanding too much restraint from union members. These miners, including Communists, understood that strikes disrupted production and represented a short-term threat to coalfield security, but more than their elders saw long-term difficulty in suppressing workplace anger. Generational divergence was evident in a series of disputes in 1942 that Moffat and his officials tried to squash, mainly in Lanarkshire, but also in Fife. In a salutary case of how the enforcement of Order 1305 aggravated pressures, 24 miners at Blairhall in West Fife were prosecuted after taking unofficial strike action in March. They were in dispute with their employer, the Coltness Iron Company, over wages and output-levels.[81] At Dunfermline Sheriff Court the miners were fined £5. They were advised that they would serve 30 days in prison if the fines were not paid within a month. Despite heavy pressure from local union officials to comply with the law, the Blairhall men refused to pay the fines, convinced of the justice of their grievances. Three were arrested and taken into custody in late August. A strike of 509 Blairhall miners in their support immediately followed, and spread to the neighbouring FCC pits, Valleyfield and Comrie. More than 2,000 miners were now on strike in West Fife. The crisis was resolved only after the Blairhall union branch paid the original fines, using CPGB funds according to Ministry of Fuel & Power officials.[82] A broader challenge to the union leadership followed in 1943, when a Presidential election was forced in the Lanarkshire Miners' Union. The Militant Miners' Committee candidate, Hugh Brannan, won majorities at 22 of the 60 branches, and was defeated narrowly by the Communist incumbent, William Pearson, by 9,195 votes (54 per cent of those cast) to 7,792 (46 per cent). Pearson's victory was based principally on Blanytre and Hamilton, where Willie Allan and other Communist miners had led the struggles of 1921 and 1926; Brannan drew support from the Shotts area, and in north Lanarkshire, winning majorities at Auchengeich, Bedlay and Cardowan.[83]

It was fitting, therefore, that the most serious war-time crisis in the Scottish coalfields originated at Cardowan. A young miner refused to perform the loading work of two men on 18 May 1943, unless paid double the rate. He was sacked on the spot. The whole section of 35 men came out on a strike that lasted until 27 May. All bar one were found guilty when prosecuted under Order 1305 in June. One man's penalty was £3 or 20 days in prison; for 33 others it was £5 or 30 days. By September those who had refused to pay, 23 in total, were arrested and imprisoned. Roughly 10,000 miners at 32 pits across Lanarkshire, Stirlingshire and Dunbartonshire expressed their solidarity by joining a strike that ran from 24 September to 4 October.[84] Striking miners at Gateside in Cambuslang were led by Michael McGahey, aged 18, who was rebuked by his Communist brothers and father. Abe Moffat opposed the strike as a threat to economic security, and vilified the MMC as 'Fascists in sheep's clothing', but worked hard to end the crisis. With the permission of the Secretary of State for Scotland, he and other NUSMW officials visited the Cardowan prisoners in Glasgow's Barlinnie prison on 1 October. The jailed miners subsequently claimed that one of the officials, James McKendrick, told them that only Cardowan and Wester Auchengeich remained on strike. The true position is difficult to establish, but press reports indicate that 3,000 miners were still out, exceeding the total employed at Cardowan and Wester Auchengeich.[85] Union officials said they had told the imprisoned miners that strikers at all pits other than Cardowan were seeking to resume work, and would do so after the men's release. The fines were paid, the Cardowan miners freed and the strike ended,[86] but the details of this resolution are cloudy. Money for the fines was borrowed by Pearson from the Lord Provost of Glasgow, Patrick Dollan, on the understanding that the prisoners would repay it in instalments. The Cardowan men and their workplace representatives did not accept this: Moffat, they said, had pledged union money to reimburse Pearson, who later repaid Dollan from his own savings.[87]

The Cardowan affair fed into the rising tide of working days lost to disputes across England and Wales as well as Scotland. The causes of this unrest were debated over two days in the House of Commons in October 1943, a week after the Cardowan men's release. Conservative and Unionist MPs claimed that employers, the government and society more broadly were facing a rebellion by miners. Sir Edward Keeling, Conservative MP for Twickenham and a Director of the Wallsend and Hebburn Coal Company,[88] approvingly paraphrased an alleged statement from Abe Moffat that 'unlawful strikes were a luxury of the minority at the expense of the majority'. Keeling argued that 'indiscipline in a mine is just as dangerous as indiscipline in a ship', jeopardising those engaged in fighting the enemy.[89] This was a contentious argument. Among military personnel, at least those from manual working class backgrounds, were those who saw civilian strikers as defending the economic security which they would be reliant upon after demobilisation.[90] On the 'Home Front' Winston Churchill was more mindful of trade union and working class thinking than many Conservative and Unionist MPs during the war.[91] In the Commons debate on the coal crisis the Prime Minister said that miners were working extremely hard despite the many strains. He conceded that nationalisation was the probable future, but as a controversial question had to be shelved until the end of the war and a General Election. Labour MPs, notably Alexander 'Sanny' Sloan of South Ayrshire and Thomas Fraser of Hamilton, responded by talking about the tension between public and private interests. Regional coal controllers were drawn from the private firms. They were tolerating and even encouraging the practice of mining from less productive seams, saving easier and more profitable workings for after the war. This was probably the

underlying issue at Betteshanger in 1942, and other employers likewise exploited emergency demand by cutting more expensive coal
without compensating miners properly for the additional work
involved.[92] Nationalisation was therefore an urgent necessity, to
ensure that the industry served the war effort and the miners were
fairly rewarded.[93]

The demand for nationalisation was being articulated by older
as well as younger miners. Sloan, Secretary of the NUSMW before
winning a Parliamentary by-election in 1939, was born in 1879,[94]
and belonged to the same generation as Willie Adamson, who had
been superseded in Fife by the younger Moffats. To paraphrase Karl
Polanyi, there was a 'double movement' of generation taking place
in the early 1940s. The Village Pit generation was securing leadership of the NUSMW, succeeding elders like Sloan and Adamson.
Shortly before Abe Moffat's election as President in 1942, William
Pearson, born in 1896, had become the union's Treasurer. In 1945
Pearson attained the position of Secretary, and helped lead the
NUMSA until his death in 1956. He had first been elected onto the
NUSMW executive in 1937. James McKendrick, his fellow Lanarkshire Communist, had joined him there in 1938.[95] The New Mine
generation of miners, however, born in the 1920s, was also emerging. Fraser told the House of Commons in October 1943 that union
officials had been addressing meetings of strikers in Lanarkshire 12
or 13 times a day, and sympathised with their concerns, but could
not persuade them to return to work. Michael McGahey, having led
a group of these strikers and resisted both union and family entreaties to give up the action, was sacked by his employer. Blacklisted by
other Lanarkshire firms he was compelled to work in the Lothians
before returning 'home' in the late 1940s to Cardowan.[96]

Industrial tensions and stoppages of work continued after the
war, hampering production and contributing to a serious shortage
of coal in the winter of 1946–7. Generational differences remained
live. Miners' leaders – members of the Village Pit generation – were
urging improved effort to support the Labour government's broader
economic and social agenda, and prepare for a successful launch
of nationalisation. But miners were reluctant in the second half
of 1945 and 1946 to work harder for private owners, who seemed

more interested in maximising the terms of their compensation than increasing production.[97] The attrition effects of the war were powerful, accentuated by continued economic austerity, with food shortages and rationing. These concerns were not unique to miners in Britain. In the Ruhr, where the Nazis had brutally suppressed the rich political and organisational culture of the miners, there was great relief after the war, but likewise patchy improvement in coal output. Ruhr miners faced greater nutritional and economic constraints than British miners, but their lives were characterised by similar working class uncertainty about industrial organisation, ownership and collective economic security.[98]

Nationalisation, Generation and Communal Security

Michael McGahey advanced through the NUMSA and the CPGB in the 1950s, working closely with Abe Moffat. He nevertheless developed a sharper critique of the nationalised industry than his mentor, which he shared with others of his generation, notably Lawrence Daly, who joined the CPGB and was NUM delegate at Glencraig by the mid-1950s. Daly visited the Soviet Union as part of a TUC youth delegation and was moved especially by the still-ruined city of Stalingrad. McGahey was a Communist until he died in 1999 but Daly left the CPGB in 1956, unable to tolerate its ideological restrictions and uncritical defence of the Soviet Union. Daly formed the Fife Socialist League, through which he associated with the broader UK New Left, before joining the Labour Party.[99]

The New Left had a limited footing in the Scottish coalfields. Daly left the CPGB before the Soviet military suppressed the anti-Stalinist revolution in Hungary in November 1956. Alex Moffat was the most prominent figure in the NUMSA who left the CPGB because of this. Other Communists, including Abe Moffat, resolved to examine their doubts within the party, which retained its standing in the NUMSA.[100] In any event Alex was elected NUMSA Vice President in 1957, and later re-joined the CPGB.[101] The New Left connection is nevertheless significant. Members of the New Mine generation – including Communists – articulated a critique of nationalisation which resembled the New Left's broader dissatisfaction that post-1945 public policy offered only moderate wealth redistribution and no thorough-going extension of workplace democracy.[102] The 'voice' of manual workers, to paraphrase Albert O. Hirschmann, was heard by policy-makers and employers on a narrow range of material questions only.[103] Stronger union influence in the nationalised industry was identified by the New Mine generation as the means to improved security. This was a lesson from the early 1940s, when union officials had prioritised production and military victory too strongly over workplace problems.

The New Mine generation was particularly troubled by pit closures. Around Shotts in Lanarkshire 1,000 jobs were lost between 1949 and 1953.[104] Miners and their families were transferred east, to Clackmannan, the Lothians and Fife. The mishandling of this process was unintentionally captured in 'Replanning a Coalfield', a 10-minute short film made in 1949 for the NCB monthly *Mining Review* series shown in cinemas. Speaking directly to camera, Robert Balfour, Chairman of the NCB Scottish Division, emphasised the benefits of relocation to Fife's expanding coalfields, where there were reserves that would last for 'hundreds of years'. The film made light of the social sacrifices demanded of migrant miners and their families. In a dramatised sequence a Lanarkshire miner was shown setting out for Fife, complaining to his wife as he left the house that he would 'miss the football' because of the move. The patrician commentator, the English character actor John Slater, claimed this was a trifle: the migrant miner would 'soon find a new team to watch'.[105] This was a minor slight, perhaps, but revealing all the same. The NCB was plainly overlooking both the importance of place in the coalfields and the troubling fact of community abandonment implicit in the shift of people and resources from Lanarkshire to Fife.[106] The Board dismissively attributed the social and civic worries arising from this process to the pessimism of 'industrial psychologists and social science students'.[107]

The Shotts closures contributed to the development of moral economy thinking in the Scottish coalfields. The miners' moral economy – reinforcing the links, direct and indirect, between New Left and coalfield politics – resembled that of E. P. Thompson's eighteenth century plebeian crowd.[108] The miners' moral economy had two core elements: pit closures and job losses had to be negotiated with union representatives rather than imposed by NCB management; and the loss of pits and employment could only be accepted where communal as well as individual economic security was guaranteed. This amounted to a lowering of 'market-ness' in the coalfields, to return to theoretical interpretations of the moral economy, and a thickening of the labour market's social embeddedness.[109] In the 1950s the accent was on NCB investment in new pits, particularly the Cosmopolitan Collieries taking shape in Ayrshire, Midlothian and Fife. In the 1960s, however, this also came to involve calls for increased alternative job creation, specifically through regional assistance to bring private sector manufacturing to Ayrshire, Lanarkshire, the Lothians and Fife.[110]

The moral economy had generational dimensions. Leading members of the Village Pit generation arguably accepted closures too readily in the late 1940s, and were taken aback by the ferocity of workforce opposition to further closures after the peak of employment in 1957–8. An emblematic struggle followed the NCB's decision to close Devon Colliery in Clackmannan on economic grounds in 1959, seeking where possible to redeploy the 653 workers at neighbouring pits. Resistance was led by members of the New Mine generation. George Bolton, born in 1934, worked at Devon and led a stay-down protest that initiated a major unofficial strike across the Scottish coalfields against the closure.[111] Interviewed in 1986, when he was NUMSA Vice President, Bolton's testimony was explicitly generational, outlining a discourse of opposition to older and uncomprehending trade union officialdom as well as the NCB. Many of his Devon workmates had moved to Clackmannan after the Shotts closures and had only just established local roots. Now they resisted as illegitimate the instruction to move again.[112] Devon workers picketed pits in Lanarkshire, West Lothian and Fife as well as Clackmannan.[113] Within two days about 25,000 miners at 46 pits across Clackmannan, Stirlingshire and Fife were on unofficial strike in solidarity with the Devon men.[114]

The strike took the NUMSA executive by surprise, and resembled the Cardowan crisis of 1943. Abe Moffat and other union leaders strongly condemned the unofficial action that followed the Devon protest, but were forced to respond by the seriousness of the underlying issues, pit closures and enforced migration. Moffat was in London on union business when the strike started. He returned to

Scotland on the evening of 24 June, consulting with Devon branch officials and advising Ronald Parker, the NCB Scottish Divisional Chairman, that the union was striving to end the strike. In discussion on 29 June some NUMSA executive members expressed sympathy with the strikers, noting that the Output per Manshift record at Devon exceeded the Scottish and British averages, and acknowledging the threat of closures to community survival. But Moffat and a majority of the executive saw the unofficial strike as an unacceptable breach of discipline that would weaken the NUM's campaign against closures.[115] There was some workplace union support for this view. NUMSA officials later received a letter from the Lindsay branch in Kelty, complaining that stay-down protestors at Devon had received 'priority admission' to the miners' convalescent home at Culross in West Fife, 'to the exclusion of men' recovering from work-related injuries or illnesses.[116] Moffat nevertheless worked to resolve the dispute's immediate cause. He held further talks with the NCB's Scottish directorate, which established the miners' future right to consultation prior to closure, and this helped to secure an end to the strike. The NCB officials kept Devon open until the workforce could be transferred together in 1960 to Glenochil.[117] This drift mine was a major investment project by the NCB two miles west of Devon. Production started in 1956, but difficulties were emerging which suggest that the NCB's confidence in moving miners there from Devon was misplaced. Original projections about Glenochil's reserves had already been queried by the NCB national directorate in 1958, and it would close in 1962.[118]

In his memoirs Moffat claimed that the 1959 crisis was resolved by his intervention and the NCB Scottish Division's important concession on consultations prior to future closures.[119] It could therefore be argued that his generation was partly responsible for constructing the coalfield moral economy. But it was the unofficial action of miners resisting the initial closure at Devon that forced both NUM and NCB officials to adopt enhanced consultation mechanisms with greater guarantees of security. The New Mine generation was therefore more robust in defending security and enforcing the moral economy. Chapter 6 details this process further, analysing opposition to closures in the late 1960s. Here it is worth noting the manner in which Michael McGahey and other younger officials in Lanarkshire approached NCB proposals for the closure of Hamilton Palace Colliery in the winter of 1958–9, just before the Devon crisis. With Hamilton Palace McGahey's priority was continuity of employment for the men affected. The NCB was persuaded to defer closure until there was a position for every Hamilton Palace miner who wanted one in North Lanarkshire, chiefly at Bedlay and Auchengeich collieries. Detailed redeployment records show that more than 99 per cent of Hamilton Palace workers received job offers at other Lanarkshire pits within three months of production ending.[120] This was shortly before 47 miners were killed at Auchengeich. Seven of these men had home addresses adjacent to Hamilton Palace and were probably part of the transferred cohort.[121] But this calamity could not have been foreseen when Hamilton Palace closed, and the union officers involved in negotiating the transfers were trying to maximise collective security. For older miners in Lanarkshire there was also an emphasis on enhanced redundancy terms, which helped to preserve opportunities for younger men. In 1963 around 950 men in Lanarkshire were paid off in this way. A. Campbell, born on 31 December 1899, left Cardowan with £165 in July, and William Potter, born on 30 October 1898, left nearby Wester Auchengeich in May with £180.[122]

While opposing closures more vigorously than their elders, members of the New Mine generation pursued a distinct approach to the daily management of the workplace. It was noted in Chapter 1 that miners schooled in the antagonisms of the 1920s and 1930s were reluctant participants in the 'traditional' functions of management. By contrast, miners who entered the industry in the 1940s and 1950s, like McGahey and Daly, used the new participative mechanisms more freely to strengthen union voice and collective security. Assessing changes in employee involvement from one generation to the next is aided by a schema of measurement. Blyton and Turnbull usefully differentiate the *extent, location* and *scope* of employee involvement, with the following definitions: *extent* as 'continuum' from no worker involvement to employee control, via information dissemination, joint consultation and joint decision; *location* from low-level participation on shop floor to higher-level engagement in boardroom; and *scope* as the strategic importance of issues under discussion, moving upwards from 'work allocation' to 'major technological change' and capital investment.[123]

In the early years of nationalisation participation amounted to consultation, at workplace level, and mainly on low-order work allocation questions.[124] Evidence from two workplaces, Glenochil in Clackmannan and Glencraig in Fife, demonstrates the willingness of New Mine generation representatives to challenge managerial control of higher-order organisational questions, including production and discipline, at local level. Glenochil hosted recurrent industrial disputes in 1958 and 1959, shaped partly by the frustrating production position that contributed to closure in 1962. NUM branch leadership contended that pit-level management was heavy-handed in its approach to discipline, with an unusually large number of dismissals. The central union protagonist was Bill McLean, born in 1919. Bill's father was William McLean, elected to the NUSMW executive in 1940 with other Village Pit generation officials. Bill McLean joined the CPGB early in his working life. Part of an NUMSA delegation to France in April 1949, he visited the northern Pas de Calais coalfield and then attended the first Communist-organised World Peace Congress in Paris.[125]

McLean became NUM area agent for Fife, Clackmannan and Stirlingshire, and in this role attended a meeting at Glenochil in March 1959 with the colliery's Manager, A. Murray, and Resident Engineer, D. Archibald, to discuss the case of a dismissed miner. The man had been found back from the coal face, breaking sticks, with the presumed intention of taking them home for firewood. Archibald argued that ignoring 'petty offences' of this kind would encourage more serious misconduct. McLean rejected this claim as frivolous and counter-productive. It was common for miners to take off-cuts that otherwise had no use. Such disciplinary initiatives by management would in any case be resisted through collective action by workers, which in the long run would be far more costly to the NCB in lost production. Archibald conceded that the miner could be re-employed but would not be compensated for wages lost since his dismissal. McLean argued the issue further and the miner was reinstated with a week's wage in lieu of the 10 days he had lost. McLean secured a similar outcome in the case of two miners dismissed in August 1959 after 'actively playing draughts underground'. McLean established that the draughts board had been in situ for some time, and that the miners, young 'lads', had been sitting beside it only for a short while, awaiting the delivery of girders that would enable them to continue with their work. The miners were reinstated, with compensation for lost wages.[126]

Lawrence Daly exerted a similar brake on managerial sovereignty at Glencraig, intervening where miners had been disciplined and dismissed. Like McLean at Glenochil, he warned that 'rash' punitive actions by managers would meet collective resistance, costly to the NCB in lost time and production. Twice in 1961 he defended the same miner, who as a 'leading man' coordinated a group of face workers. In the first instance the miner was dismissed after allegedly confronting a pit deputy in the baths over a wage dispute. The Colliery Manager, Johnston, stated that the miner had drunk three pints of beer after his shift before returning to the colliery where he assaulted the deputy. Daly observed that there were no witnesses to this other than the deputy and the miner whose dismissal was therefore unjust. On the second occasion Johnston complained that the miner was continually rejecting management instructions, speaking to officials about the organisation of work on behalf of other men, and moving away from his own workplace to do so. Daly again supported the miner, claiming a right for his members to speak up on behalf of others, and on a variety of organisational questions, particularly where these potentially involved safety matters. Two other dismissed miners were reinstated after Daly's intervention in 1962, whose allegedly poor work was cited by Johnston as the cause of a roof fall. Daly showed that the men had been following directions from a deputy.[127]

The favourable outcome for workers in these Glenochil and Glencraig cases is worth emphasising. The exercise of union voice contrasts vividly with the unilateral and often harsh exercise by management and employers of discipline in the 1920s and 1930s. The benefits to union members of the nationalised industry's consultative and conciliation machinery may not have been immediately clear to workers in the 1940s, when operating under older union officials. The use of the industry's consultative machinery by New Mine generation representatives therefore showed a dynamic learning process: the practical operation of the industry was changing in the later 1950s, with participation strengthening individual and collective security. These representatives were more willing than their Village Pit predecessors to pursue the possibilities of workforce participation in managing the industry. Returning to the Blyton and Turnbull three-part formula for measuring employee involvement, in the 1950s and early 1960s – on workplace organisation and discipline, and pit closures – New Mine generation leaders increased the *extent* of participation from limited consultation to more meaningful dialogue and greater direct influence in the 1960s. In *location* terms participation expanded slightly, from workplace level to regional level, with the involvement of McLean in the Glenochil cases and McGahey's conduct of the Hamilton Palace closures, and Scottish divisional level, with the resolution of the Devon crisis. Chapter 6, examining resistance to closures, will show that the *scope* of participation would be further expanded in the later 1960s and early 1970s, from concentration on work organisation to significantly higher order strategic questions. New Mine generation leaders would establish a share in the making of NCB investment and disinvestment decisions, and influencing UK government energy policy.

Conclusion

Collective economic security was the central goal of Scottish miners across the twentieth century. This chapter, examining the miners' political learning from the 1920s to the 1950s, has shown that two different generations of miners understood security in distinct terms. The extremely harsh economic, industrial and political environment of the 1920s and 1930s – the national lockouts, the victimisation by employers of workplace leaders, the major loss of employment – inculcated important lessons for the generation schooled as young workers and trade unionists in the aftermath of the First World War. Members of this generation saw nationalisation as deliverance from the evils of private ownership. They also learned to oppose dissent within the ranks of labour. Divisions were seen as a source of weakness, limiting the labour movement's capacity to secure improved working and living conditions. The behaviour of the Moffats and others of the Village Pit generation during and then after the Second World War demonstrated this intolerance, and the particular role of Communist politics, although these were not homogeneous. Younger Communists, notably McGahey and McLean, along with Labour militants like Daly, had a different approach. This reinforces the importance of generational distinctions. The New Mine generation figures shared the view of their elders that unity was precursor to security. But both unity and security could be jeopardised by an over-bearing exercise of union authority. Unofficial strikes – in war and peace – were seen as evidence of powerful workplace and community anger that could be mobilised with more deft leadership in pursuit of greater collective security.

These generational differences were illustrated by the issue of workplace participation. Members of the Village Pit generation were reluctant to engage with the opportunities of the nationalised industry, with joint consultative committees at workplace level offering miners' representatives the prospect of closer engagement with managers on a range of organisational questions. Older miners saw this dimension of nationalisation as a potential trap. Their formative experiences shaped a preference for the certainties of adversarial workplace relationships. Younger miners and mining representatives, born in the 1920s, whose political learning started in the 1940s and 1950s, were more critical of nationalisation yet also more willing to engage with its joint consultative committee structures and activities. The important conclusion here is that nationalisation was a dynamic process. The New Mine generation moulded nationalisation to fit the security needs of miners and their communities. Moral economy arguments were central to this process. Change was accepted as a fact of coalfield development but only where it was agreed by the workers and communities affected. Consent would not be granted unless individual and collective security was guaranteed, either through transferring miners from pits that were closing to other units within daily travelling distance, or via the establishment of alternative industrial jobs. The moral economy framework also extended to govern daily life in the pits, with members of the New Mine generation placing significant limits on managerial sovereignty in the coalfields.

Notes

1. Jim Phillips, 'Economic Direction and Generational Change in Twentieth Century Britain: the case of the Scottish Coalfields', *English Historical Review*, 132 (2017), pp. 885–911.
2. Page Arnot, *Scottish Miners*, pp. 257–60, 339–40, 366–8.
3. Paynter, *My Generation*, p. 15.
4. Karl Mannheim, 'The Problem of Generations', in Karl Mannheim, *Essays on the Sociology of Knowledge* (Routledge & Kegan Paul: London, 1952), pp. 276–322, especially pp. 288–303.
5. Claudia Goldin, *Understanding the Gender Gap. An Economic History of American Women* (Oxford University Press: Oxford, 1990), pp. 5, 16–41, 138–57; William Lyons and Robert Alexander, 'A Tale of Two Electorates: Generational Replacement and the Decline of Voting in Presidential Elections', *The Journal of Politics*, 62 (2000), pp. 1014–34.
6. Mark Roseman, *Recasting the Ruhr, 1945–1958. Manpower, Economic Recovery and Labour Relations* (Berg: Oxford, 1992), p. 325; Mark Roseman, 'The generation conflict that never was: young labour in the Ruhr mining industry, 1945–1957', in Mark Roseman, ed., *Generations in conflict: youth revolt and generation formation in Germany 1770–1968* (Cambridge University Press: Cambridge, 1995), pp. 269–89.
7. Campbell, *Scottish Miners. Volume One*, pp. 26, 34, 38, 44; Oglethorpe, *Scottish Collieries*, p. 309.
8. Kirby and Hamilton, 'Sir Adam Nimmo'.
9. Outram, 'Carlow'.
10. Macintyre, *Little Moscows*, pp. 48–78.
11. Ad Knotter, '"Little Moscows" in Western Europe: The Ecology of Small-Place Communism', *International Review of Social History*, 56 (2011), pp. 475–510.
12. Gray, *Stramash*, p. 53; Fife Psychogeographical Collective, 'Searching For Storione'.
13. Moffat, *My Life with the Miners*, pp. 9–16, 26, 28–33; Paul Long, 'Abe Moffat, the Fife Mineworkers and the United Mineworkers of Scotland: Transcript of a 1974 Interview', *Scottish Labour History*, 17 (1982), pp. 5–18.

14. Ian MacDougall, ed., *Militant Miners. Recollections of John McArthur, Buckhaven; and letters, 1924–26, of David Proudfoot, Methil, to G. Allen Hutt* (Polygon: Edinburgh, 1981), pp. 5–7, 69–71, 166–7.

15. Alan Campbell and John McIlroy, 'Reflections on the Communist Party's Third Period in Scotland: the case of Willie Allan', *Scottish Labour History*, 35 (2000), pp. 35–54, and especially p. 37.

16. MacDougall, *Militant Miners*, pp. 35–6.

17. Campbell, *Scottish Miners. Volume Two*, pp. 5–8

18. Macintyre, *Little Moscows*, p. 52.

19. William McIlvanney, *Docherty* (Sceptre: London, 1996), pp. 354–5.

20. MacDougall, *Militant Miners*, p. 26.

21. Page Arnot, *Scottish Miners*, pp. 144–9.

22. Kirby and Hamilton, 'Sir Adam Nimmo', pp. 57–9.

23. Ministry of Labour, 'National Stoppage of Work in Coal Mines', *Labour Gazette*, June 1921, p. 280.

24. Page Arnot, *Scottish Miners*, pp. 151–2.

25. Ministry of Labour, 'National Stoppage of Work in Coal Mines', *Labour Gazette*, April 1921, p. 175.

26. John Foster, 'Prologue: What Kind of Crisis? What Kind of Ruling Class?', in John McIlroy, Alan Campbell and Keith Gildart, eds, *Industrial Politics and the 1926 Mining Lockout: the Struggle for Dignity* (University of Wales Press: Cardiff, 2004), pp. 7–40.

27. Campbell, *Scottish Miners. Volume Two*, p. 160.

28. Quentin Outram, 'The General Strike and the Development of British Capitalism', *Historical Studies in Industrial Relations*, 21 (2006), pp. 121–41.

29. MacDougall, *Militant Miners*, pp. 96–7.

30. Laybourn, 'Revisiting the General Strike'.

31. MacDougall, *Militant Miners*, pp. 98–102.

32. Hester Barron, 'Women of the Durham Coalfield and their Reactions to the 1926 Miners' Lockout', *Historical Studies in Industrial Relations*, 22 (2006), pp. 53–83, and especially p. 66; Annmarie Hughes, *Gender and Political Identities in Scotland, 1919–1939* (Edinburgh University Press: Edinburgh, 2010), pp. 92–5.

33. Campbell, *Scottish Miners. Volume One*, pp. 240–1, 244–8.

34. Alan Campbell, 'Scotland', in John McIlroy, Alan Campbell and Keith Gildart, eds, *Industrial Politics and the 1926 Mining Lockout: the Struggle for Dignity* (University of Wales Press: Cardiff, 2004), pp. 173–89; quote at p. 182.

35. Campbell, *Scottish Miners. Volume One*, pp. 289–92, 303.

36. Page Arnot, *Scottish Miners*, pp. 178–80; Campbell, *Scottish Miners. Volume Two*, pp. 229–32.
37. Moffat, *My Life with the Miners*, pp. 49–51.
38. MacDougall, *Militant Miners*, pp. 128–9, 165–6.
39. Itinerary of the 1934 Hunger March, Working Class Movement Library, https://www.wcml.org.uk/our-collections/protest-politics-and-campaigning-for-change/unemployment/itinerary-of-the-1934-hunger-march/wcml/en/our-collections/protest-politics-and-campaigning-for-change/unemployment/itinerary-of-the-1934-hunger-march; accessed 22 June 2017.
40. Ian MacDougall, *Voices From the Hunger Marches* (Polygon: Edinburgh, 1991), *Volume One*, pp. 118–33; and *Volume Two*, pp. 269–90.
41. Outram, 'Carlow, Charles Augustus'.
42. Page Arnot, *Scottish Miners*, p. 262.
43. MacDougall, *Militant Miners*, pp. 121–6.
44. Campbell and McIlroy, 'Communist Party's Third Period'.
45. MacDougall, *Militant Miners*, pp. 133–4.
46. Campbell and McIlroy, 'Communist Party's Third Period'.
47. Long, 'Abe Moffat', pp. 15–17.
48. Robert Duncan, 'Gallacher, William (1881–1965)', *Oxford Dictionary of National Biography* (Oxford University Press: Oxford, online, 2011).
49. MacDougall, *Militant Miners*, pp. 147–8.
50. William Gallacher, *Revolt on the Clyde: an Autobiography* (Lawrence & Wishart: London, 1936; Fourth Edition, London, 1978), pp. 270–87.
51. Terry Brotherstone and Jim Phillips, 'A Peculiar Obscurity? William Gallacher's Missing Biography and the Role of Stalinism in Scottish Labour History: a contribution to an overdue discussion', *Scottish Labour History*, 51 (2016), pp. 154–73.
52. 'Obituary: Alex Maxwell, communist, community activists and local councillor', http://www.organizedrage.com/2013/03/obituary-alex-maxwell-communist.html#!/2013/03/obituary-alex-maxwell-communist.html, accessed 8 May 2017; 'Retirement of Councillor Willie Clarke', Early Day Motion 275, House of Commons, 4 July 2016, https://www.parliament.uk/edm/2016-17/275, accessed 3 May 2017.
53. Campbell, 'Scotland', pp. 184–5.
54. Moffat, *My Life with the Miners*, p. 83.
55. Ella Egan, Interview with Willie Thompson, 28 October 1985; Neil Rafeek, *Communist Women In Scotland: Red Clydeside from the Russian Revolution to the End of the Soviet Union* (Tauris Academic Studies: London, 2008), p. 215.

56. McIlroy and Campbell, 'McGahey'.
57. Lawrence Goldman, 'Daly, Lawrence (1924–2009)', *Oxford Dictionary of National Biography* (Oxford University Press: Oxford, online, 2013); *Jean McCrindle*, Obituary, Lawrence Daly, *The Guardian*, 30 May 2009.
58. Joe Owens, *Miners, 1984–1994: a decade of endurance* (Polygon: Edinburgh, 1994), pp. 82–3.
59. Campbell, 'Scotland', pp. 179, 184–7.
60. MacDougall, *Militant Miners*, pp. 137–9.
61. McIlroy and Campbell, 'McGahey'.
62. Goldman, 'Daly'; Robert Taylor, 'McGahey, Michael [Mick] (1925–1999)', *Oxford Dictionary of National Biography* (Oxford University Press: Oxford, online, 2004).
63. Supple, *British Coal Industry*, pp. 525–6.
64. Ariane Mak, 'Conspicuous Consumption in Wartime? Welsh Mining Communities and Women in Munitions Factories', in Corinna Peniston-Bird and Emma Vickers, eds, *Gender and the Second World War: Lessons of War* (Palgrave: London, 2016), pp. 55–72.
65. James A. Jaffe, 'The Ambiguities of Compulsory Arbitration and the Wartime Experience of Order 1305', *Historical Studies in Industrial Relations*, 15 (2003), pp. 1–26.
66. Nina Fishman, '"A Vital Element in British Industrial Relations": A Reassessment of Order 1305, 1940–51', *Historical Studies in Industrial Relations*, 8 (1999), pp. 43–86.
67. Adrian Tyndall, 'Patriotism and Principles: Order 1305 and the Betteshanger Strike of 1942', *Historical Studies in Industrial Relations*, 12 (2001), pp. 109–30.
68. Ariane Mak, 'Spheres of Justice in the 1942 Betteshanger Miners' Strike: An Essay in Historiographical Ethnography', *Historical Studies in Industrial Relations*, 36 (2015), pp. 29–57.
69. Field, *Blood, Sweat and Toil*, p. 113.
70. Board of Trade, *Coal*, Cmd. 6364 (HMSO: London, 1942), pp. 5–7.
71. Field, *Blood, Sweat and Toil*, p. 117.
72. Page Arnot, *Scottish Miners*, pp. 248–9.
73. Field, *Blood, Sweat and Toil*, pp. 111–19.
74. McIlroy and Campbell, 'Beyond Betteshanger. Part 1: Politics, Prosecutions and Protest', and 'Part 2: The Cardowan Story'.
75. Gildart, 'Coal Strikes on the Home Front'.
76. McIlroy and Campbell, 'Politics, Prosecutions and Protest', pp. 40–1.
77. Field, *Blood, Sweat and Toil*, pp. 319–21.
78. TNA, LAB 10/483, Ministry of Labour & National Service note on Strike at Newcraighall Colliery, 29 May 1944; various materials on

Strike at Lingerwood, 31 May to 2 June 1944; reports submitted to Ministry of Labour & National Service by W. O. Kerr, 31 May 1944 to 10 September 1945.

79. TNA, Cabinet Papers, Labour shortage and the end of the war, War Cabinet Conclusions, 19 April 1944, http://www.nationalarchives.gov.uk/cabinetpapers/themes/labour-shortage-end-war.htm, accessed 21 July 2017.

80. Ariane Mak, *En grève et en guerre. Les mineurs britanniques au prisme des enquêtes du Mass Observation (1939–1945)*, Université de recherché Paris Sciences et Lettres, PhD, 2018, pp. 270–4.

81. 'In brief', *Manchester Guardian*, 16 April 1942, p. 3; and 'Scottish Miners' Strike', *Manchester Guardian*, 29 August 1942, p. 9.

82. Mak, *En grève et en guerre*, pp. 292–7.

83. McIlroy and Campbell, 'Cardowan Story', pp. 41–6.

84. 'Scottish Strike Spreading: 7,000 Miners Idle', *Manchester Guardian*, 29 September 1943, p. 6.

85. 'Miners Released: Scottish Strike Ending', *Manchester Guardian*, 2 October 1943, p. 6.

86. 'Miners Returning', *Manchester Guardian*, 4 October 1943, p. 6.

87. McIlroy and Campbell, 'Cardowan Story', pp. 57–8.

88. Wallsend and Hebburn Coal Co. Ltd, List of Company Directors, 1940, Durham Mining Museum, http://www.dmm.org.uk/company/w005.htm; accessed 5 June 2017.

89. *Parliamentary Debates, Fifth Series, Commons*, Vol. 392, 817–26, 833–7, 12 October 1943.

90. Field, *Blood, Sweat and Toil*, p. 284.

91. Paul Addison, *Churchill on the Home Front* (Jonathan Cape: London, 1992), pp. 332–3.

92. Mak, 'Spheres of Justice', pp. 37–8.

93. *Parliamentary Debates, Fifth Series, Commons*, Vol. 392, 920–33, 959–66, 988–98, 13 October 1943.

94. Esther Davies, 'Sanny Sloan, the Miners' MP', *Scottish Labour History*, 52 (2017), pp. 78–91.

95. Page Arnot, *Scottish Miners*, pp. 236, 244, 250, 268.

96. McIlroy and Campbell, 'Cardowan Story', pp. 74–5.

97. Tookey, 'Three's A Crowd?'.

98. Roseman, *Recasting the Ruhr*, pp. 63–93.

99. Lawrence Daly,' Fife Socialist League', *New Left Review*, 1.4 (1960), pp. 69–70; Christos Efstathiou, 'E. P. Thompson, the Early New Left and the Fife Socialist League', *Labour History Review*, 81.1 (2016), pp. 25–48.

100. Rafeek, *Communist Women*, p. 141.
101. Obituary, 'Mr Alex Moffat', *The Guardian*, 7 September 1967.
102. Campsie, 'Politics of Everyday Life'.
103. Albert O. Hirschman, *Exit, Voice and Loyalty: responses to decline in firms, organizations and states* (Harvard University Press: Cambridge, MA, 1970).
104. TNA, POWE 37/481, National Coal Board Scottish Division (NCBSD), List of Pits closed, 1949–1959.
105. 'Replanning a Coalfield', *National Coal Board Collection, Volume One, Portrait of a Miner*.
106. Heughan, *Pit Closures at Shotts*.
107. NCB Scottish Division, *Scotland's Coal Plan*, pp. 29–30.
108. Thompson, 'Moral Economy of the English Crowd'.
109. Gibbs, 'Moral Economy of the Scottish Coalfields', pp. 128–30.
110. Phillips, 'Deindustrialisation and the Moral Economy'.
111. TNA, POWE 37/481, clipping, '"Stay Down" To Save Pit', *Daily Worker*, 24 June 1959.
112. George Bolton, Interview with Willie Thompson, presumed May 1986.
113. TNA, POWE 37/481, Ministry of Power Coal Division, Note on the strike at Devon Pit, 24 June 1959.
114. 'Miners stay down pit as protest', *The Guardian*, 24 June 1959, p. 2; 'Labour Relations', *The Guardian*, 27 June 1959, p. 2; and 'Scots pit closure plan reaffirmed', *The Guardian*, 2 July 1959, p. 2.
115. NMMS, National Union of Mineworkers Scottish Area (NUMSA), Executive Committee (EC), 29 June 1959; *The Times*, 26 June 1959.
116. NMMS, NUMSA, EC, 31 August 1959.
117. NRS, CB 276/14, L. R. Milligan, Industrial Relations Director, NCBSD, to K. G. Smith, Secretary, NCBSD, 17 June 1959, and William Summers, Alloa Area General Manager, NCBSD, to K. G. Smith, Secretary, NCBSD, 15 March 1960; NMMS, National Union of Mineworkers Scottish Area (NUMSA), Executive Committee (EC), 21 March 1960.
118. Halliday, *Disappearing Scottish Colliery*, pp. 78–110.
119. Moffat, *My Life with the Miners*, pp. 185–6.
120. NRS, CB 313/19/1, NCB Scottish Division, Manpower Deployment, Hamilton Palace, May 1959.
121. NRS, CB 313/14/1, NCB Scottish Division, Central West Area, Note on Proceedings of Meeting to discuss the closure of Hamilton Palace Colliery, 18 March 1959; CB 207/39/3/2, Assistant Area Safety Engineer to J. R. Cowan, List of Casualties, 30 September 1959.
122. NRS, CB 99/24/10, Lanarkshire Redundancies, 1963.

123. Paul Blyton and Peter Turnbull, *The Dynamics of Employee Relations* (Palgrave Macmillan: Basingstoke, 2004), pp. 254–7.

124. Anderson, *Scottish Trade Unions and Nationalisation*, pp. 311–49.

125. Page Arnot, *Scottish Miners*, pp. 245, 352.

126. NRS, CB 307/5/1, Glenochil NCB-NUM Meetings, 1956–62; Minute of a Meeting held at Glenochil Colliery on Saturday 1st March 1958; Minutes of a Meeting held at Glenochil Mine, 27 August 1959.

127. NRS, CB 305/1/1, NCB, Glencraig Pit Meetings, 1961–66; Minutes of a Meeting held at Glencraig Colliery, 20 February 1961; Minutes of a Pit Meeting held at Glencraig Colliery, 12 June 1961; Notes on Pit Meeting held at Glencraig Colliery, 9 February 1962; Minutes of Pit Meeting held at Glencraig Colliery, 22 February 1962.

CHAPTER 5

Miners and the Scottish Nation: from the 1950s to the 1970s

The dominant Labour and Communist political traditions of mining trade unionism in Scotland co-existed with social conservatism and religious sectarianism in the coalfields. This tension was highlighted in an offbeat and perceptive intervention by Milton Rogovin, the social documentary photographer, who visited the Scottish coalfields in 1982. Rogovin is associated with the civil rights movement and working class culture in the USA. In Scotland he photographed miners in Ayrshire, Fife and the Lothians for his major project, *The Family of Miners*, 1981–97, which included images from the USA, Mexico, Cuba, France, Spain, the Federal Republic of Germany, Czechoslovakia, China and Zimbabwe.[1]

With the Scottish miners Rogovin used a favoured technique of twinning contrasting images. One pair encapsulates the countervailing political-cultural tendencies in Scotland's coalfields. In the first image Rogovin presents several miners relaxed and smiling, about to go underground. Centre stage is a miner in his thirties, with dark and wavy hair, wearing a donkey jacket, overalls and pit helmet. The same miner appears in the second image, this time in a domestic setting with his wife and daughter. All three are standing stiffly, unsmiling, in front of a print of King Billy, Prince William of Orange, at the Battle of Boyne in Ireland in 1690. The miner's short sleeves display an arm tattooed with the red hand of Ulster. On the wall beside King Billy is a photograph of four men in Orange Order regalia, one wearing a clerical collar. Above this is Cecil Beaton's wedding portrait of Queen Elizabeth II and the Duke of Edinburgh. Also displayed is a framed picture of a barbed-wire fence with the legend, 'At the going down of the sun and in the morning we shall remember', and a host of Rangers Football Club iconography, including faces of two players, Derek Johnstone and Robert Russell, either side of a plaque reading 'John Greig MBE Rangers', a former captain and the club's manager in 1982.

Rogovin visited the coalfields with NUMSA officials and knew their politics,[2] which were decidedly at odds with *The Family of Miners* living room. The NUMSA was avowedly internationalist, anti-militarist and anti-sectarian. The Labour-Communist leadership opposed feudalism and hereditary privilege. John McArthur, the Village Pit Communist from East Fife, characterised recipients of the Order of the British Empire as 'Our Bloody Enemy'.[3] Sectarianism and social conservatism were most evident in Lanarkshire and to an extent in Ayrshire. At Bedlay, near Glenboig in Lanarkshire, the Catholic Church was influential, and restrained the reach of Communist politics in the pit. Protestant Loyalist and Irish Republican affinities were present to a lesser extent in Stirlingshire, the Lothians and Fife, transferred from Lanarkshire with migrant miners. These divisions, surviving to be captured by Rogovin's eye in 1982, had been partly flattened by structural changes after nationalisation, with common working practices and bargaining arrangements.[4] Greater unity across boundaries of locality, ethno-religious identity and party politics was also attained directly through campaigning by miners' leaders against deindustrialisation. The miners' moral economy was central to this process, and acceptable to Orange and Green as well as Red adherents.[5] Pit closures were directed centrally by the NCB in London, operating within the framework of economic and energy policies determined by UK governments. A strongly held view emerged among Scottish miners that core decisions about working class economic security were therefore being taken remotely from the communities, families and individuals affected. Class and Nation duly became central elements in the Scottish miners' campaigning and distinct political identity, along with gender, of course, given the overwhelmingly male nature of the workforce. The composition of this class-nation-gender blend is illuminated conceptually by the term intersectionality, adapted from post-colonial and gender theory.[6] Scottish miners were working class, Scottish and male, and with this particular intersectional identity occupied a distinct position in the Scottish, British and international labour movements.

The first part of the chapter examines how the NUMSA and its political allies conceptualised deindustrialisation in national terms. The miners' annual Gala in Edinburgh, Scotland's capital, blended Scottish culture with British and International political themes. This strengthened a Scottish nation frame of reference which guided the miners to draw lessons about the linkages between political-constitutional structures in the UK on the one hand and deindustrialisation in Scotland on the other hand. This prompted the NUMSA to push constitutional questions onto the agenda of the STUC in the 1960s, a process analysed in the second part of the chapter. Generational change was important in this movement towards Home Rule, pushed by Michael McGahey and other mining leaders born in the 1920s who were more critical of extant political-constitutional as well as industrial structures than their elders. Scotland was a Nation, these miners argued. They saw the transfer of legislative powers from Westminster to a Parliament in Scotland as a means of improving economic security by slowing the contraction of industrial activity and employment.

The Scottish Nation

'He firmly believed, and his union firmly believed, that Scotland was a nation. Not a region of Britain, not a district, but a nation in its own right and entitled to demand a right to nationhood'.[7] This was McGahey, addressing the STUC at Aberdeen in April 1968. McGahey's political views were influenced by his education in the NUMSA. This included attendance at summer and weekend schools with tuition from academics and leading NUMSA officials, including Abe and Alex Moffat. The syllabus encompassed mining engineering, union organisation, social sciences and history. The schools were attended by 60 miners per annum.[8] Scotland's nationhood was emphasised in these classes by Abe Moffat, who in 1950 moved an unsuccessful resolution in favour of a Scottish Parliament at the STUC.[9] The schools continued into the 1960s and 1970s, when McGahey the tutor impressed upon young trade unionists that compromise was never a defeat. Reflecting on the faults of nationalisation, perhaps, which older union officials had been slow to identify, McGahey emphasised that 'the most important form of criticism is self-criticism'. These lessons shaped the thinking of Iain Chalmers, a Cosmopolitan Colliery miner who helped to lead the 1984–5 strike in Fife.[10]

The construction of unity among Scottish miners was pursued in many ways after nationalisation by leading members of the Village Pit generation. An influential event was Paul Robeson's visit to Edinburgh in July 1949, just months before the African-American singer was barred from travelling overseas by the US government, citing alleged Communist associations but actually punishing his civil rights activism. 'A Star Drops In', screened in cinemas within the NCB's *Mining Review* series, showed Robeson visiting Woolmet Colliery in Midlothian with Abe Moffat and other NUMSA officials. In the packed canteen Robeson sang 'Joe Hill', the union-organising anthem. Robeson performed that evening at Edinburgh's Usher Hall for miners brought from all parts of the Scottish coalfield by union-organised transport.[11]

Politicised culture was likewise central to the annual Gala, established by the Village Pit generation and held every May Day in Edinburgh's Holyrood Park. The format was influenced by the Durham Gala, which originated in 1867 and remained the largest gathering of miners from across the English, Welsh and Scottish coalfields after nationalisation.[12] The flow of miners and their families marching into the Durham Gala behind colliery banners, captured in newsreel films assembled in Bill Morrison's 2010 *The Miners' Hymns*,[13] was replicated in Edinburgh. Page Arnot, an English Communist, saw the Scottish Gala as an expression of 'gaiety and the holiday spirit' plus 'the miners' pride in their strength and unity and their hard-won victories'. The solidarities described by Page Arnot were those observable at Durham: British and International. Aneurin Bevan, hero of the Labour left and one-time South Wales coal miner, concluded his address to the 1953 Scottish Gala with the phrases, 'Long live the unity of the British working class!' and 'Long live the spirit of International May Day – workers of all lands unite!'[14] There were nevertheless distinctly Scottish elements on display. Ewan Gibbs has emphasised the significance of the setting, in Scotland's capital. Crowds processed into Holyrood Park down the Royal Mile and the Canongate, coming together in a manner that celebrated their common national and occupational identity as Scottish miners. The importance of unifying miners across territorial and ethno-religious boundaries was clear. Scottish national-cultural elements featured strongly: bagpipes, dancing, and Highland games as well as the gendered pursuits of boxing and football, while the political agenda fused working class, Scottish, and internationalist themes. The tenor shifted over time. Home Rule was presented with increasing force in the 1960s. Growing support for anti-colonialism, evident also at the STUC,[15] led to the participation of trade union representatives from Vietnam in 1969.[16] The STUC helped these delegates obtain visas and publicised their attendance as a 'rallying point for the trade union movement' to 'express its opposition to the Vietnamese war'.[17]

South Wales miners, also Communist-influenced, likewise convened an annual gala in the capital, Cardiff, blending culture and politics, with brass bands, arts and craft exhibitions and rugby union.[18] Both Welsh and Scottish national identities were only partly circumscribed by the British context of the nationalised coal industry. At the Scottish Gala miners from Scotland contested football games and boxing bouts with 'brothers' invited from other parts of the 'national coalfield'. Miners from Durham, say, or Yorkshire, were also competitors in an employment sense as the NCB paid ever-closer attention from the 1950s onwards to comparative area performance in assessing investment priorities. This led to pit closures and job losses. These accelerated in 1960 and 1961, which can be identified as a crucial transition point in the miners' understanding of economic security. Policy changes to safeguard coal communities could be implemented at UK level by a Labour government. But deindustrialisation was particularly acute in Scotland, and the continued contraction of mining employment after Harold Wilson's Labour government was elected in 1964 reinforced an emergent argument that greater policy-making autonomy in Scotland was the central prerequisite of future security.

A crisis of coalfield confidence in Scotland was precipitated in the autumn of 1961 when the NCB's Scottish Division revealed that among the pits scheduled to close in 1962 were Rothes in Fife and Glenochil in Clackmannan. These were both prestigious NCB developments in the 1950s. Rothes was the economic and industrial core of the New Town of Glenrothes, and its establishment had resulted in the closure of older pits nearby. Miners moved to Rothes with their families from Lanarkshire, attracted by new council housing as well as the prospect of more stable employment in a modern colliery. 'That's for me', thought Ian Terris, a young face worker who transferred from Cardowan.[19] Production started in 1958, but Rothes was wetter than expected with substantial geological difficulties.[20] NCB Scottish Division engineers argued that investment in deeper workings would make Rothes successful but in a falling market Lord Robens and his officials at headquarters decided on closure. Glenochil was a giant drift mine, the largest in Britain, cutting into the Ochil hills. Its opening was accompanied by the reconstruction of the village of Tullibody, with new-built council housing and a school for migrant families, mainly from Lanarkshire. As with Rothes, local pits were closed and their reserves forfeited, notably at Devon, to release labour for the new colliery. Production started in 1956 but workings were more compressed and tortuously angled than anticipated, with serious faulting.[21] Daily output in 1960 and 1961 fluctuated between 700 and 900 tons, short of the 1,750 sought by the NCB.[22]

Migration and the apparently false promise of economic security were major elements in the crisis that subsequently unfolded. Workers and union representatives articulated their anger in moral economy terms. A redundant Rothes miner told reporters that the NCB 'brought us here on false pretences', and 'should be forced to rehouse us where we came from'. But few of the ex-Lanarkshire families really wanted to leave. Glenrothes was a successful community in the making, with neighbourly solidarities in the streets, modern leisure facilities and schools. 'Anybody leaving Glenrothes . . . will do so with tears', said another redundant Rothes man. He had accepted an NCB offer of transfer to Derbyshire.[23] Sidney Ford, NUM President, told Robens in April 1962 that the NCB was ignoring its role in creating the difficulties facing Rothes and Glenochil miners. Families and whole communities in the recent past had been uprooted, 'on the advice of the Board', and 'enticed' to move to Clackmannan and Central Fife 'on the promise of secured employment'.[24] The NUM sought a public inquiry specifically into the competence of the Scottish Division's management. Mrs M. Lonsdale for the Scottish Co-operative Women's

Guild wrote to Robens endorsing this demand. Patrick Dollan, chairman of the National Industrial Fuel Efficiency Service and former Labour Lord Provost of Glasgow, told Robens that public opinion in Scotland was 'mystified' by the closures. J. McEvoy, secretary of Dunfermline Trades Council, made a similar plea to Robens, noting the 'profound sense of trepidation and bewilderment' aroused in mining communities and across Scotland. David Anderson, Bowhill Branch NUM secretary, addressed Robens as a one-time member of Attlee's Labour government. Many miners felt Robens had travelled so far from the Labour Party that he should resign from his office 'rather than carry out Tory policy'.[25]

These interventions reflected widening unease in Scotland as employment losses mounted in shipbuilding and metal production as well as coal. The Rothes-Glenochil crisis pushed the NUMSA closer to union representatives of workers in these other sectors. Joint action was coordinated by the STUC with support from the Labour Party and the CPGB. The NUMSA and the STUC were linked by individuals and common political outlook. Alex Moffat was on the STUC General Council until his election as NUMSA President in 1961. Bill McLean, who had become NUMSA General Secretary after his work as area agent for Fife, Clackmannan and Stirlingshire, took Moffat's place on the STUC General Council. He remained in both roles until his premature death at the age of 58 in November 1977.[26] McLean operated initially on the General Council's Organisation Committee, which set the STUC's annual conference and policy agenda, and in 1962 joined the Economic Committee, which articulated an increasingly critical analysis of the UK government's alleged incapacity to promote industrial growth and employment.[27] In the STUC as well as the NUMSA Communists worked in alliance with Labour figures. James Jack, General Secretary from 1963 to 1975, and his successor, Jimmy Milne, who died in office in 1986, were both Communists. Jack was born in 1910, and started his working life just before the 1926 General Strike. Milne, born in 1921, belonged to the same generation as McGahey, Daly and McLean. Their formational Communist politics were those of the Popular Front, pragmatically campaigning within a broad working class and 'progressive' alliance. Communism was important too in shaping labour movement support for Home Rule. Jack, Milne and other Communists in the STUC came to share McGahey's appreciation that Scotland was a nation as distinct from an economic region of the UK. While suspicious of the conservative potential of nationalism, these trade unionists argued that Scotland's relatively retarded economic position within the UK was a question of internal colonialism. The remedy was greater political autonomy for Scotland. In linking industrial and political campaigns the NUMSA was also supported by Labour MPs from mining constituencies. Generational change was significant in this area too, promoting closer cooperation between Labour and Communist forces. An important figure was Alex Eadie, born into an East Fife mining family in 1920. His father, Robert, was a Communist, but Alex joined the Labour Party and was a Fife County Councillor as well as NUM delegate at Lochhead Colliery. Eadie stood for the NUMSA Presidency against Alex Moffat in 1961, but after this defeat was propelled into Parliamentary politics. As MP for Midlothian from 1966 he campaigned against pit closures and for a Scottish Parliament, working closely with McGahey who he 'had grown up' with in the NUM, in the words of Tam Dalyell.[28]

The labour movement mobilisation against pit closures was therefore significant in national as well as class terms. The Rothes-Glenochil crisis was embedded by the NUMSA and the STUC in a moral economy critique of UK policy-making. The Conservative government was seeking both faster expansion across the UK and greater convergence in growth rates between Scotland and England. These goals were not self-evidently compatible. The STUC argued that without close direction of industrial investment, growth in England would be faster than in Scotland. The problem had been analysed in the 1961 Toothill Report, authored by the Chairman of Ferranti Scotland, which called for improved transport, housing, and educational infrastructure to stimulate 'science'-based manufacturing. Toothill recommended that regional policy incentives be directed to promoting 'growth points' around the New Towns rather than stabilising employment in older and more congested urban-industrial settings.[29] This agenda was debated as government policy contributed to a rapid rise of unemployment in Scotland, from 85,366 in February 1962 to 136,030 in February 1963.[30] Growth in southern and central England had created a marginal increase in inflation, which the government responded to with higher interest rates and lower public expenditure.[31] This punctured growth in Scotland, frustrating industrialists and government officials in the

Scottish Development Department.[32] The STUC criticised the slow-down too, supporting the aim of growth through greater industrial diversification. But Jack and other officials objected to the Toothill agenda's reliance on private industrial investment through public subsidy. It was 'galling', no less, that regional assistance grants and loans could be spent unsupervised by private investors with limited concern for the communities and workers abandoned by large-scale industrial change.[33]

The growing industrial employment crisis was examined by the STUC in a Conference on Scotland's Economy, held in St Andrew's Halls, Glasgow, on 18 February 1962. The 1,400 attendees included delegates from 62 unions and trades councils, officials of the Scottish Council for Development and Industry, which had sponsored the Toothill Report, and Labour MPs. The negative effects of government policy on employment in coalmining, shipbuilding and iron and steel were emphasised by the General Council in a pre-conference statement. This detailed Scottish relative economic disadvantage: one-tenth of the UK population but one-fifth of the unemployed lived in Scotland. Alex Moffat outlined the believed failings of NCB strategy. When collieries closed on economic grounds redundant miners were transferred. The 'receiving' collieries duly became less economic unless production was expanded by the same proportion as the workforce increase. Some miners at Glenochil and Rothes had already moved twice since nationalisation and were now facing a third transfer. In the 1950s the publicly owned coal industry had subsidised private industry with low-cost fuel, below the market rate. In moral economy terms Moffat claimed it was thereby incumbent on the government to direct private industry to coalfield areas. Moffat was followed by Jack Service, of the Confederation of Shipbuilding and Engineering Unions (Clyde Area), and John Irvine, of the Iron and Steel Confederation.[34] Employment in these sectors had also fallen steadily since 1957–8.[35] The conference unanimously passed a motion supporting stronger government direction of industry, and asserting the obligations acquired by private sector recipients of regional assistance to provide employment in areas of social need.[36]

The NCB rationalised the Glenochil and Rothes closures in a *Five Year Mining Review*, drafted late in 1961 after discussion between

Robens and Ronald Parker, NCB Scottish Division Chairman.[37] The *Review* was organised around productivity, measured in Output per Manshift (OMS). Productivity and OMS as specific elements of coal industry management were not used systematically until the early 1940s. Harold Wilson claimed a role in their adoption as a civil servant in the wartime Ministry of Fuel & Power. The original motive for focusing on productivity was acute labour shortage. Obtaining more value from fewer workers was essential first to the war effort and then to the economic recovery under Attlee's Labour government. Productivity then largely disappeared from policy debates until the 1960s, when linked concerns about 'decline', growth and 'modernisation' re-focused attention on output per worker as a measure of economic performance. Renewed interest in productivity is associated with Wilson's Labour administration elected in 1964,[38] and so the NCB's 1961 *Review* was slightly ahead of the policy-making trend. The NCB used OMS to identify comparative pit-level performance and thereby target cost-reducing closures. The schema defined three categories of colliery: A had substantial reserves and a satisfactory OMS; B held significant reserves but an unsatisfactory OMS; and C contained limited and dwindling reserves but a reasonable OMS. In 1961 in Scotland 10 million tons were produced by category A pits, 3.7 million by category B, and 2.1 million tons from category C. This implied that collieries supplying more than a third of Scottish output were at risk of closure on economic grounds. Average OMS in category A pits had increased from 20.5 hundredweights (cwts) in 1957 to 24.8 in 1961, and in the first quarter of 1962 was projected to rise more rapidly to 27.8 cwts with the extension of power-loading. OMS in category B pits OMS was stagnant: 19.5 cwts in 1957 and 19.8 in the first quarter of 1962. OMS in category C grew slower than in category A, up from 19.8 to 23.8 cwts.[39]

Robens and Parker used the ABC schema when discussing the Rothes-Glenochil crisis with NUM representatives in April 1962. The NUM delegation, led by Ford, included Alex Moffat and John McArthur, who was now serving the union as Fife area secretary. Moffat engaged in a lengthy disagreement with Robens and Parker about the Scottish Division's management of the industry. He revisited the NCB's decision to raise the price of Scottish coal in 1961, which placed pits and jobs in Scotland under additional pressure. Robens argued that accelerating the closure of C category pits would shape a smaller but more competitive Scottish industry and held out the prospect of retaining B category pits – with significant reserves – if their OMS positions were improved.[40] The NUM objected strenuously to this rationale. In both this meeting and a subsequent discussion with Parker, Moffat presented the argument he had put to the STUC conference. Productivity could not be raised in all pits at the same rate. Closing lower performers and transferring a portion of their workers would undermine OMS at receiving pits. The drive to greater productivity would generate further job cuts unless overall demand increased.[41]

The NUMSA executive examined the productivity paradox in detail in August 1962. Frustration was articulated, but there was a strong emphasis on the threat to collective security. There were 43 collieries in Scotland with an OMS below 24 cwts per manshift, and in the endangered B and C categories. These included units with more than 1,000 miners such as Auchengeich, Bedlay and Cardowan in Lanarkshire and Barony and Knockshinnoch in Ayrshire. NUMSA officials interpreted the problem in national terms. In the 'race for jobs, Scotland would not have many left' unless OMS increased at all pits, especially those in categories B and C which, posing even greater economic hazard, were concentrated in localities most remote from alternative employment.[42] Details of how the *Five Year Mining Review* could operate in Fife, shown by McLean to the STUC Economic Committee, underlined this latter worry. B and C collieries were largely within the Cowdenbeath-Lumphinnans-Lochgelly conurbation, where limited job opportunities outside coal were not broadened until the growth and diversification of Glenrothes later in the 1960s. B category pits included Bowhill, Glencraig and Mary, along with Rothes, which produced 140,000 tons in 1961. Among those in the C category – moderate OMS but limited reserves – were Aitken and Lindsay, both in Kelty, plus Nellie in Lochgelly, and Lumphinnans 11. All of the A category collieries were in East and West Fife. Michael and Wellesley were still the largest and most productive pits in Scotland, employing 2,450 and 1,820 miners, and produced 717,000 and 492,000 tons respectively in 1961. Frances was the third largest, and also in East Fife. A category pits in West Fife were Blairhall, Bogside, Comrie and Valleyfield.[43]

Table 5.1 NCB category A, B and C pits in Fife, showing employment and production position, 1961

	Employment	Production (tons)
A pits	9,440	2,529,000
B pits	6,170	1,352,000
C pits	3,190	943,000
Total	18,800	4,554,000

Source: GCUA, STUC General Council, Economic Committee, 7 February 1962

Production and employment data from the Fife pits by category in 1961 are summarised in Table 5.1.

So the NCB's *Review* contained particular hazards for Fife, the largest region of the Scottish coalfield. Collieries in the A category held 63 per cent of total output in Scotland in 1961, but only 55 per cent in Fife, where around half of the workforce was employed in the B and C pits. The NUM's concerns were therefore fully warranted. In September 1961 the NCB shared data with the interdepartmental Scottish Coal Committee, examined in Chapter 1, predicting the shrinkage of coal industry employment in Central Fife from 7,900 to zero by the end of 1965. A less dramatic drop, from 1,788 to 600 over the four years, was predicted for Clackmannan.[44] This pessimistic future intensified the employment crisis in Central Fife and Clackmannan caused by closing Rothes and Glenochil, reinforcing the danger of community abandonment. The NCB's Inter-Divisional Transfer Scheme, established in 1962, conceded this very point. Robens told NUM representatives in April 1962 that some mining localities in Scotland would shrink. Insensitively, he added that miners transferred to the East Midlands and Yorkshire would not be started on the piece rates they had earned in Scotland, but revert to day rates from which they might 'move up' over time.[45]

The paradox of productivity gains contributing potentially to further redundancies could not be resolved in 1962, and nor could the larger problem of pit closures be avoided. But the labour movement response in Scotland shaped a substantial reorientation of NCB and then UK government policy-making. Union-articulated moral economy arguments had a discernible impact, establishing a new political context within which deindustrialisation was understood in Scotland. This contributed to more effective resistance to closures in the later 1960s and 1970s. McGahey and other New Mine generation figures would link deindustrialisation with the unequal distribution of political power across the UK. In the short run important concessions were also obtained from the NCB, on the management of closures and transfer of miners, conceding local redeployment as a priority. The closures of Rothes and Glenochil were confirmed shortly after the meeting between Robens and industry unions in April 1962. NCB Scottish Division research showed that deeper drivages would not reach full production for five years, and there was no future guarantee of profitable operations.[46] The workforce of 809 was gradually dispersed. Reporters described 650 being found work at neighbouring mines, with clustered transfers to Frances, Michael and Wellesley. Several dozens – 58 by mid-July 1962 – accepted redeployment to Yorkshire or the Midlands.[47] An unofficial strike was staged nevertheless by a reported 3,300 miners in Fife and Alloa against the closure of Glenochil and Rothes in March 1962. As with the 1959 rebellion against Devon's closure, this was precipitated by a stay-down protest at Glenochil.[48] This action contributed to the careful and localised redeployment of the Glenochil workforce, akin to the Hamilton Place closure in 1959. NCB data on the colliery's 750 employees in June 1962 indicates that slightly more than 95 per cent were re-employed at mines in Clackmannan, Stirlingshire or West Fife, mainly to Comrie, 10 miles away. The NCB recorded the employment destinations of those leaving the industry, with a small number shifting to distilling, locally in Clackmannan, or to the British Motor Corporation commercial vehicle plant at Bathgate, 23 miles away in West Lothian. Only 33 Glenochil miners, 4.4 per cent of the total, left without a firm offer from the NCB or an identified job outside the coal industry.[49]

In Central Fife there were fewer employment alternatives to coal. This became further evident when Mary and Aitken were scheduled for closure following the circulation of the *Five Year Mining Review*. NCB managers met union representatives to discuss the future of each pit at separate consultative committee meetings in August 1962. With Mary, a B category pit, the area general manager, T. Scrimgeour, emphasised heavy financial losses and wanted the colliery closed early in 1963. McArthur for the NUM said it was unlikely that Mary's 500 miners could be redeployed effectively elsewhere in Central or East Fife, now that Rothes had gone. He pledged that the NUM would resist any closure on economic grounds until industrial alternatives were established, and was campaigning on this basis with the support of the wider trade union movement.[50] This action kept Mary open until 1966, but Aitken, a C category pit and also running at a financial loss, closed in 1963. Scrimgeour, seeking greater 'efficiency', wanted to bring employment down from 877 to somewhere between 570 and 600. Redundant men could be redeployed in other NCB divisions: outwith Scotland, in other words.[51] There had already been a major readjustment of production at Aitken in the spring of 1959, concentrating operations from double to single shift, with 174 men transferred within Fife, including 59 to Comrie and 29 to Blairhall. The NUM, led by McLean, had accepted this on the basis that Kelty would be sustained as a community in the longer-term.[52] The proposed changes just three years later transgressed this moral economy expectation. At the colliery consultative committee meeting Adam Hunter of the NUM, elected Labour MP for Dunfermline two years later, said the situation was thoroughly abhorrent: 'we were in a jungle with pits struggling against one another for survival'. McArthur, developing this critique, said that extending the life of Aitken in the manner proposed would result in closures elsewhere in Central Fife. He reprised the argument articulated in the case for saving Mary. 'Little or no attempt had been made to bring in alternative industry or to train men for a change in occupation', he said, and noted the damaging implications for viability at other pits of receiving miners transferred from Aitken.[53] As with Mary, this opposition delayed the NCB's plans for Aitken. NCB officials returned later in 1962 with alternative proposals. Instead of retaining a concentrated operation at Aitken, with a proportion of miners redeployed in Central Fife, the colliery would close altogether, and the entirety would be redeployed in West Fife and Clackmannan. Hunter and McArthur accepted this as preferable, easing the pressure in Central Fife and protecting Kelty's economic future.[54]

NUMSA and Scottish Home Rule

The framing of deindustrialisation as a distinct problem in Scotland strengthened labour movement support for Scottish Home Rule in the later 1960s. In the early 1960s it produced important changes in UK government policy. 'We need to get these factories into Scotland', Moffat said, during the NUMSA executive's discussion of the productivity imbroglio in August 1962. Diversification was a pre-requisite for further contraction of coal,[55] an argument mobilised that summer by NUM officials opposing closures and redundancies in Central Fife. The Conservative government was pressed into publishing a prospectus for industrial stimulus in 1963. Enhanced investments in transport and social infrastructure plus increased regional assistance were promised. This marked an endorsement by UK policy-makers of the Toothill agenda although Scotland's distinct political position remained unrecognised by the government, which enjoyed significant if softening support among Scottish 'Unionist' electors.[56] The new package was presented as *regional* intervention, assisting an area experiencing problems arising from the contraction of traditional industry.[57] A related initiative in north-east England reinforced the narrative of geographically targeted regeneration within the UK.[58] The government nevertheless published the claim that by increasing infrastructure expenditure in Scotland from £100 million to £140 million over two years it was targeting 11 per cent of total public service investment in the UK on 7 per cent of the population. This hinted at discrete Scottish characteristics, and selective treatment was proposed for the coalfields. Central Fife and North Lanarkshire along with the Vale of Leven and the designated New Towns were identified as in particular need for growth.[59] The 1964–70 Labour governments strengthened this commitment to restructuring. The 'sixteen-fold' increase in real terms of regional policy incentives across the UK from 1962–3 to 1969–70 had a major impact in Scotland.[60] Labour's approach was guided by *The National Plan* of 1965, supplemented by *The Scottish Economy* with its significant sub-title, *A Plan For Expansion*.[61] The stimulation of alternative employment was examined in Chapter 1. In Fife the closure of Rothes was followed by the wholesale redevelopment of Glenrothes. A core of US-owned electrical engineering firms established large-scale employment for ex-miners and many women. By 1971 almost two-thirds of male jobs and well over one-half of female jobs were in industrial categories.[62]

The STUC had criticised Toothill on the grounds that private industry was given too much leeway in its use of public funds. Closer democratic oversight of regional assistance was necessary. This trade union critique of policy-making in Scotland partly reflected the impact of decolonisation. Independence movements in Asia and Africa were supported by the STUC from the 1940s to the 1960s,[63] and inspired interest in greater political self-determination in Scotland. Of further importance were debates about internal colonialism in Britain,[64] influenced by developments in the USA, where President Johnson's War on Poverty highlighted the retarded economic condition of the south, especially the Appalachian mining territories of West Virginia and Kentucky. Parallels could be drawn between the Scottish and US coalfields, with common experiences of unemployment, low wages and inadequate social amenities, including housing. The argument articulated by some of Johnson's radical advisers in the Office for Economic Opportunity, that parts of the USA were held in poverty so that others could remain rich,[65] had echoes in Scotland, particularly in the 1960s when growth was checked by UK policy-makers to ease inflationary pressures felt only in the south and Midlands of England.[66]

STUC and the NUMSA officials presented this reasoning when lobbying the Labour government and NCB for new employment opportunities and stable coal production in Scotland. The STUC General Council held direct talks with the Prime Minister in June 1965. McLean challenged a claim made by Fred Lee, Minister of Power, that lost mining jobs were being off-set by the provision of alternatives. McLean told Wilson that in Fife 1,000 miners had been made redundant at Bowhill three months previously. Only 100 had been redeployed within the NCB or found new jobs elsewhere.[67] In discussion later in 1965 with Willie Ross, Labour's Secretary of State for Scotland, and Ronald Parker of the NCB, NUMSA and STUC officials asserted that 'new industries' were still an urgent priority in Fife, Lothians and Lanarkshire, 'to provide alternative jobs for miners displaced from work'. The NCB's continued offer of supported transfers to English collieries was described as offensive in national as well as labour terms: 'The wholesale migration of Scottish miner [sic.] to the South would not be accepted as an alternative'.[68] Ross is usually characterised as a strong advocate of distinct Scottish interests, both to protect living standards in Scotland and safeguard the integrity of the UK.[69] In this vein he told the STUC that 'he was on record as having declared that there must be no further acceleration of Scottish pit closures', and accepted the need to accelerate the construction of advance factories in the coalfields.[70]

The position in Central Fife remained acute. Lindsay Colliery closed early in 1965, when six pits remained. As McLean told Wilson, the largest of these, Bowhill,[71] followed shortly afterwards. A total of 2,400 miners were working at Glencraig, Lumpinnans 11 & 12, Mary, Minto and Kinglassie.[72] Daly and Alex Moffat blocked NCB plans to shut these collieries immediately, restating the core prerequisites for closure: comprehensive and local redeployment,[73] or comparable jobs in other industries.[74] These requirements were met, and the Central Fife pits were all closed in 1966. Chapter 1 showed the importance at this point of a Ministry of Labour promise of new industry employment in Fife, with 2,300 positions explicitly 'for males'. At the same time, and under union pressure, the NCB brought forward the build-up of employment in the Cosmopolitan Collieries of the Longannet complex in West Fife and Seafield in East Fife. At Seafield alone a projected 2,600 would be working by July 1967. [75] Consultative talks were held with the Coal Board at national level, in April 1966, where NUMSA was represented by Moffat, McGahey and McLean. The Scottish union officials insisted that the success of this venture was dependent on efficient transport arrangements. Collecting miners from various settlements on potentially circuitous routes from Kelty to Seafield could extend the working day by unacceptable lengths. Robens agreed that a fleet of buses covering a range of routes and journeys would be put in place.[76] The NCB delivered on this promise. Willie Clarke moved in 1966 from Glencraig to Seafield, which he remembers as resembling a bus garage at shift changeovers.[77]

Difficulties remained elsewhere in 1965 and 1966, however, notably in South Lanarkshire. Depopulation and even community abandonment in the Douglas Valley to the south and around

Shotts in the east were dangers recognised by Board of Trade officials in discussion with local authority representatives and Judith Hart, Labour MP for Lanark and Parliamentary Under-Secretary of State for Scotland. Further diversification was agreed as necessary,[78] but this was inhibited by macro-economic pressures and UK-level priorities. Wilson's government was intent on controlling inflation and the balance of payments deficit by removing demand from the economy. Public spending cuts were accompanied by an emergency Prices and Incomes Act in the summer of 1966. This established a six-month mandatory stop on wage increases followed by another six months of 'severe restraint', perturbing trade unionists and shop floor workers across the UK. The controls seemed to weigh more heavily on manual wage-earners than shareholders and employers.[79] The measures were nevertheless regarded as especially punitive in Scotland, reinforcing the internal colonialism narrative of UK policy-making. At the 1967 STUC Lawrence Daly said the Prices and Incomes Act violated the 'democratic right of free collective bargaining' and reinforced the unjust inequality between Scottish and English living standards. It was infuriating that wages of Scottish workers were capped to restrain inflationary pressures evident only in the wealthier areas of England.[80] Devaluation of sterling later in 1967 was accompanied by further wage controls and deflationary measures. This contributed to the fall in manufacturing employment noted in Chapter 1. Daly argued at the 1968 STUC conference that the government was stimulating unemployment and retarding social progress. He made the case for an alternative course with controls on capital exports, radical cuts in military expenditure and a more comprehensive emphasis on the redistribution of wealth.[81]

The critique of UK policy-making in national as well as class terms was also evident in related debates about industrial relations. Wilson's government in 1965 established the Royal Commission on Trade Unions and Employers' Associations, chaired by Lord Donovan, which reported in June 1968. Donovan concluded that prolonged low unemployment since the 1940s had shifted the locus of pay bargaining from industry-level to workplace. Inflationary pressures existed because local agreements often supplemented national deals, sometimes after unofficial strikes. Stronger workplace union organisation was needed along with greater education to help employees understand the harmful aggregate effects of frequent stoppages.[82] But business organisations and the Conservative opposition favoured statutory enforcement of agreements between employers and unions, and making unofficial strikes illegal.[83] Barbara Castle, Secretary of State at the Department of Employment and Productivity, which succeeded the Ministry of Labour in 1968, was pushed into publishing a White Paper, *In Place of Strife*, in January 1969. This proposed fines for unofficial strikers, membership ballots before official strikes, and government-imposed solutions to inter-union disputes that intermittently disrupted production, particularly in motor manufacturing.[84]

The labour movement at UK level opposed *In Place of Strife* as an affront to union autonomy.[85] There were shades of opinion within the Scottish labour movement, some welcoming the 'positive' agenda on union rights, but the prevailing tendency was opposition. This was led by the NUMSA which hosted an STUC General Council conference on the White Paper at the miners' convalescent home at Culross in West Fife. Further STUC General Council talks were held in February, prior to the annual conference at Rothesay in April which Castle addressed but only after delegates had first expressed their opposition to *In Place of Strife*. The General Council approved the 'positive' elements but strongly criticised the 'penal clauses'. At Rothesay McGahey and the younger Abe Moffat, speaking for SCEBTA, addressed the White Paper in excoriating terms. McGahey had experienced the coercive force of state intervention in industrial relations during the Second World War, it will be remembered, when sacked for leading unofficial strike action in support of miners prosecuted under Order 1305. Now he even disputed the STUC General Council's observation that the proposals were partly beneficial:

> What were these so-called justifiable, so-called good things, in the White Paper? The right to belong to a trade union? Who was entitled to grant anyone the right to belong to a trade union? It was like granting someone the right to breathe. It was an inherent right for every worker to belong to a trade union, and that did not require legislation. The power and strength of the trade union movement could wrest that right from the employers.

Moffat argued that *In Place of Strife* was based on a fundamental misreading of economic problems in the UK. Trade unions and workers were being held responsible for slow growth and stagnating industrial production which were actually the result of the government's deflationary economic management and private capital's under-investment. Why, he asked rhetorically, were employers not required to hold ballots before closing mines or factories?[86]

The STUC coordinated a one-day strike on Clydeside, part of a broader UK-wide mobilisation, against *In Place of Strife*.[87] The TUC agreed a number of voluntary efforts intended to resolve inter-union disputes and minimise unofficial disruption, and the government dropped the 'penal clauses' in June 1969.[88] The episode contributed all the same to the movement of opinion within the Scottish labour movement towards Home Rule, pushed onto the STUC's agenda by the NUMSA in 1968. McGahey was elected NUMSA President in 1967 after acting in this role when Alex Moffat became ill prior to early retirement on health grounds. For the miners Home Rule became even more attractive with the publication of *Fuel Policy* in November 1967, the Labour government's White Paper which is examined further in Chapter 6. The trend to devolution in some areas of policy was being countered in the coalfields, with the NCB centralising control over its various territorial divisions. NCB officials in Scotland became less influential, negating the NUMSA's lobbying power. This became brutally clear when NCB officials in London over-ruled the Scottish Division's planned reopening of Michael Colliery after the disastrous fire in September 1967.[89]

McGahey frequently made the case for Home Rule on NUM platforms, including the Scottish Gala where he is seen in Figure 5. He took the argument to the 1968 STUC conference in Aberdeen's Beach Ballroom, speaking to the following resolution:

> That this Congress, recognising the desire of the Scottish people for a Scottish Parliament, calls upon the Government to introduce legislation to establish a Parliament for Scotland, the ultimate form and powers of which should be determined by the Scottish electorate.

Figure 5 Campaigning for economic security in language of class and nation: Michael McGahey at the Scottish Miners' Gala. Lawrence Daly sits alongside. © NMMS

McGahey asserted that 'decentralisation of power' would enable Scottish manual workers and trade unionists to advance their distinct material and class interests. A Scottish Parliament would strengthen economic security in the coalfields. Matters of fundamental principle were emphasised too: Scotland was a nation, entitled to self-determination. This had been said many times before by miners' representatives, he observed, among them Keir Hardie and Bob Smillie in the late nineteenth and early twentieth centuries. McGahey distanced the Scottish miners from the SNP, which had won the Hamilton by-election in November 1967. The NUMSA opposed 'separation' from the UK and rejected any 'theory of a classless Scotland'. Scottish miners had 'more in common with the London dockers, the Durham miners and the Sheffield engineers than they ever had with the barons and landlord traitors of that kind in Scotland'. Workers in Scotland nevertheless had particular problems that were exacerbated by the constitutional-political structures of the UK. McGahey concluded by claiming that a Scottish Parliament would be neither parochial nor chauvinistic. It would enable Scottish people to 'play their part in taking up the challenge of life and contributing to the strength of the international working-class movement'.[90]

The case for Home Rule was contested. R. Garland of the Amalgamated Union of Engineering & Foundry Workers (AUEW) moved a rival resolution concentrating on the dangers of nationalism and 'separation'. Working class living standards could only be improved through 'the economic framework of Great Britain' and 'national joint negotiating machinery covering Scotland, England and Wales'. In a short debate Hugh Wyper of Glasgow District Trades Council replied to Garland by pointing out that McGahey's case for Home Rule was based on opposition to 'separatism'. Wyper supported the argument that it would be 'folly' to ignore popular feelings on the national question, allowing 'the SNP to direct such aspirations in to channels which, in the long run, would be disastrous for the working people of Scotland'. A. E. Henderson of Clydebank and District Trades Council endorsed the NUMSA's motion, as did D. McGibbin of the Union of Shop, Distributive and Allied Workers, who characterised nationalism as a 'remarkable' international feature, likening the call for Scottish Home Rule to self-determination claims from Arab and African peoples, Poles and the 'Black Moslem movement in America'. Acknowledging critics of the NUMSA resolution, McGibbin called for the question to be remitted to the General Council for detailed examination before reporting back to the next conference. Garland insisted that a vote be taken, hoping this would extinguish the prospect of further discussion, but a huge majority, 1,420 to 213, supported keeping Home Rule on the STUC agenda, to be scrutinised by the General Council and debated at the following year's conference.[91]

The STUC General Council concluded in August 1968 that the NUMSA's resolution was too open, allowing for the 'separatist' interpretation articulated by Garland, as opposed to McGahey's vision of a Parliament with defined powers operating in a reformed UK polity. There were question marks about which powers would be devolved to Scotland and how the Parliament would be elected but the AUEW resolution was deemed to be out of sympathy with 'the mood of Scotland'. The General Council knew that the Labour government was planning a Royal Commission on the Constitution,[92] announced in October 1968.[93] Chaired by Lord Crowther, and then, after his death by Lord Kilbrandon, this began taking evidence in September 1969 and reported in 1973, recommending a Scottish Legislative Assembly elected by proportional representation with a Scottish Cabinet and Prime Minister, and a corresponding reduction in the number of Scottish MPs at Westminster along with the abolition of the role of Secretary of State for Scotland.[94] At Rothesay in April 1969 the STUC General Council reported on the potential advantages of a 'Scottish legislative assembly' for the STUC's 830,000 affiliated members and their families, but characterised Home Rule as just one pre-condition of greater economic security. Extended public ownership and stronger government direction of private industry were also necessary. McGahey reprised his class argument for Home Rule, telling congress that the national question could be resolved in a progressive manner, strengthening working class economic security, if the labour movement led the debate.[95] This leadership role would not come from the Labour Party. J. D. Pollock of its Scottish Council told the Royal Commission on the Constitution in May 1970 that it opposed legislative devolution. Crowther asked Pollock if this would change if the Conservatives won the coming General Election and stayed in power for a decade or more, demolishing 'the structure of socialism in this country'. Pollock replied that Scotland's success depended on socialists controlling the UK economy, but Tory rule was nevertheless preferable to 'separatism', the alleged consequence of legislative devolution.[96]

The Labour Party's official opposition in Scotland to Home Rule strengthened the importance of trade union campaigning for its delivery. The role of Communist politics and personalities remained significant. McGahey joined the CPGB national executive in 1971, and was then elected NUM Vice President in 1972. The CPGB's pro-Home Rule position exhibited the influence of McGahey and other Scottish trade unionists, including Hugh Wyper and Jimmy Reid, recently returned to work in the shipyards after lengthy full-time service for the party, and a Communist councillor in Clydebank. The CPGB's memorandum to the Royal Commission framed Home Rule as offering greater democratic control of risks to workers' security arising from changes in economic life. In Scotland the 'the key positions in electronics, motor vehicles, chemicals, oil refinery and other important growth industries' were 'held by foreign based firms'. Scottish and Welsh Parliaments would afford democratic accountability to measures of administrative devolution, which had grown considerably in the 1960s, particularly with the development of regional policy. Scottish and Welsh Parliaments would also provide enhanced economic planning, including firmer direction of industrial location. A separate memorandum submitted to the Commission by the Scottish Committee of the CPGB reprised the claims that Scotland possessed distinct culture, history, legal, housing and education systems, along with identity and 'consciousness of nationality'.[97]

Wyper and Reid were witnesses to the Commission on behalf of the CPGB. Reid emphasised the damaging human effects of economic and industrial centralisation which devolution was envisaged as remedying. There was a general north-south divide in Britain, he conceded, but the effects were particularly acute in Scotland because of its status as a distinct nation:

It is one thing to have young people being drained from Northumberland and Cumberland, but in Scotland over fifteen to twenty years a reaction has developed, because we are not a part of England or of any other country; there is a Scottish character, a Scottish national identity and aspirations which give a new dimension to the problem. When we see young people in the shipyards of Scotland being forced to uproot themselves and go to the Midlands and elsewhere, we react as people to when their national identity is diminished.[98]

Reid's reference to the shipyards was significant. Wilson's government had promoted the estuarial grouping of shipyards, believing that scale economies would improve performance and promote competitiveness. But the Upper Clyde Shipbuilders (UCS) group in Glasgow and Clydebank was burdened with huge debts, primarily incurred by John Brown in Clydebank in constructing the *QEII* for Cunard.[99] UCS sought major financial support from the UK government in 1969, which was agreed in return for redundancies affecting one-third of workforce.[100] Problems continued, and UCS entered liquidation in June 1971 when Edward Heath's Conservative government, elected in 1970, refused a request for additional working capital. Closure of the yards was resisted through the famous work-in, which after 18 months secured government support for a measure of restructuring that preserved around 6,000 jobs. The work-in was characterised by Reid, one of its leaders, as both national and class struggle, with the Clyde abandoned by 'faceless' policy-makers in Whitehall.[101]

The UCS campaign reinvigorated the Home Rule debate. The Heath government initially allowed unemployment to drift upwards. The problem particularly affected industrial sectors. The STUC countered by establishing a cross-party Scottish Assembly which met in Edinburgh's Usher Hall on 14 February 1972. In attendance with 1,300 others and speaking for greater political autonomy for Scotland were Sir William McEwan Younger and Teddy Taylor, chairman of the Conservative Party and Tory MP for Cathcart respectively, along with David Steel, Liberal MP for Roxburgh, Selkirk and Peebles, and Winnie Ewing, SNP Vice President.[102] The majority of speakers, however, were representatives of the labour movement: trade union, Labour and Communist party officials, local authority leaders and MPs.[103] James Jack said that Home Rule would bring a 'workers' Parliament', protecting economic security on labour movement terms. John Boyd of the AUEW, which opposed devolution at the 1968 STUC, said 'the only answer to Scotland's economic problems is Scottish government'.[104] The Assembly agreed a Charter of Proposals calling for an intensified regional policy effort to stimulate demand for industrial production and employment.[105]

The Assembly coincided with the climax of a six-week national strike in the coal industry, the first since 1926. McGahey spoke at the Usher Hall despite breaking his leg that morning in a struggle with a police officer during a mass picket of Longannet power station.[106] The strike, examined in greater detail in Chapter 6, focused political attention on the national question. The miners were trying to reverse the erosion of their earnings that had accumulated with falling demand for coalfield labour since the late 1950s. The underlying causes of low pay were deindustrialisation and, according to the Scottish miners, internal colonialism. Job losses and pit closures took place in Scotland because of decisions made in London by policy-makers who were remote physically and socially from the people and communities adversely affected.[107]

Energy and electoral politics changed after 1972. The new bounty of oil from the North Sea potentially strengthened the economic case for Scottish independence. But the political importance of coal also increased. The defeat of the Conservative government in 1974 was connected to another national pay dispute in the industry. Heath called a General Election during this dispute, hoping a decisive victory would equip his government to resist pay claims by other groups of workers as well as the miners, but lost. Labour formed a minority government in March 1974, and Harold Wilson, the Prime Minister once more, scraped a bare majority after another General Election, that October. The SNP won seven seats in March and 11 in October, and came second in 30 others, many held narrowly by Labour in constituencies with significant portions of working class electors. This placed heavy pressure on the new government to move the Home Rule agenda onwards. A tortuous legislative process was initiated, seeking to establish a Parliament in Wales as well as Scotland.[108]

The steps towards Home Rule were welcomed by the NUMSA, but oil was a threat. In the 1960s, when oil prices were low, mining union leaders spoke about coal's rival in moral and social terms. In focusing on 'narrow commercial considerations', Daly told an

STUC energy forum in 1968, the government ignored the costs of maintaining a military presence in the Middle East, where most of Britain's oil was sourced. The social expense of lost employment and purchasing power in the coalfields was falsely discounted.[109] The upward movement of the oil price in the early 1970s, in the context of Arab-Israeli conflict, revived the economic case for coal. But this was jeopardised in the long-term by North Sea oil. The diminished reliance on imports from politically unstable regions devalued Daly's argument about resource control and military commitments in the Middle East. North Sea oil could displace coal, not least in the generation of electricity. Power stations such as Longannet had dual-firing capacity and were adaptable for greater use of oil. In advancing the political case for independence and an SNP government, both of which ends the NUMSA opposed in class terms, North Sea oil also posed a potential risk to public ownership of industry, the progressive distribution of wealth and trade union rights. 'I am proud of the Scottish people and of the Scottish area of the NUM', said Willie Clarke of Seafield at the 1978 STUC, restating the case for Home Rule as a means of protecting security in the coalfields. He also ridiculed the SNP and the class-blind claims which it advanced for the North Sea. 'It is not Scottish oil, it is not British oil, until it is nationalised; it belongs to the monopolies, and the monopolies will determine the rate of extraction'.[110]

McGahey discussed the complexities of North Sea oil in a tripartite energy industry grouping established by the Secretary of State for Energy, Tony Benn, in 1976. The theme of union engagement in strategic policy-making was introduced in Chapter 4. The Blyton and Turnbull extent-location-scope schema for assessing employee involvement was used to evaluate the significance of this engagement, and generational elements were emphasised. Benn's energy forum showed how McGahey and others of his generation engaged policymakers on higher location and greater scope questions than their predecessors, moving beyond workplace questions and dialogue with coal industry managers. In a dedicated session on Scotland, McGahey explained that any renewed rundown of coal burn could not simply be imposed from Whitehall or Westminster. With devolution there would have to be an Energy Board for Scotland, linked to the Scottish

Parliament. At an all-British meeting McGahey developed this argument, emphasising the general principle of coordination. 'It's not a competition between coal and oil', he said, 'it's a question of how the resources of the nation are properly harnessed in the interests of the nation'. In private hands oil and gas could be depleted too rapidly, a denial of democracy, and the only other alternative to coal, nuclear power, was ecologically hazardous. Devolution provided the potential in Scotland to manage coal more carefully within a national Scottish energy plan, protecting its 'people and communities'.[111]

The path to devolution was meanwhile becoming more complicated. Trade union advocates felt that the government's approach was half-hearted, offering powers that were inadequate to the scale of Scotland's economic and social problems. *Our Changing Democracy*, published in November 1975, proposed elected Assemblies for Scotland and Wales, but without transfer of economic powers.[112] The STUC General Council criticised this arrangement,[113] which appeared unrevised in the Scotland and Wales Bill of 1976. The government's attempts to control inflation with public spending cuts exacerbated the rate of unemployment across the UK. A new post-1945 peak of 6.1 per cent was reached in January 1977, but in Scotland it was 7.4 per cent and growing more rapidly than in other parts of Britain. In any case Scottish and Welsh Labour MPs slowed the progress of the Scotland and Wales Bill, which did not reach the statute book before the end of the Parliamentary session.[114]

The NUMSA attempted to re-energise the campaign at the STUC in 1977. Eric Clarke, who succeeded Bill McLean later that year as NUMSA General Secretary, moved a resolution outlining support for the government's Bill, 'despite its weaknesses', while calling for the Assembly to have 'greater powers over Scotland's economy, trade and the universities'. He said the STUC should help Labour MPs, especially in English constituencies, to understand that denying 'the wishes of the Scottish people will drive them into the separatist camp'. Clarke's resolution was resisted by Alex Kitson of the General Council, seeking to deflect criticism of the government and the Parliamentary Labour Party. 'Devolution', Kitson conceded, 'will be a process and without doubt experience will teach the possibility of greater economic power residing with the Assembly'. Clarke remitted the NUMSA resolution.[115] Separate Scotland and Wales Bills were then introduced in November 1977. These included referenda where voters would be asked whether devolution legislation if passed should be enacted. Labour internal divisions were famously exposed by this proviso. Anti-devolutionist MPs in their number introduced by amendment a fatal hurdle: if less than 40 per cent of the total electorate voted 'Yes', the government would repeal the Scotland Act.[116] The NUMSA and STUC General Council lobbied government and Labour MPs to remove this amendment,[117] but it stood, and influenced the outcome of the subsequent referendum. On 1 March 1979 in Scotland 32.5 per cent of the electorate voted 'Yes' to devolution, 30.4 per cent 'No', and 37.1 per cent did not vote at all.[118]

The Scottish miners' campaign for a Scottish Parliament had a significant counterpoint in 1976 and 1977. Willie Clarke was among the NUMSA officials and activists who journeyed several times to the Grunwick photo-processing plant in north-west London to support workers locked out by their employer, George Ward, for seeking union recognition.[119] Bus-loads travelled from Fife, Midlothian and Stirlingshire. Rab Amos, SCEBTA delegate at Monktonhall, and John McCormack, NUM delegate at Polmaise, were among them.[120] The presence on the Grunwick picket line of McGahey, Eric Clarke and other NUMSA officials was captured in memorable photographs by Homer Sykes.[121] Grunwick was a highly 'complex encounter' in class, gender and ethnic terms, to use Ken Lunn's phrase.[122] Many of the workers were Kenyan Asian-heritage women, occupying a substantially different position in the national-class-gender matrix from Scottish miners.[123] The ways in which various groups of male trade unionists supporting the Grunwick campaign obscured the distinct ethnic and gender issues involved have been examined by McDowell, Sundari and Pearson. Their analysis warns against stereotypes but refers to 'a blunt Yorkshire miner' who told reporters that he was there 'to support the lads of Grunwick'.[124] 'Lads' is obviously a gendered term, and in literal terms excludes women. The word 'blunt' conveys directness in thought and speech, but also connotes an absence of intellectual sophistication. The implication that miners who supported the Grunwick strikers were ignorant, specifically of the fact that most of the locked out workers were women, is unfair. Trade unionists from Yorkshire, South Wales and Scotland travelled hundreds of miles to London and gave up a day's earnings or holiday. They did so generously, to express their common interest with the women and men of Grunwick in defending union rights and working class economic security.

Conclusion

Scottish miners were not entirely homogeneous in their politics, culture and identity. The Scottish Family of Miners, to borrow Milton Rogovin's motif, was composed of social conservatives and religious sectarians as well as class-conscious trade unionists and international socialists. Male chauvinism might be seen as structurally embedded in the miners' defence of an economic order that prioritised men's jobs in coal mining. Yet the miners also accepted the desirability of changes, so long as they increased the viability of coalfield communities. Over time, gender inequalities became less pronounced. The esteem of women as equal partners was emphasised in union rhetoric, and would be crucial in generating strike solidarity across the Scottish coalfields in 1984–5. The value of greater gender equality was an acknowledged element of the distinct Scottish mining identity, which the NUMSA leadership developed through political campaigning from the 1950s to the 1980s. This encompassed emphasis on the claimed values of the Scottish nation as well as solidarity with working class people across Britain and the world. The expression of class solidarity at Grunwick in 1976 and 1977 across boundaries of nationality, gender and ethnicity reinforced the Scottish miners' claim to occupy a distinct position within the broader labour movement.

The NUMSA defended security in the coalfields in collaboration with unions representing other groups of workers experiencing job losses arising from deindustrialisation. Solidarities of class were pursued with trade unionists across Britain, but miners in Scotland tended to see deindustrialisation as an acute and even distinctly Scottish problem. The manner in which it was accelerated deliberately by UK policy-makers, remote from the social effects of mine or factory closures and job losses, was emphasised. The unreformed constitutional-political structures of the UK were challenged. Scotland's national right to self-determination was asserted, and the NUMSA persuaded the STUC to adopt Home Rule as its official policy by the early 1970s. Circumstances then forced devolution onto the Labour government's legislative agenda after 1974. In the late 1950s and early 1960s alternative forms of industrial employment were demanded as the price of coal's contraction. This is where gender relationships were quietly reordered. Coalfield society had privileged male interests. The introduction of industrial alternatives benefited men but also broadened the opportunities for women, and contributed to an erosion of gender inequalities. This helped to off-set the negative consequences of deindustrialisation, but offered diminishing returns from the later 1960s, and so the NUMSA and its labour movement allies, growing impatient, reverted in moral economy terms to a defence of male employment in the coal industry. The campaign to protect jobs and communities from the later 1960s onwards is analysed in the final part of this book.

Notes

1. Milton Rogovin, Social Documentary Photographer, http://www.miltonrogovin.com, accessed 18 October 2017.
2. Mark Rogovin, Milton's son, email to author, 20 February 2012.
3. MacDougall, *Militant Miners*, p. 163.
4. Gibbs, *Deindustrialisation and Industrial Communities*, pp. 156–65.
5. Gibbs, 'Moral Economy of the Scottish Coalfields', p. 135.
6. Patricia Hill Collins, *Black Feminist Thought: Knowledge, Consciousness and the Politics of Empowerment* (Routledge: London, 2009).
7. Scottish Trades Union Congress (STUC), *71st Annual Report*, The Beach Ballroom, Aberdeen, 16–19 April 1968 (STUC: Glasgow, 1968), pp. 398–401.
8. Page Arnot, *Scottish Miners*, pp. 413–15.
9. Rafeek, *Communist Women*, pp. 57–8.
10. Iain Chalmers, in conversation with author, East Wemyss, 9 September 2017.
11. *A Star Drops In*, directed by Peter Pickering, Data Film Productions, NCB, *Mining Review*, 2nd Year, No. 11, July 1949, on BFI DVD compilation, *Land of Promise: the British Documentary Movement, 1930–1950*.
12. Beynon and Austrin, 'Sam Watson, a Miners' Leader', *Historical Sociology*, 28 (2015), pp. 458–90.

13. *The Miners' Hymns*, a film by Bill Morrison with music by Johann Johannsson, Hypnotic Pictures, 2010, BFI.
14. Page Arnot, *Scottish Miners*, pp. 420–2.
15. Esther Breitenbach, 'For Workers' Rights and Self-determination? The Scottish Labour Movement and the British Empire from the 1920s to the 1960s', *Scottish Labour History*, 51 (2016), pp. 113–33.
16. Gibbs, *Deindustrialisation and Industrial Communities*, pp. 146–54.
17. STUC, *72nd Annual Report*, The Pavilion, Rothesay, 15–18 April 1969 (STUC: Glasgow, 1969), pp. 481–2.
18. Curtis, *South Wales Miners*, p. 48.
19. Terris, *Twenty Years Down the Mines*, pp. 24, 85–7.
20. Oglethorpe, *Scottish Collieries*, pp. 157–8.
21. Halliday, *Disappearing Scottish Colliery*, pp. 65–74, 99–107.
22. NRS, CB 55/11, Minutes of Glenochil Mine Consultative Committee, 24 February 1960, 15 March 1960, 31 August 1960, 5 April 1961 and 27 December 1961.
23. '"Tombstones" of Rothes mark double death: JOB-FOR-LIFE AND HOME LOST', *The Guardian*, 12 July 1962.
24. TNA, COAL 31/96, Verbatim Notes of a Meeting between representatives of the NCB and the NUM, 26 April 1962.
25. TNA, COAL 31/96, Mrs M. Lonsdale, Scottish Co-operative Women's Guild, to Robens, 19 December 1961; Dollan to Robens, 17 November 1961; J. McEvoy, Dunfermline Trades Council, to Robens, 18 November 1961.
26. STUC, *81st Annual Report*, The Music Hall, Aberdeen, 17–21 April 1978 (STUC: Glasgow, 1978), Obituary, W. McLean, p. 394.
27. Glasgow Caledonian University Archives & Special Collections (GCUA), STUC General Council, 21 April 1961, and 9 May 1962.
28. Obituary, Alex Eadie, *The Telegraph*, 26 January 2012; Obituary, Alex Eadie, by Brian Wilson, *The Guardian*, 1 February 2012; Obituary, Alex Eadie, by Tam Dalyell, *The Independent*, 28 January 2012.
29. Toothill, *Report on the Scottish Economy*.
30. NRS, SEP 10/312, Ministry of Labour, Monthly Report on the Main Features of the Employment Position in Scotland, February 1963.
31. Jim Tomlinson, *Managing the Economy, Managing the People. Narratives of Economic Life in Britain from Beveridge to Brexit* (Oxford University Press: Oxford, 2017), pp. 188–9.
32. Phillips, *Industrial Politics of Devolution*, pp. 19–27.
33. GCUA, STUC General Council, Economic Committee, 28 December 1961; General Council Press Statement, 10 January 1962; Economic Committee, Report of Trade Union Conference, 7 March 1962.

34. GCUA, STUC General Council, Organisation Committee, 5 January 1962.
35. Gibbs and Tomlinson, 'Planning the New Industrial Nation'.
36. GCUA, STUC General Council, Resolution for Conference, 18 February 1962.
37. TNA, COAL 31/96, Parker to Robens, 4 November 1961.
38. Tomlinson, *Managing the Economy*, pp. 161–86.
39. TNA, COAL 31/96, NCBSD, *Five Year Mining Review*, 1962–6.
40. TNA, COAL 31/96, Verbatim Notes of a Meeting between representatives of the NCB and the NUM, 26 April 1962.
41. TNA, COAL 31/96, Parker to Robens, 6 August 1962, relating a meeting held that day between representatives of the NCB Scottish Division and the NUMSA Executive.
42. NMMS, NUMSA Executive Committee, 13 August 1962.
43. GCUA, STUC General Council, Economic Committee, 7 February 1962.
44. TNA, PREM 11/4451, Scottish Coal Committee, Note by NCB, September 1961.
45. TNA, COAL 31/96, Verbatim Notes of a Meeting between representatives of the NCB and the NUM, 26 April 1962.
46. TNA, COAL 89/353, NCB, Scottish Division, Fife Area, Proposals on Future Development, projecting forward to 1967 from April 1962; R. G. C. Cowe, Secretary, NCB, note, 17 May 1962.
47. '8½ M. PIT TO CLOSE', *The Guardian*, 14 March 1962, and 'Tombstones of Rothes mark double death', *The Guardian*, 12 July 1962.
48. '"GO BACK" CALL TO 3,330 MINERS', *The Guardian*, 19 March 1962.
49. NRS, CB 307/19/1, NCB, Scottish Division, Colliery Closure Manpower Deployment, Glenochil, June 1962.
50. NRS, CB 353/14/1, Notes on the Special Consultative Meeting held to discuss the future of Mary Colliery, 10 August 1962.
51. NRS, CB 201/14/2, NCB-SD, Fife Area, Notes on the Special Consultative Meeting held to discuss the future of Aitken Colliery, 14 August 1962.
52. NRS, CB 201/14/2, K. G. Smith, Secretary, NCB-SD, to Abe Moffat, 26 January 1959; Aitken Colliery Consultative Committee, Special meeting, 25 March 1959.
53. NRS, CB 201/14/2, NCB-SD, Fife Area, Notes on the Special Consultative Meeting held to discuss the future of Aitken Colliery, 14 August 1962.
54. NRS, CB 201/14/2, Scrimgeour to Milligan, NCB-SD Deputy Chairman, 1 November 1962; NCB-SD, Fife Area, Note of Special Meeting to discuss the future of the Colliery (Aitken), 28 November 1962.

55. NMMS, NUMSA Executive Committee, 13 August 1962.
56. Alvin Jackson, *The Two Unions: Ireland, Scotland, and the Survival of the United Kingdom, 1707–2007* (Oxford University Press, Oxford, 2012), pp. 259–64.
57. Scottish Development Department, *Central Scotland: Programme for Development and Growth*, Cmnd. 2188 (HMSO: London, 1963).
58. 'White Papers Soon on North', *The Times*, 31 October 1963.
59. 'Investment to rise to £140 millions: growth areas idea accepted', *The Guardian*, 15 November 1963.
60. Scott, 'Regional development and policy'.
61. Department of Economic Affairs, *The National Plan*, Cmnd. 2764 (HMSO: London, 1965); The Scottish Office, *The Scottish Economy, 1965 to 1970: A Plan For Expansion*, Cmnd. 2864 (HMSO: Edinburgh, 1966).
62. Phillips, 'Moral Economy of Deindustrialization', pp. 104–5.
63. Breitenbach, 'For Workers' Rights and Self-determination?'
64. Michael Hechter, *Internal Colonialism. The Celtic Fringe in British National Development, 1536–1966* (Routledge & Kegan Paul: London, 1975).
65. Portelli, *They Say in Harlan County*, pp. 281–5.
66. Phillips, *Industrial Politics of Devolution*, pp. 35–45.
67. TNA, PRO EW8/294 'Meeting between PM and his colleagues and representatives of the STUC', 2 June 1965, appendix F.
68. STUC, *69th Annual Report*, The Music Hall, Aberdeen, 19–22 April 1966 (STUC: Glasgow, 1966), pp. 34–5.
69. Jackson, *Two Unions*, pp. 275–8.
70. STUC, *69th Annual Report*, pp. 37–8.
71. NRS, SEP 14/1894, Scottish Development Department note relating phone call from Ronald Parker, NCB Scottish Divisional Chairman, 26 March 1965.
72. NRS, CB 305/5/1, NCB Scottish Division, Closure of Glencraig, no date, presumed March 1966.
73. NMMS, NUMSA, EC, 9 May 1966.
74. NRS, CB 305/5/1, Note of proceedings at the Meeting between representatives of the NCBSD and the NUMSA and SCEBTA [tradesmen's union], 18 January 1966, and Minute of Meeting on the Proposed Closure of Glencraig Colliery, 11 March 1966.
75. NRS, CB 305/5/1, NCB Scottish Division, Closure of Glencraig, no date, presumed March 1966.
76. NRS, CB 305/5/1, NCBSD, Colliery Closures – Glencraig, Note of a meeting between representatives of the NCB and the NUM, 27 April 1966.

77. Willie Clarke, Interview.
78. NRS, SEP 14/894, Note of a meeting between Minister of State, Board of Trade, Darling, and deputation from Lanarkshire County Council led by Judith Hart MP, 20 December 1965.
79. Robert Taylor, *The Trade Union Question in British Politics* (Blackwell: Cambridge, 1993), pp. 138–47.
80. STUC, *70th Annual Report*, Queen's Hall, Dunoon, 18–21 April 1967 (STUC: Glasgow, 1967), pp. 416–30.
81. STUC, *71st Annual Report*, pp. 318–21.
82. *Royal Commission on Trades Unions and Employers' Associations 1965–1968*, Cmnd. 3623 (HMSO: London, 1968).
83. Michael Moran, *The Politics of Industrial Relations* (Macmillan: London, 1977), p. 68; Alastair J. Reid, *United We Stand. A History of Britain's Trade Unions* (Penguin: Harmondsworth, 2004), pp. 299–300; 'A Report to Forget', *The Economist*, 15 June 1968, pp. 16–17.
84. Department of Employment and Productivity, *In Place of Strife. A Policy for Industrial Relations*, Cmnd. 3888 (HMSO: London, 1969), pp. 28–9.
85. Lewis Minkin, *The Contentious Alliance. Trade Unions and the Labour Party* (Edinburgh University Press: Edinburgh, 1992), pp. 114–16.
86. STUC, *72nd Annual Report*, pp. 153–6, 412–13, 421–2.
87. Angela Tuckett, *Scottish Trades Union Congress* (Mainstream: Edinburgh, 1986), pp. 381–7.
88. 'In Place of Government', *The Economist*, 21 June 1969, front page and editorial matter.
89. Halliday, *Disappearing Scottish Colliery*, pp. 71–5.
90. STUC, *71st Annual Report*, pp. 398–401.
91. STUC, *71st Annual Report*, pp. 401–9.
92. GCUA, STUC General Council, 14 August 1968.
93. Peter Jenkins, 'A rubber boner?', *The Guardian*, 1 November 1968.
94. *Royal Commission on the Constitution: Volume 1, Report*, Cmnd. 5460 (HMSO: London, 1973), pp. 335–44.
95. STUC, *72nd Annual Report*, pp. 230–5.
96. *Royal Commission on the Constitution. Minutes of Evidence, Volume IV, Scotland* (HMSO: London, 1970), pp. 23–39.
97. *Commission on the Constitution. Evidence, Volume IV*, pp. 57–64.
98. *Commission on the Constitution. Evidence, Volume IV*, pp. 65–71.
99. Lewis Johnman and Hugh Murphy, *British Shipbuilding and the State: a political economy of decline* (University of Exeter: Exeter, 2002), pp. 163–68, 184.

100. TNA, EW 7/1456, Extract, Cabinet Ministerial Committee on Economic Policy, 6 May 1969.
101. John Foster and Charles Woolfson, 'How Workers on the Clyde Gained the Capacity for Class Struggle: the Upper Clyde Shipbuilders' Work-In, 1971–2', in John McIlroy, Nina Fishman and Alan Campbell, eds, *British Trade Unions and Industrial Politics. Volume Two: The High Tide of Trade Unionism, 1964–79* (Ashgate: Aldershot, 1999), pp. 297–325.
102. John Kerr, 'Right to work call unites the Scots', *The Guardian*, 15 February 1972.
103. GCUA, STUC General Council, Scottish Assembly on Unemployment, 14 February 1972, List of Speakers.
104. STUC, *75th Annual Report*, Queen's Hall, Dunoon, 18–21 April 1972 (STUC: Glasgow, 1972), pp. 258–61.
105. GCUA, STUC General Council, Charter of Proposals for the Scottish Assembly, 14 February 1972.
106. *Scottish Miner*, March 1972.
107. Jim Phillips, 'The 1972 Miners' Strike: Popular Agency and Industrial Politics in Britain', *Contemporary British History*, 20 (2006), 2006, pp. 187–207.
108. Christopher Harvie, *No Gods and Precious Few Heroes: Scotland since 1914* (Edinburgh University Press: Edinburgh, 1993), p. 90.
109. GCUA, STUC Economic Committee, Meeting with Representatives of Unions with membership engaged in the Fuel Industries, Trade Union Centre, Glasgow, 26 November 1968.
110. STUC, *81st Annual Report*, pp. 620–1.
111. TNA, COAL 31/166, Tripartite Meeting on Electricity Coal Burn in Scotland, 5 February 1976; Coal and Electricity, Informal Note of a meeting held at Church House, Westminster, Friday 20 February 1976, and Department of Energy, Tripartite Energy Consultations, p. 15.
112. *Our Changing Democracy: Devolution to Scotland and Wales*, Cmnd. 6438 (HMSO: London, 1975), pp. 28–9, 55–6.
113. STUC, *79th Annual Report*, The City Hall, Perth, 19–23 April 1976 (STUC: Glasgow, 1976), pp. 200–1.
114. *The Times*, 26 January 1977.
115. STUC, *80th Annual Report*, The Pavilion, Rothesay, 18–22 April 1977 (STUC: Glasgow, 1977), pp. 794–5.
116. Vernon Bogdanor, *Devolution in the United Kingdom* (Oxford University Press: Oxford, 1999), pp. 186–7.
117. *STUC, 81st Annual Report*, pp. 254–9, 617–23.

118. Henry Drucker and Gordon Brown, *The Politics of Nationalism and Devolution* (Longman: London, 1980), pp. 120–1.
119. Willie Clarke, Interview.
120. Amos, Interview; John McCormack, Fallin, in Owens, *Miners*, p. 115.
121. Homer Sykes, http://homersykes.photoshelter.com/gallery/GRUN-WICK-STRIKE-STOCK-IMAGES-PHOTOS-PHOTOGRAPHY-LON-DON-1977-1970s-UK/G0000MmrftXBGUt0, accessed 26 November 2010 and 7 February 2011.
122. Kenneth Lunn, 'Complex Encounters: Trade Unions, Immigration and Racism', in Alan Campbell, Nina Fishman, John McIlroy, eds, *British Trade Unions and Industrial Politics, vol. Two: the high tide of trade unionism, 1964–79* (Ashgate: Aldershot, 1999), pp. 70–90.
123. Jack McGowan, '"Dispute", "Battle", "Siege", "Farce"? – Grunwick 30 Years On', *Contemporary British History*, 22 (2008), pp. 383–406.
124. Linda McDowell, Anitha Sundari, and Ruth Pearson, 'Striking Narratives: class, gender and ethnicity in the "Great Grunwick Strike", London, UK, 1976–1978', *Women's History Review*, 23.4 (2014), pp. 595–619, with quote at p. 612.

Part Three

Organise: for Jobs, Wages and Communities

CHAPTER 6

Resisting Closures and Winning Wages in the 1960s and 1970s

On 21 November 1967 NCB officials in London announced that Michael Colliery in East Wemyss would be closed permanently after the calamitous fire on 9 September which had killed nine miners and caused significant underground damage.[1] It is a common misapprehension, repeated in media coverage of the 50th anniversary of the disaster in 2017, that the fire *caused* the closure.[2] NCB Scottish Division officials had in fact devised a programme of action to rescue the colliery. With investment of around £4 million, production would restart early in 1969. There would be an annual profit of £750,000 by 1970–1, with 1,500 miners still employed.[3] The closure was therefore politically driven, the decision taken by Lord Robens in London after the publication one week earlier of *Fuel Policy*. Employment in the coal industry had more than halved since 1958. Now it would halve again by 1975, to under 200,000.[4] Robens said that within this inhospitable policy environment there was no justification for re-investment at Michael, when diminished demand for coal could be met from other collieries.[5]

This was a grim scenario, for miners in East Fife and in Scotland generally. The economic position in the coalfields was perhaps more precarious than at any point since nationalisation. Yet Michael's closure was followed by an improvement in security for Scottish miners and their communities. It was the last colliery to be closed against organised opposition from NCB employees and their trade union representatives until the winter of 1982–3. The slowdown of closures and redundancies from 1968 onwards was examined in Chapter 1, emphasising two structural factors: the NCB had largely completed the mechanisation of coal-getting; and the stabilisation of employment in coal was a deliberate response to the falling growth of alternative industrial jobs in mining areas. Meanwhile the politics of energy were shifting in coal's favour, at least temporarily. *Fuel Policy* was premised on a future of low oil prices, but these rose significantly in the early 1970s: coal became more attractive, consolidating the safety of mining jobs.

One other factor in creating greater security after 1967 was vital: the activism of union representatives. The politics of generation and nation were prominent. In the summer of 1967 Alex Moffat retired as NUMSA President on health grounds and died just weeks later, on 6 September, after 45 years in the trade union movement.[6] It has already been noted that Michael McGahey replaced Moffat in an acting capacity and then permanently after winning the Presidential election later in the year.[7] This was a significant generational transfer of leadership with implications for union policy. In March 1967 Moffat had persuaded an NUMSA Delegate Conference to accept additional closures on economic grounds, arguing this would safeguard a smaller but more viable industry. Under McGahey's direction the NUMSA reversed this position three months later, pledging to protect remaining coalfield employment on social as well as economic grounds.[8] McGahey's New Mine generation enlarged the scope of the NUMSA's activism. Moral economy imperatives were imposed on policy-makers and *Fuel Policy*'s targets for reduced production and employment coal reduction were missed. Scheduled closures were delayed or abandoned altogether, exemplified by the important case of Cardowan in Lanarkshire, targeted by the NCB in 1969 but kept open by union pressure until 1983.

The chapter is structured in two parts. The miners' mobilisation against *Fuel Policy* is examined first. This picks up the issue of closures, examined in Chapters 1 and 5. The chronological coverage is brought forward from the mid-1960s and with greater focus on pit-level developments. Michael's closure combined with the generational transfer of leadership in the NUMSA to intensify resistance to deindustrialisation and 'market-ness' in energy policy. Closures were accepted on occasion but managed carefully. Additional coal burn was achieved by the NCB under labour movement pressure, reinforcing the sense that the New Mine generation was more ambitious in its policy-shaping interventions than the Village Pit generation. An examination of collective action for increased wages from 1969 to 1974 forms the second half of the chapter. The NUMSA influenced the left turn in British mining politics more broadly from the late 1960s. This movement is usually understood in terms of wage militancy, and with good reason. Scottish miners wanted to reverse the decline of their wages relative to those of other manual workers. But the underlying issues were deindustrialisation and collective security. Campaigning on these questions brought McGahey and Lawrence Daly to national prominence in the UK. Daly was elected General Secretary of the NUM in 1968 and McGahey came a close second to Joe Gormley in the NUM Presidential election of 1971 before winning the position of Vice President in 1972. The distinct politics of Scotland retained a powerful position in the coalfields. Deindustrialisation was still being related by Scottish miners to internal colonialism within the UK. The victories of 1972 and 1974 were a boost to younger miners, the Cosmopolitan Colliery generation, raising their moral economy expectations and securing the ground that they would defend in the 1980s.

Resisting Closures

In December 1966 the NCB advised industry unions that it wanted to close Wellesley in Buckhaven, East Fife. Productivity was relatively high, but geological conditions were becoming difficult. Wellesley, an A category colliery in 1962 was now reclassified as C category: reasonable OMS but limited workable reserves. Bill McLean for the NUMSA insisted that the 1,000 men be redeployed locally, to Seafield or Michael, and in blocks, preserving work-groups to maintain morale. The NCB acceded and the colliery closed in June 1967.[9] Wellesley's closure passed the NUM's moral economy test: local employment was preserved, but the challenges to coalfield security across Scotland were mounting. This was recognised at the STUC in April 1967, meeting in Dunoon, which passed unanimously a motion moved by A. G. Merker of West Lothian Trades Council and seconded by McGahey, outlining opposition to closures on economic grounds. Merker warned that the trend in government policy would lead to the closure of all Scottish pits, bar Seafield and Michael in Fife, Bilston Glen and Monktonhall in Midlothian, Barony and Killoch in Ayrshire, and Cardowan in Lanarkshire.[10] If anything this was understating the dangers posed by *Fuel Policy*, published that November. Government files on the drafting of this White Paper provide rich detail. Ministry of Power officials reckoned that in Scotland by 1980 only Michael, employing just over 2,000 miners, and the Longannet pits, with perhaps 6,000, would still be open.[11] At the Department of Economic Affairs it was emphasised that damaging employment losses would be encountered in Ayrshire by the end of the 1960s, and in all other areas during the 1970s. The Board of Trade, examining the prospects in Midlothian, noted that alternative job creation was unlikely to off-set the losses that would arise from the closures of Bilston Glen and Monktonhall.[12]

This difficult future shaped responses to the disaster at Michael, and the closure announcement which followed. Michael employed 2,184 miners in September 1967, almost 6 per cent of the NCB Scottish Division's workforce. The colliery was still the biggest producer in Scotland, and a major source of economic activity in East Fife. Its employees amounted to one-fifth of the local employment exchange area's insured adult male population, drawn from the towns of Buckhaven, Methil and Leven, and the villages of Coaltown of Wemyss, Coaltown of Balgownie, Windygates and Kennoway as well as East Wemyss.[13] Male unemployment in the local employment exchange area reached 7.2 per cent after the closure, three times the UK average in February 1968.[14] The NUMSA executive met in emergency session on 11 September, two days after the fire, agreeing to demand that Michael re-open as quickly as possible and the workforce be retained while the Board of Trade took 'urgent measures' to direct new industry to the area, with re-training facilities where necessary. Lawrence Daly communicated this position to Anthony Crosland, the Labour government's President of the Board of Trade.[15] Daly and McLean discussed the crisis with the STUC General Council two weeks later, emphasising the centrality of Michael to economic life in East Fife.[16] Three days later James Jack, STUC General Secretary, attended a scheduled meeting with Willie Ross, Secretary of State for Scotland, accompanied by McLean. The union officials told Ross that the sense of economic insecurity in East Fife was acute. McLean stressed the political dangers of inaction, with women in the coalfields especially forceful in criticising the Labour government and mining unions for inadequately defending pits and jobs. The women 'were claiming – and justifiably so – that if the Government could make money available for private enterprise development in Scotland, there was no reason whatsoever for failing to provide similar funds for the mining industry'. Ross was non-committal, accepting that the situation was difficult, but asking the union representatives to await the outcome of a meeting taking place that day between Harold Wilson and NUM officials at the Labour Party Conference in Scarborough.[17]

Wilson talked to Robens about pit closures in Downing Street on 28 September, the day before this Scarborough meeting, along with Richard Marsh, Minister of Power, and Peter Shore, Secretary of State at the DEA. The Ministry of Power's note of the meeting with Robens refers to an understanding that closures could be accelerated if employment alternatives were being created more quickly than anticipated. This implied that the converse might also be applicable: where alternatives were emerging more slowly than expected, closures could be delayed. This much was admitted in the Wilson-Robens meeting: the DEA would be empowered to initiate consultations on individual closures with the NCB and the Ministry of Power where a significant increase in unemployment was threatened. In such cases the DEA could recommend deferring closure. At Scarborough the NUM delegation included Daly and McGahey, and Wilson again accompanied by Marsh and Shore. The discussion was dominated by broader concerns about closures and the likely contents of *Fuel Policy*, but Daly and McGahey raised the question of Michael. Wilson agreed that a discussion of industrial diversification in East

Fife should be prioritised, between Ross and McGahey in the first instance.[18]

McGahey and Ross met two weeks later, on 16 October. McGahey wanted the government to contribute to the financial cost of re-opening Michael. Such investment was warranted by the colliery's scale and value as an employer and producer. McGahey also sought more incentives for manufacturing firms to locate in the area.[19] This higher-location lobbying continued three days later, when McLean put the case for rescuing Michael directly to Wilson in Glasgow's St Enoch Hotel as part of an STUC General Council delegation. McLean noted the 'bleak' implications for the community of losing Michael's jobs, and reiterated the colliery's prospects on the basis of recent development and massive reserves. Wilson replied only that the government was working to devise means of narrowing the unemployment gap 'between the less and more prosperous regions', and gave no guarantee that Michael could be saved.[20]

It is unsurprising, close to the publication of *Fuel Policy*, that the government was unwilling to fund Michael's revival, but a positive case for increased regional assistance to East Fife was constructed. This ignored the basic premise of McLean's argument when meeting Ross on 29 September that it was perverse to refuse financial support to the nationalised coal industry while investing significantly in private manufacturing. Lord Hughes, Under-Secretary of State at the Scottish Office and responsible for regional policy in Scotland, met representatives of local authorities, the NCB and trade unions in Buckhaven on 14 November, the very day that *Fuel Policy* was published. Hughes said the government would provide rent-free Board of Trade accommodation for five years for firms offering 'suitable employment' in East Fife.[21] Michael's closure was confirmed one week later. This was strenuously opposed by Michael's workforce, the various local authorities affected, and trade union officials. Direct appeals were made to both Wilson and Robens,[22] and McGahey secured joint NCB-union talks at Scottish Divisional level. He queried the NCB's claim that the costs of re-opening the pit would exceed £5 million. But even this sum McGahey characterised as a 'worthwhile investment' given the pit's profitability and extensive reserves of 40 to 50 million tons, in thick and easily workable seams. The workers and their representatives restated the damaging community effects of closure.[23] Parker, NCB Scottish Division Chairman, conveyed these sentiments to Robens.[24]

The closure was a serious transgression of the miners' moral economy. It will be remembered that this had two core elements: changes had to be arrived at by agreement, and were only accepted if consistent with collective economic security. The final decision was taken by managerial fiat against workforce and union opposition, and announced in London. McLean told NCB officials in Scotland that this violated established consultation rights.[25] The NUMSA and the STUC held a Scottish Mining Protest Rally in Edinburgh on 9 December, linking Michael's closure to the broader threat posed by *Fuel Policy* to coalfield security. The distinct national question in Scotland was prominent.[26] McGahey wrote to Ross afterwards. Further closures would surely follow, he stressed, and were most likely in localities with limited employment alternatives such as West Lothian and East Ayrshire.[27]

An STUC Economic Committee deputation including McLean obtained separate meetings in London with Robens and Marsh in mid-December. Robens, knowing the STUC officials would be seeing Marsh the following morning, said that government policy was responsible for Michael's closure. Marsh did not deny this, but said that rescuing Michael would result in job losses elsewhere. The way forward for East Fife and other coalfield areas was industrial diversification.[28] Such an approach was accepted as desirable by D. S. Davidson of Buckhaven and Methil Town Council, but the local authority still sought the colliery's preservation, lobbying the Scottish Office to support this end.[29] Ross and Gwyneth Dunwoody, Parliamentary Secretary at the Board of Trade, met the Mining Group of Labour MPs at the Scottish Office in Whitehall in January 1968. Social costs and moral economy arguments were emphasised by Alex Eadie, former East Fife miner and union official. 'This was not a depressed or depressing area', Eadie said, 'and a great deal had been invested in social capital', including the development of high-achieving local authority schools.[30] Ross told the MPs – contradicting Marsh's remarks to the STUC Economic Committee – that decisions about pit closures were taken by the NCB, and he was powerless to intervene. Ross reiterated this position a fortnight later when meeting NUMSA officials in Edinburgh, arguing that his role was confined to mitigating the effects of closures, chiefly through the regional policy changes outlined in November.[31]

Within East Fife hope that Michael could be rescued was gradually extinguished. Among various practical difficulties, McLean told STUC colleagues in October 1969, was the incremental dispersal of the workforce.[32] The workers' moral economy arguments were not entirely set aside, however. Local and Scottish-wide labour movement pressure resulted in the government fulfilling its promise to bolster economic security in East Fife, with support from the NCB. In October 1970 half the men employed at Michael in 1967 were working in other collieries. Most of these miners, 844, were still in East Fife, including 179 who were at Frances and 478 at Seafield by February 1968. Another 109 were in West Fife. Six more had moved to the Lothians or Ayrshire and 60 had transferred to England, mainly to Nottinghamshire and Yorkshire. Another quarter of the 1967 workforce, 303 men aged 55 to 59 and 206 aged 60 and over, had received early retirement and access to their pensions. Only one in four had been made redundant, and most of these were reckoned by the Scottish Office to be working in other sectors in 1970.[33] This latter point bears emphasis. The employment situation in East Fife although less promising than in Scotland and the UK overall was not hopeless. Regional policy adjustments made in response to the crisis had a positive effect. Of lasting significance was the arrival in Leven in 1969 of Distillers Company (Ltd), employing 1,000 workers by 1973.[34] The blending and bottling plant embodied at local level the broadly successful trend in regional policy, with Scottish Gross Domestic Product per capita increasing from 87.7 per cent of the UK level in 1962 to 91.1 per cent in 1966–73 and then 96.0 in 1973–9.[35]

The stabilisation of economic activity in East Fife was part of a general pattern across Scotland's coalfields after 1967, likewise arising from changes in government and NCB strategy. These adjustments were a response to expectations of security in the coalfields, articulated and defended by union representatives from the New Mine generation. In November 1968 the NCB employed about 36,000 miners in Scotland. Ministry of Power officials at this point provided ministers with a further briefing on future employment prospects. There would be a drop of one-third to 24,700 in Scotland by March 1971, followed by further retrenchment to 15,000 in 1975 and 8,000 in 1980. The productivity paradox which had emerged earlier in the 1960s was still a live concern. Average OMS had improved from 22.9 hundredweights in 1961 to 35.4 in 1968,[36] but this had eliminated mining employment because overall demand had fallen.[37] In February 1969 the Scottish Office reviewed the status of pits identified as category B and C in 1962. Most had either closed or were expected to soon, including Lady Victoria in Midlothian and Cardowan in Lanarkshire, with over 1,000 miners facing redundancy at each colliery.[38] Yet Lady Victoria remained open until 1981, and Cardowan until 1983. Jobs were lost in Scottish coal at less than half the overall NCB rate from 1969 to 1972, when almost 30,000 miners were still employed in Scotland.[39] Employment fell far more slowly than the NCB predicted in 1968. The NCB employed 24,000 in Scotland in 1975, compared with the forecast 15,000, and more than 20,000 in 1980, compared with the projected 8,000.[40]

How did this slowdown happen? The case of Cardowan in Lanarkshire is instructive, highlighting the successful impact of union activism. A total of 1,539 were employed at the colliery in March 1969. Closure was planned by the NCB, with limited scope for redeployment. While perhaps 430 could move to neighbouring Bedlay, the remaining 1,100 would be redundant. Sixty per cent of the Cardowan workers travelled from the Hamilton area, a legacy of closures in the late 1950s and early 1960s. The remainder lived in the East Glasgow-Kirkintilloch-Kilsyth corridor, where local unemployment was 6.3 per cent, on par with East Fife after Michael's closure, and nearly three times the UK average.[41] One of Cardowan's main customers was the British Steel Corporation (BSC), which refused an entreaty from the NCB to pay more for its coal. Union representatives were advised in September 1969 by the NCB that the pit was officially in jeopardy. The prospect of transfers to Bedlay was now less likely as this colliery was also in jeopardy, threatening another 910 jobs. A hundred miners could be offered transfer to distant Polmaise in Stirlingshire and Kinneil in West Lothian, and another 433 further away still, to pits in Alloa and Fife. The vast majority of the 2,000 Lanarkshire miners threatened with redundancy would only stay in the coal industry if they moved to England.[42]

The NUMSA refused to accept this. NUM officials persuaded the NCB at a meeting in November 1969 that Cardowan could become more 'viable', proposing an increased daily output from 1,700 to 2,250 tons. McGahey wrote to NCB Scottish South Area officials after this meeting in remarkable terms. Bedlay would be removed from jeopardy status and Cardowan taken off the closure list. That, he said, was 'the decision' made by the NUMSA executive for the NCB to implement.[43] McLean advised STUC colleagues that closure would not be accepted by the union or the workforce.[44] The NCB did not alter the official status of either Bedlay or Cardowan, but both continued operating through 1970 and into 1971. Cardowan's performance improved, although short of the planned daily target of 2,250 tons. In March 1971 NCB officials in London discussed the position at Cardowan. 'The union seems already to have assumed the colliery is out of jeopardy', one official noted, recommending that the threat of closure to both Lanarkshire pits be officially rescinded. This would spare a difficult and potentially unwinnable argument with the workers and their representatives. 'Yes', another official replied: 'let them de-jeop!' Meeting NCB officials in June 1972, McGahey claimed this outcome as vindication of the union's argument that closures were not permissible on economic grounds alone.[45]

The decisive moral economy factor in Lanarkshire was the absence of local employment alternatives for miners facing redundancy. Closures were accepted by the NUMSA on economic grounds but only where jobs in other industrial sectors were available or where local redeployment was achievable. Such was the case with Blairhall in West Fife which closed in May 1969 after a four-month dialogue involving local and Scottish management and union representatives. There were 652 men on the books on 2 February 1969. Age and fitness were elements in the case for closure and redeployment: 117 were in the 55–59 age cohort and 61 were 60-plus years old. In all age cohorts 69 men were absent, long-term sick. McLean examined the issue with William Rowell, NCB Scottish North Director, focusing largely on the fit men who were younger than 60. McLean requested and received a list of vacancies at collieries in daily travelling distance from Blairhall. There were 546 openings at the Longannet trio of Bogside, Castlehill and Solsgirth plus 42 at Comrie and another 90 at Dollar. McLean wanted to see the residential profile of the Blairhall workforce as well. About one-sixth of the 645 men still employed at the pit on 28 February 1969 lived in Central Fife, transferred four or five years earlier when the Kelty–Cowdenbeath–Lochgelly–Cardenden closures took effect. Finer-grain data was also gathered on occupation and age group. McLean was concerned about safeguarding the higher earnings of Blairhall face workers, clustered in the 31–45 age group.[46] McLean established that Longannet vacancies were largely for non-face workers.[47] Blairhall's NUM delegate, James Carr, claimed the existence of an earlier NCB promise that his face-working members would receive priority treatment if transferred to Longannet. McGahey intervened at this point, in April 1969, obtaining a meeting with NCB officials which he attended with Carr and McLean. The NCB admitted that promises made to the Blairhall face workers had been broken to accommodate ex-Michael miners at Longannet in the spring of 1968. McGahey, McLean and Carr negotiated an agreement with the NCB that a further build-up of production and employment at Longannet would be brought forward. This enabled 253 Blairhall men to go to Solsgirth and 164 to Castlehill, with another 55 heading to Comrie and Dollar.[48] Crucially, all established earnings were to be protected, and NUMSA officials accepted Blairhall's closure on this basis. Economic security was emphatically maintained.[49]

Blairhall was one of just two collieries that closed in Scotland in 1969. There was a single closure in 1970 and none at all in 1971; three shut in 1972, then four in 1973, one in 1974, three in 1975, one in 1976, and none in 1977.[50] The 1970 closure was Lochhead in East Fife, accepted by the workforce and union representatives because of continued employment build-up at Seafield and the Longannet complex.[51] NCB officials organised a visit for Lochhead miners and their wives contemplating a move to Solsgirth in February 1970. This included meetings with pit management and union representatives for 'the men' and a tour of local authority housing in Saline, Sauchie and Kincardine for 'the ladies'. There was lunch afterwards at the Castle Campbell Hotel in Dollar to discuss the terms of transfer.[52] The outcomes at Lochhead and especially Blairhall illustrated the assertive manner in which NUMSA officials of the New Mine generation used the structures of the nationalised industry, extending its reach from the workplace, and broadening its scope from work organisational issues, the less ambitious terrain favoured by officials of the Village Pit generation.

The Longannet connection also restates the importance of union engagement with public policy. It was in direct response to pressure from the NUMSA that the NCB lobbied the government successfully to secure coal as the prime energy source at this and two other South of Scotland Electricity Board (SSEB) power stations built on either side of the Firth of Forth in the 1960s, Kincardine and Cockenzie.[53] The establishment of Kincardine prevented the closure of Manor Powis Colliery in Stirlingshire, which the NCB had scheduled in 1967, saving 480 redundancies.[54] With this new customer the pit remained open for another six years.[55] McGahey advised the STUC in November 1968 that the SSEB had wanted to generate a greater share of electricity at the new plants through oil burn, but this was vetoed by the government under pressure from the NUM as well as the NCB. The protection of employment in West Fife was specifically cited by McGahey as a factor in securing coal burn at Longannet.[56] At Cockenzie proposed coal usage was stepped up rapidly, from 1,010,000 tons in 1967 to 2,510,000 tons in 1970.[57] Economic security in the coalfields was being strengthened through the NUM's exercise of louder voice in policy-making. Before the generational transfer of leadership this had focused on lobbying for enhanced regional assistance to stimulate economic diversification in the coalfields. Now this effort switched back – as the contrasting Cardowan and Blairhall cases indicate – to protection of existing coal industry employment. UK Ministry of Power officials commented on this privately, seeing the NCB's willingness to slow contraction in Scotland as the direct consequence of union pressure inspired by the falling increase of alternative job creation.[58]

Losses in coal were stemmed further by two external factors: the devaluation of sterling in November 1967, coinciding with the publication of *Fuel Policy*, and the rising cost of oil imports.[59] A major crisis in oil supply followed the escalation of Israeli-Arab conflict in 1973. But the intensified lobbying of policy-makers by union representatives and the slowed contraction of coal preceded much of the cumulative oil price rise. Returning to the Blyton and Turnbull formula for assessing worker participation, this implied a substantial extension and broadened scope of trade union influence, to the point where unions could veto as well as delay NCB closure plans. Although *Fuel Policy* had made the case for moving away from coal, to minimise electricity-generation costs, separate Scottish and UK-level union delegations to the Ministry of Power in 1967 secured an undertaking that the government would support the coal industry's effort to soak up surplus labour in coalfield areas characterised by slower economic activity. Marsh was briefed to tell the Scottish delegation: 'There is no question of the Scottish coalfield taking the especially heavy knocks expected in some other coalfields. That it is reasonably placed derives from a substantial planned increase in coal consumption at Scottish power stations.'[60]

Winning Better Wages

The defence of pits and jobs was accompanied by the growing willingness of miners to take collective action for better wages. Industry-wide tensions, reflected in national disputes, were aggravated by union-management disagreements at workplace level. At Bilston Glen in October 1969 the colliery's Assistant Manager, W. Taylor, attempted to suppress the NUM District practice of holding pithead meetings with members before the start of a shift. J. Young, an NUM official, claimed that Taylor had sought to break up a meeting because passageways were blocked, delaying a contraband search. Taylor ordered Young to leave the premises, saying that otherwise the police would be called. McGahey discussed the matter with the NCB's Scottish South Area management. He conceded that pit-head meetings should not exceed 10 minutes nor interfere with production, but claimed they were a legitimate part of the industry's dialogical culture. Area management accepted that 'good common sense should prevail in situations like this' as well as the essence of McGahey's position, that his officials had a right to address their members in the workplace.[61]

The Bilston Glen pit-head meeting in October 1969 had been discussing a looming national dispute, which resulted in a two-week unofficial strike across Scotland, beginning that very day at nearby Monktonhall. Miners at Bilston Glen and other Scottish pits joined the strike two days later. Other areas of the UK coalfield were involved, chiefly Yorkshire and South Wales. The specific trigger was the demand for a paid 20-minute meal break within the eight-hour day for surface workers, which the NCB was resisting. 'Hours are money as cash in the pay packet is money', said Robens, appearing on BBC TV's *Panorama* in front of a studio audience including unofficial strikers. The surface workers' conditions were being negotiated within the annual pay award bargaining talks. The NUM national executive had recommended acceptance of the NCB offer, which excluded the meal break for surface workers. Daly, now NUM General Secretary, appeared alongside Robens on *Panorama*, rationalising the executive's position while empathising with the surface workers' claim. The programme ended with Daly and a group of Yorkshire and Welsh strikers debating the union's rules, specifically the proviso that a national strike could only proceed with the support of a two-thirds majority in a membership ballot. 'I didn't make the rules', Daly said, 'you [meaning the membership of the union] and the pioneers made them, these are the rules, two-thirds by ballot'.[62]

Some Yorkshire miners called for Daly to resign along with the union President, Sir Sidney Ford.[63] The General Secretary's longer-term credibility was damaged, according to Vic Allen.[64] Andrew Taylor disagrees, arguing that Daly's constitutional duty to defend national executive policy did not stop him from advocating strike action for wage increases.[65] Allen's claim appeared in a profile of trade union militancy, published in 1981, which emphasised the NUM's crucial shift to the left in the late 1960s.[66] Outwardly the miners looked weak in collective bargaining terms in the late 1960s, supporting Allen's argument that a change of political outlook at the top of the NUM was vital to the victories in 1972 and 1974. The relative position of miners in the wages league for manual workers had slowly declined since the 1950s in the context of closures, lost members and the growth of energy alternatives to coal. From an entirely different perspective Edward Heath's Conservative government, surprised by the shift in the miners' politics, also identified the role of union leadership as the key factor in 1972 and 1974. In his memoirs Heath referred to the union's 'spasm of militancy'.[67] The government was, however, over-dependent for trade union intelligence on 'moderate' union officials such as Joe Gormley, the NUM President from 1970 to 1982. Gormley was 'outed' as a former police special branch informant in 2002, nine years after his death.[68] In the summer of 1973 the NUM President held private talks with the Prime Minister, without the knowledge of other union officials, including Daly and McGahey, seeking to resolve the miners' pay claim within the government's anti-inflationary economic strategy.[69]

This reliance on Gormley contributed to the government's inability to see trade unions as responsive organisations with leaders subject to direction by their members. This was a failing of the government in its broader approach to organised labour, embodied in the Industrial Relations Act of 1971. This provided unprecedented statutory regulation of trade union behaviour on the misapprehension that this was controlled by executives and officials.[70] Ahead of the 1974 strike Heath wrote to Gormley twice, hoping the NUM President could avert action supported by 81 per cent of the union members who had voted in a national ballot.[71] In attempting to comprehend coalfield militancy Heath alighted on the Communist politics of many NUM officials. McGahey's role in particular was scrutinised, partly because of his intervention as union Vice President in talks between the NUM and the Prime Minister in November 1973, when the government was seeking to avert a national strike. McGahey told Heath that he was committed to driving the Conservative government out of office, meaning through the mobilisation of public opinion behind a Labour victory at the next General Election. But Heath and many others constructed an alternative interpretation of McGahey's remarks, as a call to subvert Parliamentary structures through industrial action alone.[72]

Numerous historical interpretations follow both Allen and Heath in presenting the 1972 and 1974 strikes as driven by left-shifting trade union leadership.[73] The strikes were, however, major social movements, with deep roots in the protracted process of deindustrialisation since the late 1950s. Such is the conclusion of an alternative if varied body of literature, which this author has contributed to, emphasising longer-run trends in coalfield employment and energy politics, along with the importance of workplace mobilisation. Pressure from below forced the leftward move within the NUM.[74] This was implicitly acknowledged by members of the security services detailed to investigate the role of NUM officials after the 1972 strike, including McGahey. The intelligence officers concluded that the CPGB had not guided events in any significant way.[75]

The impact of deindustrialisation on miners' strike-willingness is worth elaborating. There was a strong correlation between falling coal industry employment in the 1960s and the slipping value of miners' real wages, despite the growth of productivity. In 1970, submitting an annual pay claim to the NCB, the NUM stated that productivity had increased by 34.3 per cent since 1964. In the same period the cost of living had risen by 35.9 per cent but wages had only gone up 28.1 per cent. The proposed single year rise of 23 per cent would improve this position, where miners were sixteenth in the wages league.[76] Peter Downie, who worked at Bedlay at the time, remembers discussing wages with other Rangers fans at Ibrox. Those who worked at the Chrysler car plant in Linwood were earning £35 a week, to his £22-10s.[77] This earnings gap with car workers was raised as both perverse and unjust by miners in the Midlands of England, speaking to reporters in the late autumn of 1973. Chrysler was offering £52 a week for assembly work and £45 'to sweep floors' while the NUM was seeking £40 and £45 weekly minima for underground workers and power-loaders.[78]

Wage discontent united miners across the UK in pursuit of greater economic security. The concentration of production in larger collieries helped to cement the solidarity and effectiveness of the strikes, particularly as electricity was being generated from a relatively small number of power plants. Interruptions of coal production could lead quickly to power cuts, strengthening the miners' hand in negotiations. Both the developing solidarity of miners in the face of deindustrialisation and their unexpected acquisition of bargaining leverage were evident in the 1969 strike. To recap, in Scotland this commenced on 14 October at Monktonhall,[79] which drew miners from wide catchment areas in Edinburgh, East Lothian and Midlothian, a glimpse of their daily travel routine captured in Figure 6.

Figure 6 Miners at Monktonhall, Midlothian, home of the 'young team' in the 1970s. © NMMS

The Monktonhall union branch was led by members of the Cosmopolitan Colliery generation, known as the 'young team' according to one of their number, David Hamilton.[80] Workers at other pits came out in increments: six by 16 October and another nine by 22 October when 16,000 miners were on strike in Scotland.

The majority of pits, 19, but a minority of workers, 14,000, were still at work, indicating greater strike-willingness at Cosmopolitan Collieries and other large units.[81] Miners in all parts of the UK coalfield returned to work on 25 October, and a Special Conference of union delegates on 30 October agreed to a national ballot on the NCB's offer, which Daly characterised as amounting to the largest single-year increase since nationalisation. A big majority of 82 per cent accepted,[82] on the understanding, McGahey claimed, that the union would maintain pressure on the NCB to increase wages further and meet the surface workers' demand for paid meal breaks.[83]

McGahey and the Scottish miners pushed the NUM national leadership to further militancy in 1970. Vigilance on wages was emphasised at the union's annual conference in the summer which paralleled McGahey's campaign for the national Presidency, won by Gormley. The miners' pay claim that autumn exceeded the newly elected Conservative government's voluntary pay cap of 10 per cent. The government presented inflation, rising steadily since 1967, as a major economic problem and diagnosed wage growth as its largest approximate source. The wage-push narrative of inflation was compatible with another Conservative political narrative gaining traction, trade union 'power', which the 1972 and 1974 strikes superficially illustrated.[84] An incomes policy was implemented to control pay growth with statutory footing from November 1972. But the government's analysis of inflation was highly problematic. There were multi-varied triggers, most notably the upward movement in global commodity prices, especially oil,[85] and the wage-push explanation was largely bogus in the miners' case, with wages rising across the 1960s more slowly than both living costs and productivity gains.

A national ballot on the NCB's annual pay offer in 1970 produced a 55.5 per cent majority for strike action.[86] This fell short of the two-thirds majority necessary for a strike. There were clear territorial divisions on the issue. Big strike votes were recorded in South Wales, with 83 per cent, and in Scotland, with 70 per cent. There were smaller majorities in Yorkshire (60 per cent), Durham (53 per cent), Derbyshire and the North West (both 50 per cent). Significant majorities *against* strike action were cast in the Midlands, with 62 per cent, and Northumberland, with 60 per cent. These area differences preoccupied officials at the Department of Energy, the Ministry of Power's renamed successor. Output data for the 1969–70 financial year was grouped by area and voting outcome, to gauge the potential impact on energy endurance of unofficial strikes on the same pattern as 1969. The weekly output of Wales, Scotland, Yorkshire and Kent amounted to 1.25 million tons, 0.5 million of which supplied power stations. This loss could be tolerated for two weeks, but a longer strike would 'put us deeply in the mire', with effects that would last deep into the winter and possibly beyond. A two-month stoppage throughout the industry would lead to the exhaustion of all reserves.[87] Ministry of Technology officials took the same view, fearing that a strike lasting between six and eight weeks 'would virtually close down the economy'. For all the changes in the energy mix since the 1950s, three-quarters of electricity was still coal-generated.[88]

The result of the 1970 NUM ballot was announced on 23 October. Unofficial stoppages began in the strike-majority areas on 26 October. On 27 October the NCB increased its pay offer, acknowledging the result of the ballot, perhaps, and the supply dangers identified by government officials. The revised offer was accepted by the NUM national executive, subject to a further national ballot, but before this took place unofficial action became generalised in the pro-strike areas. Production stopped entirely in Scotland, Yorkshire and South Wales by 2 November. Department of Energy officials reckoned that this strike, if it lasted a month, would necessitate the cessation of coal exports and increased oil burn at power stations. The strike peaked on 13 November, a Friday, but the Yorkshire miners returned to work over the weekend that followed, and most pits in Scotland were back at work by 18 November. The NCB's improved terms were accepted by 77 per cent in a national ballot held on 17–20 November. The two-week strike had cost a total of 3 million tons, exceeding the 1969 losses by 0.5 million tons, equivalent to a single week's output across the entire NCB network.[89]

The 1969 and 1970 unofficial strikes provided evidence of division as well as unity across the UK coalfields. McGahey and other NUM officials, including many outside Scotland, saw the two-thirds hurdle as unachievable and therefore a threat to the union's integrity. At the 1971 NUM annual conference in Aberdeen a compromise rule change was agreed, slightly favouring those calling for a simple majority over those wanting to retain the two-thirds proviso: a new threshold for national strike action of 55 per cent. The NUM's next pay claim, in the autumn of 1971, proposed a 25 per cent rise to improve the miners' relative position. A counter-offer of 7.5 per cent from the NCB, close to the maximum permissible under the government's operating norm of 8 per cent, which had tightened since 1970,[90] was rejected by the NUM's executive. An overtime ban was established to reduce stocks at power stations, and a national ballot held on industrial action. This produced a strike vote of 58.8 per cent, bolstered by 75 per cent in Yorkshire and 65.5 per cent in South Wales. The majority in Scotland was 59.5 per cent, lower than 1970 but nevertheless indicative of substantial support for collective action in pursuit of improved security.[91] On 9 December the NUM national executive issued the statutory one month's notice for strike action to commence on 9 January 1972.[92] The government examined urgently the potential economic effects of the strike, but Robert Carr, Secretary of State for Employment, told Heath that his Department believed the miners would be unable to endure for longer than six weeks. The strikers would return to work defeated, with the pay policy intact. Sir Dennis Barnes, Permanent Secretary at Employment, told a meeting of inter-departmental and NCB officials that power stations were well-stocked. The worries expressed by Department of Energy officials in October 1970 were seemingly forgotten. Even in the case of a prolonged stoppage by the miners there was unlikely to be any interruption of electricity supply.[93]

These predictions foundered on the solidarity of UK labour. This was partly generated by the broader unease within the labour movement arising from the government's economic and industrial relations policies. Unemployment had been allowed to escalate from 2.7 per cent in 1970 to more than 4 per cent in 1971,[94] and the Industrial Relations Bill, circumscribing union freedoms, had passed through Parliament. The NUM's union allies in road transport and on the railways largely halted the movement of coal between collieries and power stations.[95] Some transfers of coal were sanctioned. Willie Clarke recalled in 2009 that the union committee at Seafield was responsible for governing distribution across large areas of eastern and north-eastern Scotland. Provision was made for deliveries to medical facilities and schools, and to elderly and other vulnerable domestic customers but, as elsewhere, conventional sales were blocked.[96] Electricity-generating boards responded with additional oil burn, including at Longannet, normally producing a third of the SSEB's power but nearing 50 per cent during the strike.[97] Oil was brought up the Firth of Forth to breach a large picket at the plant's road entrance. A bold but unsuccessful attempt to delay a Danish tanker was devised by Tam Coulter, NUM delegate at Manor Powis, using a fishing trawler.[98] The STUC General Council examined other ways of tightening the pressure. Alex Kitson used International Transport Workers' Federation contacts to reach the Danish seamen's union, seeking an embargo on oil transfers, and electricity industry union members in power stations were asked to refuse to work with supplies that had breached NUM pickets.[99] At Cockenzie union stewards responded to this call positively. The SSEB Edinburgh Works Committee, chaired by Ron Brown, later the Labour MP for Leith, advised members to join the miners on the picket lines and support their fight 'for decent wages and conditions'.[100]

At Longannet the picketing intensified four weeks into the strike. The Scottish miners, sensing victory, were emboldened by the symbolic triumph at the West Midlands Gas Board coke depot in Saltley on 10 February, closed by a mighty crowd of Birmingham engineering workers, numbering more than 10,000, which joined a picket of mainly Yorkshire miners marshalled by their area official, Arthur Scargill. NUM members from Derbyshire, South Wales and Scotland were present too.[101] At Longannet by 6 a.m. on 14 February there were more than 2,000 miners, brought from all parts of the Scottish coalfield on buses organised by the NUMSA. A police force of 400 officers kept the road open, just, pushing the pickets back and making numerous arrests. It was in this melee that McGahey sustained a broken leg. Thirteen pickets – 11 miners plus a socialist activist and a student supporter from Edinburgh – were charged with the serious public order offence of mobbing and rioting. This carried stiffer penalties than breach of the peace, the standard legal weapon against strikers. The mass picketing and punitive projected sanction recalled the disorder and class conflict of the inter-war lockouts. Indeed one legal scholar noted at the time that the mobbing and rioting charge had not been used in Scotland in an industrial dispute since 1921.[102] But the politics of the coalfields had changed since the 1920s, remade by the combined efforts of the Village Pit and New Mine generations. Outrage was expressed by NUMSA officials and political representatives at the severity of the charges. There is circumstantial evidence that the government's senior law officers at this point intervened, including Norman Wylie, the Lord Advocate, to lower the social heat. The 13 were released from custody. The Procurator Fiscal insisted on maintaining the charges to trial, held in Dunfermline in June 1972, but all 13 were cleared after what seemed an unusually short period of deliberation by the jury.[103]

The government was over-whelmed by the strike in 1972. Power cuts and a State of Emergency were introduced early in February, and a Court of Inquiry established under Lord Wilberforce, a High Court judge, to examine the miners' pay claim. The NUM's evidence to Wilberforce was presented by Daly, whose detailed analysis of the low pay and harsh working environment of the industry has been likened by Taylor to the miners' determined approach to the 1919 Sankey Commission.[104] Wilberforce recommended a two-stage increase to accommodate both the government's anti-inflation pay controls and the miners' claim for substantial improvement.[105] In direct and lengthy negotiations with Heath and the Cabinet that followed, the NUM executive secured the terms of the original claim in full.[106] The settlement was ratified by a national ballot and the strike ended on 28 February.[107] These gains were then largely swallowed up, however, by escalating inflation, driven by the abrupt increase in the price of oil from $2 a barrel in January 1972 to $11 a barrel in January 1974.[108] Wage consciousness among miners was strengthened in this economic environment. This was the conclusion of a thoughtful NCB Scottish Area research paper, referenced in Chapters 1 and 2, which developed the theme of industrial alienation arising from mechanisation and the concentration of employment in Cosmopolitan Collieries. It is no coincidence that this paper was written in the summer of 1973, 18 months after the successful 1972 strike with price inflation approaching an average annual rate of 10 per cent.

The balance in coal industry workplaces was shifting from 'intrinsic' to 'extrinsic' rewards, these terms consciously borrowed from the well-known *Affluent Worker* sociological study,[109] meaning that miners were increasingly motivated by wage claims to mitigate the threat that price inflation posed to their economic security.[110]

The rising oil price tilted the balance of energy politics further in the miners' favour. An overtime ban was called by the NUM on 25 October 1973. The government responded by declaring a State of Emergency on 13 November and then, as coal stocks were run down, an official three-day industrial week from 13 December, scheduled to run into the New Year. The NCB was largely usurped from its negotiating role by Heath and his ministers who were defending an ever-tighter anti-inflationary policy. Talks in December 1973 and January 1974, involving also the leadership of the TUC, produced no settlement. On 31 January and 1 February 1974 NUM members voted overwhelmingly for strike action from 9 February in support of the NUM's claim: £40 a week for underground workers and £45 for power-loaders. Parliament was dissolved and the 'Who Governs' election followed on 28 February. The Conservatives lost their Commons majority and Harold Wilson formed a minority Labour government which settled the miners' claim on terms explicitly designed to strengthen their real wages. In partnership with the government and the NCB the NUM was then involved in the *Plan For Coal*, a long-term strategy of investment. Renewed support for coal was rationalised by various actors in terms of the changing energy terrain exemplified by the oil price hike.[111]

The 1972 and 1974 strikes demonstrated the value to Scottish miners of pursuing enhanced security through collective action at UK level. The *Plan For Coal* seemed to confirm this. In Scotland 1975 was the biggest production year since 1968, and employment remained steady. A new NCB Scottish Area Director, James Cowan, noted that investment plans developed under the *Plan For Coal* included an addition to the Longannet complex, Castlebridge in Clackmannan, plus underground connections between Bogside and Kinneil, beneath the Forth, and between Seafield and Frances in East Fife.[112] Within this programme of renewed growth the NUM accepted the closure of Valleyfield in 1978, its workforce redeployed within West Fife.[113] The Labour government's involvement of union representatives in policy-planning and commitment to devolution, both examined in Chapter 5, provided a promising basis for longer-term economic security in the Scottish coalfields. But there was an important countervailing tendency which jeopardised cross-coalfield unity and threatened this progress, namely the introduction of area incentive pay schemes in 1977. This innovation had been identified by NCB officials during the 1973–4 dispute as a potential means of undermining union militancy and solidarity. A crucial advocate was Wilfred Miron, former Chairman of the NCB East Midlands Area. Support for area-based schemes was expressed in 1974 by NUM officials and members in Leicestershire, Nottinghamshire and South Derbyshire but met strong opposition from miners and their representatives in Scotland, South Wales, Kent and Yorkshire. This was an ideological question, transgressing the unity of miners across the coalfields, but geological differences were an important aggravating factor. Underground conditions were generally more complex in the 'peripheral areas', making it unlikely that power loaders in Scotland, for instance, could match the increases in output that might be obtained in Nottinghamshire. A national incentives framework was rejected in a ballot of NUM members by 62.7 per cent to 37.3 per cent in November 1974, but Gormley and his allies on the national executive authorised the introduction of area incentives in 1977, despite miners in Scotland, South Wales, Kent and Yorkshire reiterating the criticism that these schemes would prove unjust and divisive.[114] This circumvention of national opinion to satisfy sectional interest in the English Midlands was resented by miners in Scotland, and became an important trope in 1984, used to legitimise the area-by-area path to a national strike which by-passed opposition in Nottinghamshire, Leicestershire and elsewhere.[115]

Conclusion

Economic security in the coalfields was strengthened after 1967. The miners' moral economy was enforced vigorously by members of the New Mine generation. The closure of Michael Colliery, imposed on workers, union and community, was the last of its kind until the winter of 1982–3. Two structural factors weighed in the miners' favour: the NCB had attained substantial advances in mechanisation by 1967, and economies of scale had been achieved with the establishment of the Cosmopolitan Collieries. But the miners' mobilisation was nevertheless crucial in averting the significant erosion of employment envisaged in *Fuel Policy*, the Labour government's 1967 White Paper. Miners' union officials engaged closely with policy-makers at Scottish and UK level, supported by their allies in the wider labour movement, led by the STUC. Increased coal burn at the new suite of SSEB power stations in West Fife and East Lothian was secured. As the creation of jobs in new industries slowed, so did the rate of employment loss in coal. Pits closed only where the interests of mining localities were carefully protected. There was scope for accommodating miners from Blairhall at nearby collieries in West Fife, on protected wages, and so its closure was ratified in 1969. At Cardowan and Bedlay in Lanarkshire the moral economy indicators pointed the other way: the vast majority of men could not be assimilated by the NCB within daily travelling distance and so the NUM blocked these proposed closures. This mobilisation was encouraged by labour movement claims about Scotland's distinct national needs which buttressed moral economy arguments about the obligations of policy-makers to protect security in the coalfields. The Labour government was compelled in the late 1960s to respect and honour these claims. This involved high-level contacts between NUMSA officials and the Prime Minister as well as the Secretary of State for Scotland, who were both wary of transgressing public and labour movement opinion in Scotland, and bolstered security in mining areas accordingly.

Security was also pursued by Scottish miners at UK level, specifically through industrial action for improved wages from 1967 onwards. The New Mine generation in Scotland was instrumental in shifting the politics of the NUM to the left, and Scottish miners were prominent in the major unofficial strikes of 1969 and 1970. The crucial rule change, reducing the national ballot threshold for strike action from two-thirds majority to 55 per cent, was achieved at the NUM conference in Aberdeen in 1971. This enabled the miners to fight across Britain and win significant pay increases in 1972 and 1974. The effectiveness of the national strikes surprised the Conservative government, and there is a tendency in the literature to over-emphasise the agency and motives of a small cohort of union officials in moving the NUM to the left. But McGahey, Daly and others were elected to union office because they reflected the ambitions of the broad mass of miners for more trenchant resistance to deindustrialisation. The national strikes of 1972 and 1974 were prefaced by an upsurge of activism evident in 1969 and 1970. Cross-occupational working class and trade union solidarity was also significant in 1972 and 1974, itself reflective of more general labour movement concerns – across the UK as well as in Scotland – about deindustrialisation and unemployment. The Labour government established in 1974 was a harbinger of stronger security. There was partnership between unions and the state, and NCB production and employment were steadied in Scotland, reinforcing the apparent value to Scottish miners of UK-level action. But the trend to unity across the coalfields was tempered by the recrudescence of territorial loyalties, with the introduction of area incentive schemes. This privileging of local interests anticipated the difficulties that would be evident in the 1980s, as the NUM struggled to construct effective resistance to a new and much harsher attack on coalfield security from the Conservative government and its allies at the NCB. The prominence of these territorial divisions reinforced the Scottish labour movement's argument that deindustrialisation and economic security were phenomena with distinct national features in Scotland.

Notes

1. NRS, CB 260/14/1, NCB, Michael Colliery, Press Statement, 11.30 a.m., 21 November 1967.
2. Cheryl Peebles, 'Fifty years on community remembers Michael Colliery disaster which killed nine', *The Courier*, 11 September 2017.
3. NRS, CB 360/21/1, NCB, SNA, Michael Colliery: Brief Report on Future Prospects, 18 September 1967.
4. Cmnd. 3428, pp. 36, 71.
5. NRS, CB 360/13/14/5, Minute of Meeting on Michael Colliery, 6 December 1967.
6. GCUA, STUC, General Council, 6 September 1967.
7. MHC, L-15-9, clipping, 'Safety Is Our Resolution in 1968', *Scottish Miner*, January 1968.

8. NMMS, NUMSA, Special Delegate Conferences, 27 March and 14–16 June 1967; thanks to Ewan Gibbs for this reference.

9. NRS, CB 423/14/2, NCB Scottish Division, Fife/Alloa Area, Brief for senior officials of the NCB for the meeting to be held on 21 December 1966; Notes of the Special Consultative Committee held on 21 December 1966 to discuss the future of Wellesley Colliery; R. H. Tucker to G. Gillespie, Acting Chief Mining Engineer, 23 June 1967.

10. STUC, *70th Annual Report*, pp. 325–7.

11. TNA, POWE 52/113, DEA Working Group on Regional Implications of Fuel Policy and Natural Gas, Possible Reductions in Employment Opportunities through Colliery Closures, Note by the Secretary, A. J. Surrey, 30 May 1967.

12. TNA, POWE 52/113, DEA Working Group on Regional Implications of Fuel Policy and Natural Gas, 'Coal Closures', Scotland, 7 June 1967.

13. NRS, SEP 4/2332, Board of Trade Office for Scotland, 'Note on the Leven and Methil Employment Exchange Area and the Surrounding Travel to Work Area', 13 September 1967.

14. NRS, SEP 4/2334, Miss M. J. Alexander, Regional Development Division, 'The Closure of Michael Colliery and Industrial Development in the Leven Area of Fife', 19 October 1970.

15. TNA, POWE 52/202, Lawrence Daly to Anthony Crosland, 12 September 1967.

16. GCUA, STUC General Council, Report of a Meeting of Representatives of Mining Unions with the Economic Committee, 26 September 1967.

17. GCUA, STUC General Council, Report of a Meeting of Economic Committee with the Secretary of State for Scotland, 29 September 1967.

18. TNA, PREM 13/1610, Meeting to discuss colliery closures, Cabinet room, 28 September 1967; Meeting between Prime Minister and NUM, Scarborough, 29 September 1967.

19. NRS, SEP 4/2336, Note of a meeting held in the Map Room, St Andrew's House, 16 October 1967, between the Secretary of State and a deputation of officials from the mineworkers' unions.

20. GCUA, STUC General Council, Report of a Meeting with Prime Minister, 19 October 1967.

21. NRS, SEP 4/2333, Michael Colliery: meeting between Lord Hughes and representatives of Fife local authorities, NCB and Mineworkers' unions, Buckhaven, 14 November 1967.

22. TNA, POWE 52/202, John Fotheringham, Joint TU Committee, Michael Colliery, to the Prime Minister, 7 December, 1967, and NRS, CB 260/14/1, Fotheringham to Lord Robens, 23 November 1967.

23. NRS, CB 360/13/14/5, Minute of Meeting on Michael Colliery held in Lauriston House, 6 December 1967.
24. NRS, CB 260/14/1, R. W. Parker, Divisional Chairman, to Robens, 6 December 1967, and Parker to D. J. Skidmore, Director, NCB, SNA, 7 December 1967.
25. NRS, CB 360/13/14/5, Minute of Meeting on Michael Colliery held in Lauriston House, 6 December 1967.
26. GCUA, STUC General Council, Economic Committee, 5 December 1967.
27. NRS, SEP 4/2336, McGahey to Ross, 21 December 1967.
28. GCUA, STUC General Council, Report of meeting between Economic Committee members and Robens, 14 December 1967; Report of meeting between Economic Committee members and Minister of Power, 15 December 1967.
29. NRS, SEP 4/2334, D. S. Davidson, Town Clerk, Burgh of Buckhaven and Methil, to J. Cormack, Private Secretary, Scottish Office, 12 January 1968.
30. NRS, SEP 4/2334, Note of a meeting held in Dover House on Thursday 4 January 1968.
31. NRS, SEP 4/2336, Note for the record: Secretary of State's meeting with the Scottish Area NUM on Friday 19 January 1968.
32. GCUA, STUC, Economic Committee, Minutes, 28 October 1969.
33. NRS, CB 260/14/1, James Hamill, Scottish Development Department, to J. E. Pardoe, NCB, SNA, Deputy Director, 28 July 1970, and Pardoe reply, 5 August 1970.
34. NRS, CB 360/14/1, National Coal Board, Scottish North Area, Statement showing the deployment of manpower from Michael Colliery, 12 February 1968; and SEP 4/2334, Miss M. J. Alexander, Regional Development Division, 'The Closure of Michael Colliery and Industrial Development in the Leven Area of Fife', 19 October 1970.
35. Scott, 'Regional development and policy', p. 338.
36. TNA, EW 7/826, Secretary State Brief, Colliery Closures, November 1968.
37. Tomlinson, *Managing the Economy*, p. 186.
38. TNA, EW 7/826, Scottish Economic Planning Board, Analysis by areas of possible run-down in Colliery Manpower up to March 1971, February 1969.
39. NCB, *Report and Accounts for 1971–2*, House of Commons 445 (HMSO: London, 1972), p. 31
40. Oglethorpe, *Scottish Collieries*, p. 20.
41. TNA, EW 7/826, NCB Colliery Closure Programme, Scotland, March to December 1969, Note by Scottish Office, March 1969.

42. TNA, EW 7/826, Ministry of Power, Note on current colliery closure cases in Scotland, 30 September 1969.

43. TNA, COAL 89/103, William Summers, NCB Scottish North Area, to K. S. Jeffers, NCB Secretary, 17 April 1970; and Michael McGahey to R. D. Glass, NCB Scottish South Area, 27 November 1969.

44. GCUA, STUC General Council, Economic Committee, 25 November 1969.

45. TNA, COAL 89/103, K. S. Jefferies to W. V. Shepherd, NCB, 22 March 1971, and W. V. S. reply, 23 March 1971; NCB Scottish North Area, Minutes of Meeting with Trade Union representatives, Alloa, 28 June 1972.

46. NRS, CB 235/5/5, NCB Scottish North Area, Blairhall: estimated manpower, 4 February 1969; McLean to Rowell, 11 February 1969; NCB Scottish North Area, Closure – Blairhall Colliery, estimated vacancies at collieries within daily travelling distance; Place of Residence by Categories, Blairhall, 28 February 1969; Ages of Workmen Employed at Blairhall Colliery, 22 February 1969; Minutes of Meeting regarding closure of Blairhall Colliery, 11 March 1969.

47. NMMS, NUMSA, EC, 8 April 1969.

48. NRS, CB 235/5/5, McGahey to Rowell, 23 April 1969; Minutes of Meeting to discuss the position of the men affected by the Blairhall Closure, 29 April 1969; Blairhall Colliery Closure – redeployment proposals, 7 May 1969.

49. NMMS, NUMSA, EC, 12 May 1969.

50. Oglethorpe, *Scottish Collieries*, p. 28.

51. NRS, CB 346/5/5, Special Colliery Consultative Meeting at Lochhead Colliery, 19 August 1969.

52. NRS, CB 346/19/1, NCB Scottish North Area, Pre-Transfer Visit to Solsgirth and Dollar Mines – Saturday 28 February 1970.

53. Halliday, *Disappearing Scottish Colliery*, pp. 142–54.

54. NRS, CB 352/14/1, Chairman, NCB Scottish Division, to P. J. L. Holman, Board of Trade, 1 February 1967; J. A. Field, Secretary, NCB Scottish Division, to William Baxter MP, 16 February 1967.

55. Oglethorpe, *Scottish Collieries*, p. 245.

56. GCUA, STUC General Council, Meeting of Economic Committee with representatives of unions with membership engaged in the Fuel Industries, 26 November 1968.

57. TNA, POWE 52/137, Ministry of Power projections, Cockenzie Power Station Schedule, Supply of Coal, 1966–1980, no date.

58. TNA, POWE 52/271, D. J. Turner, Ministry of Power, Edinburgh, to C. G. Thorley, Ministry of Power, Coal Division, 24 January 1967.

59. Tomlinson, *Managing the Economy*, p. 222.
60. TNA, POWE 52/277, Brief for the Minister's meeting with the Scottish Trades Union Congress to discuss the current problems of the coal mining industry in Scotland 15 Dec 1967, Note by R. E. Dearing, 12 December 1967.
61. NRS, CB 51/1, Bilston Glen Colliery Consultative Committee, NCB Scottish South Area, Meeting held on 5 December 1969 to discuss pithead meeting at Bilston Glen Colliery on 14 October 1969.
62. TNA, POWE 63/645, Transcript, BBC TV *Panorama*, 20 October 1969, 8 p.m.
63. Keith Harper, 'Miners extend strike', *The Guardian*, 20 October 1969.
64. V. L. Allen, *The Militancy of British Miners* (The Moor Press: Shipley, 1981), pp. 162–220.
65. Taylor, *NUM and British Politics. Volume 2*, p. 27.
66. Allen, *Militancy of British Miners*, pp. 162–220.
67. Edward Heath, *The Course of My Life* (Hodder & Stoughton: London, 1998), p. 350.
68. Richard Norton-Taylor, 'Gormley and Buckton named as special branch informers', *The Guardian*, 24 October 2002, https://www.theguardian.com/politics/2002/oct/24/uk.past2, accessed 10 November 2017; Ray Buckton was General Secretary of ASLEF, the train drivers' union, from 1970 to 1987, and died in 1995.
69. Taylor, *NUM and British Politics. Volume 2*, p. 83.
70. Fred Lindop, 'The Dockers and the 1971 Industrial Relations Act, Part 1: Shop Stewards and Containerization', *Historical Studies in Industrial Relations*, 5 (1998), pp. 33–72.
71. TNA, PREM 15/2127, Heath to Gormley, 23 January 1974, and PREM 15/2128, Heath to Gormley, 7 February 1974.
72. John Campbell, *Edward Heath* (Pimlico: London, 1993), pp. 574–97.
73. Kevin Jefferys, *Finest and Darkest Hours. The Decisive Events in British Politics from Churchill to Blair* (Atlantic Books: London, 2002), pp. 168–78; Morgan, *People's Peace. British History*, pp. 346–9; Paul Routledge, *Scargill: the unauthorized biography* (HarperCollins: London, 1993), pp. 90–5.
74. Andy Beckett, *When The Lights Went Out. What Really Happened to Britain in the Seventies* (Faber and Faber: London, 2009), pp. 53–88, 125–50; Tony Hall, *King Coal: Miners, Coal and Britain's Industrial Future* (Penguin: Harmondsworth, 1981), pp. 166–96; Malcolm Pitt, *The World on our Backs: The Kent Miners and the 1972 Miners' Strike* (Lawrence and Wishart: London, 1979); Phillips, '1972 Miners' Strike: popular agency and industrial politics'.

75. TNA, PREM 15/986, Secret Service, 'Influence of Subversive Organisations in the NUM and the Miners' Strike', 24 February 1972.
76. Taylor, *NUM and British Politics. Volume 2*, pp. 36–7.
77. Gibbs, *Deindustrialisation and Industrial Communities*, pp. 92, 106.
78. 'The miners don't dare to call a ballot', *The Economist*, 28 November 1973, pp. 87–8.
79. TNA, POWE 52/249, Newstape, 14 October 1969.
80. Hamilton, Interview.
81. TNA, POWE 52/249, Newstape 16 October 1969; K. M. Tait, Ministry of Power, Coal Division, 21 October 1969; P. S. Ross, Coal Division, 22 October 1969.
82. Taylor, *NUM and British Politics. Volume 2*, pp. 32–3.
83. TNA, POWE 52/249, Newstape, 27 October 1969.
84. Paul Smith, 'Order in British Industrial Relations: From Donovan to Neoliberalism', *Historical Studies in Industrial Relations*, 31–2 (2011), pp. 115–54.
85. Tomlinson, *Managing the Economy*, pp. 189–90.
86. Taylor, *NUM and British Politics. Volume 2*, pp. 36–7.
87. TNA, FV 19/65, Department of Energy, Coal Implications of Limited Industrial Action, 28 October 1970; Le Cheminant, Note, 13 October 1970.
88. TNA, POWE 63/645, Ministry of Technology, Threatened Coal Strike, 13 October 1970.
89. TNA, FV 19/65, Department of Energy, Le Cheminant, Coal Effects of Unofficial Strikes, 7 November 1970; A. T. Gregory to Le Cheminant, 16 and 18 November 1970; handwritten note, 'Strikes', 19 November 1970.
90. Beckett, *When the Lights Went Out*, p. 63.
91. National Library of Scotland (NLS), Acc. 9805.234, Bill McLean to NUMSA Branch Secretaries and Delegates, 3 December 1971.
92. Taylor, *NUM and British Politics. Volume 2*, p. 53.
93. TNA, LAB 77/84, Carr to Heath, 6 January 1972, and Sir Dennis Barnes, Minute of a Meeting at the DTI, 13 January 1972.
94. Tomlinson, *Managing the Economy*, pp. 145–8.
95. Hall, *King Coal*, pp. 180–1.
96. Willie Clarke, Interview.
97. NRS, HH 56/97, Cabinet Official Emergencies Committee, 14 February 1972.
98. 'Tam and his merry men take to the sea', *Scottish Miner*, March 1972; NRS, HH 56/95, Scottish Development Department, Situation Reports, 24 and 27 January 1972.
99. GCUA, STUC General Council, 9 February 1972.

100. NRS, HH 56/96, Chief Constable, Lothian and Peebles Constabulary, to Chief Constable, Edinburgh City Police, 15 February 1972, with copy of SSEB Works pamphlet.
101. Beckett, *When the Lights Went Out*, pp. 71–84.
102. Peter Wallington, 'The case of the Longannet miners and the criminal liability of pickets', *Industrial Law Journal*, 1 (1972), pp. 219–28.
103. Phillips, *Industrial Politics of Devolution*, pp. 129–36.
104. Taylor, *NUM and British Politics, Volume 2*, pp. 69–70.
105. Ashworth, *British Coal Industry*, pp. 310–11.
106. TNA, PREM 15/986, Note for the Record: Discussion, 10 Downing Street, Saturday 19 February 1972.
107. NLS, Acc. 9805.235, Telegram from Gormley, Schofield and Daly, to McLean, 25 February 1972.
108. Beckett, *When the Lights Went Out*, p. 129.
109. Goldthorpe, Lockwood, Bechhofer and Platt, *Affluent Worker: Industrial Attitudes and Behaviour*.
110. TNA, COAL 101/488, Melanby Lee, A paper for consideration by the Scottish Area Monday and Friday Absence Committee, meeting 8 August 1973.
111 Taylor, *NUM and British Politics. Volume 2*, pp. 88–94, 113–17.
112. James R. Cowan, 'National Coal Board: Scottish Area in the 1980s', *Mining Technology* 62, No. 711 (January 1980), pp. 20–1.
113. Phillips, *Miners' Strike in Scotland*, p. 113.
114. Allen, *Militancy of British Miners*, pp. 272–80; Taylor, *NUM and British Politics. Volume 2*, pp. 122–33.
115. Steve McGrail with Vicky Patterson, *Cowie Miners, Polmaise Colliery and the 1984–85 Miners' Strike* (Scottish Labour History Society: Glasgow, 2017), p. 22.

CHAPTER 7

Campaigning for Jobs and Communities in the 1980s

Economic security in the coalfields was challenged and then substantially weakened in the 1980s. The miners' strike of 1984–5 was an unsuccessful attempt to reverse the change in economic direction driven in the UK by Margaret Thatcher's Conservative governments, first elected in 1979. Market-ness was heightened significantly, and the social-embeddedness of economic activity thinned.[1] This shift is often characterised as neoliberal, although the state retained a powerful role under Thatcher, not least in the realms of public order and military defence.[2] Moreover, government expenditure as proportion of Gross Domestic Product increased after 1979, partly because of greater social security payments arising from faster deindustrialisation and job elimination. These were unintended consequences of a new emphasis on limiting the money supply and reducing inflation. Diminished demand combined with a prolonged increase in the cost of borrowing to exert downward pressure on industry. The rising value of sterling, boosted by augmented government revenue from North Sea oil, contributed to the further elimination of industrial jobs as manufacturing exports became less competitive. The change in economic direction was signalled by lower government expenditure on trade and industry. There was less support for the regional stimuli that had sustained employment diversification in the coalfields since the 1950s.[3]

The emphasis by Thatcher's governments on society as a marketplace populated by individual actors competing for scarce resources was deeply ideological, with a lasting negative impact on the public realm, social solidarity and collective economic security.[4] Income tax cuts and VAT rises symbolised Thatcherism's regressive nature. Privatisation of publicly owned industries and utilities,[5] and the restoration of the 'right of management to manage', liberated from state regulation and the trade union 'veto', were other key elements.[6] Britain became a more unequal society, with the Gini coefficient for income distribution increasing by about 50 per cent in just 10 years, from 0.23 in 1977 to 0.34 in 1987. Similarly, wages' share of Gross Domestic Product was consistently above 58 per cent across the 1950s, 1960s and 1970s, but fell to 54 per cent in 1988, where it has more or less remained for three decades.[7]

The miners' strike of 1984–5 was conducted on this changing economic and political terrain. It was contentious and remains subject to competing interpretations. A complicated range of questions were involved: energy politics and prices; coal industry finances; policing, public order and civil liberties; and the strategy and tactics of the strikers.[8] These were all important facets of the strike but the really significant issues, generally overlooked, were trade union voice in policy-making and working class economic security. The danger of misdirection in discussing the strike was elegantly described by Raymond Williams in the late 1980s. 'In the cutting of coal there is noise and dust and unwanted stone', he wrote. 'Similarly', he continued, 'in the coal strike there are central issues of great importance to the society, but around them, and often obscuring them, are the noise and dust and stone of confused, short-term or malignant argument.'[9] Union voice and collective security, the hidden 'central issues', were core elements of the miners' moral economy that was assaulted by Thatcherism. 'This is a steak-pie strike', said John McCormack, NUM delegate at Polmaise Colliery in Stirlingshire, shown in Figure 7. Defeat for the strikers would result in the death of their industry.[10]

The destabilisation of economic security in the coalfields after 1979 is examined in the first part of this chapter. An important element of this pre-history of the strike, the anti-trade union turn in NCB management, had distinct features in Scotland. The second part analyses the industrial politics of the strike. The government's assault on the moral economy of the coalfields is detailed. The miners in Scotland were defending what they saw as viable collective

Figure 7 'This is a steak-pie strike': fighting to preserve the life of Polmaise, Stirlingshire, the last Villlage Pit. © NMMS

resources: their workplaces and jobs. The final part of the chapter examines community. In economic terms mining communities were diminished by the strike and its brutal aftermath, the accelerated closure of pits and further losses of manufacturing employment. But in ideological terms these communities became stronger, partly because the strike and subsequent deindustrialisation were such painful experiences. There were two important ingredients in the make-up of coalfield resilience: the role of women, which encouraged further progressive changes to gender relations that were already developing; and a renewed movement towards Home Rule prompted by the revived concern that deindustrialisation had a distinctly negative impact on Scotland that constitutional-political reforms might arrest.

Thatcherism and Coalfield Insecurity

The Conservative government elected in 1979 recast coal miners in discursive terms, from working class heroes deserving of special protection to greedy self-seekers whose opposition to pit closures was a social menace.[11] In March 1983 *The Sunday Times* claimed, just before an NUM ballot on industrial action, that since the 1972 and 1974 strikes miners had 'fought their way to the top of the wages tree and have acquired more security in their jobs than most of the rest of us'. The social costs of this alleged transformation were emphasised. 'Every man, woman and child in Britain contributes £10 a year in subsidy to the industry', the editorial asserted. 'If the miners see now to use their power to gouge even more from the public purse, they will lose public support, and without that they will lose their fight'.[12] The ballot resulted in an anti-strike majority across England, Wales and Scotland of 61 to 39 per cent.[13] This clipping was collected in the personal papers of Sir Ian MacGregor, the Scots-American businessman who was appointed chairman of the NCB in 1983.[14] McGregor moved to the NCB from the British Steel Corporation where employment had been reduced from 166,000 to 71,000 since a lengthy national strike in 1980.[15] He was regarded widely as an 'American butcher of British industry' and championed Thatcherite managerial sovereignty. 'I don't think the unions should manage a business', he told reporters. Although MacGregor was paid the same salary as his predecessor, Norman Siddall, starting at £59,325, he was a very expensive public asset. The government had to pay Lazard Freres bank in New York £1.5 million to compensate for the continued loss of his services.[16]

The Sunday Times editorial of 1983 echoed the government's 'rhetorical framing' of coal mining and industrial relations. This encompassed three linked narratives. First, miners were privileged and their leaders were unrealistic in defending employment at pits that in economic terms were inefficient and even redundant. Second, the government was protecting a national interest against the sectional aspirations of striking workers.[17] Third, striking workers were illegitimately exploiting trade union power. For recent evidence of this Thatcherites pointed to the 1972 and 1974 miners' strikes,[18] and the 1978–9 'Winter of Discontent', when the Labour government's anti-inflationary incomes policy was breached by disputes involving manual workers in public services and private sector manufacturing.[19] This latter narrative was developed in 'real time' in the early months of 1979 and contributed that May to Thatcher's first General Election victory, although in Scotland support for Labour solidified from a 36.3 per cent vote share in October 1974 to 41.5 per cent. The 'union power' narrative was recurrently reiterated to rationalise legislative changes which narrowed the scope for effective industrial action. Union participation in policy-making was likewise excoriated and marginalised.[20]

Security in mining communities was challenged by the Coal Industry Act of 1980, requiring the NCB to become self-financing by 1984. The doubling of unemployment between 1979 and 1982 to three million highlighted the acceleration of deindustrialisation, which lowered demand for coal-fired electricity and materials, notably steel, that were produced in energy-intensive conditions.[21] Adjusting supply to fit falling demand meant closing pits where production was most expensive. The threat to jobs was especially felt in Scotland, Northumberland, Durham, South Wales, parts of Yorkshire, and Kent. Comparatively difficult geological conditions in these areas elevated production costs and reduced support in the 1970s for incentive payment schemes. At the Scottish Miners' Gala in Edinburgh in June 1980, and the NUMSA Conference that followed at Rothesay, McGahey promised to resist closures through a 'mass campaign in the coalfield'.[22] In that autumn's annual pay negotiations the NCB admitted that large-scale closures were being contemplated. Area divisions were evident in a ballot on the NCB's offer. Fifty-six per cent favoured acceptance, but in Scotland 73 per cent were against, as were majorities in South Wales, Yorkshire and Kent.[23] In February 1981 miners in these areas joined an unofficial strike against NCB plans to reduce production by 10 per cent. Endangered pits included Cardowan plus Highhouse and Sorn in Ayrshire.[24]

The 1981 strike coincided with a major industrial crisis in Scotland, the closure of the Linwood car plant with 4,800 job losses. When the STUC General Council met Linwood union officials and stewards, George Bolton, NUMSA's Vice President, argued for 'concerted trade union action' to resist the government's deflationary economic policy which he said was the chief threat to employment in car production as well as coal mining. Linwood's closure, he warned, would further reduce demand for Scottish steel and coking coal.[25] Still heavily reliant on NCB coal, the government relaxed cash limits and the unofficial strike ended,[26] but the retreat was temporary: coal was stockpiled and the growth of nuclear-, oil- and gas-generated electricity was accelerated.[27] The government then appointed the Monopolies and Mergers Commission (MMC) to investigate NCB finances. The Commission scrutinised production performance of each coalfield area and every colliery. This widened serious divisions already evident between the NCB and the NUM, which boycotted the industry's National Consultative Council from November 1982 to March 1983.[28] Another telling sign was a sudden increase in the industry's serious reportable injury rate. This doubled from 0.87 per 100,000 man shifts in 1979–80 to 1.69 in 1981–2 and 1.82 in 1983–4, above even the annual average of 1.59 experienced from 1930–3, under private ownership and at the bottom of the depression. Mercifully, the rate of fatal accidents remained low by historic standards, although also rose from 0.06 per 100,000 man shifts in 1979–80 to 0.09 in 1982–3.[29]

A new NCB Area Director in Scotland, Albert Wheeler, took up his post in 1980–1 and told miners they could only enjoy security by producing coal at competitive prices. In pursuit of this objective

Wheeler transgressed established industrial relations procedures.[30] This new approach in Scotland preceded MacGregor's appointment as NCB chairman by more than two years. Wheeler's micromanagement style emphasised pit-level performance. Quarterly accountability meetings were held with pit managers who had to explain various economic indicators: saleable output, productivity, spending on materials and electricity, and manpower. In June 1981 the manager of Comrie, T. Clark, was asked why expenditure on incentive payments to miners had crept up in the previous quarter when overall output had slightly declined.[31] Wheeler was abrasive with union representatives who he targeted as obstacles to the achievement of more ambitious production targets. In Midlothian Wheeler said to the NUM delegate at Monktonhall, David Hamilton, 'I'm going to break you', meaning the union, and its share of workplace authority.[32]

Bedlay was closed by agreement in the winter of 1981–2, with transfers to Cardowan, Polkemmet and the Longannet complex.[33] The pioneering anti-union turn within NCB management in Scotland was then experienced with full force, at Kinneil in West Lothian in December 1982. This was the first closure in Scotland against workforce, community and union opposition since Michael in 1967. Kinneil's miners and union representatives resisted in moral economy terms, pointing to the colliery's large reserves of 160 million tonnes. McGahey criticised the proposed voluntary redundancies: 'We will not trade jobs for money', he told reporters.[34] NUMSA and SCEBTA officials invoked industry procedures and appealed against the Scottish Area decision at NCB headquarters in London,[35] but an attempted strike across Scotland's coalfields in defence of Kinneil gathered limited support. Miners in the Lothians and West Fife reportedly crossed picket lines to work normally.[36] The difficulty of mustering effective collective resistance to individual closures was further illustrated after Wheeler announced in May 1983 that production would end at Cardowan, where 1,400 were employed.[37] This case attained a high political profile given the proximity of the coming General Election in June. Nigel Lawson, Secretary of State for Energy, made reference to the colliery in a campaigning speech. He stated that it was the 'economics of the madhouse' to produce coal at financial loss. 'Generous' redundancy terms were available, as were transfers to other NCB pits.[38] These were disingenuous claims. The redundancy offer transgressed the coalfield moral economy on two related grounds. First, it was made to individual workers, over the heads of union representatives and outwith established procedure. Second, it commodified jobs on an individualised basis that were regarded by many miners as the collective property of their community.[39]

The proposed transfers were also contentious. Cardowan's SCEBTA delegate was Nicky Wilson, a member of the Cosmopolitan Colliery generation. Interviewed in 2009 he remembered the anger of other younger men. The offered redeployment was mainly to the Longannet complex. For Cardowan miners this was a distance from home to work of between 30 and 40 miles but the probable alternative was unemployment, given the scarcity of local job opportunities.[40] There were two other problems. First, the transfers were resisted at 'receiving' collieries because Wheeler and his officials ignored established consultation procedures.[41] Second, the NUM regarded those miners who left Cardowan before its closure was confirmed as 'renegades'.[42] The transfers duly forced a lengthy lockout at Polmaise and shorter stoppages at Bogside, Frances and Polkemmet. Wheeler confirmed the closure of Cardowan in late August. The remaining 750 employees voted by a majority of three to two against industrial action in further defence of the colliery.[43] In discussion with other NUMSA officials McGahey saw this defeat in terms of management 'duplicity' and the damaging impact on morale of mass unemployment in industrial communities.[44]

The MMC report was published after the Conservative government's re-election in June 1983. It recommended a 10 per cent cut in capacity by closing pits with the highest losses per tonne.[45] The NUM claimed that there was a secret 'hit list' of 75 collieries scheduled to close with the loss over three years of 64,000 of the industry's 200,000 jobs. Documents released in 2014 confirmed that Thatcher discussed such a list on 15 September 1983 with Lawson, who was now Chancellor of the Exchequer, plus Peter Walker, Secretary of State for Energy, and Norman Tebbit, Secretary of State for Employment. But in 1983 the government and NCB both obfuscated, conceding only that perhaps 20 pits might be lost.[46] Ewan

Gibbs has analysed the Department of Energy's detailed plans from this period. Officials favoured a rapid run-down to meet the government's intended withdrawal of subsidy from the industry, and concentrate production on those collieries which yielded financial profit and might thereby serve as attractive future resources for privatisation.[47] The NCB finances that formed the basis for these policy discussions and the substance of the MCC report were questioned by Andrew Glyn and several other economists who challenged government claims that production costs made coal an uncompetitive source of energy. Glyn observed that the supposed costs of current production included legacy charges: compensation to neighbours arising from subsidence or to ex-miners of working age who had left the industry because of accident or illness. The NCB was also paying 6.3 per cent interest on capital loans from the government, double the average rate for nationalised industries, and another burden exaggerating the overall bill for coal.[48]

The 'high cost' narrative was strong enough by 1983 to withstand such criticism. The MMC report compounded the new insecurity of the coalfields. There were losses at all collieries in Scotland although most of these had only emerged recently. Comrie and Monktonhall were among those reporting significant profits in 1979–80. In 1981–2 losses at the Cosmopolitan Collieries were generally low and barely registered at the Longannet complex.[49] While the MMC data was hardly compelling as evidence of a long history of inefficiency in Scotland, Wheeler and NCB Area management nevertheless intensified the pressure on individual collieries. The resulting transformation of workplace relations can be traced in the NCB's pit-level consultative committee records. Polkemmet in West Lothian is an illuminating example. In 1977 management and worker representatives discussed various questions in an open and constructive manner. Management complaints about instances of vandalism were taken seriously by the union delegate, who signed a joint letter to workers about the damage to production arising from disabled equipment. Management likewise accepted worker complaints about the poor quality of safety clothing – 'the gloves were pure rubbish' – and displayed an ambition to improve the environment as well as the performance of the colliery. Real tensions only emerged after 1980. Workforce representatives were concerned about the unavailability of spare parts for machinery and a ban on recruitment. Was the pit being run down, they asked, to lengthen the lives of Bedlay and Cardowan?[50] In the summer of 1982 Wheeler installed a new general manager at the pit, William Kennedy, who was highly confrontational. The colliery was losing money, he told his first consultative committee, and worker performance had to improve. He wanted a daily output of 1,600–1,800 tonnes but was only obtaining 1,500 tonnes in December, and early in 1983 he threatened closure of selected faces which were 'gobbling up manpower with very little result'. Kennedy left in June 1983 to manage Monktonhall. His Polkemmet successor, D. R. Steele, demanded even-greater effort to meet a notional daily target now raised to 2,000 tonnes.[51]

Contestation at Polkemmet was part of a broader pattern. At Bilston Glen a new manager was also appointed in 1982, T. Clarke, late of Comrie, who told worker representatives that the colliery was falling 'deeper into the mire'. He blamed this on workforce 'apathy'. Wheeler contributed directly to rising tension at Bilston Glen. Attending a colliery consultative committee later that summer, he claimed there were no geological or technical explanations for an alleged shortfall in production.[52] At Seafield antipathy was also heightened after the arrival of a new manager in May 1983, George Caldow, who hectored and lectured his way through numerous consultative committee meetings in the summer, autumn and winter that followed. He alleged that workers were indifferent to the colliery's competitive position, and threatened dismissal of those who questioned his authority.[53] Antagonism was even more overt at Monktonhall where Kennedy, having moved from Polkemmet, literally tore up the document outlining various joint agreements in the presence of David Hamilton, NUM delegate.[54] Kennedy claimed in August 1983 that output could not be improved because of poor worker performance, with a 'lack of urgency, bad workmanship, supervision and attitudes'.[55] Development work was suspended; 63 men were accused of withholding effort and threatened with dismissal; and 300 voluntary redundancies were sought without consulting union representatives. In September 150 men arrived a few minutes late after attending a pit-head meeting to examine these problems. They were sent home, losing the shift's pay. This was a lockout, which the union responded to locally by declaring a strike which lasted until the first week of November.[56] When the Monk-tonhall miners returned to work Kennedy made further inroads into existing agreements by insisting that Hamilton undertake a full-time workload underground. There was no scope as before for union activity in normal hours.[57]

Escalating industrial warfare was therefore a strong characteristic of the Scottish coalfields *before* the great strike against pit closures began on 12 March 1984. This is an important qualifier to the standard Anglo-centric observation that the 'national' strike 'began' when the NCB announced the closure of Cortonwood Colliery in Yorkshire.[58] In January 1984 Wheeler announced his intention to close Polmaise, Scotland's last Village Pit.[59] With an NUM overtime ban in place from November 1983 onwards, in furtherance of a national pay claim, several pits were vulnerable to weekend flooding. Wheeler was insisting that management staff would not perform safety duties in the absence of NUM members. The manager at Barony in Ayrshire, T. Gaw, told union officials that operating this machinery was not management's job.[60] Bogside experienced significant damage in February and the NCB declared that it would also be closed.[61] At Seafield Caldow unilaterally suspended the consultative committee in January 1984 and initiated a lockout after sending home 30 men who reported one minute late.[62] At Polkemmet Steele said the men's 'attitudes' needed to change. The workers' representative, Neilson, replied that members were gravely demoralised by over-bearing management and worries about future security.[63] At this point, in the first week of March, a majority of Scotland's miners were locked out, on strike or otherwise engaged in dispute with local management. All territorial areas within Scotland were affected. Margaret Thatcher's characterisation of the strike, 'Mr Scargill's Insurrection',[64] referring to the NUM President elected in 1982, is a clear but instructive misdirection. Like Heath before her, Thatcher was unable to see the social movement dimensions of industrial action. The strike came 'from below', to defend union voice and economic security which were threatened by Wheelerism as well as Thatcherism.[65]

The strike was also a generational struggle. In Figure 8 men in their twenties and thirties are prominent among those marching towards Holyrood Park and the Scottish Miners' Gala in 1984.

Figure 8 A movement of youth as well as class: Gala Day procession of strikers and supporters, Edinburgh, May 1984. © NMMS

The average age of NCB employees had gradually increased after nationalisation: 40.5 years in 1957, 42.1 in 1965 and 44.2 in 1973–4, when it peaked. The trend then reversed, markedly, to 40.6 in 1978–9 and 38.7 in 1982–3.[66] Almost one miner in five was 24 years old or younger in March 1984.[67] This reflected a concerted effort by the NCB to reduce manpower to align production with demand, according to Ned Smith, its Director of Industrial Relations. This effort was concentrated on older miners, and relatively few over the age of 50 were still employed by 1984. The younger age profile of the workforce was a crucial factor, Smith believed, in the strikers' subsequent endurance.[68] A notional average age miner in 1984 of 38 had been born in 1946, at the point of nationalisation. His working life commenced in 1961 or 1962, after coal industry employment had peaked. Early experiences in Scotland probably included the closure of his local pit and negotiated transfer to a Cosmopolitan Colliery. At the end of the 1970s, aged 33 or 34, he anticipated another 20 years of employment. In moral economy terms the Village Pit had been relinquished because the Cosmopolitan Colliery guaranteed long-term security. Generational factors were also evident in the fractious workplace struggles of 1983–4. Full-time union officials of the New Mine generation were keenly aware of the dangers posed by the Thatcher government's economic strategy. Bolton's comments on the Linwood crisis at the STUC General Council in February 1981 demonstrate this. Yet they were slow to spot Wheelerism's threat to workplace trade unionism. Willie Clarke, an NUM branch official at Seafield, remembers that he and other workplace representatives, men born in the 1940s, had to persuade both Bolton and McGahey that there was a serious industrial relations emergency unfolding in 1983. Members of the Cosmopolitan Colliery generation compelled their elders to protect pits and jobs through strike action in 1984. This resembled the manner in which members of the New Mine generation had pushed Village Pit generation officials three decades earlier to accept the urgency of stronger resistance to closures.[69]

The Industrial Politics of the Strike

The national strike began on Monday, 12 March 1984. Its legality in Scotland was established in the High Court in Edinburgh in

September 1984. The NUMSA had carefully constructed the action within its rules, members being consulted at pit-head meetings ahead of an executive meeting and delegate conference in February which authorised the action.[70] The strike was broadly solid until November 1984, when attrition effects plus major financial incentives from the NCB – including tax-free bonuses – softened endurance, particularly in Ayrshire. Before this the only significant breach in the strike in Scotland was at Bilston Glen, where a small minority were working from June.[71]

The national strike across England, Wales and Scotland was weakened by internal NUM divisions. The union's most serious problem was that all but 3,000 of 40,000 miners in Nottinghamshire worked continuously throughout the strike. Working miners in Nottinghamshire are usually depicted as acting in economically rational terms. Their pits were relatively good producers with strong pre-1984 performance records. These miners worked because they perceived no threat to security on economic grounds.[72] This established narrative has been queried, with recent research emphasising pit-level patchiness in overall performance in Nottinghamshire, and the incidence of closures in the 1970s and early 1980s. Its 'peculiar history' has also been stressed, including the impact of migration from Durham and Scotland in the 1960s and 1970s. 'Where did they fight for my job?', asked these migrants in 1984.[73] An area ballot in Nottinghamshire rejected a strike by an approximate factor of three to one. NUM area and pit-level representatives who supported the strike were ousted, including Jimmy Hood, the Lanarkshire migrant at Ollerton.[74] Hood and the Nottinghamshire minority maintained a defiant strike infrastructure, including women's support groups. Three coachloads of strikers and supporters visited the Scottish Gala in May 1984, staying with families of ex-Cardowan workers.[75]

The majority who had worked in Nottinghamshire left the NUM after the strike, forming a rival organisation, the Union of Democratic Mineworkers (UDM) in the summer of 1985. The history of the strike in Nottinghamshire and its aftermath is contested, with competing interpretations,[76] and has contributed to individual and communal difficulties in coming to terms with deindustrialisation. Some Nottinghamshire miners, including strikers, feel excluded from collective memories of the industry.[77] In Yorkshire especially anti-UDM feeling remains intense, reflected in the construction of a narrative claiming that the NUM's rival was active *during* the strike. This falsified history was displayed on a pair of banners carried at a rally in Knottingley marking the closure of Kellingley Colliery in December 2015, Britain's last site of deep coal mining.[78] It was recently articulated also by David Donovan, the South Wales NUM pit delegate whose links with lesbian and gay supporters of the strike in London were depicted in the 2014 feature film *Pride*.[79]

Despite the emergence of contested historical interpretations, there was a strong positive correlation in Nottinghamshire between profitable pre-strike performance and low strike commitment. Examination of NCB data in the 1983 MMC report shows that nine of North Nottinghamshire's 14 pits were in financial surplus in 1981–2, and in South Nottinghamshire there was only one serious 'loser', Babbington. In North Nottinghamshire OMS was 3.17 tonnes and in South Nottinghamshire it was 2.68 tonnes. This exceeded the industry OMS average of 2.4 tonnes. In Scotland average OMS was 2.0 tonnes.[80] Lower average OMS and higher financial losses in Scotland may therefore suggest confirmation of the same performance-strike propensity correlation as Nottinghamshire: Scottish miners were defending 'inefficient' jobs by striking and Nottinghamshire miners were defending 'efficient' jobs by working. But pit-level differences in Scotland offer an alternative interpretation. Pre-strike performance in Scotland was strongest at the Longannet trio of Bogside, Castlehill and Solsgirth, where the OMS of 3.19 tonnes exceeded the North Nottinghamshire average. Strike endurance at these pits was as strong as anywhere else in Scotland from March 1984 until March 1985. Miners within the Longannet complex saw their collieries as 'resources of hope', to paraphrase Raymond Williams: prime assets that had to be defended against the dubious economics of Wheelerism and Thatcherism.[81] Strike endurance was also impressive until February 1985 at Seafield, another Cosmopolitan Colliery with a strong pre-1984 production record.[82]

The strategy pursued by miners in defence of these assets and their collective security remains contentious. In separate reviews of my 2012 book on the strike, Bob Eadie, son of Alex, and Quentin Outram each identified three issues which they saw as compromising the NUM's action. First, there was no national ballot beforehand, weakening its legitimacy. Second, picketing of major economic units like the Ravenscraig steel mill in Motherwell threatened the jobs of other workers, breaching labour movement solidarity and forfeiting support. Third, the leadership was inflexible in its negotiations with the NCB. Eadie argued that an agreement on revised pit closure procedures could have been secured if McGahey rather than Scargill had been NUM President.[83] Peter Ackers has made similar observations. Without a national ballot the NUM leadership deployed the union's federal structure, enabling Scotland, Yorkshire and other constituents to declare area strikes in March 1984. These areas followed McGahey's 'domino' strategy, seeking to persuade or compel others to join. This led to conflict at pits in Nottinghamshire, picketed by strikers from other areas, including Scotland. Similar tensions arose later in Scotland, where pickets at Bilston Glen included strikers from Northumberland on occasion. Ackers argues that the disorder associated with this picketing contributed to the NUM's political isolation, inhibiting the construction of a larger anti-Conservative alliance in defence of miners' jobs. The economic and social damage of coalfield deindustrialisation might have been deferred, he emphasises, if the NUM had retreated by accepting some closures.[84]

The charge that miners isolated themselves is exaggerated. Diminished solidarity at peak-level between the NUM, the TUC and other unions was accompanied by the strong bonds within the labour movement which miners formed at the level of workplace and community. These links were often 'trans-local', connecting South Wales miners with trade unionists in London, for example. They were also reciprocal. Miners received financial and moral support from people in communities outside the coalfields whose activism was bolstered by the political inspiration which they received from the strikers.[85] In Scotland the trade union movement helped to establish support groups in major urban and industrial centres. Valuable connections were formed between Ayrshire and Glasgow, and between Fife and Dundee.[86] Miners also made common cause with black and ethnic minority activists as well as gay and lesbian rights campaigners.[87]

Criticisms of NUM strategy are further qualified by new evidence detailing the character and extent of the government's determination to impose a heavy defeat on the strike and trade union influence in public policy-making. This is contained in papers released in 2014 that Ackers, Eadie and Outram did not have sight of when going to print, which has since been analysed in detail.[88] The government was seeking to defeat the NUM and remove meaningful union voice from the coal industry with important 'demonstration effects' for workers and unions in other sectors. Ralph Miliband's 'class struggle from above' thesis is highly apposite.[89] In this combat the government was supported by a range of social and business elites, including those in the largely anti-trade union print and broadcast media.[90] Business leaders, especially in industry, were sometimes frustrated by Thatcher's economic management but as a body they welcomed the 'creation of a climate where being the boss counted for something', as Adeney and Lloyd put it in 1986.[91] The war against the miners should therefore be understood as a key 'stepping stone' in the government's broader campaign to enfeeble unions, bolster employers, and heighten market-ness in the economy. The government pursued this strategy carefully by isolating enemies in the labour movement and confronting them incrementally.[92] Detailed plans were involved, as mounting documentary evidence confirms. Lord Younger, Secretary of State for Scotland in 1984–5, wrote to Thatcher in November 2002, contrasting the determined effort that their Cabinet had undertaken in 1984 with the then Labour government's allegedly lax approach to a national strike by the Fire Brigades Union.[93]

The combative character of government strategy is illustrated by its willingness to absorb the extremely high financial costs of the strike. Estimates generally coalesce around the figure of £6 billion – about £18 billion in 2018 values – in lost production and tax revenues, replacement coal stocks and additional oil burn charges, along with reduced economic activity plus the significant expense of policing strikers and their communities. The £6 billion figure outweighs the NCB's projected financial losses for producing coal in the financial year of 1984–5, some £100 million, by a factor of *60 to 1*. This was a 'worthwhile investment', according to Lawson,[94] but a colossal premium only explicable with reference to the scale of the government's hostility to the miners and their trade union. In David Peace's novel *GB84* a group of South Yorkshire strikers discuss this very point in July 1984:

> They go on about uneconomic pits and then they spend sixty-five million quid a week on police, compensation costs to industry, alternative power and lost income tax. Sixty-five million fucking quid. Every week. That's nigh on ten million fucking quid a day. It's been over a hundred days. Hundred days at ten million quid a day. Never spent a bloody penny round here before. Think about it, said Billy. Ten million quid a day for a hundred days. Fucking hell, she must really hate us. Really fucking hate us.[95]

The scale and character of the government's commitment surely dilutes the argument that the NUM lost the strike because of failings in its own strategy. A national ballot would not have changed the outcome. The likeliest result, based on national ballots in 1982 and 1983, is that the 55 per cent strike threshold would not have been reached. In this situation miners already on strike would probably still have remained out for a lengthy period. Their isolated action would have ended amid internal union bitterness, accompanied by government and NCB demands for revised procedures for handling closures, with diminished union voice. The alternative scenario of the ballot reaching the 55 per cent threshold would have made the situation more delicate from the government's perspective. With a larger portion of Nottinghamshire's miners on strike coal reserves would have fallen more rapidly. In such case, however, the government would have spent even more money to make good the fuel 'gap', increasing coal imports and escalating oil burn in power stations. Miners in Nottinghamshire, fearing redundancy in the face of this counter-attack, would have been drawn back to work.

These many 'would haves' and 'would not haves' underline the hazards of counter-factualism. What is clear, however, is that the government's war against the miners narrowed the scope for effective alternative action by the NUM, especially its capacity to reach a negotiated settlement with meaningful union voice intact. From March to December 1984 Thatcher chaired the government's

Cabinet Ministerial Group on Coal. Minutes from these twice-weekly meetings demonstrate the serial manner in which the government destabilised negotiations between the NCB and the NUM. Thatcher told the group in May 1984 that an agreement would only be permissible if the NUM accepted that pits would be closed on economic grounds, and the NCB obtained ultimate authority to determine where such grounds existed. The Prime Minister reiterated this position ahead of talks in July 1984: 'it was important that the terms [of any resolution] should be seen to permit the closures sought by the NCB before the strike'. When negotiations restarted in September she returned to the same theme: the 'most important requirement would be an agreement that would not in any way fetter the NCB in arranging the closure, as and when necessary, of uneconomic pits'.[96]

Thatcher was seeking to dismantle the joint-regulatory mechanisms that had protected economic security in the coalfields since nationalisation. The moral economy of the coalfields was being dismantled. Strategic retreat by the NUM in these circumstances was extremely difficult. An agreement providing the NCB with unilateral powers to determine future closures could not be accepted by the strikers. McGahey understood this. The July talks, for example, were derailed by the NCB's insistence that pits would close when reserves could no longer be 'beneficially developed'. McGahey recognised that 'beneficially' had an 'economic connotation': 'if a colliery was not beneficial in terms of profits, it was not economically viable', so the NCB would close it. The NUM would not tolerate this, he told comrades on the NUMSA's Strike Committee, and neither could he, 'rejecting any concept of uneconomic closures, this being the basic, fundamental and central question of the whole dispute'.[97] This is worth reiterating: the absence of a negotiated settlement was not the result of the NUM's inflexibility but the government's disabling veto of any type of agreement that retained meaningful union voice.

The government's strategy and resolve are revealed elsewhere in the minutes of the Cabinet Ministerial Group on Coal. Eadie, Outram and Ackers have depicted the miners' picketing of Ravenscraig in April and May 1984 as counter-productive because it jeopardised support for the strike among steel and transport workers and other potential allies. This action was undeniably a source of difficulty within the labour movement, but it was successful in placing substantial pressure on the government. Norman Tebbit, who had become Secretary of State for Trade and Industry in October 1983, viewed coal shortages at Ravenscraig as the government's outstanding economic difficulty at the end of April. Steel production was threatened, endangering supply to a range of industrial customers.[98] The NUM's squeeze was tightened when 3,000-plus NUM pickets tried to block BSC's supply of coal by road to Ravenscraig from the Clyde terminal at Hunterston. Government officials believed by 8 May that production at Ravenscraig would cease within three days.[99] A crucial Prime Ministerial intervention followed that very day in a meeting of the Cabinet Ministerial Group on Coal. Thatcher asked George Younger, Secretary of State for Scotland, why Scottish chief constables had not replicated the practice in England of stopping pickets from reaching their targets. Younger was instructed to ask Scottish chief constables this specific question.[100] On 10 May officers of Strathclyde Police arrested 290 miners from West Fife, Clackmannan and Stirlingshire on the A80 at Stepps.[101] The miners spent the day in police stations in and around Glasgow, not knowing they had been apprehended after a direct intervention by the Prime Minister.[102] The NUM, protecting its members from further legal entanglements and penalties, lifted the siege at Ravenscraig where supply was restored and production preserved.[103]

Ravenscraig and Hunterston witnessed sporadic disorder as miners and their supporters struggled with police officers. Hundreds of Scottish miners were also involved in the major confrontation in June at Orgreave, the BSC coke works in South Yorkshire, when mounted and heavily armed police officers attacked pickets. This episode was notorious for the physical violence inflicted on striking miners by the state.[104] But the malevolence ran wider. South Yorkshire Police officers fabricated evidence to substantiate the serious criminal charge of riot against 55 miners that collapsed in court in a trial heard in 1985. Involving conspiracy to construct false evidence, systematic perjury and actions designed to obstruct justice, this malpractice foreshadowed the same constabulary's behaviour during the 1989 Hillsborough Stadium outrage.[105]

From June 1984 onwards picketing in the Scottish coalfields was increasingly focused on collieries, notably Bilston Glen, as miners started returning to work. Strikers also acted occasionally at the homes of working miners. A van belonging to Jim Pearson, the first miner to return to work in Fife, at Longannet, was repeatedly vandalised.[106] The relative absence of assaults on NCB property was a notable contrast with the lockouts of 1921 and 1926, when miners imposed costs on the owners by disabling mine equipment and machinery. There were no events in Scotland comparable to the remarkable insurrection in Easington, County Durham, in August 1984 where picketing miners, angered by a combined NCB-police operation to bring a single strike-breaker into the colliery, invaded the property and caused significant material damage.[107] Nor were there the protracted scenes of social disturbance seen in Yorkshire villages, provoked by police officers principally from London and Manchester who entered pubs and shops, ostensibly searching for allegedly law-breaking pickets, but arguably seeking to intimidate strikers and their local supporters, who fought back.[108] In Scotland the strikers broadly adhered to the moral economy position that the collieries belonged to the community. It would have been surprising if strikers had attacked assets which their struggle was defending.[109]

Violence was arguably being applied from the other direction. Economic security in the coalfields was decomposed within the rule of law and norms of British Parliamentary democracy, but the conscious abandonment of communal resources – the 'people's coal', as McGahey called it – was experienced in many coal settlements as an extended and disastrous act of violence, inflicted by hostile external forces.[110] The NCB's 'back to work' campaign was itself a moral economy transgression. It breached established custom by encouraging strike-breaking during an industrial dispute. The initiative included direct contact with strikers by NCB managers at local level, over the heads of union representatives. This approach came from the top, including letters sent by Ian MacGregor to miners at their homes. These were addressed 'Dear Colleague', encouraging strikers to return to work and criticising their union's officials.[111]

In the 1974 strike a potentially catastrophic flood had been averted at Valleyfield by union members. 'The men deserve every credit for coming out' to save the colliery, James Cowan, NCB Scottish Area Director, had told reporters.[112] In 1984 around 600 NUM members were providing safety cover every week in Scotland, usually on a rota basis, to protect collieries so that normal production would resume after the strike. The NUM national executive, provoked by the back-to-work campaign, resolved to withdraw safety cover because this was now helping to produce coal and so break the strike. This decision divided opinion among strikers, especially in Scotland because Wheeler reiterated the position adopted during the 1983–4 overtime ban. Management staff would not undertake safety work: 'their job is to manage', he told reporters.[113] In a notable inversion of the 1921 and 1926 disorder, Wheeler's managers disabled pumping machinery so that Polkemmet in West Lothian was catastrophically flooded over the last weekend of August 1984. Local union attempts over three agonising days to gain underground access were thwarted by pit managers. In West Lothian this is remembered as a sinister episode.[114] It is believed that UK security service officers planned a three-stage sequence of destruction: an initial handful of likely strike-breakers were identified and encouraged to enter the colliery as workers, goading the union locally into withdrawing safety cover; management would accordingly switch off the pumping machinery in line with Wheeler's instruction; and the pit would then be flooded.[115] Coal was never produced again at Polkemmet, which closed in 1986.[116]

The strike ended in March 1985, by which time its focus had shifted. Realising there could be no meaningful settlement some union officials and activists – including in Scotland – sought a return to work in exchange for the NCB reinstating the many miners sacked for alleged offences on picket lines and in communities. Even this compromise was not secured, however, and union delegates controversially voted in London on the first Sunday in March 1985 to end the strike without any agreement in place. Victimisation was a special difficulty in Scotland where 206 miners, amounting to 1.5 per cent of the strikers, were dismissed in 1984–5. Only 0.6 per cent of the strikers in England and Wales were sacked.[117] There was an echo here of the disproportionate volume of prosecutions of strikers in Scotland under Order 1305 during the Second World War, but more significantly this pattern reflected the distinct anti-union turn within NCB Scottish management under Wheeler since 1980–1. At Polkemmet two miners were convicted for criminal damage to the colliery office, smashing windows in their anger after the flooding controversy in August. In November they asked the colliery manager, Steele, for clemency. He was unforgiving, stating that one of them 'had a deplorable attendance record' and the other was 'a thorn in everybody's flesh'. Their employment was terminated with immediate effect.[118] Sackings included men who had been arrested but never actually convicted. A typical case was John Swain of Polmaise, charged in August, sacked in November, and admonished in March.[119] In an echo of the 1940s as well as the 1920s, Michael McGahey's son, also Michael, a miner at Bilston Glen, was sacked following arrest on picket-line duty.[120] David Hamilton, NUM delegate at Monktonhall, was arrested for strike-related activities and held on remand in Edinburgh's Saughton prison for several weeks in the autumn of 1984 but eventually exonerated of all charges. He was sacked all the same, and unable to find work for several years.[121] Other NUM delegates were likewise targeted and dismissed: Jackie Aitchison at Bilston Glen, after being falsely accused of entering NCB property during a picket,[122] and Tam Mylchreest at Castlehill, following arrest on a picket line.[123] There is strong circumstantial evidence that many of the sacked men were subsequently blacklisted by non-coal employers, notably in the construction industry. Intelligence on these and hundreds of labour activists in other sectors was gathered by private consultants, possibly through contacts in the police and security services, and purchased by anti-trade union employers.[124]

Communities and the 1984–5 Strike

In economic terms mining communities were desperately punished by the strike. Household finances, lowered by the lengthy overtime ban from November 1983,[125] were severely straitened by losing male earnings for a whole year. Intense material hardship was common, but softened by two important factors that made the costs of striking bearable. First, it was noted in Chapter 2 that 74 per cent of households in Scottish coalfield settlements were local authority renters in 1981. Labour councils in Fife, the Lothians, Lanarkshire and Ayrshire all deferred or lowered rents for striking miners. Second, female wages provided a basic survival platform, and the proportion of married women in employment was slightly higher in the coalfields than in Scotland as a whole. Younger men who lived on their own were the most vulnerable to economic hardship, although larger families encountered serious difficulties too. These were compounded by the Department of Health and Social Security's decision to reduce supplementary benefits to miners' dependents on the assumption, which officials enforcing the policy knew to be incorrect, that the NUM was providing strike pay.[126]

Security in mining communities was further diminished after the strike when the trend to authoritarian management and deindustrialisation was emphatically confirmed. Working conditions were particularly oppressive at 'Castlehell' and 'Belsen Glen'.[127] NCB Scottish management even attempted, unsuccessfully, to establish the NUM's post-strike union rival, the UDM, at some collieries.[128] At Comrie, Fife's only surviving New Mine, where just one miner had broken the strike,[129] production ended in September 1986.[130] About half of the colliery's 678 redundant men lived in West Fife, with significant clusters in Dunfermline and Oakley. A total of 245 were resident in the Cowdenbeath to Kelty conurbation and 60 more in Alloa and adjacent villages. The New Mine of the 1930s had become a Cosmopolitan Colliery in residential terms as workers arrived from pits shutting in the 1960s, widening the negative effects of closure.[131] Bogside also closed in 1986, followed in 1987 by Killoch and Polmaise, and in 1988 by Seafield and Frances.[132] Barony closed in 1989, as did Bilston Glen, where management harried union representatives and workers until the very end.[133] Two of the Longannet pits, Solsgirth and Castlehill, closed in 1990. Monktonhall stopped producing in 1988, when the vast majority of its employees were made redundant, although 30 were retained on a care and maintenance basis, and a workers' cooperative was active in the mid-1990s. The colliery closed and was destroyed in 1998.[134] Industrial archaeologists were able to preserve the headframes at Barony and Frances, but there was a rush by policy-makers at local as well as national government level to eradicate mining's visible symbols, an impediment, it was claimed, to future economic development.[135] Longannet continued to burn locally mined coal, from a small pit immediately adjacent to the power station, but this flooded and closed in 2002, and from Castlebridge in Clackmannan, which opened shortly after the strike and operated until 1999.[136]

This rundown was imposed by managerial fiat, with limited alternative economic activity and employment available in the coalfields, and no attempt by government – as there had been from the 1950s to 1970s – to offset mining job losses with regional policy-assisted alternatives. Instead, the social security system incentivised older miners to withdraw from economic activity altogether on grounds of disability, obscuring the 'real' level of unemployment in ex-coal localities. This was often double the official figure given for unemployment benefit claimants. In 1991 unemployment among men aged 16–64 inclusive in the ex-coalfields of Fife and Lanark-shire was officially 13.5 per cent, but 'really' 21.2 per cent including those classified as 'permanently sick'.[137] The trend was lasting. In the whole of Fife in 2001 6 per cent of working age men were registered unemployed, just above the UK male average of 5.6 per cent. But a further 7.1 per cent were 'permanently sick' and uninvolved in economic activity.[138] Sickness benefits were higher than unemployment benefits and not means-tested, so were unaffected by the earnings of other household members. This cushioned the material impact of deindustrialisation on older ex-miners, but the long-term consequence of heavy employment losses in the coalfields was nevertheless substantial economic and social deprivation.[139]

The common experience of enduring hardship in 1984–5 contributed to a strengthening of solidarity in mining communities which united against the common anti-working class foes of Tory government and NCB management. The activism of the dozens of local strike centres was highly important. A daily hot meal and weekly shopping bag were vital especially to single miners, and it was in the 'soup kitchens' in welfare clubs that men and women consolidated the strike.[140] 'Food on the table' was a 'political statement', according to Rab Amos, SCEBTA delegate at Monktonhall, and more important than anything else in sustaining the strikers' belief that they could survive and emerge victorious.[141] In school holidays this provision was bolstered by local authorities providing daily lunches for children. In Lanarkshire and Ayrshire this came through Strathclyde Regional Council's Social Work department.[142] In East Fife the Dysart centre collected food, crockery and cutlery from Regional Council stores in Glenrothes and distributed them to local centres.[143] Maintaining a dignified family life remained difficult, especially at Christmas, but this challenge reinforced community feeling, chiefly due to the hard work and imagination of women. In Midlothian pantomime tickets were obtained after lengthy lobbying of theatres by women who also negotiated special discount gift vouchers with British Homes Stores on Princes Street in Edinburgh.[144] Elsewhere the Christmas campaign was bolstered by material support from the STUC and other trade unions in Scotland, UK and across Europe, with toys, food and other groceries from France, the German Democratic Republic and the Soviet Union.[145]

The social and ideological cohesion of coal communities was stretched nevertheless. Not everyone was a manual worker or identified with collective working class interests. In *Coal Is Our Life* Dennis, Henriques and Slaughter noted the implications for the minority who stood apart from the majority, particularly in times of crisis. Individuals opposed to collective action would be coerced or shunned: 'made to feel the weight of the community's displeasure'.[146] Daniel Wight observed similar disciplinary forces in the early 1980s in Cauldmoss.[147] The solidarity of the strike in 1984–5 demonstrated the NUMSA's success in developing a common identity based on the class and national integrity of Scottish miners, but the coercive force of community was important too. In Cowie in Stirlingshire strikers who failed to report for picket duty were fined by their local committee. Men found to be claiming sickness benefit during the strike were ostracised in moral economy terms as cheats. They were denied access to the strike centre's communal feeding and support network. Strikers broke off contact with friends or family members who returned to work.[148] In South Wales strike-breakers are remembered in moral terms as 'wife-beaters, reprobates'.[149] In Scotland they were denounced in a similar manner. To fit the dominant narrative of class solidarity those who returned to work were socially distanced as deviants, or 'wasters', the pejorative term used in Scotland to shame those who allegedly transgress communal values.[150] The intersectional language of gender and nation was prominent in this process. The Bilston Glen working miners in 1984 were 'not men', and they were 'not Scottish miners', according to strikers in Stirlingshire. The lone strike-breaker at Longannet, Pearson, was a 'professional scab' and 'not a miner' either, but 'a JCB driver'.[151]

This vocabulary is reproduced in Scottish coalfield memory, bringing to mind what oral historians call the 'cultural circuit', where individual recollection is based upon and reinforces dominant social narratives.[152] In the 2000s and 2010s strike-breakers were still remembered as 'weak' individuals: problem drinkers, gamblers, poor workers. Often in trouble with management, their jobs had been defended by union intervention before the strike, deepening their moral reprehensibility in returning to work in 1984.[153]

Women played a key role in the shunning of strike-breakers in Scotland in 1984–5, according to Jean Stead of *The Guardian*. Stead saw the strike's effects on gender relations as significant. She called her book *Never The Same Again*,[154] implying agreement with Beatrix Campbell's pre-strike assessment that coalfield gender relations in the north-east of England were barely altered from the 1950s or even the 1930s.[155] In Scotland thousands of coalfield women joined the campaign to protect economic security by defending collieries threatened with closure. Women established contacts with supporters beyond the coalfields, speaking at trade union, workplace and community meetings and rallies, including events held by their national organisation, Women Against Pit Closures. Yet the extent to which gender relations and politics were transformed in 1984–5 was exaggerated, partly, it has been argued, by feminist-socialist women who supported the strike from larger towns and cities outwith coal communities. Coalfield women were an established force in labour movement campaigning before the strike began. Some of these activists presented themselves knowingly as political newcomers to meet non-coalfield expectations of naïve miners' wives and so attract supporters who might otherwise have been indifferent to the strike.[156]

The characterisation of an unchanging world before the strike also overlooked evidence that moderate progress was discernible as early as the 1950s, with widening labour market opportunities encouraging women to hold less restricted social, emotional and sexual attitudes.[157] The further extension of female paid employment combined with wider cultural and social changes to reduce gender inequalities at least in some localities, in Scotland as elsewhere. Women before the strike were not passive victims of gender oppression. Nor were men homogeneously chauvinistic.

The defence of male jobs in the coalfields by the NUMSA in the 1960s and 1970s co-existed with a clearer commitment to narrowing inequality between men and women than exhibited by mining trade unionists elsewhere in Britain. In these decades *Scottish Miner* admittedly included exploitative photographic images of young women, wearing swimsuits or other clothing highlighting the wearer's physical shape, and accompanied by risible editorial text. Similar material was carried in the Young Communist League's periodical at the time. The editors of each publication believed that this was fashionably in tune with the 'swinging' cultural strand of the time, and a means of engaging younger readers.[158] But the practice was dismal, and discontinued by *The Scottish Miner* in 1974. Women thereafter were increasingly portrayed in progressive and non-objectified terms. During the 1984–5 strike the newspaper characterised women as leading – and not merely supporting – the communal defence of jobs and pits.[159]

So in Scotland the strike marked a transition rather than a departure in gender relations.[160] There was some degree of gender role reversal in mining households, with men engaged in child care and other aspects of domestic life, and women occupied in public-facing strike activities. Margaret Wright's 2008 film, *Here We Go. Women Living the Strike*, features a number of protagonists from Fife, the Lothians and Lanarkshire who emphasise the liberating nature of their activism, including speaking to large audiences of workers, trade unionists and citizens outwith the coalfields.[161] The scope and geographical range of this female activism was varied, however. It was difficult for women in the small mining settlements of Stirlingshire and Ayrshire to assert their voices in the face of male chauvinism.[162] Women in Mauchline, East Ayrshire, a few miles north of Killoch Colliery, said that the strike suffered as a result.[163] Sexism among men remained a regrettable feature of social relations throughout the Scottish coalfields, confronting women activists in communities and sometimes even at home. So their determined provision of moral leadership as well as material support was all the more remarkable, according to Ella Egan, who convened the NUMSA Women's Support Group. After the strike the NUMSA wanted to acknowledge gender parity in industrial struggle by opening union membership to women on the same terms as men.

The initiative was blocked at a federal level in the union nationally, but in Scotland the area leadership supported it unconditionally. 'A working class movement without women is like a bird with one wing', McGahey is remembered as saying: 'it winnae fly'.[164]

The attempt to organise women within the union reinforced the Scottish miners' claims to a distinct national identity. This involved more progressive gender politics, and also contributed to the emergence of stronger public support for political devolution in Scotland after the strike. The miners and other trade unionists campaigned for a Parliament in the second half of the 1980s within a broader cross-class and cross-party movement for constitutional change. This included large numbers of professionals who were formed generationally by the social democratic values embedded in Scottish comprehensive schooling by the 1960s. Lindsay Paterson has pointed out that members of this generation were employed by the 1980s in teaching, medicine and other areas of the social services. Dismayed by the Thatcherite assault on the public sector, these professionals shared the labour movement's appetite for a Parliament in Edinburgh that would be more responsive than Westminster to Scotland's distinct economic interests, and more active in preserving the social democratic values which had enhanced their life chances.[165]

The STUC coordinated this cross-party movement. It gained momentum after the 1987 General Election, when the Conservative Party lost support and more than half of its Parliamentary representation in Scotland but held ground in England to form another majority government with Thatcher as Prime Minister. The 'democratic deficit' argument developed serious traction. Moral economy sentiment was further offended by continuing industrial closures and the government's regressive policies, most notably the Community Charge, or 'Poll Tax'. This reform of local government financing in 1988–9 was deeply unpopular: flat-rate charges absorbed a greater proportion of low income and were introduced in Scotland a year before England and Wales. A dynamic 'Can't Pay Won't Pay' campaign of civil disobedience developed within working class communities which drew organisational impetus from miners' support groups formed in 1984. This embarrassed the STUC and the Labour Party in Scotland which opposed the Tax but were committed to 'constitutional' methods and the public services which non-payment jeopardised.[166] The STUC's General Secretary, Campbell Christie, and Deputy General Secretary, Bill Speirs, managed these difficulties carefully, linking the Tax with the urgency of Scottish Home Rule, and positioned the labour movement at the heart of a social democratic 'Civic Scotland' which drew in various anti-Conservative political parties, local authorities, Churches and pressure groups.[167] These forces were brought together in the Scottish Constitutional Convention from 1989 which formed the basis for the Parliament established in 1999.[168] Michael McGahey retired as NUMSA President in 1987, succeeded by George Bolton. When McGahey died in January 1999, less than four months before the first Scottish Parliament Election, the NUM's central role in pushing Home Rule on to the labour movement's agenda in Scotland was emphasised by a number of trade union officials and political activists.[169]

Conclusion

Economic security in the coalfields was challenged, compromised and then permanently violated in the 1980s by the UK government and its allies within the NCB. Trade unions were targeted as an obstacle to the government's strategic goals of heightening marketness in economic and social life. The coal industry was identified as an inefficient operator and high cost prisoner of the NUM. The 1984–5 strike in defence of collieries, jobs and communities was prefigured by a lengthy struggle at workplace level, initiated in Scotland ahead of other areas of the British coalfields by an anti-union turn within NCB management. More than half of Scotland's miners were in dispute with their local management when the national strike began in March 1984. Generation and the moral economy of the coalfields were central features of this resistance. The strike was led by men and women of the Cosmopolitan Colliery generation, animated and activated by formative experience. Their families and communities had been compelled to abandon Village Pits, often with workable reserves of coal, in favour of the Cosmopolitan Collieries which they accepted on the basis of long-term sustainability.

They would not relinquish these assets easily, and fought to preserve them in 1984–5.

The NUM's strategy during the strike was contentious and is still being criticised. More willingness from union leaders to seek accommodation on closures could, it is argued, have delayed deindustrialisation, retaining coal industry jobs and wages in mining communities for a longer period. These criticisms are substantially qualified by new evidence presented in this chapter. The government was committed to removing union voice from the industry. The Prime Minister's intervention at Ravenscraig in May 1984, breaking the miners' siege to maintain steel production, illustrates this commitment. The government strategy included two key elements: destabilising the NUM-NCB negotiations, to prevent a settlement that preserved meaningful union voice; and absorbing colossal economic costs, which outweighed the purported financial losses of producing coal across the UK in 1984–5 by a factor of 60 to 1. Thatcher and her ministers paid an enormous premium in pursuit of their struggle against the miners, which was also a war against the trade union movement and the working class more generally.

Mining communities were grievously affected in economic terms by the strike and its aftermath. The existence of strike-breakers, even in Scotland, demonstrated that coal communities were not ideologically homogeneous. In the longer run, however, these communities emerged from the crisis of the strike and the closures that followed with renewed solidarity. Gender relations had slowly evolved from the 1960s as employment opportunities for women increased. They changed in further progressive ways during the strike, partly as a result of women's political activism. This strengthened the longer-term cohesion of mining communities and had a positive influence on progressive politics in Scotland more broadly. The narrative of a distinct Scottish national commitment to social justice, under assault from a UK government without democratic or moral mandate, was given much greater force by the anti-Thatcherite resistance of men and women in the coalfields. This renewed the campaign for a Scottish Parliament, which came to successful fruition in 1999.

Notes

1. Gibbs, 'Moral Economy of the Scottish Coalfields', pp. 128–9.
2. Andrew Gamble, *The Free Economy and the Strong State: the Politics of Thatcherism* (Macmillan: Basingstoke, 1994).
3. Tomlinson, *Managing the Economy*, pp. 74–80, 229–30.
4. Peter Fleming, *The Death of Homo Economicus: work, debt and the myth of endless accumulation* (Pluto Press: London, 2017).
5. James Meek, *Private Island: Why Britain Now Belongs to Someone Else* (Verso: London, 2014), pp. 8–24.
6. Chris Howell, *Trade Unions and the State: the Construction of Industrial Relations Institutions in Britain, 1890–2000* (Princeton University Press, Princeton, NJ: 2005), pp. 131–73.
7. Atkinson, 'Distribution of Income'; Larry Elliot, 'Income inequality is getting wider', *The Guardian*, 4 December 2017; Howard Reed and Jacob Mohun Himmelweit, *Where Have All the Wages Gone? Lost pay and profits outside financial services* (TUC: London, 2012), pp. 9–11.
8. Peter Ackers, 'Gramsci at the Miners' Strike: Remembering the 1984–1985 Eurocommunist Alternative Industrial Relations Strategy', *Labor History*, 55 (2015), pp. 151–72; Andrew Glyn, 'The Economic Case Against Pit Closures', in D. Cooper and T. Hopper, eds, *Debating Coal Closures: economic calculation in the coal dispute, 1984–5* (Cambridge University Press: Cambridge, 1988), pp. 57–94; David Howell, 'Defiant Dominoes: Working Miners and the 1984–5 Strike', in Ben Jackson and Robert Saunders (eds), *Making Thatcher's Britain* (Cambridge University Press: Cambridge, 2012), pp. 148–64.
9. Williams, 'Key Words in the Miners' Strike', pp. 120–7.
10. McGrail, *Cowie Miners*, p. 61.
11. Jörg Arnold, '"The Death of Sympathy." Coal Mining, Workplace Hazards, and the Politics of Risk in Britain, ca. 1970–1990', *Historical Social Research*, 41 (2016), pp. 91–110.
12. University of Glasgow Archives (UGA), ACCN 1786/4/3, clipping, 'Miners' strike would be a foolish tragedy', *The Sunday Times*, 6 March 1983.
13. *The Times*, 9 March 1983.
14. M. W. Kirby, 'MacGregor, Sir Ian Kinloch (1912–1998)', *Oxford Dictionary of National Biography* (Oxford University Press: Oxford, online, 2016).
15. Charlie McGuire, '"Going for the Jugular": The Steelworkers' Banner and the 1980 National Steelworkers' Strike in Britain', *Historical Studies in Industrial Relations*, 38 (2017), pp. 97–128.
16. UGA, ACCN 1786/4/3, clippings, 'Must it be confrontation over coal?', and Jane McLoughlin, 'Mac the nice', both in *Manchester Guardian Weekly*,

3 April 1983, and 'Robert L. Millar, 'Britain Names Ian MacGregor Coal Board Chief', *The Wall Street Journal*, 29 March 1983.

17. Martina Steber, 'Fundamentals at Stake: the Conservatives, Industrial Relations and the Rhetorical Framing of the Miners' Strike in 1984–85', *Contemporary British History*, 32.1 (2018), pp. 60–77.

18. Peter Dorey, 'Conciliation or Confrontation with the Trade Unions? The Conservative Party's "Authority of Government Group", 1975–1978', *Historical Studies in Industrial Relations*, 27/28 (2009), pp. 135–51.

19. Colin Hay, 'The Trade Unions and the "Winter of Discontent": A Case of Myth-Taken Identity', *Historical Studies in Industrial Relations*, 36 (2015), 181–203; Tomlinson, Managing the Economy, pp. 199–205.

20. Paul Smith and Gary Morton, 'The Conservative Governments' Reform of Employment Law, 1979–97: 'Stepping Stones' and the 'New Right' Agenda', *Historical Studies in Industrial Relations*, 12 (2001), pp. 131–47.

21. Ashworth, *British Coal Industry*, pp. 414–15.

22. *Scottish Miner*, June–July 1980.

23. *Scottish Miner*, December 1980.

24. *The Times*, 11 and 19 February 1981.

25. GCUA, STUC General Council, Special Meeting to discuss Talbot/Linwood Car Plant, Congress Office, Sunday 15 February 1981.

26. 'How the coalmen defeated the government', *The Economist*, 21 February 1981, pp. 35–6.

27. Taylor, *NUM and British Politics. Volume Two*, pp. 155–62; Adeney and Lloyd, *Loss Without Limit*, pp. 78–9.

28. TNA, COAL 74/4783, Coal Industry National Consultative Council, 9 November 1982, 11 January 1983, 1 February 1983, 8 March 1983, 10 May 1983.

29. National Coal Board, *Report and Accounts, 1983/4* (NCB: London, 1984), pp. 28–9.

30. Andrew Perchard and Jim Phillips, 'Transgressing the Moral Economy: Wheelerism and Management of the Nationalised Coal Industry in Scotland', *Contemporary British History*, 25 (2011), pp. 387–405.

31. NRS, CB 121/4, NCB Scottish Area, Minutes of the Accountability Meeting, 24 February 1981; CB 121/6, NCB Scottish Area, Minutes of the Accountability Meeting, 24 June 1981.

32. Hamilton, Interview.

33. NMMS, NUMSA, Executive, 23 September 1981; Gibbs, 'Moral Economy of the Scottish Coalfields', p. 145.

34. NRS, CB 335/14/3, clipping, John Lloyd, 'Scottish pit closure move angers miners', *Financial Times*, 20 September 1982.

35. *The Times*, 4 October 1982.

36. Terry Brotherstone and Simon Pirani, 'Were There Alternatives? Movements from Below in the Scottish Coalfield, the Communist Party, and Thatcherism, 1981–1985'. *Critique*, 36–7 (2005), pp. 99–124, with Kinneil detail at p. 107.

37. TNA, COAL 89/103, NCB Central Secretariat, Colliery Closures, 13 May 1983, and Public Relations Department, NCB Scottish Area, Closure Cardowan, 13 May 1983.

38. TNA, COAL 89/103, Extract from Mr Lawson's proposed speech today, 13 May 1983.

39. Gibbs, 'Moral Economy of the Scottish Coalfields', pp. 146–7.

40. Nicky Wilson, Interview with Author, Scottish Miners' Convalescent Home, Blair Castle, Culross, 18 Aug. 2009.

41. *The Scotsman*, 7 July 1983.

42. NMMS, NUMSA, EC, 12 July 1983, and Minute of Special Conference of Delegates, 12 July 1983.

43. *The Scotsman*, 26 and 27 August 1983.

44. NMMS, NUMSA, EC, 29 August 1983.

45. Monopolies and Mergers Commission (hereafter MMC), *National Coal Board. Volume One*, pp. 363–6.

46. Nick Higham, 'Cabinet papers reveal "secret coal pits closure plan"', BBC News, 3 January 2014, http://www.bbc.co.uk/news/uk-25549596.

47. Ewan Gibbs, *The Meaning and Memory of Coalfields: Deindustrialisation and Scottish Nationhood* (University of London: London, forthcoming, 2019).

48. Glyn, 'Economic Case Against Pit Closures'.

49. MMC, *National Coal Board. Volume Two*, Appendix 3.5 (a), NCB Deep Mines. Operating Results 1981–82 – Scottish Area, and Appendix 3.6 (a), NCB Deep Mines. Colliery operating surplus/(loss), 1976–77 to 1981–82, Scottish Area.

50. NRS, CB 380/3/2, Polkemmet Colliery Consultative Committee, 1 February and 6 September 1977, 8 September and 13 October 1981.

51. NRS, CB 380/3/2, Polkemmet CCC, 8 September, 13 October and 24 November 1982; 9 February, 22 June, 12 and 26 October 1983.

52. NRS, CB 229/3/1, Bilston Glen CCC, 31 March, 26 May, 26 July, 11 August and 8 September 1982.

53. NRS, CB 398/3/2, Seafield CCC, 24 May, 28 June, 12 July, 27 September and 8 November 1983.

54. Hamilton, Interview.

55. NRS, CB 363/3/8, Monktonhall CCC, 24 August 1983.

56. *Scottish Miner*, November 1983.

57. Hamilton, Interview.

58. Paul Foot, 'Introduction', in Roger Huddle, Angela Phillips, Mike Simons and John Sturrock, *Blood, Sweat & Tears: Photographs from the great miners' strike* (Artworker Books: London, 1985), pp. 7–9; Richards, *Miners on Strike*, pp. 100–10; J. Winterton and R. Winterton, *Coal, Crisis and Conflict: The 1984–85 Miners' Strike in Yorkshire* (Manchester University Press: Manchester, 1989), pp. 64–72.

59. NRS, CB 382/14/1, D.G. Brandrick, secretary, NCB, to Lawrence Daly, [outgoing] General Secretary, NUM, 6 February 1984.

60. NRS, CB 221/3/4, Barony CCC, 29 November 1983.

61. *The Scotsman*, 28 January 1984, and *Courier & Advertiser*, 31 January and 1 February 1984.

62. Kirkcaldy Art Gallery and Museum (hereafter KAGM), Iain Chalmers, Strike Diary, 14, 17, 18, 23 and 27 February and 5 March 1984.

63. NRS, CB 380/3/2, Polkemmet CCC, 25 January 1984.

64. Margaret Thatcher, *The Downing Street Years* (HarperCollins: London, 1993), pp. 339–78.

65. Jim Phillips, 'Containing, Isolating and Defeating the Miners: the UK Cabinet Ministerial Group on Coal and the three phases of the 1984–5 Strike', *Historical Studies in Industrial Relations*, 35 (2014), pp. 117–41.

66. Ashworth, *British Coal Industry*, Table A1 and commentary on pp. 163, 250, 298.

67. NCB, *Report and Accounts, 1983/4*, pp. 18–19.

68. Ned Smith, *The 1984 Miners' Strike: The Actual Account* (Oyster: Whitstable, 1997), pp. 12–15.

69. Willie Clarke, Interview.

70. NMMS, NUMSA, EC and Minute of Special Conference of Delegates, both 20 February 1984; Eric Clarke, with Bob McLean, 'The Mineworkers' Strike 1984–5: the Role of the Scottish Area as Banker to the Union', *Scottish Affairs*, 49 (2004), pp. 138–50.

71. Phillips, *Miners' Strike in Scotland*, pp. 110–42.

72. Richards, *Miners on* Strike, pp. 175–92; Taylor, *NUM and British Politics: Vol. 2*, pp. 188–9.

73. Griffin, '"Notts. have some very peculiar history"', pp. 90–1.

74. 'Jimmy Hood: Obituary', by Brian Wilson, *The Guardian*, 5 December 2017.

75. Joan Witham, *Hearts and Minds. The Story of the Women of Nottinghamshire in the Miners' Strike, 1984–1985* (Canary Press: London, 1986), pp. 120–3, 146–7.

76. David Amos, *The Miners of Nottinghamshire. Volume 4: 1980–1985* (Union of Democratic Mineworkers: Mansfield, 2013); Harry Paterson,

Look Back in Anger. The Miners' Strike in Nottinghamshire 30 Years On (Five Leaves Publications: Nottingham, 2014).

77. Jay Emery, 'Belonging, memory and history in the north Nottinghamshire coalfield', *Journal of Historical Geography*, 59 (2018), pp. 77–89.

78. Jörg Arnold, '"Like Being on Death Row": Britain and the End of Coal, c. 1970 to the present', *Contemporary British History*, 32.1 (2018), pp. 1–17.

79. David Featherstone and Diarmaid Kelliher, eds, *London and the 1984–5 Miners' Strike* (University of Glasgow: Glasgow, 2018), p. 11.

80. MMC, *National Coal Board. Volume Two*, Appendix 3.5 (a), NCB Deep Mines. Operating Results 1981–82 – South Nottinghamshire Area and North Nottinghamshire Area, and Appendix 3.4 (b), NCB Deep Mines. Area operating results – OMS – 1976–77 to 1981–82.

81. Williams, *Resources of Hope*.

82. Phillips, *Miners' Strike in Scotland*, pp. 119–29.

83. Bob Eadie, 'The Miners' Strike in Scotland', *Scottish Affairs*, 23.1 (2014), pp. 153–5; Quentin Outram, Review, *Scottish Labour History*, 48 (2013), pp. 194–6.

84. Ackers, 'Gramsci at the Miners' Strike'.

85. Diarmaid Kelliher, 'Contested Spaces: London and the 1984–5 Miners' Strike', *Twentieth Century British History*, 28 (2017), pp. 595–617.

86. GCUA, STUC General Purposes Committee, 19 December 1984, and General Council, 9 January 1985; Phillips, *Miners' Strike in Scotland*, pp. 116–17.

87. Diarmaid Kelliher, 'Solidarity and Sexuality: Lesbians and Gays Support the Miners, 1984–5', *History Workshop Journal*, 77.1 (2014), pp. 240–62; Daryl Leeworthy, 'The secret life of us: 1984, the miners' strike and the place of biography in writing history "from below"', *European Review of History*, 19.5 (2012), pp. 825–46.

88. Phillips, 'Containing, Isolating and Defeating the Miners'.

89. Ralph Miliband, *Divided Societies: Class Struggle in Contemporary Capitalism* (Clarendon: Oxford, 1989), pp. 115–66.

90. Granville Williams, ed., *Settling Scores: The Media, the Police and the Miners' Strike* (Campaign for Press and Broadcasting Freedom: London, 2014); Seumas Milne, *The Enemy Within: the Secret War Against the Miners* (Verso, 4th edition: London, 2014), pp. 364–7.

91. Adeney and Lloyd, *Loss Without Limit*, pp. 3–4.

92. Peter Dorey, 'The *Stepping Stones* programme: The Conservative Party's struggle to develop a Trade Union Policy, 1975–79', *Historical Studies in Industrial Relations*, 35 (2014), pp. 89–116.

93. Margaret Thatcher Foundation, Viscount Younger to Baroness Thatcher, 28 November 2002, https://www.margaretthatcher.org/document/111443, accessed 10 December 2017; thanks to Paul Hardman of the NUM for this reference.

94. Peter Dorey, '"It was Just Like Arming to Face the Threat of Hitler in the late 1930s". The Ridley Report and the Conservative Party's Preparations for the 1984–85 Miners' Strike', *Historical Studies in Industrial Relations*, 34 (2013), pp. 173–214.

95. David Peace, *GB84* (Faber and Faber: London, 2004), p. 158.

96. TNA, CAB 130/1268, CMGC, 30 May, 11 July and 12 September 1984.

97. NMMS, NUMSA, Strike Committee Minutes, 23 July 1984.

98. TNA, CAB 130/1268, CMGC, 30 April 1984.

99. NRS, SEP 4/6028, Sit Rep, 8 May 1984.

100. TNA, CAB 130/1268, CMGC, 8 May 1984.

101. NRS, SEP 4/6028, Scottish Office Daily Situation Report, 10 May 1984; NMMS, NUMSA, Box 10, Area Coordinating Committee, Reports, Thursday 10 May 1984.

102. John McCormack with Simon Pirani, *Polmaise: the Fight for a Pit* (Word Press, 2015 edition, https://polmaisebook.wordpress.com), p. 36.

103. GCUA, STUC General Council, General Purposes Committee, 16 May 1984.

104. McGrail, *Cowie Miners*, pp. 55–8; Guthrie Hutton, *Coal Not Dole. Memories of the 1984/85 Miners' Strike* (Stenlake: Catrine, 2005), pp. 26–8; West Lothian Trade Union Council, *Unity Is Strength: West Lothian Memories of the Miners' Strike, 1984–85* (West Lothian TUC, 2015), p. 49.

105. David Conn, 'The Scandal of Orgreave', *The Guardian*, 18 May 2017.

106. NRS, SEP 4/6027, Scottish Office Daily Situation Reports, 28 and 29 June, 26 and 27 July 1984.

107. Paul Brown, 'Riot police face pickets as rebel smuggled into pit', *The Guardian*, 23 August 1984, p. 24.

108. TMI, DDA, Papers relating to 1984/5 miners' strike, Box 2, David Waddington, 'Maltby: a study in community resistance', Coal and Community Conference, Sheffield, 7–9 March 1986.

109. Willie Clarke, Interview.

110. Andrew Perchard, '"Broken Men" and "Thatcher's Children": Memory and Legacy in Scotland's Coalfields', *International Labor and Working Class History*, 84 (2013), pp. 78–98.

111. TNA, COAL 26, NCB Industrial Relations Department, drafts of letters from Ian MacGregor to NCB employees; thanks to Arne Hordt for this reference.

112. 'Miners in fight to save pit', *The Guardian*, 11 February 1974, p. 28.

113. Peter Hetherington, 'Safety work splits miners', *The Guardian*, 7 August 1984, p. 2.

114. West Lothian TUC, *Unity Is Strength*, pp. 52–6.

115. Milne, *Enemy Within*, pp. 319–22.

116. Oglethorpe, *Scottish Collieries*, pp. 264–5.

117. Phillips, *Miners' Strike in Scotland*, p. 152.

118. NRS, CB 380/15/17/2, NCB Polkemmet Colliery, Minute of a Meeting held at the Colliery on 6 November 1984.

119. McGrail, *Cowie Miners*, pp. 124–5.

120. Michael McGahey, in Owens, *Miners*, pp. 82–3.

121. Hamilton, Interview.

122. *Scottish Miner*, October 1984.

123. McGrail, *Cowie Miners*, p. 92.

124. Dave Smith and Phil Chamberlain, *Blacklisted: The Secret War between Big Business and Union Activists* (New Internationalist: London, 2015).

125. McGrail, *Cowie Miners*, pp. 46–7.

126. Phillips, *Miners' Strike in Scotland*, pp. 120–1.

127. McGrail, *Cowie Miners*, p. 93; *Scottish Miner*, October 1984.

128. Eric Clarke, Interview.

129. NRS, SEP 4/6029, Scottish Office Situation Report, 4 February 1985.

130. NRS, CB 267/14/1, J. E. Addison, NCB, circular to industry unions, 2 October 1986.

131. Fife Federation of Trades Councils with Richard Saville and George Kerevan, *Comrie Colliery: The Fight for the Future!* (Fife Federation of Trades Councils, no date, presumed 1986), p. 2.

132. NRS, CB 398/14/1, J. E. Addison, Head of Staff, British Coal Corporation, Scottish Area, to Eric Clarke, 19 January 1988.

133. NRS, CB 229/3/1, Bilston Glen CCC, 1 March 1988 and 15 May 1989.

134. Amos, Interview.

135. John Hume, Interview with Valerie Wright and author, Lilybank House, University of Glasgow, 23 November 2017.

136. Oglethorpe, *Scottish Collieries*.

137. Beatty and Fothergill, 'Labour Market Adjustment in Areas of Chronic Industrial Decline', pp. 627–40.

138. *Scotland's Census 2001. Key Statistics for Council Areas and Health Boards Across Scotland* (HMSO: Edinburgh, 2003); 'Unemployment rate in

the UK by gender from 2000 to 2017', *statista*, https://www.statista.com/statistics/280236/unemployment-rate-by-gender-in-the-united-kingdom-uk-year-on-year, accessed 20 March 2018.

139. Foden, Fothergill and Gore, *State of the Coalfields*.
140. Alex Maxwell, *Chicago Tumbles: Cowdenbeath and the Miners' Strike* (Alex Maxwell: Glenrothes, 1994), pp. 41–2.
141. Amos, Interview.
142. NMMS, NUMSA Strike Coordinating Committee, Box 10, 29 June 1984.
143. KAGM, 75.3/1/1, NUM Dysart Strike Centre, Reports, 27 March and 5 July 1984.
144. Guthrie, *Coal Not Dole*, pp. 45–7; Ian MacDougall, *Voices From Work and Home* (Mercat Press: Edinburgh, 2001), pp. 143–4.
145. Amos, Interview; McGrail, *Cowie Miners*, pp. 38–9.
146. Dennis, Henriques and Slaughter, *Coal Is Our Life*, p. 88.
147. Wight, *Workers Not Wasters*, pp. 87–112.
148. McGrail, *Cowie Miners*, p. 32.
149. Curtis, *South Wales Miners*, pp. 232–3.
150. Wight, *Workers Not Wasters*, *passim*.
151. McGrail, *Cowie Miners*, pp. 59–60.
152. Alistair Thomson, 'Anzac Memories: putting popular memory theory into practice in Australia', in Robert Perks and Alistair Thomson, eds, *The Oral History Reader* (Routledge: London, 1998), pp. 300–10.
153. Wilson, Interview; Hutton, *Coal Not Dole*, pp. 48–52; West Lothian TUC, *Unity Is Strength*, pp. 33–4.
154. Jean Stead, *Never the Same Again. Women and the Miners' Strike* (The Women's Press: London, 1987).
155. Beatrix Campbell, *Wigan Pier Revisited: poverty and politics in the eighties* (Virago: London, 1984).
156. Sutcliffe-Braithwaite and Thomlinson, 'National Women Against Pit Closures'.
157. Dennis, Henriques and Slaughter, *Coal Is Our Life*, pp. 232–3.
158. Willie Thompson, *The Good Old Cause: British Communism, 1920–1991* (Pluto: London, 1992), pp. 165–6.
159. *Scottish Miner*, October 1967, January and February 1974, and June 1984.
160. Spence and Stephenson, 'Side By Side With Our Men?'
161. *Here We Go. Women Living the Strike*, Presented and Directed by Margaret Wright, TV2DAY, Independent Video Production, 2009.
162. McGrail, *Cowie Miners*, pp. 79–82; Ayrshire strike leaders, Interview with Willie Thompson, 9 December 1985.

163. Catriona Levy and Mauchline Miners' Wives 'A Very Hard Year'. *1984–5 Miners' Strike in Mauchline* (Workers' Educational Association: Glasgow, 1985).

164. Ella Egan, Interview; Willie Clarke, Interview.

165. Lindsay Paterson, *Education and the Scottish Parliament* (Dunedin Academic Press: Edinburgh, 2005), pp. 21–7, and *Scottish Education in the Twentieth Century* (Edinburgh University Press: Edinburgh, 2003), pp. 130–54.

166. Ewan Gibbs, '"Civic Scotland" vs Communities on Clydeside: Poll Tax Non-Payment c. 1987–1990', *Scottish Labour History*, Vol. 49 (2015), pp. 86–106.

167. Jim Phillips, 'Christie, Campbell (1937–2011), trade unionist and political campaigner', *Oxford Dictionary of National Biography* (Oxford University Press: Oxford, online, 2016).

168. James Mitchell, *The Scottish Question* (Oxford University Press: Oxford, online, 2014), Chapter 10, 'Here's to the Next Time'.

169. 'One of the greats has gone', *The Herald*, 1 February 1999.

Legacy and Conclusion

On 9 September 2017 a service of remembrance was held in East Wemyss for the nine miners killed in the disastrous fire at Michael, exactly 50 years previously. The service was organised by the Fife Mining Heritage Preservation Society (FMHPS), and held at the village memorial, a miniature replica of Michael's No. 3 pit headframe. The service was attended by a multi-generational assembly of about 450. It was introduced by Duncan Gilfillan and Elizabeth McGuire, Chair and Secretary of the FMHPS, and led by the Reverend Wilma Cairns of Buckhaven and East Wemyss Parish Church. The Reverend Cairns spoke warmly about the nine miners who were still mourned by the families who lost them: Hugh Gallacher, aged 61, Alexander Henderson, 41, James Mackay, 59, Henry Morrison, 36, Johnston Smith, 60, James Tait, 41, Andrew Taylor, 43, Andrew Thomson, 55, and Philip Thomson, 64. She remembered these men as skilled workers, loving husbands, fathers and sons, helpful colleagues, friendly drinking buddies and pals who went to the football. Family flowers were joined on the village memorial by tributes from the Scottish Mines Rescue Training Centre in Crossgates, Fife, which had assumed a leading role in the difficult recovery operation in 1967, and representatives of Fife Trades Union Council, present with their banner, along with Peter Grant, MP for Glenrothes, and David Torrance, MSP for Kirkcaldy.

Nicky Wilson, President of the NUMSA, laid a wreath of white carnations. He spoke about the 311 men who had left their homes on the evening of 8 September, preparing for the night shift, to put food on the table for their families. Wilson said that the lives and deaths of the lost Michael men encapsulated the huge contribution made by mineworkers to the economic wealth of society, over decades and generations. The immense price of coal in human life was still being paid. Wilson followed two other speakers. Robert Balfour, Lord Lieutenant of Fife, commented on the values of community in coal localities, which had survived despite the loss of deep mining, and recalled the bravery and skill of the rescuers. Councillor Jim Leishman, Provost of Fife and Honorary President of the FMHPS, was a thirteen-year-old boy in Lochgelly in 1967, and spoke in 2017 as the proud son of a coal miner who had died shortly after retirement from Solsgirth Colliery. Provost Leishman remembered miners gathering in Lochgelly, waiting anxiously for news and boarding buses for East Wemyss where they helped the rescue effort. He also dwelt on the particular pain experienced by the families of the three miners whose bodies had not been recovered, and stressed the social solidarity of all Fifers. The service concluded with a walk through the village to an informal gathering on the site of the colliery baths, led by the Buckhaven and Methil Miners' Brass Band.

The memorial service was reported by national television and newspapers in Scotland. The Scottish Television coverage made extensive use of 1967 news footage.[1] Watching the old pictures from East Wemyss evoked a sense of national as well as local crisis, the reporter speaking urgently to camera with the pithead and baths in the background, and exhausted miners and rescuers emerging into the daylight. The media attention in 2017 was also a reminder that mining deaths usually received attention outwith the coalfields only when incidents with multiple casualties occurred. The attrition effects of smaller accidents went unremarked. The continued low-key presence of fatal danger after nationalisation was an important factor, according to David Selway, writing about South Wales, in limiting the establishment of memorials to those killed in major disasters. These came only after deindustrialisation, from the 1980s onwards.[2] In Scotland the historical position was similar, although multiple-victim accidents like Michael assumed a greater impact on the overall volume of fatalities after nationalisation in 1947. Selway's broader contention, that memorialisation has followed deindustrialisation, is consistent with experience in Scotland, where several community markers to miners killed in historical disasters were established after the closure of local mines. These include a cairn at Knockshinnoch, near New Cumnock, a statue representing an Auchengeich miner in Moodiesburn, North Lanarkshire, the replica of the Michael head-frame in East Wemyss, and a large headstone in Loanhead, Midlothian.

All industrial memorials are politicised and contentious. Clark and Gibbs distinguish civic memorials instituted by local authorities from community memorials organised by voluntary groups. They argue that civic memorials to heavy industry in Inverclyde and Lanarkshire symbolise the ambiguous class politics of 'New Scotland' in the 2010s which emphasise 'social justice' but conceal past as well as present conflict between labour and capital.[3] The politics of memorialisation are also gendered, as Jackie Clarke has observed, privileging remembrance of male labour, and connected to the ways in which localities characterise themselves.[4] It might be argued that there are not enough public memorials to coal miners, but there are even fewer to workers engaged in other forms of industry, particularly women, despite their intense deployment in textiles, one of Scotland's historic staples, and the widening of female employment opportunities in manufacturing after the Second World War. Three community mosaics were installed in Dundee in 2017, commemorating female and male employment at Timex, the US-owned multinational manufacturer in the city of watches and electronics from 1947 to 1993. These reinforce the Clark-Gibbs contrast between civic and community memorials. There are no local authority-founded memorials to assembly goods manufacturing in Scotland, so far as can be established, and certainly none comparable with those marking coal mining or other heavy industries. This downplays the involvement of women in industrial employment, and the impact on female workers of deindustrialisation.

The complexity of memorialisation is embodied by the Loanhead head-stone in Midlothian, which is dedicated to the 15 miners who died at Bilston Glen Colliery between 1960 and 1988. Each man was killed in a separate accident. The memorial would be characterised in the Clark-Gibbs model as community in provenance, established by the Loanhead Retired Miners Branch of the NUM, and also commemorates those killed at other pits in Midlothian. It was unveiled on 23 August 2008 by George 'Dod' Crawford, NUM Branch official at Bilston Glen from 1982 to 1988. Beneath the names of those killed 'THE TRUE PRICE OF COAL' is emphasised in large capitals. On the reverse of the memorial, looking from the top down, there is an image of a miners' helmet, the lamp switched on, the words, LET THERE BE LIGHT, then a 1961 photograph showing empty coal trucks in front of the colliery, followed by the lyrics of 'The Miners Song', re-arranged by Rab Brough:

> It's a working man I am and I've been down underground and I swear to God if I ever see the sun, or for any length of time I can hold it in my mind I never again will go down Bilston Glen
>
> At the age of 16 years with my father close to tears as he vowed never again to send his son to the dark recess of the mine where you age before your time and the coal dust hangs heavy on your lungs
>
> At the age of 65 I pray to God I'm still alive, and the wheels above the mine no longer wind, and they finally closed the hole where for years we clawed for coal I never again will go down Bilston Glen

'THE TRUE PRICE OF COAL' acknowledges but subverts the economic arguments used to rationalise closures, particularly in the 1980s. It reclaims the narrative which in Scotland arguably retained greater public traction than in other parts of the UK: miners paid heavily for the energy enjoyed by society. There is a link through the NUM to the miners' communal politics and collective social achievements. But 'The Miners Song' emphasises the damage that coal inflicted on physical health. It suggests consolation in deindustrialisation, and raises an important question. As coal mines were dangerous places, have Scottish workers become healthier without them?

There is no definitive answer to this question. Coal mines were clearly dangerous workplaces before the Second World War but then became safer after nationalisation through public ownership and stronger trade union voice.[5] Deindustrialisation, moreover, has not led to the harmonisation of health outcomes between ex-mining communities and the rest of society. The long-term consequences of lost employment in mining were summarised in a report published by the Coalfields Regeneration Trust report in

2014. In Ayrshire and Lanarkshire 6.9 per cent of the population were recorded as reporting bad or very bad general health, above the Great Britain average of 5.4 per cent.[6] Perchard has analysed the despondency among young men deprived of meaningful opportunities in the ex-coal communities of Ayrshire,[7] and a recent study of this part of the ex-coalfield emphasises the linkage between deindustrialisation on the one hand and elevated exposure to poor mental as well as physical health.[8] Alessandro Portelli, writing of Harlan County in the ex-coalfields of Kentucky, says 'survival is not just a word'. Lives are destabilised by dependence on prescription opiates and shortened in other ways, notably by suicide and gun violence.[9] Human life in the Scottish ex-coalfields is not as unforgiving, but the regionalised patterns of ill-health and material inequality arising from deindustrialisation are clear enough. In August 2013 across Great Britain the out of work benefit claimant rate, aggregating incapacity benefit, job seekers' allowance and income support, was 10.9 per cent. In the coalfields as a whole it was 14.1 per cent. In the ex-coal communities of Fife and Ayrshire/Lanarkshire it was 15.7 per cent and 15.2 per cent respectively.[10]

Community memorials to coal disasters and coal lives are therefore reflective of deindustrialisation's 'half-life', a long process of recovery and endurance generated by the closure of collieries, factories and mills everywhere.[11] Memorialisation is accompanied by a communal desire to salvage positive social fabric from the painful recent past, moving past the shock of closure and its immediate aftermath to reflect more carefully on the good times as well as the hard times associated with industrial employment and communities.[12] The difficulties, including the punishing experience of much industrial work, cannot be discounted. In linking the human casualties of the coal industry to the Thatcher government's narrative that was used to rationalise colliery closures, the Loanhead memorial, like many others in ex-industrial communities, provides evidence of what Steven High terms 'the wounds of class'. It recognises that industrial employment was both dangerous and rewarding. And it is also a cautionary reminder that deindustrialisation was not a passive development, with an accidental legacy of ruined buildings and broken lives in ex-industrial locations. Given the centrality of disinvestment decisions by policy-makers and business leaders, deindustrialisation was actually a dynamic process, involving the active ruination of lively and liveable industrial communities.[13]

The political consequences of deindustrialisation have been complicated. Voting patterns across the UK indicate that the process has been unpopular in ex-industrial localities, and by many is understood either as the consequence or ineffectiveness of government policy. Thatcher's governments did not seek the loss of industrial jobs, but pursued deregulation, privatisation and the removal of trade union voice from policy-making. These were barriers to deindustrialisation. Without them the erosion of industrial activity and employment accelerated. The 'policy consequence' understanding of deindustrialisation explains why in ex-coalfield territories there has been a move away from support for the Conservative Party, although less so in England and perhaps Wales than in Scotland, and in England less so in Nottinghamshire and even Yorkshire than in Northumberland and Durham. In the Nottinghamshire constituencies of Sherwood and Mansfield, each with substantial mining interests, increased Conservative voting in the 1987 General Election was influenced by the strike in 1984–5, which the majority of local miners had not supported. A trend back to Labour was evident in the General Elections of 1992 and 1997, but was reversed subsequently. Popular support for the Labour Party, in Nottinghamshire as elsewhere, was gradually reduced by the 'policy ineffectiveness' understanding of deindustrialisation. The Coalfields Regeneration Trust, a social enterprise and charity established in 1999 with encouragement from the Labour government, sponsored new business and employment growth, along with skills training, particularly among younger people.[14] Labour acquired limited political credit from this. In England in the summer of 2016 the long-term political consequences of deindustrialisation included substantial working class disaffection with mainstream parties and existing structures in ex-coalfield localities. In the referendum on UK membership of the European Union there were large majorities in favour of leaving in Nottinghamshire, Derbyshire and Yorkshire: 70.9 per cent in Mansfield, 70.8 per cent in Bolsover, and 68.3 per cent in Barnsley. The leave share of the vote, 51.9 per cent, was also exceeded in the north-east: 57.5 per cent in Durham and 54.1 per cent in Northumberland. But in Scotland there were significant majorities for remain in all of the ex-coalfields, the lowest at 58.3 per cent in Ayrshire and the highest at 63.1 per cent in North Lanarkshire. This followed the national pattern in Scotland, where remain secured 62 per cent of the vote.[15]

The 2016 referendum reinforced the sense that the long-term political impact of deindustrialisation in Scotland has been different. The move away from Labour in the coalfields involved greater support for Scottish nationalism and independence, with the political-constitutional structures of the UK seen as an economic threat to everyday material security. In 2013 Margaret Thatcher's death was celebrated, this verb consciously emphasised, by ex-miners and their supporters interviewed by reporters in Midlothian. The former Prime Minister had 'destroyed' Scotland through policies that destabilised and then destroyed industrial production and employment. A clear national narrative was evident, although class politics were present too. There was similar 'rejoicing' in Durham and Yorkshire.[16] 'Thatcher dead', texted Ken Capstick, former Vice President of the NUM Yorkshire Area, to his friend, Arthur Scargill, the former President of the NUM, in April 2013. 'SCARGILL ALIVE', came the reply.[17]

The politics of nation in Scotland were more prominent on the thirtieth anniversary of the strike, competing with a class and trade union narrative in the framing of public memory. Labour MSPs Iain Gray and Neil Findlay secured a debate in March 2014 in the Scottish Parliament to discuss the anniversary. Gray and Findlay revisited the strike in class terms, focusing on the solidarity of mining communities and the injustice experienced by miners in all parts of the coalfield, including Scotland. Findlay spoke about the campaign for an inquiry into policing at Orgreave in South Yorkshire in June 1984, and called for an examination of policing and the operation of the law in Scotland during the strike. He pointed to the substantial circumstantial evidence that criminal justice was used by the state to discipline the strikers in Scotland, and weaken the effectiveness of their actions. The Scottish government opposed such investigation in 2014. SNP Ministers and MSPs were uninterested in the class dimensions of the strike, which they characterised as an imposition on Scottish coal communities by twin external forces, the Thatcher governments and the NUM's national leadership.[18] This blindness to class arguably demonstrated the continued defects of nationalism from a trade union perspective, highlighted by Michael McGahey and other NUMSA leaders when arguing for devolution in the 1960s and 1970s. It was difficult, however, to present the Scottish government as chauvinistic in nationalist terms by the later 2010s. The commitment to social justice was more than rhetorical, supported by significant initiatives on the living wage, measures mitigating UK government welfare spending cuts, and a progressive agenda on equality issues.[19]

The distinct political legacy of deindustrialisation in Scotland was further borne out by the referendum in September 2014 on Scottish Independence. Regional results indicated extensive popular acceptance of the view that deindustrialisation and its legacy were as much a question of nation as class. Overall 44.7 per cent of voters cast their ballots for Yes to Scottish Independence. The Yes vote exceeded this in five of the ex-coalfield local authority areas: East Ayrshire, North Lanarkshire, where there was a Yes majority, South Lanarkshire, Clackmannan, and Fife.[20] The SNP share of the vote in a number of ex-coalfield constituencies also exceeded the national average in the Scottish Parliament Election of 2016. Yet class was not eclipsed entirely. Labour's share fell relatively softly in ex-mining areas. The complexities of deindustrialisation's political legacy were encapsulated in the constituencies of Airdrie & Shotts in Lanarkshire, where closures had been initiated by the NCB in the late 1940s and early 1950s, and Cowdenbeath in Fife, the core of the old 'Little Moscows', where restructuring in the 1960s had shut the Village Pits. In each of these constituencies there was a healthy showing for SNP and Labour, and their combined share of the vote was 82 per cent, suggesting that some element of class alignment survived alongside a greater emphasis on distinctly Scottish priorities.[21] Such remained the case even in the UK General Election of 2017. In the context of a Conservative – or, more accurately, a Unionist – 'resurgence' in Scotland, the combined SNP-Labour share of votes in both constituencies still exceeded 73 per cent. Economic security in the ex-coalfields remained a priority, and social democratic Labour and SNP candiates were seen as its best defenders.[22]

In June 2018 Michael Matheson, the Scottish government's Cabinet Secretary for Justice, reversed the SNP's earlier thinking and announced an independent review of the impact of policing on affected communities in the 1984–5 strike. A kind of social democratic consensus seemed to be coalescing, emphasising the collective harm caused in the coalfields by the agents of the UK state and the broader process of deindustrialisation. The review, chaired by John Scott QC, and assisted by Dennis Canavan, former Labour MP and MSP for coalfield constituencies in Stirlingshire, Jim Murdoch, Professor of Public Law at the University of Glasgow, and Kate Thomson, former Assistant Chief Constable in Police Scotland, began collecting evidence in August 2018. Public consultation meetings were held across the ex-coalfields in mining welfare institutes between October and December 2018. Former strikers provided vivid testimony of police harassment, intimidation and physical violence. They told of being arrested, some of them young men still in their teenage years, and being placed under very heavy pressure by police officers to plead guilty to alleged offences, or face lengthy spells in prison on remand. Some pleaded guilty, with the union paying their fines, simply in order to get back into the community where they could support the strike. The unusually vindictive punishments in sheriff courts were also emphasised, along with the suspected collusion between police and NCB to secure the dismissals from employment of strike activists.[23] The review was due to submit an interim report to Matheson's successor as Secretary for Justice after a Scottish Cabinet reshuffle, Humza Yousaf, early in 2019, with a final report expected later in the same year.[24]

* * *

The Auld Union Banner carried by miners from Barony and Killoch collieries in Ayrshire identified three steps to the goal of socialism: legislate, educate, organise. This book has defined the miners' socialism in terms of security: stable jobs, safe workplaces, and viable communities. The miners articulated their pursuit of security primarily in terms of class, but the distinct national interests of Scottish workers were continually reasserted. Gender and community were additional elements in an intersectional coalfield social identity. The four dimensions of class, nation, gender and community were fluid and changed over time, interacting with a variety of dynamic material contingencies: economic structure; ownership of the coal industry; the strength of union voice; workplace scale, safety and production technique; pit closures and deindustrialisation. Community had a double meaning in the coalfields: economic localities where mining absorbed a dominant share of male employment; and ideological communalities where citizens adhered to agreed social values. Economic restructuring and deindustrialisation gradually eroded community as economic locality, but moral economy feeling in the coalfields was bolstered by this process. Community in ideological terms was duly fortified in the 1960s and 1970s, and further strengthened in response to deindustrialisation in the 1980s and 1990s, particularly as gender relations incrementally became less unequal.

There was one additional factor in the miners' changing social identity over time: generation. Three distinct generations have been identified in this book. They were structured by changes to the predominant form of production regime in the Scottish coal industry. Each generation understood economic security in distinct terms, and pursued it in different ways. Nationalisation of the coal industry was the key ambition of the Village Pit generation, whose members came of age in the volatile economic and industrial conditions of the 1920s. Private ownership was seen as an obstacle to security. Employment was continually interrupted; communities were destabilised by wage-cutting, the coal masters' default response to market competition; and mining in Scotland was more dangerous than elsewhere in the UK, through a combination of forced-pace mechanisation, financial cost-reduction, and the suppression of trade union voice. Key activists like Abe and Alex Moffat were sacked and victimised after the 1926 lockout. They only secured a return to underground employment with rearmament and the Second World War. Nationalisation was a major achievement won by the Village Pit generation. Safety was much improved by the transfer from private to public ownership. The NCB accepted the value of close dialogue with the NUM and other industry unions, and the exercise of worker voice had a highly positive impact. In Scotland under private ownership there were on average 0.46

deaths per 100,000 man-shifts per annum from 1932 to 1941, but only 0.25 deaths per 100,000 man-shifts per annum under public ownership from 1947 to 1956.

Nationalisation was not an unambiguous triumph, however. Insecurity remained in the coalfields, directly encountered by the thousands of miners who experienced redundancy or redeployment in the 1950s and 1960s, as the NCB concentrated production in a dwindling number of pits. Community abandonment in Lanarkshire was implicit in this restructuring, which the Village Pit generation of miners' leaders was not equipped ideologically or practically to resist. The Moffats and their peers – in England and Wales as well as Scotland – had been reluctant to accept responsibility for a greater share in the managerial structures of the industry, preferring the certainties of adversarial bargaining. The New Mine generation, born in the 1920s, attained adulthood in the military and industrial conflict of the Second World War, where its members found themselves at odds with Village Pit union officials as well as employers and the state. The early problems of nationalisation consolidated generational distinctions. New Mine generation workers and union representatives were more willing than their elders to criticise the new regime and engage with the NCB and UK policy-makers on higher-order strategic questions. The miners' moral economy approach to industrial change, articulated initially by the Village Pit generation, was enforced more strongly by the New Mine generation. In conceptual terms, market-ness in the coalfields was appreciably lowered, and the economic dimension of work was more thickly embedded in the social requirements of mining communities. This involved an acceptance of industrial restructuring, so long as collective economic security was maintained, and on the basis of social dialogue. Closures of pits and losses of jobs in mining were acceptable where local and comparably paid alternatives were organised. There were two possibilities: transfers to other collieries, within daily travel distance, or employment in new factories established by private sector manufacturers, usually with government regional assistance.

New industry jobs helped to reshape gender relations in the coalfields in a progressive manner. Inequality between men and women was an important legacy of the privately owned industry.

The poverty of workplace amenity placed a burden on women domestically, to launder clothing and prepare baths for men, often in badly equipped and over-crowded housing. Public sector initiatives in housing from the 1940s therefore also contributed in the longer run to reduced gender inequality. A distinct Scottish pattern was evident. At the insistence of the miners, local authorities and not the NCB, as elsewhere in the British coalfields, took the lead in expanding housing provision. This separation of the roles of coalfield employer and landlord was vital, providing households with greater security of tenure in times of social crisis, as in 1984–5. Public sector and local authority employment provided additional opportunities for women, along with the new jobs in manufacturing. In 1981 the rate of employment among married women in coalfield communities was above the national Scottish average. Male chauvinism remained an unpleasant characteristic of coalfield social relations, but a strong countervailing trend was embedded in the politics of mining trade unionism before 1984. The strike gave further impetus to greater equality between women and men. In Fife and the Lothians especially, partly reflecting the influence of Communist politics, women helped to lead the defence of economic security, strengthening community cohesion and resilience. The additional personal and collective confidence acquired by many women contributed to enhanced female participation in political and public life after the strike, into the 1990s and the twenty-first century.

The general solidarity of the strike illustrated the depth of moral economy feeling in the coalfields. This was linked to an understanding of power in the UK state. Miners from the 1950s onwards were arguing that Scotland was a nation, with distinct economic interests and social characteristics. Security in the coalfields also required the redistribution across class boundaries of wealth in the UK, which Scottish workers had helped to create over centuries. Home Rule was a means of reconciling these competing interests: separate political structures on national lines but shared resources within the UK. The NUMSA – especially its New Mine generation leaders in the 1960s and 1970s – persuaded the Scottish labour movement, through the STUC, to support Home Rule. This was consistent with an internationalist view that emphasised the liberating value of decolonisation. Scotland was a nation with the right to self-determination in the same way as the new states being formed in Africa and Asia. The presence of North Vietnamese trade union representatives at the NUMSA Gala in Holyrood in 1969 was important symbolically. New Mine generation activism utilised Scottish nation arguments to stabilise employment in the coal industry. This dropped sharply from 1957 to 1967, but then fell much more slowly until 1979. The radical cuts envisaged in the Labour government's *Fuel Policy* White Paper of 1967 were resisted. Scotland's distinct economic interests were conceded by policy-makers, with enhanced public investment in coal-fired power stations, and the Labour Party at UK level broadly persuaded of the need for Home Rule. Devolution was blocked in the late 1970s, in part by Labour MPs in Westminster. Within the Scottish labour movement and a broader Civic Scotland coalition it was revived and emboldened as a political issue in 1984–5, and the debates about deindustrialisation and the democratic deficit that followed.

The miners' success in achieving significant pay rises through collective action in the early 1970s reflected the emergence of the Cosmopolitan Colliery generation, its members born in the late 1940s and 1950s, and beginning their working life in the 1960s. These workers were assembled in larger industrial units, and typically spent an hour or so each day travelling between work and home. They were conscious of having traded valued local assets, Village Pits and even New Mines, for the small number of giant Cosmopolitan Collieries. These were resources with a future, which striking miners defended in 1984–5. In the 1970s miners successfully improved their wages position, partly in the context of changing energy politics. The surge of the oil price gave them a short-term advantage. But oil was also identified as a long-term threat to security in the coalfields by McGahey and the New Mine generation in the 1970s. The rapid exploitation of the North Sea in the 1980s contributed to deindustrialisation. Rising oil prices did not shelter coal from production and job cuts. Tax revenues from the North Sea elevated the value of sterling, damaging the competitiveness of manufacturing industry and eliminating industrial jobs. The ensuing fall in demand for coal placed renewed pressure on miners' jobs; the capacity for collective working class and trade union resistance was diminished by rising unemployment. The miners enjoyed effective practical as well as moral and financial support from other unionised workers in the national strikes of 1972 and 1974 but this could not be reproduced on the same scale in 1984–5.

The chief characteristic of the 1984–5 strike was the attack on union voice by the UK government and its confederates in the NCB. There was a war against the miners. The military metaphor is carefully chosen and not an over-statement. The government was intent on reordering society, upwardly distributing wealth and authority, and narrowing the practical basis of democracy. Without meaningful working class participation in policy-making, Britain in the 1980s rapidly became a far more unequal society. This was the process that the Cosmopolitan Colliery generation of coalfield men and women were resisting. Deindustrialisation accelerated after the strike, with many damaging results. But moral economy feeling in coalfield and then ex-coalfield communities in Scotland was intensified rather than extinguished. Thatcherism in this sense was unsuccessful. In ideological terms ex-mining communities have not been defeated. Their social values survive, and continue to shape Scotland's distinct politics in the twenty-first century. The memorial service for the miners of Michael Colliery in September 2017 demonstrated the hardiness and optimism of these communities, and their continued commitment to collective economic security and social solidarity.

Notes

1. 'Mining Disaster: Village marks 50 years since colliery fire', https://stv.tv/news/features/1397346-mining-disaster-marks-50th-anniversary-with-memorial/, accessed 13 September 2017; 'Fife pays tribute to victims of the 1967 East Wemyss colliery disaster', *The Scotsman*, 9 September 1967, http://www.scotsman.com/news/politics/fife-pays-tribute-to-victims-of-1967-east-wemyss-colliery-disaster-1-4555758, accessed 13 September 2017.
2. Selway, 'Mining Accidents and Memory in South Wales'.
3. Andy Clark and Ewan Gibbs, 'Voices of social dislocation, lost work and economic restructuring: Narratives from marginalised localities in the "New Scotland"', *Memory Studies*, 2017, early online publication, 21 pp.

4. Jackie Clarke, 'Afterlives of a Factory: Memory, Place and Space in Alençon', in Steven High, Lachlan MacKinnon and Andrew Perchard, eds, *The Deindustrialized World: Confronting Ruination in Postindustrial Places* (University of British Columbia Press: Vancouver, 2017), pp. 111–25, and especially pp. 112–13.

5. McIvor, 'Deindustrialization Embodied'.

6. Foden, Fothergill and Gore, *State of the Coalfields*, p. 16.

7. Perchard, '"Broken Men" and "Thatcher's Children"'.

8. Mhairi MacKenzie, Chik Collins, John Connolly, Mick Doyle and Gerry McCartney, 'Working-class Discourses of Politics, Policy and Health: "I don't smoke; don't drink. The only thing wrong with me is my health"', *Policy and Politics*, 45.2 (2017), pp. 231–49.

9. Portelli, *They Say in Harlan County*, p. 311.

10. Foden, Fothergill and Gore, *State of the Coalfields*, pp. 22–3.

11. Tim Strangleman, 'Deindustrialisation and the Historical Sociological Imagination: making sense of work and industrial change', *Sociology*, 51 (2017), pp. 466–82.

12. Shelley Condratto and Ewan Gibbs, 'After Industrial Citizenship: Adapting to Precarious Employment in the Lanarkshire Coalfield, Scotland, and Sudbury Hardrock Mining, Canada', *Labour/Le Travail*, 81 (Spring 2018), pp. 213–39.

13. Steven High, '"The Wounds of Class": A Historiographical Reflection on the Study of Deindustrialization, 1973–2013 ', *History Compass*, 11 (2013), pp. 994–1007.

14. The Coalfields Regeneration Trust, http://www.coalfields-regen.org.uk/, accessed 30 April 2016.

15. Matthew Godwin, 'Labour's core voters no longer share its progressive values', *The Guardian*, 24 June 2016; Ian Jack, 'First the elite ignored the estates. Now the estates have turned on the elite', *The Guardian*, 25 June 2016.

16. Severin Carrell, 'Scottish miners celebrate Thatcher's funeral with whisky and morbid jokes', *The Guardian*, 17 April 2013; Simon Hattenstone, 'Lady Thatcher's funeral: no tears at Easington colliery', *The Guardian*, 17 April 2013; Helen Pidd and David Conn, 'Margaret Thatcher's death greeted with little sympathy by Orgreave veterans', *The Guardian*, 8 April 2013.

17. John Harris, 'In Search of Arthur Scargill: 30 years after the strike', *The Guardian*, 28 February 2014.

18. The Scottish Parliament, *Official Report. Meeting of the Parliament.* Thursday 20 March 2014, http://www.scottish.parliament.uk/parliamentarybusiness/28862.aspx?r=9054&mode=html#iob_81837.

19. BBC News, Scotland Business, 'Scottish government unveils "living wage nation" plans', 12 November 2017, http://www.bbc.co.uk/news/uk-scotland-scotland-business-41956518, accessed 13 November 2017; Scottish Government, 'Stark reality of UK Government welfare cuts', 29 June 2017, https://beta.gov.scot/news/stark-reality-of-uk-government-welfare-cuts, accessed 13 November 2017.

20. Roderick McInnes, Steven Ayres and Oliver Hawkins. *Scottish Independence Referendum 2014: analysis of results* (House of Commons Library: London, 2014), p. 4.

21. Scottish Parliament 2016 Results, *The Guardian*, 7 May 2016.

22. General Election Results, *The Guardian*, 10 June 2017.

23 Author notes of Public Consultation Meeting, Fallin Miners Welfare Society and Social Club, 5 December 2018.

24. Scottish Government, 'Independent review of policing during Miners' Strike', 7 June 2018, https://news.gov.scot/news/independent-review-of-policing-during-miners-strike, accessed 13 June 2018.

Bibliography

Interviews

Unless otherwise indicated, these were conducted by the author in the homes of interviewees, with union position and colliery affiliation where appropriate in parenthesis.

Rab Amos (SCEBTA, Monktonhall), Roslin, 23 February 2011.
Iain Chalmers (NUM, Seafield), Cowdenbeath, 30 July 2009.
Eric Clarke (NUMSA General Secretary), Scottish Mining Museum, Newtongrange, 25 August 2009.
Councillor Willie Clarke (NUM, Seafield), Ballingry, 13 November 2009.
David Hamilton MP (NUM, Monktonhall), Parliamentary Advice Office, Dalkeith, 30 September 2009.
John Hume, Interview with Valerie Wright and author, Lilybank House, University of Glasgow, 23 November 2017.
Nicky Wilson (SCEBTA, Cardowan), Scottish Miners' Convalescent Home, Blair Castle, Culross, 18 August 2009.

Willie Thompson Interviews

Willie Thompson generously provided recordings of interviews he conducted in 1985–6.

Ayrshire strike leaders (Barony and Killoch), 9 December 1985.
George Bolton (NUMSA Vice President), undated, but presumed late 1985.
Ella Egan (COSA, and convenor of NUMSA Women's Support Group), 28 October 1985.

Archive Materials

Glasgow Caledonian University Archives

Scottish Trades Union Congress, General Council Papers: 1961–2, 1967–9, 1972, 1981.

Kirkcaldy Art Gallery and Museum

NUM, Seafield and Frances Strike Committee, Dysart Strike Centre, Reports, March 1984 to July 1984.
Iain Chalmers, Strike Diary, 1984.

Methil Heritage Centre, Fife

L-15-8   Wellesley Colliery
L-15-9   Michael Colliery

The Mining Institute, Newcastle

David Douglass Archives

The National Archives, Kew

BX 6   Coal Industry Social Welfare Organisation: Division General.
CAB 130   Cabinet Miscellaneous Committees.
COAL 26   NCB, Industrial Relations Department.
COAL 29   NCB, Production Department.
COAL 31   NCB, Chairman's Office.
COAL 74   NCB, Minute Series.
COAL 75   NCB, Minute Series: Divisional.
COAL 89   NCB, Secretary's Department: Colliery Files.
COAL 101 NCB, Operational Research Executive and predecessors.
EW 7   Department of Economic Affairs: Regional Policy.
EW 8   Department of Economic Affairs: Growth, Incomes and Prices Policy Division.
FV 19   Ministry of Fuel and Power, Statistics Division and Successors: Registered Files.
LAB 10   Department of Employment and Predecessors: Industrial Relations.
LAB 77   Department of Employment and Predecessors: Private Office Papers.

POWE 37   Ministry of Fuel and Power, Coal Division, and Successors: Registered Files.

POWE 52   Ministry of Fuel and Power, Coal Division, and Successors: Registered Files.

POWE 63   Ministry of Power, Petroleum Division, and Successors: Registered Files.

PREM 11   Prime Minister's Office: Correspondence and Papers, 1951–64.

PREM 13   Prime Minister's Office: Correspondence and Papers, 1964–70.

PREM 15   Prime Minister's Office: Correspondence and Papers, 1970–4.

National Library of Scotland, Edinburgh

Acc. 9805   NUMSA, Papers and Correspondence.

National Mining Museum of Scotland, Newtongrange

Lothian Coal Company, Records.
NUMSA, Executive Committee Minutes.
NUMSA, Delegate Conference Minutes.
NUMSA, Strike Committee, Minutes, 1984–5.
NUMSA, Strike Coordinating Committee.

National Records of Scotland, Edinburgh

CB 3   Fife Coal Company, records.
CB 51   NCB, Scottish Division, Output and Manpower statistics.
CB55   NCB, Scottish Division, Colliery Committees.
CB 65   Coal Industry, Histories.
CB 121   NCB, Scottish Area, Colliery Accountability Meetings.
CB 99   NCB, Scottish Division, Colliery Consultative Committee papers.
CB207   NCB, Scottish Division, Auchengeich Colliery.
CB 229   NCB, Scottish Area, Bilston Glen Colliery.
CB 235   NCB, Scottish Division, Blairhall Colliery.
CB 243   NCB, Scottish Division, Bothwell Castle Colliery.
CB 260   NCB, Scottish Division, Closure of Colliery records.
CB 267   NCB, Scottish Division, Comrie Colliery.
CB 276   NCB, Scottish Division, Devon Colliery.
CB 305   NCB, Scottish Division, Glencraig Colliery.
CB 307   NCB, Scottish Division, Glenochil Colliery.
CB 313   NCB, Scottish Division, Hamilton Palace Colliery.
CB 335   NCB, Scottish Area, Kinneil Colliery.

CB 346   NCB, Scottish Division, Lochhead Colliery.
CB 352   NCB, Scottish Division, Manor Powis Colliery.
CB 353   NCB, Scottish Division, Mary Colliery.
CB 360   NCB, Scottish Division, Michael Colliery.
CB 363   NCB, Scottish Area, Monktonhall Colliery.
CB 380   NCB, Scottish Area, Polkemmet Colliery.
CB 382   NCB, Scottish Area, Polmaise Colliery.
CB 398   NCB, Scottish Area, Seafield Colliery.
CB 420   NCB, Scottish Division, Valleyfield Colliery.
DD 10   Scottish Home Department, Papers.
HH 56   Scottish Home Department, Civil Emergencies Files.
SC 21   Dunfermline Sheriff Court, Records.
SEP 2   Industry Department of Scotland, Papers.
SEP 4   Board of Trade Office for Scotland and Successors, Papers.
SEP 10   Ministry of Labour, Reports.
SEP 14   Scottish Development Department, Papers.
SEP 17   Secretary of State for Scotland, Correspondence.

University of Glasgow Archives

GB 248, ACCN 1786   Papers of Sir Iain Kinloch MacGregor, Industrialist.

Official Publications

Board of Trade, *Coal*, Cmd. 6364 (HMSO: London, 1942).
Census 1961 England & Wales. County Report, Nottinghamshire (HMSO: London, 1964).
Census 1971 England & Wales. Country Report, Nottinghamshire, Part II (HMSO: London, 1973).
Census 1981 England & Wales. County Reports, Nottinghamshire, part 1 (HMSO: London, 1982).
Employment Policy, Cmd. 6527 (HMSO: London, 1944).
Department of Economic Affairs, *The National Plan*, Cmnd. 2764 (HMSO: London, 1965).
Department of Employment and Productivity, *In Place of Strife. A Policy for Industrial Relations*, Cmnd. 3888 (HMSO: London, 1969).
Department of Trade and Industry, *Extensive Fall of Roof at Seafield Colliery Fife, 10 May 1973, Report by J. W. Calder, Chief Inspector of Mines and Quarries*, Cmnd. 5485 (HMSO: London, 1973).
General Registry Office, *Census 1951 Scotland. Volume IV: Occupations and Industries* (HMSO: Edinburgh, 1956).

General Registry Office, *Census 1961 Scotland. County Reports* (HMSO: Edinburgh, 1963–4).

General Registry Office, *Census 1961 Scotland. Volume Six. Occupation, Industry and Workplace. Part III Workplace Tables* (HMSO: Edinburgh, 1966).

General Registry Office, Edinburgh, *Census 1971 Scotland. Economic Activity: County Tables, Part II* (HMSO: Edinburgh, 1975).

McInnes, Roderick, Steven Ayres and Oliver Hawkins. *Scottish Independence Referendum 2014: analysis of results* (House of Commons Library: London, 2014).

Mines Department, *Explosion at Cardowan Colliery, Lanarkshire, on 16 November 1932, by Sir Henry Walker, C.B.E., H.M. Chief Inspector of Mines*, Cmd. 4309 (HMSO: London, 1933).

Ministry of Fuel and Power, *Accident at Knockshinnoch Castle Colliery, Ayrshire, 7 September 1950, by Sir Andrew Bryan, H.M. Chief Inspector of Mines*, Cmd. 8180 (HMSO: London, 1951).

Ministry of Labour, *Labour Gazette* (HMSO: London).

Ministry of Power, *Explosion at Cardowan Colliery, Lanarkshire, on 25 July 1960, by H. R. Houston, C.B.E., H.M. Deputy Chief Inspector of Mines and Quarries*, Cmnd. 1260 (HMSO: London, 1961).

Ministry of Power, *Explosion at Kames Colliery, Ayrshire, 19 November 1957, Report by Sir Harold Roberts*, Cmnd. 467 (HMSO: London, 1958).

Ministry of Power, *Explosion at Lindsay Colliery, Fifeshire, 14 December 1957, by Sir Harold Roberts*, Cmnd. 485 (HMSO: London, 1958).

Ministry of Power, *Fire at Michael Colliery, Fife, 9 September 1967. Report by H. S. Stephenson, H.M. Chief Inspector of Mines and Quarries*, Cmnd. 3657 (HMSO: London, 1968).

Ministry of Power, *Fuel Policy*, Cmnd. 3428 (HMSO: London, 1967).

Ministry of Power, *Underground Fire at Auchengeich Colliery, Lanarkshire, 18 September 1959, by T. A. Rogers, H.M. Chief Inspector of Mines and Quarries*, Cmnd. 1022 (HMSO: London, 1960).

Monopolies and Mergers Commission, *National Coal Board. A Report on the efficiency and costs in the development, production and supply of coal by the National Coal Board, Volume One* and *Volume Two*, Cmnd. 8920 (HMSO: London, 1983).

NCB, *Report and Accounts for 1950*, HC 188 (HMSO: London, 1951).

NCB, *Report and Accounts for 1957*, HC 181 (HMSO: London, 1958).

NCB, *Report and Accounts for 1967–68*, HC 401 (HMSO: London, 1968).

NCB, *Report and Accounts for 1968–69*, HC 446 (HMSO: London, 1969).

NCB, *Report and Accounts for 1969–70*, HC 130 (HMSO: London, 1970.

NCB, *Report and Accounts for 1971–72*, HC 445 (HMSO: London, 1972).

NCB, *Report and Accounts, 1983/4* (NCB: London, 1984).

NCB Scottish Division, *Scotland's Coal Plan* (NCB: Edinburgh, 1955).

Our Changing Democracy: Devolution to Scotland and Wales, Cmnd. 6438 (HMSO: London, 1975).

Parliamentary Debates, Fifth Series, Commons (HMSO: London).

Registry General Scotland, *Census 1981 Scotland. Reports for Central Region, Fife Region, Lothian Region*, and *Strathclyde Region, Volumes 1 and 4* (HMSO: Edinburgh, 1982).

Registry General Scotland, *Census 1981. New Towns. Volume 1* (HMSO: Edinburgh, 1983).

Royal Commission on the Constitution. Minutes of Evidence, Volume IV, Scotland (HMSO: London, 1970).

Royal Commission on the Constitution: Volume 1, Report, Cmnd. 5460 (HMSO: London, 1973).

Royal Commission on Safety in Coal Mines. Report, Cmd. 5890 (HMSO: London, 1938).

Royal Commission on Trades Unions and Employers' Associations 1965–1968, Cmnd. 3623 (HMSO: London, 1968).

Scotland's Census 2001. Key Statistics for Council Areas and Health Boards Across Scotland (HMSO: Edinburgh, 2003).

Scottish Development Department, *Central Scotland: Programme for Development and Growth*, Cmnd. 2188 (HMSO: London, 1963).

The Scottish Office, *The Scottish Economy, 1965 to 1970: A Plan For Expansion*, Cmnd. 2864 (HMSO: Edinburgh, 1966).

The Scottish Office, *Scottish Abstract of Statistics*, No. 9/1980 (HMSO: Edinburgh, 1980).

The Scottish Parliament, *Official Report* (HMSO: Edinburgh).

Industry and Labour Publications

Committee of Inquiry appointed by the Scottish Council (Development and Industry) under the Chairmanship of J. N. Toothill, *Report on the Scottish Economy* (SCDI: Edinburgh, 1961).

Cowan, James R., 'National Coal Board: Scottish Area in the 1980s', *Mining Technology* 62, No. 711 (January 1980), pp. 20–1.

Cunningham, Andrew S., *The Fife Coal Company Limited. The Jubilee Year, 1872–1922* (Fife United Press Limited: Leven, 1922).

Fife Federation of Trades Councils with Richard Saville and George Kerevan, *Comrie Colliery: the Fight for the Future!* (Fife Federation of Trades Councils, no date, presumed 1986).

Muir, Augustus, *The Fife Coal Company Limited: A Short History* (Fife Coal Company: Leven, approximately 1948).

Reed, Howard and Jacob Mohun Himmelweit, *Where Have All the Wages Gone? Lost pay and profits outside financial services* (TUC: London, 2012).

Scottish Miner.

STUC, *69th Annual Report*, The Music Hall, Aberdeen, 19–22 April 1966 (STUC: Glasgow, 1966).

STUC, *70th Annual Report*, The Queen's Hall, Dunoon, 18–21 April 1967 (STUC: Glasgow, 1967).

STUC, *71st Annual Report*, The Beach Ballroom, Aberdeen, 16–19 April 1968 (STUC: Glasgow, 1968).

STUC, *72nd Annual Report*, The Pavilion, Rothesay, 15–18 April 1969 (STUC: Glasgow, 1969).

STUC, *79th Annual Report*, The City Hall, Perth, 19–23 April 1976 (STUC, Glasgow, 1976).

STUC, *80th Annual Report*, The Pavilion, Rothesay, 18–22 April 1977 (STUC: Glasgow, 1977).

STUC, *81st Annual Report*, The Music Hall, Aberdeen, 17–21 April 1978 (STUC: Glasgow, 1978).

UCATT, False Self Employment, https://www.ucatt.org.uk/false-self-employment, accessed 15 March 2017.

West Lothian Trade Union Council, *Unity Is Strength: West Lothian Memories of the Miners' Strike, 1984–85* (West Lothian TUC, 2015).

Coal Communities Ephemeral Literature and Online Collections

Ayrshire History, http://www.ayrshirehistory.com

The Coalfields Regeneration Trust, http://www.coalfields-regen.org.uk

Durham Mining Museum, http://www.dmm.org.uk

Fife Psychogeographical Collective, 'Searching For Storione – A walk with the ghosts of Little Moscow', posted 25 May 2013, http://fifepsychogeography.com/2013/05/29/searching-for-storione-a-walk-with-the-ghosts-of-little-moscow

Homer Sykes, Photographer, http://homersykes.photoshelter.com/gallery

Margaret Thatcher Foundation, https://www.margaretthatcher.org

Milton Rogovin, Social Documentary Photographer, http://www.milton-rogovin.com

Working Class Movement Library, https://www.wcml.org.uk

Levy, Catriona and Mauchline Miners' Wives *'A Very Hard Year'. 1984–5 Miners' Strike in Mauchline* (Workers' Educational Association: Glasgow, 1985).

Newspapers

The Courier
The Daily Telegraph
The Economist
Glasgow Herald and *The Herald*
The Guardian and *Manchester Guardian*
The Observer
The Scotsman
The Times

Television, Film and DVDs

Cinema Action, *UCS 1* (1971); available on *Tales from the Shipyard*, a two-disc DVD set published by the British Film Institute in 2011.

Gaumont British Instructional Films, *The New Mine* (1945), directed by Irene Wilson and produced by Donald Carter.

Here We Go. Women Living the Strike. Presented and Directed by Margaret Wright, (TV2DAY, Independent Video Production, 2009).

The Miners' Hymns, a film by Bill Morrison with music by Johann Johannsson, Hypnotic Pictures, 2010, BFI.

NCB Collection, Volume One, Portrait of a Miner (London, 2009).

Safety First, directed by Peter Pickering, Data Film Productions, NCB, *Mining Review*, 2nd Year, No. 11, July 1949.

The Spirit of '45 (Sixteen Fly Limited/The British Film Institute, 2013), directed by Ken Loach.

A Star Drops In, directed by Peter Pickering, Data Film Productions, NCB, *Mining Review*, 2nd Year, No. 11, July 1949.

Secondary Literature

Ackers, Peter, 'Gramsci at the Miners' Strike: Remembering the 1984–1985 Eurocommunist Alternative Industrial Relations Strategy', *Labor History*, 55 (2015), pp. 151–72.

Ackers, Peter and Alastair J. Reid, 'Other Worlds of Labour: Liberal-Pluralism in Twentieth-Century British Labour History', in Peter Ackers and Alastair J. Reid, eds, *Alternatives to State-Socialism in Britain: other Worlds of Labour in the Twentieth Century* (Palgrave: London, 2017), pp. 1–27.

Addison, Paul, *Churchill on the Home Front* (Jonathan Cape: London, 1992).

Adeney, Martin and John Lloyd, *The Miners' Strike, 1984–5: Loss Without Limit* (Routledge & Kegan Paul: London, 1986).

Allen, V. L., *The Militancy of British Miners* (The Moor Press: Shipley, 1981).

Amos, David, *The Miners of Nottinghamshire. Volume 4: 1980–1985* (Union of Democratic Mineworkers: Mansfield, 2013).

Aprile, Sylvie, Matthieu de Oliveira and Béatrice Touchelay, 'Introduction', in Sylvie Aprile, Matthieu de Oliveira, Béatrice Touchelay and Karl-Michael Hoin, *Les Houillères entre l'État, le marché et la société* (Septentrion Presses Universitaires: Villeneuve d'Ascq, 2015), pp. 17–19.

Amos, David and Natalie Braber, *Coal Mining in the East Midlands* (Bradwell Books: Sheffield, 2017).

Anderson, Benedict, *Imagined Communities: reflections on the origins and spread of nationalism* (Verso: London, 1983).

Arnold, Jörg, '"The Death of Sympathy." Coal Mining, Workplace Hazards, and the Politics of Risk in Britain, ca. 1970–1990', *Historical Social Research*, 41 (2016), pp. 91–110.

Arnold, Jörg, '"Like Being on Death Row": Britain and the End of Coal, c.1970 to the present', *Contemporary British History*, 32.1 (2018), pp. 1–17.

Arnold, Jörg, 'Vom Verlierer zum Gewinner – und zurück. Der Coal Miners als Schlüsselfigure der Britishen Zeitgeschichte', *Geschichte und Gesellschaft*, 42 (2016), pp. 266–97.

Ashworth, W., *The History of the British Coal Industry, Volume Five, 1946–1982: the nationalised industry* (Oxford University Press: Oxford, 1986).

Atkinson, A. B., 'The Distribution of Income in the UK and OECD Countries in the Twentieth Century', *Oxford Review of Economic Policy*, 15 (Winter 1999), pp. 56–75.

Barron, Hester, *The 1926 Miners' Lockout: meanings of community in the Durham coalfield* (Oxford University Press: Oxford, 2010).

Barron, Hester, 'Women of the Durham Coalfield and their Reactions to the 1926 Miners' Lockout', *Historical Studies in Industrial Relations*, 22 (2006), pp. 53–83.

Beatty, Christine and Stephen Fothergill, 'Labour Market Adjustment in Areas of Chronic Industrial Decline: The Case of the UK Coalfields', *Regional Studies*, 30 (1996), pp. 627–40.

Beatty, Christine, Steve Fothergill and Tony Gore, *The real level of unemployment 2012* (Centre for Regional Economic and Social Research, Sheffield Hallam University: Sheffield, 2012).

Beckett, Andy, *Promised You a Miracle. Why 1980–82 Made Modern Britain* (Allen Lane: London, 2015).

Beckett, Andy, *When The Lights Went Out. What Really Happened to Britain in the Seventies* (Faber and Faber: London, 2009).

Beynon, Huw and Terry Austrin, 'The Performance of Power. Sam Watson, a Miners' Leader on Many Stages', *Journal of Historical Sociology*, 28 (2015), pp. 458–90.

Blyton, Paul and Peter Turnbull, *The Dynamics of Employee Relations* (Palgrave Macmillan: Basingstoke, 2004).

Bogdanor, Vernon, *Devolution in the United Kingdom* (Oxford University Press: Oxford, 1999).

Booth, Alan, 'New Revisionists and the Keynesian Era: an Expanding Consensus?', *Economic History Review*, 56 (2003), pp. 125–30.

Brotherstone, Terry and Jim Phillips, 'A Peculiar Obscurity? William Gallacher's Missing Biography and the Role of Stalinism in Scottish Labour History: a contribution to an overdue discussion', *Scottish Labour History*, 51 (2016), pp. 154–73.

Brotherstone, Terry and Simon Pirani, 'Were There Alternatives? Movements from Below in the Scottish Coalfield, the Communist Party, and Thatcherism, 1981–1985', *Critique*, 36–7 (2005), pp. 99–124.

Breitenbach, Esther, 'For Workers' Rights and Self-determination? The Scottish Labour Movement and the British Empire from the 1920s to the 1960s', *Scottish Labour History*, 51 (2016), pp. 113–33.

Bulmer, Martin, 'Sociological Models of the Mining Community', *Sociological Review*, 23 (1975), pp. 61–92.

Campbell, Alan, 'Reflections on the 1926 Mining Lockout', *Historical Studies in Industrial Relations*, 21 (2006), pp. 143–81.

Campbell, Alan, 'Scotland', in John McIlroy, Alan Campbell and Keith Gildart, eds, Industrial Politics and the 1926 *Mining Lockout: the Struggle for Dignity* (University of Wales Press: Cardiff, 2004), pp. 173–89.

Campbell, Alan, *The Scottish Miners, 1874–1939. Volume One: Work, Industry and Community;* and *Volume Two: Trade Unions and Politics* (Ashgate: Aldershot, 2000).

Campbell, Alan and John McIlroy, 'Reflections on the Communist Party's Third Period in Scotland: the case of Willie Allan', *Scottish Labour History*, 35 (2000), pp. 35–54.

Campbell, Beatrix, *Wigan Pier Revisited: poverty and politics in the eighties* (Virago: London, 1984).

Campbell, John, *Edward Heath* (Pimlico: London, 1993).

Campbell, John, *Margaret Thatcher. Volume One: The Grocer's Daughter* (Vintage: London, 2001).

Campsie, Alexandre, 'Mass-Observation, Left Intellectuals and the Politics of Everyday Life', *English Historical Review*, 131 (2016), pp. 92–121.

Carswell, Jeane and Tracey Roberts, *Getting the Coal: impressions of a twentieth century mining community* (Alden Press: Oxford, 1992).

Chalmers, Iain, Untitled Manuscript Talk on The Scottish Colliers, 1606 to 1799, undated; copy in author's possession.

Chan, A., 'A "race to the bottom": globalisation and China's labour standards', *China Perspectives*, 46 (2003), pp. 41–9.

Church, Roy A., *The History of the British Coal Industry. Vol. 3, 1830–1913: Victorian pre-eminence* (Oxford University Press: Oxford, 1986).

Clark, Andy and Ewan Gibbs, 'Voices of social dislocation, lost work and economic restructuring: Narratives from marginalised localities in the "New Scotland"', *Memory Studies*, 2017, early online publication, pp. 21.

Clarke, Eric, with Bob McLean, 'The Mineworkers' Strike 1984–5: the Role of the Scottish Area as Banker to the Union', *Scottish Affairs*, 49 (2004), pp. 138–50.

Clarke, Jackie, 'Afterlives of a Factory: Memory, Place and Space in Alençon', in Steven High, Lachlan MacKinnon and Andrew Perchard, eds, *The Deindustrialized World: Confronting Ruination in Postindustrial Places* (University of British Columbia Press: Vancouver, 2017), pp. 111–25.

Collins, Patricia Hill *Black Feminist Thought: Knowledge, Consciousness and the Politics of Empowerment* (Routledge: London, 2009).

Condratto, Shelley and Ewan Gibbs, 'After Industrial Citizenship: Adapting to Precarious Employment in the Lanarkshire Coalfield, Scotland, and Sudbury Hardrock Mining, Canada', *Labour/Le Travail*, 81 (Spring 2018), pp. 213–39.

Cowling, David, *An Essay For Today: Scottish New Towns, 1947–1997* (Rutland Press: Edinburgh, 1997).

Crafts, Nicholas, 'Economic growth during the long twentieth century', in R. Floud, J. Humphries and P. Johnson, eds, *The Cambridge Economic History of Modern Britain, Vol. II, 1870 to the present* (Cambridge University Press: Cambridge, 2014), pp. 26–59.

Curtis, Ben, *The South Wales Miners, 1964–1985* (University of Wales Press, Cardiff, 2013).

Daly, Lawrence,' Fife Socialist League', *New Left Review*, 1.4 (1960), pp. 69–70.

Dalyell, Tam, 'Dick Marsh', in Greg Rosen, ed., *Dictionary of Labour Biography* (Politicos: London, 2001), pp. 381–3.

Davies, Esther, 'Sanny Sloan, the Miners' MP', *Scottish Labour History*, 52 (2017), pp. 78–91.

Dennis, Norman, Fernando Henriques and Clifford Slaughter, *Coal Is Our Life: an Analysis of a Yorkshire Mining* Community (Tavistock: London, 1969).

Dorey, Peter, 'Conciliation or Confrontation with the Trade Unions? The Conservative Party's "Authority of Government Group", 1975–1978', *Historical Studies in Industrial Relations*, 27/28 (2009), pp. 135–51.

Dorey, Peter, '"It was Just Like Arming to Face the Threat of Hitler in the late 1930s". The Ridley Report and the Conservative Party's Preparations for the 1984–85 Miners' Strike', *Historical Studies in Industrial Relations*, 34 (2013), pp. 173–214.

Dorey, Peter, 'The *Stepping Stones* programme: The Conservative Party's struggle to develop a Trade Union Policy, 1975–79', *Historical Studies in Industrial Relations*, 35 (2014), pp. 89–116.

Drucker, Henry and Gordon Brown, *The Politics of Nationalism and Devolution* (Longman: London, 1980).

Duncan, Robert, 'Gallacher, William (1881–1965)', *Oxford Dictionary of National Biography* (Oxford University Press: Oxford, online, 2011).

Duncan, Robert, *The Mineworkers* (Birlinn: Edinburgh, 2005).

Eadie, Bob, 'The Miners' Strike in Scotland', *Scottish Affairs*, 23.1 (2014), pp. 153–5.

Efstathiou, Christos, 'E. P. Thompson, the Early New Left and the Fife Socialist League', *Labour History Review*, 81.1 (2016), pp. 25–48.

Emery, Jay, 'Belonging, memory and history in the north Nottinghamshire coalfield', *Journal of Historical Geography*, 59 (2018), pp. 77–89.

Featherstone, David and Diarmaid Kelliher, eds, *London and the 1984–5 Miners' Strike* (University of Glasgow: Glasgow, 2018).

Field, Geoffrey G., *Blood, Sweat and Toil. The Remaking of the British Working Class, 1939–1945* (Oxford University Press: Oxford, 2011).

Fishman, Nina, '"A Vital Element in British Industrial Relations": A Reassessment of Order 1305, 1940–51', *Historical Studies in Industrial Relations*, 8 (1999), pp. 43–86.

Fleming, Peter, *The Death of Homo Economicus: work, debt and the myth of endless accumulation* (Pluto Press: London, 2017).

Foden, Mike, Steve Fothergill and Tony Gore, *The State of the Coalfields: economic and social conditions in the former mining communities of England, Scotland and Wales* (Coalfields Regeneration Trust and Sheffield Hallam University: Sheffield, 2014).

Foot, Paul, 'Introduction', in Roger Huddle, Angela Phillips, Mike Simons and John Sturrock, *Blood, Sweat & Tears: Photographs from the great miners' strike* (Artworker Books: London, 1985), pp. 7–9.

Foreman-Peck., J. and R. Millward, *Public and Private Ownership of British Industry, 1820–1990* (Clarendon: Oxford, 1994).

Foster, John, 'Prologue: What Kind of Crisis? What Kind of Ruling Class?', in John McIlroy, Alan Campbell and Keith Gildart, eds, *Industrial Politics and the 1926 Mining Lockout: the Struggle for Dignity* (University of Wales Press: Cardiff, 2004), pp. 7–40.

Foster, John and Charles Woolfson, 'How Workers on the Clyde Gained the Capacity for Class Struggle: the Upper Clyde Shipbuilders' Work-In, 1971–2', in John McIlroy, Nina Fishman and Alan Campbell, eds, *British Trade Unions and Industrial Politics. Volume Two: The High Tide of Trade Unionism, 1964–79* (Ashgate: Aldershot, 1999), pp. 297–325.

Foster, John and Charles Woolfson, *The Politics of the UCS Work-in: Class Alliances and the Right to Work* (Lawrence and Wishart: London, 1986).

Fox, Alan, *Industrial Sociology and Industrial Relations. Royal Commission on Trade Unions and Employers' Associations, Research Papers, 3* (HMSO: London, 1966).

Fraser of Allander Institute, *The Scottish Economy: Main Trends, 1964–1973,* https://pure.strath.ac.uk/portal/files/38985955/FEC_1_1_1975_Scottish_Economy.pdf, accessed 25 February 2017.

Gallacher, William, *Revolt on the Clyde: an Autobiography* (Lawrence & Wishart: London, 1936; Fourth Edition, London, 1978).

Gamble, Andrew, *The Free Economy and the Strong State: the Politics of Thatcherism* (Macmillan: Basingstoke, 1994).

Gibbs, Ewan, '"The Chance Tae Move Anywhere in Britain": Scottish Coalfield Restructuring and Labour Migration, c. 1947–74', *'By the People, for the People': The Nationalisation of Coal and Steel Revisited;* first workshop of the Coal and Steelworkers' Study Group, National Coal Mining Museum for England, 7–8 December 2017.

Gibbs, Ewan, '"Civic Scotland" vs Communities on Clydeside: Poll Tax Non-Payment c. 1987–1990', *Scottish Labour History,* 49 (2015), pp. 86–106.

Gibbs, Ewan, *The Meaning and Memory of Coalfields: Deindustrialisation and Scottish Nationhood* (University of London: London, forthcoming, 2019).

Gibbs, Ewan, 'The Moral Economy of the Scottish Coalfields: Managing Deindustrialization under Nationalization, c. 1947–1983', *Enterprise and Society,* 19.1 (2018), pp. 124–52.

Gibbs, Ewan and Jim Tomlinson, 'Planning the new industrial nation: Scotland, 1931–1979', *Contemporary British History,* 30.4 (2016), pp. 585–606.

Gilbert, David, *Class, Community and Collective Action. Social Change in Two British Coalfields, 1850–1926* (Oxford University Press: Oxford, 1992).

Gildart, Keith, 'Coal Strikes on the Home Front: Miners' Militancy in the Second World War', *Twentieth Century British History,* 20.2 (2009) pp. 121–51.

Gildart, Keith, 'Mining Memories: Reading Coalfield Autobiographies', *Labor History,* 50 (2009), pp. 139–61.

Glyn, Andrew, 'The Economic Case Against Pit Closures', in D. Cooper and T. Hopper, eds, *Debating Coal Closures: economic calculation in the coal dispute, 1984–5* (Cambridge University Press: Cambridge, 1988), pp. 57–94.

Goldin, Claudia, *Understanding the Gender Gap. An Economic History of American Women* (Oxford University Press: Oxford, 1990).

Goldman, Lawrence, 'Daly, Lawrence (1924–2009)', *Oxford Dictionary of National Biography* (Oxford University Press: Oxford, online, 2013).

Goldthorpe, John, David Lockwood, Frank Bechhofer and Jennifer Platt, *The Affluent Worker: Industrial Attitudes and Behaviour* (Cambridge University Press: Cambridge, 1968).

Goldthorpe, John, David Lockwood, Frank Bechhofer and Jennifer Platt, *The Affluent Worker in the Class Structure* (Cambridge University Press: Cambridge, 1969).

Goldthorpe, John, David Lockwood, Frank Bechhofer and Jennifer Platt, *The Affluent Worker: Political Attitudes and Behaviour* (Cambridge University Press: Cambridge, 1968).

Gray, Daniel, *Stramash. Tackling Scotland's Towns and Teams* (Luath: Edinburgh, 2010).

Griffin, Colin, 'Not just a case of baths, canteens and rehabilitation centres: The Second World War and the recreational provision of the Miners' Welfare Commission', in N. Hayes and J. Hill, eds, *'Millions Like Us'? British Culture in the Second World War* (Liverpool University Press: Liverpool, 1999), pp. 262–94.

Griffin, Colin, '"Notts. have some very peculiar history": Understanding the Reaction of the Nottinghamshire Miners to the 1984–85 Strike', *Historical Studies in Industrial Relations*, 19 (2005), pp. 63–99.

Hall, Peter, *Governing the Economy: The Politics of State Intervention in Britain and France* (Polity: Cambridge, 1986).

Hall, Tony, *King Coal: Miners, Coal and Britain's Industrial Future* (Penguin: Harmondsworth, 1981).

Halliday, Robert S., *The Disappearing Scottish Colliery* (Scottish Academic Press: Edinburgh, 1990).

Hannah, Leslie, 'A failed experiment: the state ownership of industry', in Roderick Floud and Paul Johnson, eds, *The Cambridge Economic History of Modern Britain. Volume III, Structural Change and Growth, 1939–2000* (Cambridge University Press: Cambridge, 2004), pp. 84–111.

Harvie, Christopher, *No Gods and Precious Few Heroes: Scotland since 1914* (Edinburgh University Press: Edinburgh, 1993).

Hay, Colin, 'The Trade Unions and the "Winter of Discontent": A Case of Myth-Taken Identity', *Historical Studies in Industrial Relations*, 36 (2015), pp. 181–203.

Heath, Edward, *The Course of My Life* (Hodder & Stoughton: London, 1998).

Heavyside, Tom, *Fife's Last Days of Colliery Steam* (Stenlake: Ochiltree, 2014).

Hechter, Michael, *Internal Colonialism. The Celtic Fringe in British National Development, 1536–1966* (Routledge & Kegan Paul: London, 1975).

Heughan, Hazel, *Pit Closures at Shotts and the Migration of Miners* (Edinburgh University Press: Edinburgh, 1953).

High, Steven, '"The Wounds of Class": A Historiographical Reflection on the Study of Deindustrialization, 1973–2013', *History Compass*, 11.11 (2013), pp. 994–1007.

Hirschman, Albert O., *Exit, Voice and Loyalty: responses to decline in firms, organizations and states* (Harvard University Press: Cambridge, MA, 1970).

Hoggart, Richard, *The Uses of Literacy* (Penguin: London, 1957).

Hood, Neil and Stephen Young, *Multinationals in Retreat: the Scottish Experience* (Edinburgh University Press: Edinburgh, 1982).

Howell, Chris, *Trade Unions and the State: the Construction of Industrial Relations Institutions in Britain, 1890–2000* (Princeton University Press: Princeton, NJ, 2005).

Howell, David, 'Defiant Dominoes: Working Miners and the 1984–5 Strike', in Ben Jackson and Robert Saunders, eds, *Making Thatcher's Britain* (Cambridge University Press: Cambridge, 2012), pp. 148–64.

Hughes, Annmarie, '"A clear understanding of our duty": Labour women in rural Scotland, 1919–1939', *Scottish Labour History*, 48 (2013), pp. 136–57.

Hughes, Annmarie, *Gender and Political Identities in Scotland, 1919–1939* (Edinburgh University Press: Edinburgh, 2010).

Hutton, Guthrie, *Coal Not Dole. Memories of the 1984/85 Miners' Strike* (Stenlake: Catrine, 2005).

Hutton, Guthrie, *Fife: the Mining Kingdom* (Stenlake: Ochiltree, 1999).

Jackson, Alvin, *The Two Unions: Ireland, Scotland, and the Survival of the United Kingdom, 1707–2007* (Oxford University Press: Oxford, 2012).

Jackson, Ben, 'The Think-Tank Archipelago: Thatcherism and Neo-Liberalism', in Ben Jackson and Robert Saunders, eds, *Making Thatcher's Britain* (Cambridge University Press: Cambridge, 2012), pp. 43–61.

Jaffe, James A., 'The Ambiguities of Compulsory Arbitration and the War-time Experience of Order 1305', *Historical Studies in Industrial Relations*, 15 (2003), 1–26.

Jefferys, Kevin, *Finest and Darkest Hours. The Decisive Events in British Politics from Churchill to Blair* (Atlantic Books: London, 2002).

Johnman, Lewis and Hugh Murphy, *British Shipbuilding and the State: a political economy of decline* (University of Exeter: Exeter, 2002).

Kelliher, Diarmaid, 'Contested Spaces: London and the 1984–5 Miners' Strike', *Twentieth Century British History*, 28 (2017), pp. 595–617.

Kelliher, Diarmaid, 'Solidarity and Sexuality: Lesbians and Gays Support the Miners, 1984–5', *History Workshop Journal*, 77 (2014), pp. 240–62.

Kelly, Pat, *Scotland's Radical Exports. The Scots Abroad – How They Shaped Politics and Trade Unions* (Grimsay Press: Edinburgh, 2011).

Kerr, C. and A. Siegel, 'The Interindustry Propensity to Strike: An International Comparison', in A. Kornhauser, R. Dubin and A. Ross, eds, *Industrial Conflict* (McGraw-Hill: New York, 1954), pp. 189–212.

Kirby, M. W., 'MacGregor, Sir Ian Kinloch (1912–1998)', *Oxford Dictionary of National Biography* (Oxford University Press: Oxford, online, 2016).

Kirby, M. W. and S. Hamilton, 'Sir Adam Nimmo', in A. Slaven and S. Checkland, eds, *Dictionary of Scottish Business Biography. Volume 1: The Staple Industries* (Aberdeen University Press: Aberdeen, 1986), pp. 57–9.

Kitson, Michael and Jonathan Michie, 'The De-industrial Revolution: The Rise and Fall of UK Manufacturing, 1870–2010', in R. Floud, J. Humphries and P. Johnson, eds, *Cambridge Economic History of Modern Britain*, vol. 2, *1870 to the Present* (Cambridge University Press: Cambridge, 2014), pp. 302–29.

Knox, W. W. and A. McKinlay, 'American Multinationals and British Trade Unions', *Labor History*, 51.2 (2010), pp. 211–29.

Knotter, Ad, '"Little Moscows" in Western Europe: The Ecology of Small-Place Communism', *International Review of Social History*, 56 (2011), pp. 475–510.

Kourchid, Olivier, 'Les Mineurs du Nord et du Pas-De-Calais face à la silicose, à la pneumoconiose at aux insuffcances respiratoires: techniques de soins et politiques de la santé dans les années 1990', in Sylvie Aprile, Matthieu de Oliveira, Béatrice Touchelay and Karl-Michael Hoin, *Les Houillères entre l'État, le marché et la société* (Septentrion Presses Universitaires: Villeneuve d'Ascq, 2015), pp. 99–114.

Laybourn, Keith, 'Revisiting the General Strike', *Historical Studies in Industrial Relations*, 21 (2006), pp. 109–20.

Leeworthy, Daryl, 'The secret life of us: 1984, the miners' strike and the place of biography in writing history "from below"', *European Review of History*, 19 (2012), pp. 825–46.

Lindop, Fred, 'The Dockers and the 1971 Industrial Relations Act, Part 1: Shop Stewards and Containerization', *Historical Studies in Industrial Relations*, 5 (1998), pp. 33–72.

Long, Paul, 'Abe Moffat, the Fife Mineworkers and the United Mineworkers of Scotland: Transcript of a 1974 Interview', *Scottish Labour History*, 17 (1982), pp. 5–18.

Lunn, Kenneth, 'Complex Encounters: Trade Unions, Immigration and Racism', in Alan Campbell, Nina Fishman, John McIlroy, eds, *British Trade Unions and Industrial Politics, Vol. Two: the high tide of trade unionism, 1964–79* (Ashgate: Aldershot, 1999), pp. 70–90.

Lyons, William and Robert Alexander, 'A Tale of Two Electorates: Generational Replacement and the Decline of Voting in Presidential Elections', *The Journal of Politics*, 62 (2000), pp. 1014–34.

McCormack, John with Simon Pirani, *Polmaise: the Fight for a Pit* (Word Press, 2015 edition, https://polmaisebook.wordpress.com).

MacDougall, Ian, ed., *Militant Miners. Recollections of John McArthur, Buckhaven; and letters, 1924–26, of David Proudfoot, Methil, to G. Allen Hutt* (Polygon: Edinburgh, 1981).

MacDougall, Ian, *Voices From the Hunger Marches. Volume One* and *Volume Two* (Polygon: Edinburgh, 1991).

MacDougall, Ian, *Voices From Work and Home* (Mercat Press: Edinburgh, 2001).

McDowell, Linda, Anitha Sundari, and Ruth Pearson, 'Striking Narratives: class, gender and ethnicity in the "Great Grunwick Strike", London, UK, 1976–1978', *Women's History Review*, 23.4 (2014), pp. 595–619.

McGowan, Jack, '"Dispute", "Battle", "Siege", "Farce"? – Grunwick 30 Years On', *Contemporary British History*, 22 (2008), pp. 383–406.

McGrail, Steve with Vicky Patterson, *Cowie Miners, Polmaise Colliery and the 1984–85 Miners' Strike* (Scottish Labour History Society: Glasgow, 2017).

McGuire, Charlie, '"Going for the Jugular": The Steelworkers' Banner and the 1980 National Steelworkers' Strike in Britain', *Historical Studies in Industrial Relations*, 38 (2017), pp. 97–128.

McIlroy, John and Alan Campbell, 'Beyond Betteshanger: Order 1305 in the Scottish Coalfields during the Second World War, Part 1: Politics, Prosecutions and Protest', *Historical Studies in Industrial Relations*, 15 (2003), pp. 27–72, and 'Part 2: The Cardowan Story', *Historical Studies in Industrial Relations*, 16 (2003), pp. 39–80.

McIlroy, John and Alan Campbell, 'McGahey, Michael (Mick), (1925–1999)', in Keith Gildart and David Howell, eds, *Dictionary of Labour Biography. Volume XIII* (Palgrave Macmillan: Basingstoke, 2010), pp. 242–51.

McIlvanney, William, *Docherty* (Sceptre: London, 1996).

Macintyre, Stuart, *Little Moscows: Communism and Working-Class Militancy in Inter-war Britain* (Croom Helm: London, 1980).

McIvor, Arthur, 'Deindustrialization Embodied: Work, Health and Disability in the United Kingdom since the Mid-Twentieth Century', in Steven High, Lachlan MacKinnon and Andrew Perchard, eds, *The Deindustrialized*

World: Confronting Ruination in Postindustrial Places (University of British Columbia Press: Vancouver, 2017), pp. 25–45.

McIvor, Arthur, and Ronald Johnston, *Miners' Lung: A History of Dust Disease in British Coal Mining* (Ashgate: Aldershot, 2007).

McIvor, Arthur and Ronald Johnson, 'Voices From the Pits: Health and Safety in Scottish Coal Mining Since 1945', *Scottish Economic and Social History*, 22 (2002), pp. 111–33.

McKean, Charles, *The Scottish Thirties. An Architectural Introduction* (Scottish Academic Press: Edinburgh, 1987).

MacKenzie, Mhairi, Chik Collins, John Connolly, Mick Doyle and Gerry McCartney, 'Working-class Discourses of Politics, Policy and Health: "I don't smoke; don't drink. The only thing wrong with me is my health"', *Policy and Politics*, 45.2 (2017), pp. 231–49.

McKibbin, Ross, *Classes and Cultures: England, 1918–1951* (Oxford University Press: Oxford, 1999).

McKinlay, Alan, 'Jimmy Reid: Fragments From a Political Life', *Scottish Labour History*, 46 (2011), pp. 37–52.

McKinlay, Alan and Bill Knox, 'Working for the Yankee Dollar. US Inward Investment and Scottish Labour, 1945–1970', *Historical Studies in Industrial Relations*, 7 (1999), pp. 1–26.

Mak, Ariane, 'Conspicuous Consumption in Wartime? Welsh Mining Communities and Women in Munitions Factories', in Corinna Peniston-Bird and Emma Vickers, eds, *Gender and the Second World War: Lessons of War* (Palgrave: London, 2016), pp. 55–72.

Mak, Ariane, 'Spheres of Justice in the 1942 Betteshanger Miners' Strike: An Essay in Historiographical Ethnography', *Historical Studies in Industrial Relations*, 36 (2015), pp. 29–57.

Mannheim, Karl, 'The Problem of Generations', in Karl Mannheim, *Essays on the Sociology of Knowledge* (Routledge & Kegan Paul: London, 1952), pp. 276–322.

Marquand, David, *Mammon's Kingdom. An Essay on Britain, Now* (Allen Lane: London, 2014).

Mates, Lewis, *The Great Labour Unrest: Rank and file movements and political change in the Durham Coalfield* (Manchester University Press: Manchester, 2016).

Maxwell, Alex, *Chicago Tumbles: Cowdenbeath and the Miners' Strike* (Alex Maxwell: Glenrothes, 1994).

Meek, James, *Private Island: Why Britain Now Belongs to Someone Else* (Verso: London, 2014).

Miliband, Ralph, *Divided Societies: Class Struggle in Contemporary Capitalism* (Clarendon: Oxford, 1989).

Milne, Seumas, *The Enemy Within: the Secret War Against the Miners* (Verso, 4th edition: London, 2014).

Minkin, Lewis, *The Contentious Alliance. Trade Unions and the Labour Party* (Edinburgh University Press: Edinburgh, 1992).

Mitchell, James, *Conservatives and the Union. A Study of Conservative Party Attitudes to the Union* (Edinburgh University Press: Edinburgh, 1990).

Mitchell, James, *The Scottish Question* (Oxford University Press: Oxford, online, 2014).

Moffat, Abe, *My Life With the Miners* (Lawrence & Wishart: London, 1965).

Moran, Michael, *The Politics of Industrial Relations* (Macmillan: London, 1977).

Morgan, Kenneth O., *The People's Peace: British History, 1945–1990* (Oxford University Press: Oxford, 1992).

Morgan, W. John, 'The Miners' Welfare Fund in Britain, 1920–1952', *Social Policy & Administration*, 24.3 (1990), pp. 199–211.

Ó Discin, Liam, 'Philip Murray: Scotland and the formation of an American union leader', *Scottish Labour History*, 51 (2016), pp. 95–112.

O'Neill, Matt, *Lanarkshire's Mining Disasters* (Stenlake: Catrine, 2011).

Oglethorpe, Miles K., *Scottish Collieries. An Inventory of the Scottish Coal Industry in the Nationalised Era* (Royal Commission on the Ancient and Historical Monuments of Scotland: Edinburgh, 2006).

Orwell, George, *The Road To Wigan Pier*, in *Orwell's England*, edited by Peter Davison (Penguin: Harmondsworth, 2001).

Outram, Quentin, 'Carlow, Charles Augustus (1878–1954)', *Oxford Dictionary of National Biography* (Oxford University Press: Oxford, online, 2016).

Outram, Quentin, 'The General Strike and the Development of British Capitalism', *Historical Studies in Industrial Relations*, 21 (2006), pp. 121–41.

Outram, Quentin, Review, *Scottish Labour History*, 48 (2013), pp. 194–6.

Owens, Joe, *Miners, 1984–1994: a decade of endurance* (Polygon: Edinburgh, 1994).

Page Arnot, R., *A History of the Scottish Miners* (George Allen & Unwin: London, 1955).

Paterson, Harry, *Look Back in Anger. The Miners' Strike in Nottinghamshire 30 Years On* (Five Leaves Publications: Nottingham, 2014).

Paterson, Lindsay, *Education and the Scottish Parliament* (Dunedin Academic Press: Edinburgh, 2005).

Paterson, Lindsay, *Scottish Education in the Twentieth Century* (Edinburgh University Press: Edinburgh, 2003).

Paynter, W., *My Generation* (Allen & Unwin: London, 1972).

Peace, David, *GB84* (Faber and Faber, London, 2004).

Perchard, Andrew, *The Mine Management Professions in the Twentieth-Century Scottish Coal Mining Industry* (Edwin Mellan, Lampeter and Lewiston: 2007).

Perchard, Andrew, '"Broken Men" and "Thatcher's Children": Memory and Legacy in Scotland's Coalfields', *International Labor and Working Class History*, 84 (2013), pp. 78–98.

Perchard, Andrew and Keith Gildart, '"Buying brains and experts": British coal owners, regulatory capture and miners' health, 1918–1946', *Labor History*, 66 (2015), pp. 459–80.

Perchard, Andrew and Jim Phillips, 'Transgressing the Moral Economy: Wheelerism and Management of the Nationalised Coal Industry in Scotland', *Contemporary British History*, 25 (2011), pp. 387–405.

Phillips, Jim, 'Christie, Campbell (1937–2011), trade unionist and political campaigner', *Oxford Dictionary of National Biography* (Oxford University Press: Oxford, online, 2016).

Phillips, Jim, *Collieries, Communities and the Miners' Strike in Scotland, 1984–85* (Manchester University Press: Manchester, 2012).

Phillips, Jim, 'Containing, Isolating and Defeating the Miners: the UK Cabinet Ministerial Group on Coal and the three phases of the 1984–5 Strike', *Historical Studies in Industrial Relations*, 35 (2014), pp. 117–41.

Phillips, Jim, 'Deindustrialization and the Moral Economy of the Scottish Coalfields, 1947 to 1991', *International Labor and Working Class History*, 84 (Fall 2013), pp. 99–115.

Phillips, Jim, 'Economic Direction and Generational Change in Twentieth Century Britain: the case of the Scottish Coalfields', *English Historical Review*, 132 (2017), pp. 885–911.

Phillips, Jim, *The Industrial Politics of Devolution: Scotland in the 1960s and 1970s* (Manchester University Press: Manchester, 2008).

Phillips, Jim, 'The Meanings of Coal Community in Britain since 1947', *Contemporary British History*, 32.1 (2018), pp. 39–59.

Phillips, Jim, 'The 1972 Miners' Strike: Popular Agency and Industrial Politics in Britain', *Contemporary British History*, 20 (2006), pp. 187–207.

Phillips, Jim, 'Participation and Nationalization: the case of British coal from the 1940s to the 1980s', in Stefan Berger, Ludger Pries and Manfred Wannöffel, eds, *The Palgrave International Handbook of Workers' Participation* (Palgrave Macmillan: Basingstoke, 2018), pp. 187–204.

Pitt, Malcolm, *The World on our Backs: The Kent Miners and the 1972 Miners' Strike* (Lawrence and Wishart: London, 1979).

Polanyi, Karl, *The Great Transformation: the political and economic origins of our time* (Beacon Press: Boston, MA, 1944).

Portelli, Alessandro, *They Say in Harlan County* (Oxford University Press: Oxford, 2011).

Rafeek, Neil, *Communist Women in Scotland: Red Clydeside from the Russian Revolution to the End of the Soviet Union* (Tauris Academic Studies: London, 2008).

Reid, Alastair J., *United We Stand. A History of Britain's Trade Unions* (Penguin: Harmondsworth, 2004).

Reid, William, 'Sir Charles Carlow Reid', in Anthony Slaven and Sydney Checkland, eds, *Dictionary of Scottish Business Biography. Volume 1: the staple industries* (University of Aberdeen Press: Aberdeen, 1986), pp. 60–2.

Richards, Andrew J., *Miners on Strike. Class Solidarity and Division in Britain* (Berg: Oxford, 1996).

Robertson, James, *And The Land Lay Still* (Hamish Hamilton: London, 2010).

Rollings, Neil, 'Cracks in the Post-War Keynesian Settlement? The Role of Organised Business in the Rise of Neoliberalism before Margaret Thatcher', *Twentieth Century British History*, 24 (2013), pp. 637–59.

Roseman, Mark, 'The generation conflict that never was: young labour in the Ruhr mining industry, 1945–1957', in Mark Roseman, ed., *Generations in conflict: youth revolt and generation formation in Germany 1770–1968* (Cambridge University Press: Cambridge, 1995), pp. 269–89.

Roseman, Mark, *Recasting the Ruhr, 1945–1958. Manpower, Economic Recovery and Labour Relations* (Berg: Oxford, 1992).

Routledge, Paul, *Scargill: the unauthorized biography* (HarperCollins: London, 1993).

Roy, Kenneth, 'Fear of the Famous', *Scottish Review 2012*, http://www.scottishreview.net/KennethRoyJuly003a.html, accessed 20 July 2017.

Samuel, Raphael, 'Introduction', in Raphael Samuel, Barbara Bloomfield and Guy Bonas, eds, *The Enemies Within: Pit Villages and the Miners' Strike of 1984–5* (Routledge & Kegan Paul: London, 1986), pp. 6–12.

Savage, Michael, *The Dynamics of Working-Class Politics. The Labour Movement in Preston, 1880–1940* (Cambridge University Press: Cambridge, 1987).

Savage, Mike, 'Working Class Identities in the 1960s: revisiting the Affluent Worker Studies', *Sociology*, 34 (2005), pp. 929–46.

Scott, Peter, 'Regional development and policy', in Roderick Floud and Paul Johnson, eds, *The Cambridge Economic History of Modern Britain. Volume III, Structural Change and Growth, 1939–2000* (Cambridge University Press: Cambridge, 2004), pp. 332–67.

Scott, W. H., Enid Mumford, I. P. McGivering and J. M. Kirby, *Coal and Conflict. A Study of Industrial Relations at Collieries* (Liverpool University Press: Liverpool, 1963).

Smith, Dave and Phil Chamberlain, *Blacklisted: The Secret War between Big Business and Union Activists* (New Internationalist: London, 2015).

Smith, Ned, *The 1984 Miners' Strike: The Actual Account* (Oyster: Whitstable, 1997).

Smith, Paul, 'Order in British Industrial Relations: From Donovan to Neoliberalism', *Historical Studies in Industrial Relations*, 31–2 (2011), pp. 115–54.

Smith, Paul and Gary Morton, 'The Conservative Governments' Reform of Employment Law, 1979–97: 'Stepping Stones' and the 'New Right' Agenda', *Historical Studies in Industrial Relations*, 12 (2001), pp. 131–47.

Smith, Roger, 'The New Town Ideal for Scottish Miners: the Rise and Fall of a Social Ideal (1945–1948)', *Scottish Economic and Social History*, 9 (1989), pp. 71–9.

Selway, David, 'Death Underground: Mining Accidents and Memory in South Wales, 1913–74', *Labour History Review*, 81.3 (2016), 187–209.

Spence, Jean and Carol Stephenson, '"Side By Side With Our Men?" Women's Activism, Community and Gender in the 1984–5 British Miners' Strike', *International Labor and Working Class History*, 75 (2009), pp. 68–84.

Standing, Guy, *Basic Income: and how we can make it happen* (Penguin: London, 2017).

Standing, Guy, *The Precariat: the New Dangerous Class* (Bloomsbury: London, 2011).

Standing, Guy, *Work After Globalization. Building Occupational Citizenship* (Edward Elgar: London, 2009).

Stead, Jean, *Never the Same Again. Women and the Miners' Strike* (The Women's Press: London, 1987).

Steber, Martina, 'Fundamentals at Stake: the Conservatives, Industrial Relations and the Rhetorical Framing of the Miners' Strike in 1984–85', *Contemporary British History*, 32.1 (2018), pp. 60–77.

Strangleman, Tim, 'Deindustrialisation and the Historical Sociological Imagination: making sense of work and industrial change', *Sociology*, 51 (2017), pp. 466–82.

Strangleman, Tim, 'Networks, Place and Identities in Post-Industrial Mining Communities', *International Journal of Urban and Regional Research*, 25.2 (2001), pp. 253–67.

Supple, Barry, The *History of the British Coal Industry, Volume Four, 1913–1946: the political economy of decline* (Oxford University Press: Oxford, 1987).

Sutcliffe-Braithwaite, Florence and Natalie Thomlinson, 'Women's Activism During the Miners' Strike: Memories and Legacies', *Contemporary British History*, 32.1 (2018), pp. 78–100.

Taylor, Andrew, *The NUM and British Politics. Volume 2: 1969–1995* (Ashgate: Aldershot, 2005).

Taylor, Robert, 'McGahey, Michael [Mick] (1925–1999)', *Oxford Dictionary of National Biography* (Oxford University Press: Oxford, online, 2004).

Taylor, Robert, *The Trade Union Question in British Politics* (Blackwell: Cambridge, 1993).

Terris, Ian, *Twenty Years Down the Mines* (Stenlake: Ochiltree, 2001).

Thatcher, Margaret, *The Downing Street Years* (HarperCollins: London, 1993).

Thatcher, Margaret, *The Path to Power* (HarperCollins: London, 1995).

Thompson, E. P., 'The Moral Economy of the English Crowd in the Eighteenth Century', *Past and Present*, 50 (1971), pp. 76–136.

Thompson, Willie, *The Good Old Cause: British Communism, 1920–1991* (Pluto: London, 1992).

Thomson, Alistair, 'Anzac Memories: putting popular memory theory into practice in Australia', in Robert Perks and Alistair Thomson, eds, *The Oral History Reader* (Routledge: London, 1998), pp. 300–10.

Todd, Selina, 'Affluence, Class and Crown Street: Reinvestigating the Post-War Working Class', *Contemporary British History*, 22 (2008), pp. 501–18.

Todd, Selina, *The People: the Rise and Fall of the Working Class* (John Murray: London, 2014).

Tomlinson, Jim, 'De-industrialization not Decline: a New Meta-Narrative for Post-War British History', *Twentieth Century British History*, 27.1 (2016), pp. 76–99.

Tomlinson, Jim, *Democratic Socialism and Economic Policy: the Attlee Years, 1945–1951* (Cambridge University Press: Cambridge, 1997).

Tomlinson, Jim, 'A "failed experiment"? Public Ownership and the Narratives of Post-war Britain', *Labour History Review*, 73 (2008), pp. 199–214.

Tomlinson, Jim, *The Labour Governments, 1964–70. Volume 3: Economic policy* (Manchester University Press: Manchester, 2004).

Tomlinson, Jim, *Managing the Economy, Managing the People. Narratives of Economic Life in Britain from Beveridge to Brexit* (Oxford University Press: Oxford, 2017).

Tomlinson, Jim, 'Re-inventing the Moral economy in post-war Britain', *Historical Research*, 84 (2011), pp. 356–73.

Tomlinson, Jim, 'Tale of a Death Exaggerated: How Keynesian Policies Survived the 1970s', *Contemporary British History*, 21 (2007), pp. 429–48.

Tookey, Mark, 'Three's A Crowd?: Government, Owners, and Workers during the Nationalization of the British Coalmining Industry, 1945–47', *Twentieth Century British History*, 12 (2001), pp. 486–510.

Tuckett, Angela, *Scottish Trades Union Congress* (Mainstream: Edinburgh, 1986).

Turner, Angela and Arthur McIvor, '"Bottom dog men": Disability, Social Welfare and Advocacy in the Scottish Coalfields in the Interwar Years, 1918–1939', *Scottish Historical Review*, 96.2 (2017), pp. 187–213.

Turner, Royce Logan, 'Post-War Pit Closures: The Politics of De-Industrialisation', *Political Quarterly*, 56.2 (April 1985), pp. 167–74.

Tyndall, Adrian, 'Patriotism and Principles: Order 1305 and the Betteshanger Strike of 1942', *Historical Studies in Industrial Relations*, 12 (2001), pp. 109–30.

Wallington, Peter, 'The case of the Longannet miners and the criminal liability of pickets', *Industrial Law Journal*, 1 (1972), pp. 219–28.

Watson, Don, *Squatting in Britain: Housing, Politics and Direct Action, 1945–1955* (Merlin Press: London, 2016).

Webster, Charles, *The Health Services Since the War. Volume I: Problems of Health Care: the National Health Service Before 1957* (HMSO: London, 1988).

Whiting, Richard, 'Affluence and Industrial Relations', *Contemporary British History*, 22 (2008), pp. 519–36.

Wight, Daniel, *Workers Not Wasters. Masculine Respectability, Consumption and Employment in Central Scotland* (Edinburgh University Press: Edinburgh, 1993).

Williams, Granville, ed., *Settling Scores: The Media, the Police and the Miners' Strike* (Campaign for Press and Broadcasting Freedom: London, 2014).

Williams, Raymond, 'Mining the Meaning: Key Words in the Miners' Strike', in Robin Gable, ed., *Resources of Hope: Culture, Democracy, Socialism* (Verso: London, 1989), pp. 120–7.

Williamson, J. N., 'Ten Years of Safety Work in a Scottish Colliery Group. Safety Record of the Fife Coal Company, Ltd., 1936–1945', *Transactions of the Institution of Mining Engineers*, 106 (1946–47), pp. 231–69.

Winterton, J. and R. Winterton, *Coal, Crisis and Conflict: The 1984–85 Miners' Strike in Yorkshire* (Manchester University Press: Manchester, 1989).

Witham, Joan, *Hearts and Minds. The Story of the Women of Nottinghamshire in the Miners' Strike, 1984–1985* (Canary Press: London, 1986).

Woolfson, Charles and John Foster, *Track Record: the story of the Caterpillar Occupation* (Verso: London, 1988).

Young, Hilary, 'Being a Man: Everyday Masculinities', in Lynn Abrams and Callum G. Brown, eds, *A History of Everyday Life in Twentieth-Century Scotland* (Edinburgh University Press, Edinburgh, 2010), pp. 131–52.

Zahn, Rebecca, 'German Codetermination without Nationalization, and British Nationalization without Codetermination: Retelling the Story', *Historical Studies in Industrial Relations*, 26 (2015), pp. 1–28.

Theses

Anderson, Ian Gareth, *Scottish Trade Unions and Nationalisation, 1945–1955: a Case Study of the Coal Industry*, University of Glasgow PhD, 1999.

Cronin, Jenny, *The Origins and Development of Scottish Convalescent Homes, 1860–1939*, University of Glasgow PhD, 2003.

Gibbs, Ewan, *Deindustrialisation and Industrial Communities: The Lanarkshire Coalfields c.1947–1983*, University of Glasgow PhD, 2016.

Kelliher, Diarmaid, *Solidarity, Class and Labour Agency: Mapping Networks of Support between London and the Coalfields during the 1984–5 Miners' Strike*, University of Glasgow, PhD, 2016.

Mak, Ariane, *En grève et en guerre. Les mineurs britanniques au prisme des enquêtes du Mass Observation (1939–1945)*, Université de recherché Paris Sciences et Lettres, PhD, 2018.

Index

Note: where applicable, the position of individuals in the coal industry or trade unions is denoted in parenthesis